THE

APOSTLES' SCHOOL

OF

PROPHETIC INTERPRETATION:

WITH

ITS HISTORY DOWN TO THE PRESENT TIME.

BY

CHARLES MAITLAND,

AUTHOR OF "THE CHURCH IN THE CATACOMBS."

"Remember ye not, that, when I was yet with you, I told you these things? And now ye know what withholdeth." — 2 *Thess.* ii. 5.

WIPF & STOCK · Eugene, Oregon

Wipf and Stock Publishers
199 W 8th Ave, Suite 3
Eugene, OR 97401

The Apostles' School of Prophetic Interpretation
With Its History Down to the Present Time
By Maitland, Charles
ISBN 13: 978-1-60608-752-7
Publication date 6/8/2009
Previously published by Longman, Brown, Green, and Longmans, 1849

ADVERTISEMENT.

In this work it has been attempted to collect together everything that the Apostles taught the Church on the subject of unfulfilled prophecy: to ascertain all that the primitive believers might know as Jews, and all that they believed as Christians. This school of prophecy is next traced historically, through its fallings-off and its revivals, down to the present time. An Appendix contains a short notice of the principal counter-interpretations, from the sophistries of the infidel Porphyry to the recent speculations of the Futurist Lacunza.

CONTENTS.

INTRODUCTORY ESSAY.

THE Apostles profess to have taught the Church the meaning of the principal prophecies, Page 1. Which teaching, as reported to us by their followers, has never been falsified by history, though parts of it have been abandoned, 3. The anciently acknowledged meaning of the "Letting Power," 7. Chief point of difference between the ancient and modern systems of interpretation : — the ancients received the written explanations of the symbols as final, 14.; the moderns often reject them, 15.

On what principle certain prophecies have been successfully explained, 18. The recognised elements of *prophetic*, or, perhaps, *poetic* style, 24. Prophetic time always literal, 28. Judæo-Christian explanation of the seventy land-weeks, 31. Mutual relation between certain prophetic periods, 33. Account of the year-day theory, 34. By the failure of all such speculations, we are encouraged to stand fast by Scripture, 40.

Point of junction between the histories of Babylon and of Antichrist, 41. Modern attempts to apply to the Pope nearly all the denunciations of prophecy, 44. What is usually meant by the "Protestant Interpretation," 47. Importance of rigidly adhering to Scripture, 49.

Case of prophecies which, in the absence of inspired or Apostolic explanations, the Church has by itself attempted to expound, 50. As, for instance, the first seal, 50–58.

viii CONTENTS.

What first broke up the primitive system of exposition? Answer: Not the year-day, but the historical scheme, 58, which appears to be founded on an assumption that the predicted events cannot happen as they are described, 63. Contrast between the historical and the primitive methods of interpreting prophecy, 65.

CHAPTER I.

THE INTERPRETATION OF PROPHECY IN THE JEWISH CHURCH.

Jaddus and Alexander, 68. The Septuagint translators, 70. The Maccabees, 75. Ben-Sirach, 77. Philo, 77. Josephus, 78. The 2300 evenings and mornings (1150 days), 80. Remaining Jewish writers, 83. Summary of the Jewish system, 85. New Testament testimony to its truth, 86. Combined Judæo-Christian scheme of the four beasts and metals, 87–95.

CHAPTER II.

THE CHRISTIAN INTERPRETATION IN THE PRIMITIVE AGE.

Summary of the primitive prophetic creed, 97. Old Testament prophecies explained in the New, 103. What the Apostles said about the times and seasons, 106. Publication of the Apocalypse, 107. Destruction of Jerusalem, 110. St. Barnabas, on the little horn, 111; on the millennium, 113. Hermes, 114. Pseudo-Esdras, 119. Papias, 121. School of St. John, 122. Ignatius, 125. Polycarp, 126. Pseudo-Sibylline oracles, 126. False Neros, 132. Revolt of Barchochebas, 133. Celsus ridicules the expectation of an Antichrist, 136. Justin Martyr, 137–9. How Jews and Christians have since changed sides about the millennium, 138. Elias and the second Witness, 140. Ten days' persecution at Smyrna, 142. What the Church of Lyons thought about Antichrist, 144.

CONTENTS. ix

Irenæus, 145–154. On the number of the Beast, 146. Serpent of Dan, 155–159. Tertullian, 159–165. On the fifth seal, 163. Judas, 165. Clement of Alexandria, 166. Hippolytus, 166–170. The Sun-clothed Woman, 169. Origen, his reply to Celsus, 170. Dionysius of Alexandria, 173. Cyprian, 174. Victorinus, 177–189. Explanation of the seals, 179–184. Methodius, 189. Porphyry, 191–7. His wife Marcella, 192. His attack upon Daniel, 193–7. Lactantius, 197. Summary of primitive writers on the millennium, 201.; on the last half week, 202.

CHAPTER III.

THE INTERPRETATION OF PROPHECY IN THE PATRISTIC AGE.

Eusebius, 207. Constantine, 208. Whence he learnt to support the Church by the State, 209. Arianism, 210. Hilary, 211. Cyril of Jerusalem, 212. Catechism for Prince Antiochus, 215. Ephrem Syrus, 216. Ambrose, 219. Apollinarius, &c., 220. Chrysostom, 221–5. Why Antichrist will be permitted to come, 223. Jerome, 225–245. Transition from Antiochus to Antichrist, in Daniel xi., 229–233. The spiritual Sodom and Egypt, 234. Babylon, 234. Era of matrons, 235. Paula and her daughter, 236–240. Marcella, 240. Algasia, 241. Ageruchia, 244. The Donatists, 245. Tychonius, 247. Augustine, 249–257. Sulpitius, 257. Theodoret, 258. How the Stone smote the Image, 259–261. Review of the history of the four empires, 261. Eudoxius, 260. Prosper, 262. The rise of Papal Rome; Leo I. and Andreas, 263–6. Cassiodorus, 270. Primasius, 270. Table of writers on the three days and a half, 271. Justinian and the Pope, 272. Gregory the Great, 273. Pretended decree of Phocas, 275. Aretas, 276.

a

CHAPTER IV.

THE INTERPRETATION OF PROPHECY IN THE MIDDLE AGES.

How the monks expounded Scripture, 278. Summary of their account of the Witnesses' death, 280. Collection of passages relative to "the great city spiritually called Sodom and Egypt," 283. Christian Rome enters upon her career of Babylon, 285, by the help of idolatry, 286, and by the abuse of spiritual power, 287. Second council of Nice, 289. Forged Donation of Constantine, 292. Coronation of Charlemagne, 294. Bede, 296. Damascenus, 297. False Christs and prophets, 298. Panic about the end of the world, 300–306. Adso, 301. Gherbert, 303. Hildebrand, 307. Expositions of mystical Babylon, 299–313. Fluentinus, 312. Bernard, 313. Hildegarde, 315. Church-history scheme of the seals, 315. Anselm of Havilsburgh, 316. Geroch, 318. Joachim, 320–3. King Richard I., 321, 2. Crusades, 323. Innocent III., 324. The Inquisition, 326. Confessional, 327–9. Eberhard, 330. Greathead, 332. The Schoolmen, 333–6. The Franciscans, 337–342. Peter John of Olivi, 339. Beguins, 341. Petrarch and Dante, 342. Hervey and Bridget, 344. Flight of the Popes to Avignon; Clemangis, 347. Berengaud and the Block-book, 349. Vincent of Ferrers, 351. Pope Pius and the Turk, 354.

CHAPTER V.

REMAINS OF THE PRIMITIVE INTERPRETATION IN MODERN TIMES.

The Jesuits, after the manner of the ancient Fulguratores, undertake to avert the omen of the Apocalyptic denunciations, 358. Summary of the current exposition of the Scarlet Beast, 358–362. Of the Sun-clothed Woman, 362–7. Procession of Leo X., 367. John of Kemnitz, 370. Reformation and the Church of England, 371. Bellarmine attacks the year-day theory, &c., 373–6. Ribera and

Viegas, on Rome's future apostacy, 376. Her recent cruelties, 380. Paramus on the Inquisition, 381. Cornelius A Lapide, 383. The French Revolution and Napoleon, 387. Lacunza (Ben-Ezra), 392. Messrs. Burgh and S. Maitland, 394. Mr. C. D. Maitland, 396. Glance at the present condition of the study of prophecy, 398.

CHAPTER VI.

THE TIMES OF ANTICHRIST - - - Page 402

APPENDIX.

SKETCH OF THE LEADING COUNTER-SYSTEMS OF INTERPRETATION.

Antiochus the little horn, 428. The Saracens or the Turks the little horn, 430. The Papal Antichrist and year-day scheme, 431. The Præterists, 445. The Futurists, 447.

INDEX TO PASSAGES OF SCRIPTURE EXPLAINED, 451.
INDEX TO AUTHORS AND PROPER NAMES, 458.

THE
APOSTLES' SCHOOL

OF

PROPHETIC INTERPRETATION.

INTRODUCTORY ESSAY.

"These things we believe: we leave posterity to see them fulfilled."— PROSPER.

SINCE the time of the Apostles, the study of unfulfilled prophecy has never held so low a place in theology as during the last two centuries. For the humble position now assigned to it, a reason may be found in the variety of opinions prevailing among interpreters: a state of confusion which seems to render hopeless every attempt to master even the outline of the prophetic scheme.

No such difficulty was felt by the ancients. There had been handed down to them, side by side with the written word, an unwritten explanation of the leading prophecies contained in it. Of this, part was derived from the verbal teaching of the Apostles; part inherited from the synagogue, together with the Book of Daniel; finally, by the publication of the Apocalypse, this floating tradition was confirmed, receiving in almost every particular the seal of direct inspiration.

The supposition cannot be unreasonable, that what the Apostles taught their followers about prophecy may be worth our knowing also; and that they who were to be guided into all truth, might know something of this portion of truth. But we now prefer to suppose that the Apostles themselves might not have understood prophecy; or that, if they did, they probably taught their converts nothing about it. But these speculations are not supported by their own writings: "Ye have heard that Antichrist shall come," writes one,—the first time that the word Antichrist occurs in Scripture. Therefore the church must already have heard about him by word of mouth. "When I was yet with you," writes another, "I told you these things:" that is, about the Man of sin and the Letting power. It is therefore idle to repeat that the ancients *could* know nothing about prophecy: the Apostles say that they *did*.

Nor can we successfully urge the excuse that the inspiration of the twelve was confined to their writings, and that their oral teaching possessed no authority. For what they had taught by word of mouth they afterwards confirm by epistle: pen in hand, they have nothing to retract, nothing to add but a caution against forgetfulness. Down to the end of the Apocalypse, they do not once say,—All that we told you about Antichrist was wrong: all that Barnabas said in his epistle was wrong: there is no literal millennium, no Judaizing Antichrist, no great tribulation under the little horn, no shortening of the days of the eleventh king. On the contrary, they confirm what they had said, and bid their disciples remember it: "Hold the traditions which ye have been taught, whether by word or our epistle."*

This primitive tradition, having so long remained unfalsified by history, comes before us with yet further claim to attention. For the future is not so easily guessed as to come right for every prognosticator; and, to judge by the fate of modern theories, a system of interpretation must be of more than human origin if it can survive the changes and chances of eighteen centuries. The expectation of the ancients did not indeed include many occurrences of the intermediate time; but it was in no way contradicted by the public establishment of Christianity, by the repeated translations of the Roman empire, or by the rise and fall of the Turkish power. They profess, indeed, to know little of the details of the trumpets, vials, and locusts; of the birth of the man-child, and of the history of the scarlet beast: but, on the other hand, they tell us confidently what they have learnt about the metallic statue and the four beasts; also about the person described as the man of sin and the little horn. They explain to us the Western Babylon, the prospects of the Roman empire, and the thousand years of the heavenly kingdom. All this they believed as a settled part of Christianity; much of it was taught to catechumens, and some portions, not altogether safe to be divulged, were at times disclosed to the heathen.

But parts of this creed were, in later ages, successively abandoned. In the fourth century the pub-

---

* 2 Thess. ii. 15.

lic establishment of Christianity threw out of sight the doctrine of the millennium. In the fifth, the Western world, and in the seventh the Eastern, dazzled by Rome's new pretensions, closed their eyes to the inscription which marks her forehead. The West rushed blindfold into her arms, and "Zion, late Babylon," was thenceforth to be her title. The millennium was now more hopelessly shut out than ever: the voice that proclaimed a new Jerusalem to be sent down from heaven, jarred with the pretensions of one that sprang from earth. Image-worship struck the next blow: it was made treason to speak of Babylon's idolatries in her own house. "Anathema to those that call the holy images idols."*

A thousand years passed away, and still the Master came not. To fill up the interval, some sought present accomplishments of prophecies till then understood to belong only to the end. In this way was produced the historical school of interpreters, which has since flourished uninterruptedly, and bids fair to flourish, till the first sound of Apocalyptic judgment shall dispel the dream, and Prophecy, too long degraded and trifled with, shall appeal from the visionaries of the closet to the consent of a terror-stricken world.

In most ages there has been felt a temptation to abandon the plain sense of the prophecies, in favour of some meaning capable of adaptation to existing events. First, Pagan persecution invited the church to believe that Antichrist was come already. She

---

* Second Nicene Council, Act. v. The references, when not given in this introductory chapter, may be found elsewhere in the work.

made no sign of assent, but while struggling with the present, prepared for a more dismal future. Next came Arius, with his denial of the Father and the Son: again, the temptation was resisted. This might be the "falling away first," but it was not the revelation of the man of sin. Thirdly, the Mahomedan power perilled her existence: here some wavered, for Maometis was found to contain the number of the Beast, and the Turks were treading under foot the holy city. Fourthly, the iron of papal tyranny entered into her soul: in the struggle for liberty more of the primitive belief was lost. The Reformers of England prudently held their ground in silence, confident of one thing only, that Babylon was Rome. Luther partly gave way to the pressure: Calvin broke loose altogether, setting up Præterism and independence of interpretation. Rome for the moment reformed a little: to prevent worse, she allowed that she would once more become Babylon in time for her destruction by Antichrist. Fifthly, the church, again slumbering, was aroused by the infidel outbreak in France: she now bethought herself of the Scriptures, and consulting them in haste, found among the marks of Antichrist the denial of the Father and the Son.

But this storm blew over like the rest. Rome, recovering from her Reformation terrors, first shut up the Apocalypse, and then left the Inquisition to settle the question about Babylon. Meanwhile, a new danger had menaced the primitive belief.

The Præterism of Calvin was not long in spreading to the Jesuits, and thence back to the Continental Protestants. Their system was continually improving: Nero was found to act the little horn better than

Julius Cæsar; Barchochebas made a better Antichrist than Simon Magus. In this way the warning voice of the Apocalypse was effectually silenced: that great witness against Rome and Antichristianity lay dead. The critics rejoiced, relieved from the pressure of controversial difficulties: they sent gifts one to another, new names of the Beast and new little horns*— mere toys, not worth quarrelling about, and easily replaced if thrown aside. Thus the very credit of the Apocalypse was undermined: the prophecy of things future was degraded to a drama of the past, barely true in outline, and altogether imaginary in details.

In this wreck of human systems one resource remains. The school of the Apostles is open to us: Barnabas remains unrefuted; we may still "salute Hermes;" the tradition held fast by the Thessalonians may be made our own.

The primitive believers, living so near the time in which prophecy was given, looked upon it as a thing in itself stupendous and supernatural, and expected a fulfilment of corresponding importance. To them it was no marvel that the Babylonish monarch, the head of gold, whose very dreams ran upon universal empire, should fall upon his face before the Hebrew captive; nor that Daniel himself, after foreseeing the desolation of his people, should have fainted and been sick certain days. Nor did the repetition of the visions lessen the marvel; for in childlike eagerness the beloved disciple exceeds both Daniel and his king.

* See Appendix, Section IV.

The opening of the sealed book is for a moment delayed; and he who has grown old in sorrows, who has watched on Calvary, has passed through boiling oil, and is now wearing out his last years an exile in the mines, bursts into tears: "I wept much."

But the occasion justified both the Apostle's impatience and the old man's tears: he had seen what he might least have expected to see in that dismal region, his risen Lord. The vision was mercifully adapted to the desolate condition of the seer: Daniel, a monarch's favourite, might endure the prospect of abomination and desolation; but the weary breaker of ores needs something more consoling. He looks on till he sees a city descending from above: and upon one of its twelve foundations he reads a name, proscribed indeed on earth, but already engraved in heaven,— his own.

For our knowledge of one subject we are entirely dependent upon the ancients: the true meaning of the expression, "He that letteth." (2 Thess. ii.) Here, however reluctantly, we must sit at their feet: if we are to solve their riddle, we must plough with their heifer. For on this point St. Paul and the Thessalonians understood each other: "Ye know what withholdeth." And how had they learnt it? "When I was yet with you I told you these things." They knew something not directly expressed in Scripture: and this knowledge they were told to hand down together with the epistle. In the primitive church, therefore, there was no doubt of the meaning of that saying. If put as a question, it was only as by way of catechism. Tertullian scarcely condescends to answer it: "What but the *Roman* status?" he asks in reply, so placing the words as to throw the emphasis upon *Roman*. (Quis nisi Romanus status ?) But, if St. Paul meant no more than this, why not say plainly in the epistle, That man will not come so long as the Roman order of things continues? A fair question, remarks Chrysostom, who is the first to ask it; for before his time the reason was self-evident.

From its beginning Christianity had come into apparent collision with the interests of the Roman state. Pilate thought it impossible to befriend Christ, and yet to continue Cæsar's friend. The same feeling hurried on the Jews to their last great act of apostacy: " The Romans will come," said the politicians of the Sanhedrim. It was pretended to be against the decrees of Cæsar, to say that there was another king, one Jesus. But the Jewish rulers feared for their own sake also. Herod's jealousy of his infant rival must be quenched in the blood of Ramah and the tears of Rachel. From the first, the kings of the earth stood up, when another King was about to be set upon the holy hill of Zion.

This jealousy was met by prudence and a reasonable submission. The Babe was carried into Egypt, from the face of Herod: the King's children were directed to pay the tribute-money, " lest we should offend them." The Apostles were not less prudent: one, speaking " of the mouth of the lion," leaves us to guess the fangs of Nero: two style Rome, Babylon. Even Daniel, though he had spoken freely of Medes and Persians, and even of the king of Grecia, kept silence about the Roman name. " In the fourth beast," says Chrysostom, " he describes the Romans, but he mentions no names. And why? Because, had he made the account too plain, most persons would have destroyed the Bible."* The same reserve was maintained by the first rabbinical writers, who called the Roman the "wicked kingdom;" the later gloss says *Roman*. The idea is also preserved by Barnabas, who applies to the fourth beast the epithet *wicked*. So far have some carried the principle of suppressing the Roman name, as thus to account for the representation of that empire by a nameless beast.†

In the New Testament writings, any appearance of intentional obscurity may suggest an allusion to Rome or the empire. On all other subjects the Apostle of the Gentiles uses great plainness of speech; when he lowers his voice it is lest the Romans should hear. When the danger was past the reason of this obscurity became a matter of history. What Lactantius knew too well, Chrysostom found it needful to explain; and this brings us to the answer which he gives to his own question: "Had the Apostle said that the Roman empire would presently be overturned, they would instantly have despatched him as seditious, and with him all the faithful, as persons who lived and fought under him."

The Apostle's successors were equally cautious: Irenæus betrays the secret by little more than one word, "Latinus." After Constantine, the reserve, no longer needful, was laid aside; yet so late as the fifth century, Jerome was called to account for his remarks

---

* Chrysost. in Dan. vii.

† So Titus Bostrensis: "Since this part of the prophecy was to be cleared up in the time of the Romans, he leaves the beast anonymous, that the Empire might not feel itself insulted." This Titus lived soon after Constantine.

upon the clay mixed with the Roman iron. They must settle their dispute, he says, with Daniel: "Non mihi imputent, sed prophetæ."

But why so much fear of speaking against the perpetuity of the state? " He does not choose," answers Jerome, "to foretel openly the destruction of the Roman empire, which its rulers think to be eternal." Thus did Christianity clash with the political creed of Rome: a grave offence, for upon that creed was supposed to be based, in great measure, the stability of the imperial throne.

For, to secure the permanence of Roman rule, prudent statesmen had availed themselves of superstition. Rome was made a goddess, her supremacy a matter *de fide:* "invicta et æterna" was the first article of her creed. With these principles she had grown up: for that one virtue was Varro thanked by the people, that though he had rashly ventured upon a battle, and had left the bones of his army upon the plains of Cannæ, yet in that disastrous hour he had proved himself no apostate from the national faith; " he had not despaired of the welfare of the republic."

The Romans, accustomed to augur defeat if their charging legions wavered in their shout, knew better than to tolerate for a moment political scepticism. But the Christians refused to recognise in the empire any peculiar principle of permanency: they knew well that, like other empires, it was to end; to be followed by the short reign of Antichrist, and that then the saints would take the kingdom. By most, this belief was carefully concealed from the Pagans. " They ridicule us," says Lactantius, "because we do not publicly maintain these things; but, in obedience to God, keep His secret in silence."*

Yet, notwithstanding all their caution, the secret was very early betrayed. It was found too good to keep, and was therefore told anonymously. About the year 135 there appeared a fictitious work entitled "Sibylline Oracles," in which the coming of the Eastern Antichrist was connected with the ruin both of Rome and of the empire. " Then," said the disguised Christian, "then shall perish the flourishing empire of Rome, the ancient queen of neighbouring cities; no more shalt thou possess the fertile plains of Rome, when the Strong one shall come in arms from Asia." †

Of this tradition, the earliest versions are given by the Pseudo-Sibyl, Tertullian, and Lactantius. "The Roman name," says Lactantius, "will be taken from the earth, and empire will revert to Asia." Tertullian, the best lawyer and politician of the three, declares that the Roman status is the thing to be removed.

All this is easily verified from Scripture. Antichrist, according to St. John, will destroy Rome so completely, that he may be said to take away its very name from the earth. At that time she will no more rule "the fertile plain of Latium." But, perhaps, Tertullian's Roman status is more precisely the meaning of the Apostle. In what sense, then, does this still exist, so as to be incompatible with the establishment of Antichrist's kingdom?

* Institutiones, lib. vii. c. 26.
† Sibylline Oracles, lib. 8.

To this question many think it enough to answer, that the title of Roman Emperor has existed without interruption from the time of Augustus Cæsar to our own. They think it enough to appeal unto Cæsar; and, while there is a Cæsar to answer for himself, they are content. For, owing to the restoration of the Western Empire during the rule of the Byzantine Cæsars, the world has never since been without one or two emperors of the Romans. The present Austrian emperor, though holding scarcely a province of Adrian's, is the direct successor of Charlemagne, who was crowned in Rome, Emperor of the Romans, the sixty-ninth from Augustus. Bellarmine, tracing in history the existence of the iron legs and feet of the vision, remarks that, between East and West, the statue has always had a leg to stand upon. Moreover, during the middle ages, the Emperor's claims against the Pope were enforced upon the old ground of literally rendering to Cæsar the things that were Cæsar's; and lastly, the Roman bishop and emperor still form an essential part of the European constitution. To this day, therefore, throughout a large portion of the civilised world, the petition rises every year, " Mercifully regard the Roman Empire." *

But, with the help of Daniel†, we may assign to

---

* Missale Romanum, ed. 1840. "Almighty and everlasting God, in whose hand are the powers of all men, and the rights of all kingdoms, mercifully regard the Roman Empire; that the nations who trust in their fierceness may through thy power be restrained." —*Service for Good Friday.*

† We turn to Daniel with the better hope of assistance, as St. Paul's discourse in Thessalonica seems to have been an exposition of Daniel. Eusebius thinks almost as much: "'Remember ye not,' &c. Thus did the admirable apostle, in his discourses, teach

the letting power a somewhat wider meaning. Antichrist will change four things: times, laws, religion, and the seat of empire. All these may be massed together as the Roman status.

The times and laws now existing are Roman. The canon and civil law are based upon the codes of Justinian and Theodosius; the names of the months, the calends of the calendar, all are Roman. But this order of things Antichrist will change: for though it is only said, " He will *think* to change times and laws," this form of speech seems to be a reservation in favour of the Divine prerogative, since it belongs to God alone truly to change times and seasons. (Daniel, ii. 21.) Antichrist may call things by new names, but he can neither change the times, nor alter the immutable laws which bind mankind.*

He will set up a new religion, abolishing all worship but his own. Or, if any besides himself is the " god of forces," it will be a god that his ancestors knew not. He will deny the Father and the Son: he will deny that Jesus Christ has come in the flesh. Therefore, till the government of Asia and Europe is entirely wrested from the hands of Trinitarian princes, Antichrist cannot have come.

Lastly, he will change the seat of empire, planting

---

them about the end of the world, confirming what Daniel had said about Antichrist, and about our Saviour's glorious kingdom." — *Mai, Vet. Scriptores*, tom. i. pt. i. p. 206.

* Of these changes, a faint image was seen in the last century, in the enactments of the French Republic, when, detesting alike Christianity and the Roman order of things, its members thought to change times and laws. The week was then broken up into a decade, and the years were dated, not from the Incarnation of Christ, but from the birth of the atheistical republic.

the tabernacles of his palace in the holy mountain. During his reign Jerusalem will be occupied by his followers, for they will tread under foot the holy city forty and two months. Where the Lord was crucified, there he will slay the witnesses: he will set up the abomination in the holy place. All prophecy agrees in pointing out Jerusalem as the seat of Antichrist's kingdom.

So much for the nature of the assistance to be derived from tradition; we come now to a yet more important subject, the use to be made of the explanations contained in Scripture. On this point the ancients and the moderns are at variance. The primitive writers made it the basis of their system, that when a symbol is accompanied by an inspired explanation, that explanation embodies its true and final meaning. They no more thought of inventing another meaning of their own, than of applying the parable of the tares to the Incarnation, or that of the sower to the judgment of the world. But from this restraint most modern expositors of prophecy think it allowable to free themselves, urging that all prophecy is figurative, and that it must mean something different from what it says.

The explanations in question are such as these: that the great horn of the he-goat is the first king of Grecia; that the great city of the witnesses' death is the city where the Lord was crucified. The three frogs are the spirits of devils working miracles; the woman Babylon is the seven-hilled city that ruled the world in the days of Domitian.

It is little suspected by the world at large, that in this our Bible-reading country there are to be found writers who deliberately set aside most of these inspired explanations, and advance others directly opposed to them. The reader, not aware of this practice, wonders to see so many grave and studious men at variance: and, if cut off from access to the ancients, probably laments that the prophecies should be so difficult and obscure, while in reality most of the difficulty lies in the system pursued by the expositors themselves.

Symbols left uninterpreted in Scripture must be studied by the help of whatever light can be brought to bear upon them. But when there is given an explanation, as plain as words can make it, how can we hope to understand anything, if we reject the help thus given us? If we reckon *such* things obscure, we may, as Augustine remarks, expect to find nothing plainly revealed in Scripture.*

To fix upon an instance. In the twelfth chapter of the Apocalypse there is seen a red dragon, explained to be the old serpent, the Devil, and Satan. Its history is carried on through the book: nor is there any other explanation of the symbol, excepting in chap. xx., where it is again declared to be the old serpent, the Devil, and Satan. In these passages there might appear to be no obscurity or contradiction. But our expositors have decided otherwise.

Clarke.—" That the Dragon is the symbol of the heathen Roman empire, is the opinion of most commentators."

Bishop Newton.—" That the Roman empire was here figured, the characters and attributes of the Dragon plainly evince."

Mede.—" The Dragon, a sign and image of the dragon-worshipping heathen Roman empire."

* Civitas Dei, lib. xx. cap. 17.

Elliott.— " What is added, of the Dragon now seen by St. John, having seven heads and ten horns, designated it, though bearing the strange badge of Asiatic royalty, as distinctively the persecuting power of pagan Rome."

Galloway.— " The great red Dragon does not here refer to the pagan emperors, as former commentators have thought, but to the Pope."

It cannot even be said, in excuse, that this mode of interpreting is absolutely required by their system. One of the same school has distinctly stated his opinion that in these cases Scripture ought to be followed: " Where an interpretation," says Dean Woodhouse, " is expressly given in the vision, that interpretation *must* be used as the key to the mystery, in preference to all interpretations suggested by the imagination of man."*

Throughout the Apocalypse, the same neglect of the inspired explanations has been carried out. The " great city" of Apoc. xi., though explained to be the city where the Lord was crucified, is in turn made to mean Germany, Rome, France, Constance, and even Paris. The whole ancient world took it to be Jerusalem: but the ancients, we shall be told, knew nothing about prophecy. If by understanding prophecy is meant being wiser than Scripture, truly the ancients *were* ignorant of prophecy: but if, as Dean Woodhouse supposes, the inspired explanation is the true key to the mystery, then the neglect of that help may furnish the key to another mystery, the present deplorable condition of our prophetic studies.

The history of this corruption is easily traced: human inventions were placed, first side by side with

---

* Woodhouse on the Apoc. ch. xii.

Scripture, afterwards above it. The ancients, as a matter of course, received the inspired explanation of the red Dragon. "His colour," quaintly remarks Victorinus, "is worthy of his work, for he was a murderer from the beginning." The monks also followed St. John in expounding the Dragon; but they must needs speculate acutely upon its tail. The tail, said some, is hypocrisy, "quia turpia celat." Others, equally bent upon refinement, made it the hindmost and baser part of our nature: quoting the words of the Apostle, "Forgetting those things that are *behind*." Late in the sixteenth century, Aretius first set the example of admitting human speculations as an alternative to Scripture: if the Dragon, he says, be the Roman empire, his tail is the Papacy; if the Pope, his tail is the clergy; "but if the Devil, as he is, his tail is some false teacher." From that time modern inventions gained ground upon Scripture, till matters came to their present condition. And yet the Apocalypse holds out no encouragement to those who would take from it, or add to it.*

The writers who thus unintentionally exalt their own modern systems, extend their favour to some parts of the primitive and apostolic tradition: but, unlike

---

* In justice to our own age, it must be added that a few still resist the stream. So Mr. S. R. Maitland: "What meaning is there in language, or how are we to expect assurance from a written revelation, if we can make the Dragon anything but the great enemy of man?" (*Second Inquiry*, p. 24). Also Pareus, in 1608: "The Dragon is called the old Serpent, the Devil, and Satan: and who this is, nobody is ignorant." In the fifth century this was known even by the African catechumens: "that this Dragon is the Devil," says their catechist, "not one of you is ignorant." — *Sermo alius de Symbolo*, inter opp. Augustini.

the ancients, they do not keep the unwritten teaching in subordination to the inspired word. Many now say, and perhaps justly, that the identity of the fourth beast with the Roman Empire is " almost an article of faith:" but if this human, though venerable, tradition be *almost* an article of faith, should not the revealed identity of the red Dragon with Satan be made *quite* an article of faith?

To explain truly the meaning of a prophecy *before* its fulfilment is the highest honour permitted to the expositor. Thus Daniel, learning from Jeremiah that seventy years were to be accomplished in the desolations of his people, knew by books the end of the time. Second to this honour is that of interpreting a prophecy *after* its fulfilment; a measure of success less uncommon. So kings, poets, and pastors, reading what had been said of Babylon, applied it to the city of Rome. They learnt from the angel that Babylon meant a city, that this city was seated on seven hills, and that it was regnant in the time of the Apostle. Next came the discovery that Rome had seven hills: requiring no great ingenuity, since the Pagan Symmachus could use the fact proverbially, commending a Roman not for being " de septem montibus," but " deseptæ mentis." * Putting these things together, they contrived to explain the vision; but are we never to improve upon this, never

---

* Symmachi Epist. lib. ii. ep. 9. The name of *seven-hilled*, once made proverbial, became independent of the existing number of hills. For, as the Jesuit Tyrinus remarks, Rome was still called "the seven-hilled" after three new hills were added to the city. (*Tyrinus in Apoc.* xvii).

to perceive the meaning of a prophecy till all history is ringing with its fulfilment?

And now, if never before, let us look forward. Let us say;—we have been right about Babylon. Prophecy has been wonderfully exact and wonderfully literal about Rome, let us trust it in the matter of Antichrist. If we are to gain any credit as expositors, let us at once say boldly, Antichrist will certainly rule the world for three years and a half: he will indeed work great miracles; he will undoubtedly reign in Jerusalem; and, though none of these things as yet seem likely, though the fig-tree does not blossom, nor fruit appear in the vine, yet we will trust in that Word which has never failed us; we will do our utmost to demolish the boast of the infidel, that prophecy means nothing distinct till the time comes, but then—may be fitted to anything.

To secure for ourselves that highest honour, we must pursue the method which has led to the right understanding of other prophecies. Had we lived in the time of Alexander, by what means could we have shared with Jaddus the power of pointing out to the conqueror the coming triumphs of his nation?

First, we must have brought ourselves to believe that the Grecia of the prophet meant neither India nor Ethiopia, but Grecia proper; that the Persia to be conquered was none other than the kingdom of Darius; that a king meant a king; and that the kingdom would be broken by literal combats of horse and foot. We might be told that this was no interpretation at all, that prophecy is always figurative, and the like. But we should not be kept long in suspense: the sword of Alexander soon cuts this Gordian knot, and in the triumph share both Daniel and Jaddus, and the principle of literal interpretation.

But it is a small matter to foretel the exploits of the son of Philip; let us attempt a higher subject, even the first coming of the Son of God.

We transport ourselves to the temple during the last year of the Saviour's preaching. We will suppose a group of rabbis to be discussing this passage of Zechariah: "Thy king cometh unto thee: he is just, and having salvation; lowly, and riding upon an ass, and on a colt the foal of an ass." The prophecy throws them into confusion. One, mystically inclined, is bent upon explaining it generally, in reference to God's spiritual guidance of man. For man is the wild ass's colt, and the Messiah, presiding over such a one, is just, and brings with Him salvation.

The majority of our rabbis, we may suppose, are anxious to find some meaning more specific, and yet not so literal as to seem unworthy of the prophecy. With the help of our new methods of developing the sense, all would be easy. The riding upon an ass is the event of a single day; the fulfilment, therefore, may be expected to occupy a year. The ass must be magnified, in proportion, to a war horse, or even to a triumphal procession: so that, according to the modern rule of symbolic miniature, the Messiah may be expected to enter Jerusalem with chariots and horses, that He may sit upon the throne of His father David. By the rule of allusive contrast, the prophecy may be explained in direct opposition to its natural sense; or, it may describe allusively the coming of some false messiah, who will attempt to gain credit by assumed humility. And, on the Præterist principle, it may be applied to Israel's temporal saviours: "Speak, ye that ride on white asses, ye that sit in judgment." Therefore, as a judge, some future king of Judah will come, just, and bringing salvation from the Roman yoke.

To these arguments one shall be made to object, that other prophecies have been fulfilled literally. He quotes instances from Daniel and Jeremiah; but the general feeling is against him. If we take the ass literally, they reply, what shall we do with the thirty pieces of silver? what with the stripes of the man of sorrows?—the vinegar and the gall?—the lots to be cast upon his vesture? Allow the ass to be figurative, or you will be forced to apply all these degrading particulars to our glorious Messiah.

Our literalist, though not convinced, is silenced. He is not prepared to carry out his system with the piercing of the hands and the feet. But not long after, while walking towards the Mount of Olives, he is met by a rustic procession. The daughter of Zion seems to be rejoicing; yea, for once, the daughter of Jerusalem is shouting. And, as the crowd approaches, he discovers the cause of so much transport,—a Man of humble condition, lowly, and riding upon an ass, and upon a colt the foal of an ass.

Thus the methods now employed to evade the natural meaning of the prophecies about Antichrist, would have enabled the Jews to evade all that was predicted about the first coming of Christ. By such means they might have persuaded themselves that there would be no personal and literal Christ, working miracles and finally ruling in Jerusalem; but, instead of this, a succession of anointed high priests, lasting through many centuries, destitute of supernatural power, and performing, in a low and far-fetched sense, some few of the things foretold of the true Messiah. And, were it objected to them that this supposed order of priests had never set foot in the holy city, we might supply them with the means of evading this difficulty also.

When history has falsified any part of a prognostication professing to be derived from Scripture, the mistake will be found, not in the over-literalness of the interpretation, but in its not being literal enough. Petrarch styled Avignon the Western Babylon, because the Papal court was then fixed there. Petrarch, we shall say, was wrong. And why? because he did not keep closely enough to the literal seven hills, and to the mark of reigning in the time of the Cæsars. In a few years the Papal court returned to Rome, and the honour of the literal sense was once more vindicated.

About the same time another mistake was made. From the flight of the Papal court to Avignon, Clemangis ventured to infer the approaching ruin of Rome. But Clemangis, on his own principles, ought to have known better; for he believed that the church had been expelled from Rome on account of its profligacy: this migration, therefore, could not be called "God's people coming out of Babylon."

When the literal sense is duly observed, the future is not always impenetrably veiled. Were it so, there would be some capital error in ourselves, defeating the intentions of that book which is entitled "The Unveiling," from its professing to show us things that must come to pass. In the year 1280, it was given out by a Franciscan monk that Rome would become yet more depraved, in order to fulfil all that is said about Babylon. The name of this obscure expositor was Peter John, of Olivi. The church of Rome, he argued, is not yet bad enough to merit the vengeance then to be inflicted on her: Christ's honour demands that she should still more openly oppose the truth. There must first be, he continued, a reformation, a revival of Gospel principles; by opposing this, the "Church Carnal" of Rome will appear in her true colours, justifying her subsequent destruction by the antichristian kings. The inquisitors, not wise in their generation, extracted this passage in order to condemn it. Thanks to their labours, we now possess it, with the assurance that it was written more than two centuries before the Reformation.

Excepting in the matter of Antichrist, inferences drawn from Scripture concerning the future have been for the most part doubtfully expressed. Thus the friar Hervey, who lived in 1320, in commenting upon the removal of "him that letteth," suggested as possible this accompaniment to the event: "That the church of Rome may one day work iniquity, so that many churches will separate from her." Andreas of Cæsarea, writing about 500, supposed that in order to fulfil that part of the Apocalypse which declares Babylon's destruction by Antichrist, Rome might again rise to power, and Constantinople be taken out of the midst. Two events at the time most improbable: but what matters probability? The Popes brought about the one, the Turks the other. It is easy for us to say now that these events were necessary, and that Andreas should have tossed empires about more confidently, having the plain sense of the Apocalypse to back him: but which of us is in a condition to cast a stone at him?

There are some predictions which correspond with history so closely and so naturally, as apparently to refute altogether the supposition of a prophetic style. "These nations," says Jeremiah, "shall serve the king of Babylon seventy years:" and those nations did serve the king of Babylon seventy years, until the yoke was broken by the Medes and Persians, as recorded by Daniel. But, though numberless instances forbid our fixing upon any one form of speech as peculiar to the prophets, their writings contain some unusual modes of expression, in which the church has agreed to recognize the elements of a prophetic style. These forms of speech can scarcely be distinguished from ancient *poetic* style: but, by whatever name they are to be called, they may be reduced to some such classification as the following:—

1st, The past or present put for the future, noticed by Pantænus about the year 165: "The sayings of prophecy are generally to be taken aorist-wise: the present is used for the future, and also for the past."* But this style is not so much prophetic as divine: "Before Abraham was, I am."

2dly, Expressions borrowed from the symbol are sometimes carried into the plain narrative. The nominative case may be symbolic; the accusative literal; the intervening verb either common or doubtful. "It was given to the Beast to make war with the saints:" repeated from Daniel; "Another king shall arise . . . and shall wear out the saints of the Most High."

---

* In Clement of Alexandria's Eclogues, sect. 56.

Here St. John retains the literal saints and their being worn out, while he substitutes for the coming king his symbol, the beast. To these mixed prophecies a key must be sought in the unsymbolic, such as the discourse upon the Mount of Olives, and the epistle of St. Paul to the Thessalonians. From the latter we learn that the Beast is an individual man, "that man of sin," literally helped by Satan, and literally destroyed by Christ's second coming. The ancients, anxious only to discover the meaning, found these sayings not more obscure than the corresponding figures, "Beware of dogs:" — "The unclean spirit walketh through dry places:" — "After my departure shall grievous wolves enter in."

Now in these passages, the dogs, the dry places, and the wolves, though taken symbolically, are left unexplained. They need no explanation, so long as the symbols preserve their ancient meaning among mankind. But let this figurative meaning be lost or changed, and the same difficulty may arise as in the case of the uninterpreted emblems of the prophets. If, again, the old meaning should be discovered, the symbol becomes once more plain as at the first. Thus the rider of the first seal, in place of a name, has this distinguishing mark, "Going forth to conquer." At length some reader of Tacitus lights upon an account of the Jews, how they gathered from the prophets the certain promise, that at that time some should go forth from Judea to conquer. Again, Daniel sees in vision a lion with eagle's wings: from the context alone, the Church explains it as the Babylonish empire. But the ruins of Nineveh, buried from that time to the present, are at length discovered and explored: among them is found, keeping watch over the portals of the Assyrian halls, a lion with eagle's wings.*

3dly, The words king and kingdom are sometimes put for each other. "The rough goat is the king of Grecia, and the great horn between his eyes is the first king." Here the word king is used first for kingdom, afterwards for king. To this mode of speaking the ancients were not unaccustomed; Barnabas uses the words as convertible: "Ten kingdoms shall reign on the earth, and after them shall arise a little one, who will depose three: likewise of their kingdoms." Another instance is found in Daniel: "These great beasts are four kings. . . . and the fourth beast shall be the fourth kingdom upon earth." But neither Theodotion nor the Seventy felt the difficulty, since they translated without scruple, "The four beasts are four kingdoms."

* Layard's Nineveh (1848). The confirmation of Daniel's genuineness, afforded by these important discoveries, is not the least part of the advantage to be derived from them. The Assyrian eagle-winged lion has been mentioned by no writer from the time of Daniel till the recent discovery of ancient Nineveh.

The Christian will not fail to rejoice when noticing that each successive attack upon the character of Daniel has been met by the production of some new testimony to his credit. A century ago, the absence of a Septuagint Daniel was the boast of the infidel: presently the true Septuagint Daniel comes to light, authenticated by internal evidence of the strongest kind. Within fifteen years the East yields up the same treasure in the form of a Syriac translation, executed A. D. 928. Next, the scheme of the empires is assaulted; and now Mai lights upon a swarm of Greek expositors, fourteen of whom are new to the modern world. Lastly, a rude hand, within the Church, would drag Daniel from his place in history, thrusting him some centuries downwards to the end of the Grecian kingdoms. Who now shall stand his friend against Christians? The Ninevites shall rise up against this generation, and shall condemn it.

4thly, The prediction is sometimes repeated in a new form, especially when containing a fixed time. The seven years of famine were foretold to Pharoah, first by seven lean kine, and next by seven thin ears. The reason is given by Joseph: "The dream was doubled unto Pharoah twice, because the thing is established by God." So in the case of Peter on the house-top: "This was done thrice."

For, though God's mercies are sure, His threatenings, as Hezekiah and the Ninevites happily learnt, may sometimes be withdrawn. At other times God not only speaks once, but twice also we hear the same: thus, the period of the woman's wilderness-life, is expressed first in days, then in times. The duration of the desolating abomination is told to Daniel first in times, next in the fraction of a land-week, and lastly in days. And, as if to make us more abundantly certain of the accuracy of the fulfilment, the time is again expressed by St. John in the form of months.

5thly, There is found an abrupt and unexpected transition from one period to another, and even from one person to another: "I will pour out my spirit upon all flesh, and your sons and your daughters shall prophesy. . . . And I will show wonders in the heaven and in the earth, blood, and fire, and pillars of smoke." The first part is applied by St. Peter to the day of Pentecost: the last is still future.

"To proclaim the acceptable year of the Lord, and the day of vengeance of our God." At the end of the first clause the Saviour Himself shut the book: the acceptable year had come; the day of vengeance is still future. Transitions of greater difficulty occur in the cases of Solomon and of Mahershahal-hash-baz; a subject which Jerome, by his masterly handling, has almost made his own. The Jews, accustomed to living prophets, probably found in these passages little or no obscurity.

Fortunately for the student, the prophetic style is never found to affect the *times*. From Genesis to Revelation, there is no instance in which a prediction containing a set time has been fulfilled in any other measure of time. To this rule there is no exception, as may be seen by the following list, comprising all extant prophecies containing times, except those that refer to the days of Antichrist. A collation of these prophecies, if made earlier, might have saved three centuries of discord and confusion.

1. *To Noah.*—" His days shall be an hundred and twenty years." Gen. vi. 3.

2. " Yet seven days, and I will cause it to rain upon the earth forty days and forty nights." Gen. vii. 4.

3. *To Abraham.* — " They shall afflict them four hundred years." Gen. xv. 13.

4. *To Pharaoh's butler.* — " Within three days shall Pharaoh lift up thine head." Also to the chief baker. Gen. xl. 13. 19.

5. *To Pharaoh.* — " There come seven years of great plenty . . . and there shall arise after them seven years of famine." Gen. xli. 29.

6. *To another Pharaoh.* — " To-morrow about this time I will cause it to rain a very grievous hail." Ex. ix. 18.

7. *To the Israelites.* — " Your children shall wander in the wilderness forty years." Num. xiv. 33.

8. *To Joshua.* — " The seventh day ye shall compass the city . . . and the wall of the city shall fall down flat." Jos. vi. 4, 5.

9. *To Saul.*— "To-morrow shalt thou and thy sons be with me." 1 Sam. xxviii. 19.

10. *To Ahab.*— "There shall not be dew nor rain these years." 1 Kings, xvii. 1. (explained by our Lord to be three years and a half.)

11. *To Ahab.*— "At the return of the year the king of Syria will come up against thee." 1 Kings, xx. 22.

12. *To the Samaritans.*— "To-morrow about this time shall a measure of fine flour be sold for a shekel." 2 Kings, vii. 1.

13. *To the Shunamite woman.*— "A famine shall come upon the land seven years." 2 Kings, viii. 1.

14. *To Ahaz.*— "Within threescore and five years shall Ephraim be broken." Is. vii. 8.

15. *To Moab.*— "Within three years, as the years of an hireling, and the glory of Moab shall be contemned." Is. xvi. 14.

16. *To Arabia.*— "Within a year, according to the years of an hireling, and all the glory of Kedar shall fail." Is. xxi. 16.

17. *To Tyre.*— "Tyre shall be forgotten seventy years," Is. xxiii. 15. 17. (until the fall of Babylon, after the seventy years' captivity).

18. *To Hezekiah.*— "I will add unto thy days fifteen years." Is. xxxviii. 5.

19. *To Judah.*— "These nations shall serve the king of Babylon seventy years." Jer. xxv. 11, 12.

20. *To the captive Jews.*— "After seventy years be accomplished at Babylon, I will visit you." Jer. xxix. 10. (referred to by Daniel, ch. ix. 2.).

21. *To Hananiah.*— "This year shalt thou die." Jer. xxviii. 16.

22. *To Pharaoh.*— "At the end of forty years will I gather the Egyptians." Ezek. xxix. 13.

23. *Against Gog.*— "They shall burn the weapons with fire seven years." Ezek. xxxix. 9.

24. "Seven months shall the house of Israel be burying them." Ver. 12.

25. *To Nebuchadnezzar.*— "Let seven times pass over

him." Dan. iv. 16. 23. 25. 34. The Seventy translate in each place, *seven years:* also Josephus. Theodotion next restores the poetic form, reading *seasons.*

26. *To Daniel.* (ch. viii. 14.)—" Unto two thousand three hundred evenings and mornings." All the Asiatics before Theodoret agree in taking this to be the three years of Antiochus, about 1150 days, allowing for intercalation. Clement of Alexandria reckons it as 2300 days, beginning with the first invasion of Antiochus.

27. " After two days he will revive us ; in the third day he will raise us up." Hosea, vi. 2. The only Old Testament prophecy (except perhaps the type of Jonah) answering to St. Paul's reference, "rose again the third day, according to the Scriptures." Quoted for that purpose by Tertullian.

28. *To the Ninevites.* — "Yet forty days, and Nineveh shall be overthrown." Jonah, iii. 4.

29. *To the Jews.* — " The Son of Man shall be three days and three nights in the heart of the earth." Matt. xii. 40.

30. *To the Disciples.* — " The Son of Man must be slain, and be raised the third day." Luke, ix. 22.

31. *To the penitent thief.* — " To-day shalt thou be with me in Paradise." Luke, xxiii. 43.

32. *To the Jews.* — " Destroy this temple, and in three days I will raise it up." John, ii. 19.

33. *To the church of Smyrna.* —" Ye shall have tribulation ten days." Rev. ii. 10. (Fulfilled in April, A. D. 168 ; the persecution raging during the nine or ten days of the games.)

34. " They lived and reigned with Christ a thousand years." Rev. xx. 4.

These are perhaps all the prophecies that can fairly be pressed into the service. Some persons might be disposed to add the parable of the fig-tree, where the three years' barrenness might indicate the three years of our Lord's dealings with the barren synagogue. Also the three days' walking toward Jerusalem, " to-day, to-morrow, and the day following," which appear to mean nothing more definite than a few days, neither one nor two. There is, however, one more passage containing a numeral, but having no measure of time expressed.

"Seventy sevens" (in our translation, *weeks*) "are determined upon thy people and upon thy holy city." (Dan. ix.) Is it seventy times seven days, or months, or years, or jubilees? All ancient expositors, including the Seventy Translators, supply the word *years:* the Christian naturally, because this brings the time right for the cutting off of his Messiah; but the Jew, in spite of his prejudices, reads years also. Forced by some strong necessity, he supplies that word, though it convicts him of rejecting the Messiah, and places at the service of his opponents an argument of fatal power. That he was right in supplying it, the event has proved; one question only can be raised, — what led him to supply it?

The Jew enjoyed two sabbaths: the one made for man, kept on the seventh day; the other called the sabbath of the land, and kept on the seventh year. The latter, though long neglected, was again observed after the time of Daniel; and, by a grant of Alexander the Great, the seventh years' tax was remitted to the Jews.* The connection between this land-sabbath and the national captivities may be gathered from the following passages of Scripture:—

I. The appointment of the land-sabbath: "The

---

* This sabbatical year was well known to Tacitus, who makes it an argument of Jewish indolence: for, forgetting the numberless holidays of the Roman calendar, he accuses the Jews of not only resting on the seventh day, but even devoting to sloth the seventh year. — *Historiarum.* lib. v.

land shall keep a sabbath unto the Lord; six years shalt thou sow thy field . . . but in the seventh year shall be a sabbath of rest unto the land." Levit. xxv. 2. 4.

II. The numbering of the seven sevens: "Thou shalt number seven sabbaths of years unto thee, seven times seven years." ver. 8.

III. A national captivity threatened in case of disobedience: "Then shall the land enjoy her sabbaths, as long as it lieth desolate, and ye be in your enemies' land. Even then shall the land rest, and enjoy her sabbaths. As long as it lieth desolate it shall rest, because it did not rest in your sabbaths, when ye dwelt upon it." Levit. xxvi. 34, 35.

IV. Seventy years' captivity inflicted: "They were carried away to Babylon . . . until the land had enjoyed her sabbaths: for as long as she lay desolate, she kept sabbath, to fulfil threescore and ten years." 2 Chron. xxxvi. 20, 21.

In these passages both the offence and its punishment are calculated in terms of years, expressed or understood. Both the seventy and the seven sevens refer to years: therefore the Jews would naturally take the seventy sevens also to mean years. Of this reasoning a trace remains in a sermon by James of Nisibim, an Armenian writer of 340. He compares the seventy sevens of Daniel with the seventy times seven of the Christian's forgiveness; for "when the children of Israel were carried captive to Babylon, God chastened them during seventy years, and then, returning to the abundance of His mercy, brought them back to their country by the hand of Ezra the scribe. He increased and magnified His mercy upon them, even to seventy sevens, each consisting of seven years."*

Until late in the middle ages, the Jews steadfastly adhered to the custom of supplying years. At that time some pretended that *jubilees* was the word to be supplied, making the whole period 24,500 years. Bartoloccius adds, that they were ashamed to commit this extravagance to writing, but taught it privately by word of mouth.†

Sometimes a prophetic period is found to be closely connected with some other time already expired, the same numeral being found in each. Thus, Jonah's three days in the whale typified Christ's three days in the heart of the earth; the forty years' wandering were a punishment for forty days' unbelief; and Ezekiel, lying on his side for 390 days, bore the national iniquity of 390 years. Our Lord also, having preached three years, lay dead during three days. This system is carried farthest with the number seven, first introduced into the world's history at the time of the creation. The seventh day was made a sabbath, the seventh seventh a Pentecost. The seventh year was a land-sabbath, the seventh seventh a jubilee. The seventh thousand of years, says Barnabas, will be the millennium.‡ Seventy years of captivity were announced by Jeremiah, and after these was to come the most perfect of all numbers, seventy times seven.

---

* Jacobi Nisibeni, Sermo 2. cap. 13.

† Bibliotheca Rabbinica, part ii. page 365.

‡ Barnabas, Epistle, ch. xv. In chap. xvi. he appears to call the seven thousand years a week. "When the hebdomad is ended, a glorious temple shall be built unto God."

How far may this analogy be pushed in other cases? Perhaps it is best not attempted, since it can make no possible difference in the times predicted. Whether a day be given for a year, a year for a day, or a day for a day, the Israelites must wander forty years, according to the forty years foretold them; Christ rises again the third day, according to the Scriptures. It might, perhaps, be allowable to say that the witnesses, having prophesied with destructive powers during three years and a half, will *therefore* suffer a temporary defeat of three days and a half, a day for a year; or, to plunge altogether into conjecture, to say that their 1260 *days* of tormenting the earth may possibly be intended to avenge the cause of a Gospel rejected during 1260 *years*. (This seems to have been the meaning of Joachim, who gave out that there would be, from Christ to Antichrist, 1260 years.) Provided always, that we allow no speculations about an imaginary 1260 years to obscure our sight of that period, seven times declared in Scripture, the three years and a half of Antichrist's reign.

But the "year-day" theory means nothing so innocent as this; for by it the expositor, whenever it suits his purpose, understands years instead of days. The result is a multiplication of the prophetic periods by 360; in excuse for which, they are in the habit of asserting roundly, that the prophets said days when they meant years. Such ignorance of Scripture, displayed by those who enjoy the free circulation of the Bible in their mother tongue, has drawn down much ridicule from our Romish opponents.

These expositors for the most part follow that system of which we have seen a specimen in the case of the red Dragon. In the present instance, however, they profess to follow Scripture, pleading, in self-defence, first, a direct permission; and secondly, several precedents.

Their supposed permission is derived from two passages: the first in Numbers xiv., where the Israelites are sentenced to wander forty years, as a judgment for forty days of unbelief; the other is in Ezekiel, where the prophet is ordered to lie upon his side 390 days, to bear 390 years of Israel's sin; it being added, " I have appointed thee each day for a year." But on looking through their commentaries, it appears that they agree with all other Bible-readers in taking forty years as forty years, and 390 days as 390 days. There is, therefore, no difference to be discussed, no question to be argued: nobody is prepared to suppose that Ezekiel besieged the iron pan for 390 *years*, or that the Israelites wandered in the wilderness for 14,400. What these passages have to do with their reading 1260 years, for as many days, remains to be shown.

The year-day theory, as its opponents have been careful to notice, involves a plain and obvious fallacy. It assumes the identity of two things directly opposed to each other: a day of punishment mercifully *given* instead of a year, and a day *said* when a year is really intended. The first is undoubtedly observed in the case of Ezekiel: if, therefore, they think the principle too honourable to the Divine mercy to be lost sight of in the case of Antichrist, let them follow it out according to their precedent. Let them say (if they *must* be wise above what is written), God might have inflicted upon us 1260 years of Antichrist: the sins of eighteen centuries deserve no less. But God, who is rich in mercy, intends not to consign twelve centuries of our race to eternal perdition: He will punish one generation only, the unbelievers themselves. Thus he has appointed a day for a year: and since, if the days were not shortened, no flesh should be saved, He has limited the Beast's power to forty and two months. But, far from reasoning thus, the year-day expositors endeavour to lengthen out the days, maintaining that the prophecy meant one time when it said another. In defence of this strange assertion they produce still stranger precedents.

Some would persuade us that the forty days declared to the Ninevites meant forty years, and that after forty years Nineveh, perhaps, was destroyed. Rather than see their gourd wither, they would sacrifice that great city, though forgiven by God, of whose threatened judgment it was said, "He did it not." Others are reported to have argued (for this argument is now at least uncommon) that our Lord's three days in the heart of the earth meant His ministry of three years; as if Jonah must go down to the bottom of the sea to prefigure Christ preaching on the surface of the earth.

Even Christ's three days' walking towards Jerusalem have been quoted in this cause: for from those three days, "to-day, to-morrow, and the day following," they do not despair of making out the present year, the year before, and the year before that. But from St. Luke*, it appears that our Lord was then on his way to Jerusalem, a few days before the Cruci-

---

* From St. Matthew's arrangement, it seems possible that these words were spoken on that day on which it was said, "After two days is the feast of the passover."— Ch. xxvi. 2. compared with xxiii. 37.

fixion. The Pharisees had advised Him to escape for fear of Herod; but the Saviour is not to be disturbed in his work: He will do cures to-day, and to-morrow, and the third day He will be perfected, or have finished. Then follows another declaration, usually understood in this sense: I have at least three days' journey before me, that I may reach Jerusalem in time for the passover. For on that day, and in that city, I must be offered up; since it cannot be that a prophet should perish anywhere but in Jerusalem; — that Jerusalem which killeth the prophets.

But what shall be said of those who would have the seven times of Nebuchadnezzar's wandering to be not yet ended, although it is said, "At the end of the days, I, Nebuchadnezzar, lifted up my eyes unto heaven?" Not that they suppose the monarch to be at this moment eating grass with oxen near Babylon; but, by joining the vision of the metallic statue to that of the brass-bound stump, they contrive to make him, in his beast-like state, still the representative of the four empires.*

If true, the system of the 1260 years must be absolutely necessary to a right understanding of the prophecies. It completely changes the character of the great tribulation, of the man of sin, and of all the Apocalyptic visions. Yet it was never heard of till dreamed

* This interpretation is given by Mr. Elliott. "On the seven times of Nebuchadnezzar's insanity and bestialism. These, calculated after the year-day system, on the hypothesis of the Babylonish king's insanity figuring that of the great empires, which he then headed, in their state of heathen aberration from God (a point on the propriety of which I can myself feel scarce a doubt), terminate — if dated from the time, B.C. 797," &c.— *Horæ Apocalypticæ*, p. 1429.

into the world by a wild Abbot in 1190. None of the inspired writers allude to it; and, which might be conclusive against its pretensions, our Lord Himself appears to have known of no such principle. For by it the time of the end could have been determined, by reckoning 2520 years from Nebuchadnezzar, and 2300 from Antiochus. "Let him that readeth Daniel understand," says the divine Expositor, doubtless Himself understanding whatever could be learnt from Daniel. Yet the time of the end was unknown even to Himself; for, as Augustine remarks, the "day and hour" in Greek mean times and seasons generally, according to the saying of St. John, "It is the last hour."

Athanasius, with his accustomed zeal for the honour of the second Person, suggests a special reason for the declaration that "neither the Son" knoweth the times. Antichrist, he says, will do great wonders, perhaps pretending to a knowledge of times and dates, and enforcing his assertions by miraculous signs. But when he and his false prophets profess this knowledge, remember (says Athanasius), that not even the true Christ, as man, knew the times; still less shall a false Christ and a false prophet be suffered to attain to that knowledge.*

The imaginary period of 1260 years is no more to be found in history than in Scripture. That a period of this length may be fixed upon, anywhere in the course of the last eighteen centuries, cannot be denied; but, beyond this, even the writers of the year-day school are not agreed. For the first who attempted to count the 1260 years reckoned from

* Athanasius, Oratio IV. contra Arianos.

Christ's birth and resurrection; but how these events contributed to set up the desolating abomination, they left their readers to guess. The next event fixed upon was Constantine's public establishment of Christianity. These 1260 years, with a little contrivance, were made to end at the Reformation; a result which somewhat redeemed the theory. As time went on, they dated from Justinian's decree in favour of Trinitarianism, and this date also succeeded in its way; for, precisely 1260 years afterwards, Christianity was suppressed in France, and thus, in a manner, the sanctuary was cleansed.. If, as the Arians say, Trinitarianism were Antichristianity, and the worship of the Son the "strong delusion," there might be some truth in this calculation; but, to a believer in the Trinity, it is in danger of seeming itself an abomination.

The next date is 606, when Phocas is supposed to have settled the dispute for precedence in favour of the church of the mother city. This date will run out in 1866.*

* Among the number of dates thrown out, it is surprising that so few have come right by chance. One of the most successful schemes is that of Fleming, published in 1703, and twice reprinted since. The system was judiciously laid down according to the political aspect of his times : the fourth vial, he supposed, began to be poured out in 1648, upon the houses of Austria and Bourbon, the political sun. St. John describes that vial as *increasing* the power of the sun; but Mr. Fleming, belonging to the school of red Dragon notoriety, takes the opposite view, and supposes that the vial will *diminish* the power of the sun of Europe. "As to the remaining part of this vial," he continues, "I do humbly suppose that it will come to its highest pitch about 1717, and that it will run out about 1794." But the Bourbon misfortunes were at their height, not in 1717, but in 1792, 1830, and 1848; while the house of Austria suffered most disgrace in 1806 and 1848. The other

History, by continually falsifying the calculations of this school, signally avenges the cause of divine prophecy. It suffers none to go off boasting that he has attained to knowledge not possessed by the Son: slowly but surely it teaches to all this lesson, that it is enough for the disciple to be as his Master, and the servant as his Lord. But the failure of all these speculations, far from discouraging the Bible-student of prophecy, ought to raise his hopes and his confidence to the highest. For, if any system could succeed when opposed to the rules laid down for his direction, he might well stand aghast at its triumph, and doubt whether it were wise to commit himself exclusively to the guidance of Scripture. But now the choice is easy: the one path indeed demands patience, but the other leads to confusion: and such confusion as is not to be met with in any other art, mystery, or science, taught throughout the world.

To return once more to Scripture, from which, in following the year-day school, we have wandered too far. In the fulfilment of prophetic times, the current, rather than the precise mode of reckoning, appears to be observed. In this sense Christ was three days in the heart of the earth, having broken into three periods of twenty-four hours each. Yet, by Gentile reckoning, He is said to have risen again " on the third day;" for, as St. Luke delights to tell, Cleopas reminds him to his face, in proof of the failure of His mission, that " to-day is the third day since these things were done."

guesses are not nearer the mark; the sixth vial, which he makes the destruction of the Turkish power, " will probably take up most of the time between 1848 and 2000." The Pope's spiritual power is to begin to fall in 1848, his temporal power in 2000.

Sometimes, as if in acknowledgment of the divine character of prophecy, every thing is made to give way to the precision of the fulfilment. The Israelites must not stay to heat the oven, for the self-same day of the four hundred and thirty years has arrived. The Thief must be roughly despatched at sunset; he must follow his Master in haste, being promised Paradise for that very day. And despite the scoffing of the unbelieving lord, the fine flour and the barley were sold the next day in Samaria, though no window was opened in heaven to bring it about.

The two great powers whose names stand foremost in prophecy come into historical contact at a single point. Where Babylon ends, Antichrist begins: the same ten kings that destroy the first, give their power to the second. When the ten kings shall have burnt Rome, so complete will be the ruin, that no sign of life or habitation will again be found in her. Here, then, is a decisive landmark; Rome is still standing, therefore Antichrist has not yet come: we are still in the times of Babylon, whether tasting or refusing her golden cup.

Expositors have laboured to fix the precise point in the rise of Antichrist which corresponds with the fall of Babylon. From the shortness of the Beast's partnership with the ten Kings, some conclude that their work of destruction will be ended before that " one hour." Others, perceiving that Antichrist plucks up three of the ten, infer that whatever the ten do they must do before the coming of Antichrist; and, from the proclamation of Babylon's fall, issued immediately before the caution against worshipping the Beast, it appears that the danger from Babylon ends before that from Antichrist begins.

This point of junction is also the point of union between the revealed and the unrevealed times of our dispensation. When once Antichrist's supremacy is established, all delay and uncertainty of time will be ended: the three years and a half will be scrupulously reckoned, being laid down by Him who is not a man that he should lie, in months, and in times, and in days. Vainly will Antichrist think to confound that reckoning, for his time is registered beyond his reach: while he treads down the earth, its revolutions are silently numbering his days: while he lifts his hand against heaven, the sun and the moon are measuring with fatal regularity the years and the months of his long-determined sway.

A few prominent differences between these great powers may be collected from Scripture:—

BABYLON IS DESCRIBED,	ANTICHRIST IS DESCRIBED,
As a feminine power.	As a masculine power.
Seductive and abandoned, prevailing through her golden cup.	Ferocious and warlike, enforcing his claims by the sword.
Continuing from the Apostle's time till Antichrist; length of duration not revealed.	Continuing forty and two months.
Is succeeded by the ten antichristian kings.	A final apostacy, provoking Christ's second coming in vengeance.
Is burnt by the ten Kings, who afterwards fight against the Lamb.	Destroyed, together with the Kings, in the great battle with the Lamb.
Is bewailed by her accomplices in crime.	Leaves none to lament his fall.
Contains some of God's people even to the end.	Fatal to the salvation of all his followers.
Established on the seven hills.	Reigns in Jerusalem.

In a word, Antichrist's coming will be as much a deathblow to Babylon, as the present establishment of Infidelity would be to Popery. "The ten kings shall burn her with fire, and shall give their power to the Beast." That this is the broad sense of Scripture is proved by a consent of writers of every age and nation. A few specimens shall be placed before the reader.

A. D. 135. *Pseudo-Sybil.* — "No more shalt thou possess the fertile plain of Rome, when the strong one shall come in arms from Asia."

180. *Irenæus.* — "He will become the eighth among them, and they shall desolate Babylon and burn her with fire."

200. *Tertullian.* — "The harlot-city must suffer merited destruction from the ten Kings, and the beast, Antichrist, with his false prophet, make war upon the church."

270. *Victorinus.* — "They will give to Antichrist honour, and counsel, and power: of whom it is said, These shall hate the harlot, that is, the city."

300. *Lactantius.* — "The abominable tyrant who meditates the extinction of that eye" (Rome), "on the loss of which the world will stumble and fall."

500. *Andreas.* — "Babylon, a city which will reign till the coming of Antichrist."

1195. *Joachim.* — "The beast and his kings triumphing over Babylon."

1530. *John of Kemnitz.* — "Antichrist will execute God's sentence and judgment upon the great harlot Babylon."

1604. *Malvenda.* — "While the ten kings are reigning, after the ruin and destruction of Rome, Antichrist, as it appears from Scripture, will come."

1832. *C. D. Maitland.* — "The infidel power, the beast under its last head, devours Popery, — burns that great city Babylon down to the ground."

As if the doom denounced upon Babylon were not

sufficient for the warning of Christendom, many modern writers have endeavoured to amalgamate Babylon and Antichrist, hoping to identify both with the Papacy. By this rash step they unsettle every thing: in snatching at the shadow of a Papal Antichrist, they let go the substance of a Papal Babylon. For, if Antichrist is now reigning, and the ten hours can be made to mean those five Gothic kingdoms that Machiavel reckons up, and which some persons, by a process known to themselves only, expand into ten[*], Babylon must have long ceased to exist. Yet some, not content with making Babylon and Antichrist coincide in time, reckon the 1260 days to have expired already, while Babylon is still standing unconsumed.

Apparently indifferent to the way in which Scripture expounds its own symbols, these writers labour to throw at the head of the Pope nearly every denunciation contained in prophecy. He is made in turn the beast from the sea, the lamb-like beast, and the image of the first beast. Twelve centuries of Popes, including the evangelizing Gregory and the gentle Ganganelli, are made, *ex officio*, sons of perdition: the man of sin becomes three hundred men of sin. At another time, the Pope is the red Dragon or the wild Boar, the star fallen from heaven[†], the angel of the bottomless pit, and even the beast from the

---

[*] See Appendix, end of Section III.

[†] This figure of the fallen star was first applied to Gregory the Great, who was supposed to have fallen from the ecclesiastical heaven. Unfortunately for the theory, he did not *fall* from that heaven, but rather *rose* to it; so that they are mistaken, as Bellarmine has it, *toto cœlo*.

bottomless pit. The great point seems to be that the type should be something infernal. Fleming styles the Pope "Prince of incarnate devils;" Mr. Fysh, more moderate, makes him only vice-devil. Many have waded through enormous difficulties to prove that the Pope is the beast that "was and is not;" probably attracted by the words, "Goeth into perdition." But at this point they leave us to struggle with the greatest difficulty of all, how the Pope *was* before the time of Domitian, ceased to be while the angel was speaking, and was again to come up out of the bottomless pit, in which at that moment he was kept shut up.

The penetration of these writers baffles all disguise: a man lies concealed in the little horn, but his eyes are visible, and at once they recognize the Pope. Their line of proof is curious: eyes — see — seer — overseer — episcopus — bishop — Pope; and so they catch him. Sometimes, to complete their satisfaction, they accomplish a play upon a proper name: Brightman makes the martyr Antipas the Antipapal martyrs; in the black horse, Mede finds the severity of Severus. According to Mr. Elliott, the angel of Apoc. x. is Christ acting the part of Antichrist; the voice, "as of a lion roaring," being that of *Leo* the Tenth.*
To Gualterus, the wild boar out of the wood seemed a fit emblem of the Pope: but no Pope had been named Wild-boar. In this emergency he fastens upon

---

* Horæ Apoc. p. 387 to 465. See especially the heading of the pages, "Antichrist's face as the sun : Antichrist's feet on land and sea: Antichrist's cry as a lion roaring." The Protestant Daubuz had before made the same angel Luther.

Hog's-snout (Bocca di Porco), the name of Sergius the Second before his accession.*

Of this rough usage the Pope cannot fairly complain. *He* first, in that indecent warfare, made free with the bolts of heaven, attempting to fix upon his sovereign the epithet of "the Beast." The emperor, as was natural, retorted: "The Pope describes me," he complains, "as the beast coming up out of the sea, full of names of blasphemy, and marked with the spots of a pard. But I say that he is that beast of which we read, 'There went out another red horse from the sea,' (meaning the *seal*, for Frederick was not quite at home in the Apocalypse,) 'and he that sat upon him took peace from the earth.' "†

This wild mode of interpreting produces a reaction: "In the Apocalypse," says Professor Lee, "I have not been able to find any mention either of the Pope or of Popery." ‡ And that is not the only mischief: these interpretations, though little noticed at home, figure with great effect in Romish commentaries. They are found to tell well in Gath: the Jesuit or the Benedictine, dragging them in as a foil to some other speculations of his own a little less extravagant, expresses a modest gratitude that he himself is not like other commentators, or even as this Anglican. Thus Calmet, to keep himself in countenance with his "Diocles Augustus," repeats with satisfaction the

* Gualterus, Homilia in Marcum 110. (A.D. 1570.) "By which omen," says Walter, "God declared that now the fatal period was at hand, when, as the Psalmist says, the wild boar out of the wood was to lay waste His vineyard."

† Petrus de Vineis, Ep. lib. i. cap. 31. (A.D. 1240.)

‡ Professor Lee on the Study of Holy Scripture, Preface.

scheme of Potter, making the Beast's enigma an incorrect square of 25, a number supposed to be of frequent occurrence in the Roman church.*

When an interpretation of this sort is peculiarly weak, its supporters attempt to raise its credit by styling it "the Protestant interpretation." Now it cannot be denied that the Reformed churches, having suffered severely at the hands of their common assailant, have been sorely tempted to revenge themselves by controversial bitterness. Protestantism, it may safely be allowed, has been at times betrayed into rash assertions, and has been driven, by the violence of its enemies, to avail itself of some unsound arguments in its own defence. But Protestantism is not yet so besotted as this, to contradict Scripture out of spite to the Pope. It is not yet so blind as formally to maintain that denying the Father and the Son means supporting the doctrine of the Trinity, or that denying Christ's coming in the flesh means parading the historical accompaniments of that coming beyond the bounds of sober decorum. The Pope denies neither the Father nor the Son; the Arians call him Antichrist because he honours the Son even as he honours the Father. Far from denying Christ's having come in the flesh, the Pope treasures up, with superstitious fondness, even the spurious relics of the cross on which He hung: the Pope sits up all night to

---

* Calmet (in Apoc. xiii.) expresses his surprise at the praises which Protestant writers have bestowed upon this vagary. So late as 1814, Mr. Clarke writes thus: "Dr. Potter's most ingenious interpretation of the number 666, upon which Mr. Mede has passed a very high and deserved encomium."— Clarke's *Dragon and Beast*, p. 76.

worship a pretended fragment of the cradle in which He lay.*

The inspired writers, when foretelling the doctrines of Antichrist, must have been capable of so describing the Papacy as to leave no doubt of its real character. They could, had they wished it, have foreshown an Antichrist idolatrous, seductive, spreading abominable delusions, and, above all, so given to unlawful intrigues with the kings of the earth, as precisely to correspond with what our church is thinking of when she exacts from her clergy this solemn oath, — "I do swear that I do from my heart abhor, detest, and abjure, as impious and heretical, that damnable doctrine and position, that princes excommunicated or deprived by the Pope, or any authority of the See of Rome, may be deposed or murdered by their subjects, or any other whatsoever." For this spirit of bloodthirsty intrigue is literally foretold of Babylon; therefore we may be certain that had the Apostles meant to describe the Pope as Antichrist, they would have fixed upon points on which he is opposed to Scripture, not those on which he is entirely in accordance with it.

It is sometimes felt as a difficulty in the literal system, that nobody could be supposed mad enough to fulfil prophecies well known and plainly expressed. If the objector should be weary of being reminded of the Jews, who, with the prophets in their hands, still pierced and buffeted the Man of sorrows, let him accept, by way of supplementary proof, the history of Babylon. Rome, swarming with readers and expositors of the Apocalypse, nevertheless assumes the

* On Christmas eve, when the supposed relic of the Bethlehem manger is exhibited at the midnight mass.

purple, claims queenship, massacres her thousands, and, as if she had never heard the story of the Sorceress on the hills, spreads treachery and bloodshed wherever her agents succeed in obtaining power.

The year-day expositors would make the prophets no better geographers than theologians. Antichrist is said to reign over the whole world: over all kindreds, tongues, and nations. St. John's whole world need not include America, or Russia, or perhaps Great Britain; but it must include his own continent: for, excepting in the episode of Babylon, every place mentioned in the Apocalypse is Asiatic. These are Patmos, where the book was written; the seven churches to which it was sent; also Armageddon, the holy city, and the river Euphrates. A European may think Europe the world; but to an Asiatic the rest of the world is an appendage to his own continent: he would say with Demetrius of Ephesus, "all Asia and the world." To St. John and his readers Asia was, to say the least, an essential part of the "whole world;" therefore, until the Pope begins to have some power or dominion in Asia, he has not fulfilled the prophecies about Antichrist.

Let it not be objected to this rigid adherence to the language of Scripture, that better and more learned men have not thought it needful, and that we may safely trust a little to their good sense and piety. For, in conflict with antiscriptural powers, this scrupulous adherence will be found our only safety. The Church of Rome may possibly dispense with the Bible, having her Trent for doctrine, her anathemas for reproof, her inquisition for correction, and her infallible pontiff for instruction in righteousness. But with us, all these purposes must be served by Scripture. We must part with all else, if the price of that pearl should require it. As the Reformers triumphed, so must we; consigning to oblivion all that opposes the word of inspiration, and setting up over its sepulchre this epitaph, — " A fond thing vainly invented, and grounded upon no warranty of Scripture, but, rather, repugnant to the word of God." *

The prophecies hitherto considered have been either — first, those interpreted in Scripture; or, secondly, those explained by the Apostles in their oral teaching. A third class still remains; — those which were explained (to the best of its power) by the Church at large, unassisted by any inspired teacher. Against these interpretations there lies the objection, that, however finished may be the superstructure, the foundation is always weak, — they want the authority only to be imparted by an inspired voice or pen. On the other side it may be urged, that in a book named " The Revelation," the portions left unexplained may be supposed to require no explanation; so that the meaning first attached and usually adhered to is probably right. The character of these explanations may be gathered from the following sketch, comprising all extant notices of the first seal down to the Reformation: —

" A white horse," writes the Apostle, "and he that sat on him had a bow: and a crown was given to him, and he went forth conquering and to conquer." (Perhaps a Hebraism, for, he went forth to complete

---

* Article XXII. On Purgatory.

INTRODUCTORY ESSAY. 51

and decisive victory; since the early Eastern versions make no attempt to preserve the exact form of the Greek.) He tells us everything about the conqueror except his name. But what if his name were known already? What if the expression "going forth to conquer" were already appropriated to the Messiah and His religion? The Jews, says Tacitus, resisted Vespasian partly on the strength of a prophecy contained in the books of their priests, that some persons "should then go forth from Judea to conquer."* Suetonius is more explicit: "Throughout the East," he says, "there flourished an ancient and steadfast belief that the fates had declared that some persons should at that time go forth from Judea to conquer. This prediction, as the event afterwards showed, referred to the Roman Emperor; but the Jews, applying it to themselves, rose in arms."† The prophecy may have been taken from Micah, from Jacob's blessing, or from both; this, however, is certain, that the belief was so general among the Jews as to support them in the unequal contest, and at length to reach the ears of both the Roman historians. Both of these thought the prediction true, but both applied it to Vespasian, whom they had seen going forth from Judea to conquer and to receive a crown. But St. John would certainly know better. He had another king than Cæsar, and to that King of kings he would not fail to apply the prophecy, even before he was shown the second crowned and conquering rider of the white horse, having on His vesture the full length title,

* Tacitus, Histor., lib. v. cap. 13.
† Suetonius in Vespasian, c. 4. " Judæâ profecti rerum potirentur."

"King of kings and Lord of lords." Therefore, from the time of Irenæus to the year 1500, all agreed to consider Christ as the Rider of the first seal. It was received without dispute, that though John first saw the emblem, David foresaw it, even when to that horseman it was cried in his hearing, "Ride prosperously."

Irenæus, the earliest writer on the subject, says, briefly, that the rider is Christ, prevailing like Jacob. Tertullian, in his usual rapid manner, styles him "The Angel of Victory." Elsewhere he appears to identify the rider with the Prosperous Rider of the psalm: the arrows he takes to be precepts, piercing the conscience. Victorinus finds a motto for the picture: "The Gospel must be preached throughout all the world." Like Origen, he takes the white horse to be the pure word. The bow is its power of piercing the heart. He thinks the Holy Spirit to be included in the symbol.

This is all that remains from the martyr-church. Their explanation, though scanty, amounts to this, that the first seal represents Christ's victory through the first preachers of the Gospel. The rapid temporal success of Christianity, its vast conquests and its spreading dominion, soon justified their application of the triumphant symbol. And it now becomes not the least part of the explanation, that the explanation itself was first given in the martyrs' age: that by faith they snatched this crown, and made it theirs. From St. Paul downwards they claim a share in their leader's victory: they come in panting to the goal, and demand the prize. But shall we reckon them victors, so weary, so blood-stained, and so despairing of life? They have still strength to answer for themselves, and their shout of triumph has not yet died away, " In all these things we are more than conquerors."*

A habit of not distinguishing between the two white horses deprives us of some ancient comments. Jerome merely notices Christ as the rider of the white horse in the Apocalypse. Tychonius makes the rider Christ combined with the Holy Spirit; the white horse is the church. Andreas, a valuable Greek writer, enjoying access to many primitive works now lost, understands by this seal the sending forth of the Apostles to preach the Gospel. Their victory is over error, their weapons are arrows of salvation. Cassiodorus follows the track. The white horse, says Primasius, is the band of primitive preachers, by divine grace made whiter than snow; the rider is Christ, mounted, as Habbakuk foresaw Him, upon horses and chariots of salvation. Arĕtas agrees in the matter of Habbakuk, making the horse the preaching of the Apostles. The bow, he says, is now "made quite naked."

The eighth century brings with it our countryman Bede, in whose hands the interpretation takes a more substantial form. " Upon the church, through grace made whiter than snow, sits the Lord, who, bearing against the wicked the arms of spiritual doctrine,

---

* The primitive interpretation of the first seal has been lately objected to, on the ground of its supposed unsuitableness to an age of martyrdom. "It will at once be seen," says Mr. Elliott, "that to have applied the bright symbols of the first seal, in any *earthly* sense, to them, amidst their bitter sufferings, mockeries, and often tears of blood, would have been felt as an act adding insult to injury." Vol. iv. p. 548. ed. 2. Perhaps "conquering and to conquer" may be a paraphrase of the hyperbole, "more than conquerors."

does in His people win a victor's crown." Haymo understands Christ going forth in the gospel; His success is betokened by the crown. Ansbert has nothing to add. Christ, says Deacon Anselm, is here seen, borne by holy preachers, conquering in Judea, and to conquer among the Gentiles. Thus, unconsciously, he comes round to the original belief, as reported by Tacitus and Suetonius.

Bruno adds, that as often as a sinner is converted, Christ is crowned afresh.

Rupert innovates a little: the horse and rider are God and man, one Christ. There is given Him a crown — the Apostles: "Thine they were, and thou gavest them me." Richard St. Victor is more simple: the primitive elect bear forth Christ: the bow is their preaching, the crown their reward. Anselm of Havilsburg adds some touches to the picture: the apostolic church goes forth, daily increasing, multitudes being added to it; and Christ obtains the crown, going into a far country to receive a kingdom. He goes forth, already a conqueror, saying, "I have overcome the world."

Even the eccentric Joachim assents: upon the army of the primitive elect sits the King of Righteousness, crowned, as man, by God the Father. The thirteenth century brings the schoolmen, who do no great mischief. Albertus Magnus finds a text for the white horse, — "Ye are the light of the world," — thus bringing the apostolic band within the compass of a single figure. Upon this horse Christ goes forth, armed with the weapons of Scripture; and there is given Him a crown of believing followers. But a man of twenty-one folios is not to be tied down to a single meaning. Christ went forth from the Father to come into the world; also He went forth, yea, He burst forth, from the narrow confines of Judea, that He might be for salvation to the ends of the earth. But Albert vainly attempts to reckon up the goings forth of this Horseman, for they have been of old, even from everlasting.

Albert is not satisfied till he has found something more strictly appropriate to the " Lamb that had been slain." There was given Him (he says) a crown — of thorns; and He went forth — from the gate of Jerusalem; conquering — the Jews and Pilate by His patience, that He might conquer — the devil and death.

The first seal, says Cardinal Hugo, is Christ conquering through primitive preaching. To some, adds Thomas Aquinas, those arrows are a savour of life, while to others their wounding brings death. De Lyra follows closely; also De Gorram: He goes forth from Judea, conquering few, to conquer many. At that point Oremius finds room to insert the saying, " Lo, we turn to the Gentiles." Berengaud proposes a change: Christ striving with the antediluvians. He was so fortunate as to find a follower, unless the " Block-book" Apocalypse be his own production. In that collection of wood-cuts, the first living creature holds a scroll containing the words (almost copied from Berengaud), " Come and see, — that is, understand spiritually, — what thou hast read of as done before the deluge." Paradisus returns to the beaten track, and is followed by Bernardine, who copies Bede.

For some centuries they had been labouring to perfect the illustration of the bow and the crown, the conquest past, and the conquest to come. The monks, who overdid every thing, were on these points minute to a fault. The wood of the bow was made the Old Testament; the string, the more active and impelling power of the New. For the horse, some quoted the prophet: "He hath made the house of Judah his goodly horse in the battle." For, from the tribe of Judah, Christ chose those who were to bear Him forth to the conquest of the Gentiles. Of such a horse they might well affirm that "He saith among the trumpets, Aha; neither believeth he that it is the sound of the trumpet." For in the inner prison those men sang praises, their feet fast in the stocks, but their steps as firm in heaven. (Fulgentius.) And from this horse the rider never dismounts: He has promised to be with it always, even to the end of the world. But the crown and the conquest were not so easily fixed.

Whatever remains as the trophy and glory of a conquest may be called its crown. It was the crown of Eleazar, that when his work was ended and the sun went down, he could not lay aside his weapon; his hand, stiffened and swelled with the carnage, was not to be disengaged from the hilt. It was the crown of Phinehas that he was zealous for his God, and this shall be told of him to all generations for evermore. But what, in this figurative sense, is the Saviour's crown?

Some said, the glory of being believed in. Evidently a great triumph, since St. Paul reckons it among the mysteries, that Christ was believed on in the world. Others said, the believing people; "a crown of glory in the hand of the Lord." For this rewards His labour: when He sees of the travail of His soul, He is satisfied. But Christ was crowned in another sense, even for the suffering of death with glory and honour. Nor may we forget the martyr's crown, to which, as the faithful and true martyr, He is entitled. But here the mystic Bernardine dashes into the thickest of the glory, and undertakes to tell the whole story of the crown. It is, he says, four-fold. First, of flesh: the crown with which His mother crowned Him on the day of His espousals with our nature; secondly, of thorns, with which His stepmother, the synagogue, crowned Him; thirdly, a glorified resurrection body; and, fourthly, His believing people. Bernardine then dreams on, uttering in his sleep very pleasant things: how in this crown there are entwined the lilies of the pure in heart, the red roses of martyrs, and the violets of the lowly ones.

He went forth conquering and to conquer: conquering in Judea, and to conquer among the Gentiles: conquering in Himself, to conquer in His people. His first conquest might be that of which His wounds are telling: "He through death overcame death." And yet this is scarcely the first, since before it He could say, in a better sense than Alexander, "I have overcome the world."

In 1450 Dionysius sums up: the chorus of the Apostles, or the primitive church, bears forth Christ and His Gospel to the conquest of the world. To the man Christ Jesus there is given, by the blessed Trinity, a crown,—supreme felicity, dominion, and honour; also a circle of believing followers. Also, there was given Him, by the synagogue of Satan, a crown of thorns, by patiently enduring which He won that crown of glory which now adorns His brow.

He conquered the devil by humiliation, the world by poverty, the flesh by holiness; that by His power He might subdue all adversaries, wounding them either to perdition or to endless life.

At this point we may leave the horseman, before he falls into the hands of certain Jesuits, who strip him of his glory, and rob him of his divine immortality. Alcassar makes the rider Faith; Viegas styles him Caligula, but Caligula as a shadow of Christ. He has since been taken for Nerva and Constantine; Foxe and Faber make him the Babylonish empire; Wetstein, reasoning from the bow, the Parthian Artabanus. For to each of these the expositors present a crown, and decree a triumph at their own proper cost.

A symbol so generally applied to the Saviour acquires, if merely from long and hallowed association, a degree of sacredness. The accredited portrait of an earthly benefactor we do not endure to hear lightly spoken of, or pronounced to resemble some hateful and revolting character. Moreover, there seems to be a certain propriety in the symbols of prophecy: the King of kings goes forth upon a white horse; the Cæsars rage in the figure of a ten-horned beast. These emblems of the crown and the white horse, this tribute to the valour and the purity of the warrior, is it lawful to give them to Cæsar or not? Let us first inquire whose is the image and superscription.

Even among the moderns, some have sacrificed part of a favourite system rather than remove this ancient landmark. This primitive interpretation has been followed by Woodhouse, Wordsworth, Vitringa,

King James I., Pareus, Bossuet, Grotius, La Haye, Mede, Cunninghame, Walmsley, Lowman, Mulerius, Tyndal, Brightman, and others, together with the Jesuits Mariana, Ribera, Pererius, Menochius, A Lapide, and Tyrinus. Still, the meaning of the symbol, though for fourteen centuries considered fixed, is now made an open question; and, which is yet more strange, nearly the whole prophetic creed of the ancients, including the inspired explanations, has shared the same fate. The cause of this change is a subject for diligent inquiry.

Some point to the year-day theory as the origin of the confusion: not that they intend themselves to follow the natural sense, but, finding that theory unprotected by Scripture, ridiculed by the critics, and continually falsified by history, they think it fair game, and cry out upon it as the author of all the disturbance. But a little inquiry will show that the year-day theory has not this to answer for: since,—

First. It did not originally interfere with the natural interpretation; for both Joachim and Walter Brute placed the appearance of Antichrist after the end of the 1260 years.

Secondly. It was never an active principle, but one of many contrivances, resorted to by way of lengthening out the periods fixed in prophecy. Among these are a *time* for 100 years, suggested by Tychonius; a time for thirty years (Luther); a month for seven years (Foxe); and a year for 190 years, (Bengel). Bishop Horsley, with the help of more algebra than the Apostles had any idea of, reduces 1260 days to 242 years. Clearly these are not the persons to cast a stone at their year-day neighbours.

Thirdly. The 1260 years, though invented by Abbot Joachim together with the historical system, did not come into favour till long after it. Dionysius, who wrote in 1450, knew nothing of the 1260 years, but accused the historical expositors of causing the confusion. "Some," he says, "endeavour to explain the Apocalypse, in reference to the state and troubles of the church in chronological order during the Gospel dispensation, from the time of the Apostles and Christ's first coming down to the persecution of Antichrist and the end of the world. Their exposition is made out of histories and chronicles."*
The writer here pointed at is De Lyra; otherwise an excellent commentator, and a fair specimen of the unmixed historical school. On Apoc. xiv. he writes: "I saw one seated on a cloud, King Pepin; like unto the Son of Man, being conformed to Christ: having on his head a golden crown, which the Frank kings then wore. And another angel, Pope Stephen, went out of the temple of the Roman church," &c.†

This system professes to find in history the fulfilment of nearly all the Apocalypse. As time advances, the events have to be moved farther back in the book, — an operation easily performed, as there appears to be no fixed point in the system; but, as nothing has yet happened like the opening of the sixth seal, or the resurrection of the witnesses, the plan has its difficulties. Here the more prudent make a stand: these things, they say, must be still future; the great day of the Lamb's wrath cannot have passed away unnoticed,

---

* Dionysius Carthusianus, in Apoc. x.

† Nicolas De Lyra, postilla in Apoc. xiv. Such expositions, when a little out of date, begin to appear almost ludicrous.

since the universal terror is an essential part of the event. But they all profess to have found the locusts, which the ancients expected as part of the great tribulation. Here, then, we may expect a decisive explanation: if the locusts have come at all, there can be no question *when* they came.

The locusts, says Joachim, are the Waldenses, Cathari, and Paulikians. The locusts, says De Lyra, are the Arian Vandals. The locusts, thunders Luther, are the schoolmen; and their King Apollyon is Aristotle.* The locusts, says Brute, are the friars: but the friar Ubertinus hopes that they are only monks. Here Broughton steps in as moderator: the locusts, he says, are both monks and friars: their women's hair shows that they live in cloisters. The swarm now threatened to settle finally upon the monks; but, beyond all hope, a strong west wind took away the locusts. Their sudden migration may be thus explained: —

These fiery visitants, though in other respects well fitted for controversial use, possessed the disadvantage of being certain to sting those that employed them. Long after every one else had discovered this propensity, the Romanist Walmsley was incautious enough to give out that the locusts were Protestants. Be it so, answered his opponents; allow, therefore, that the Church of Rome, being tormented by them, has not the seal of God upon her forehead. Upon this the stern features of Controversy relaxed into a smile.

Since that time the locusts have been banished to the East. They are now usually explained to be

* Lutherus in librum Ambrosii Catharini.

the Saracens, sent to torment those who worshipped idols of gold, and silver, and brass; that is, the Greek church. But history says something about the Greeks having split off from the Latins on the question of image-worship; adding, that, because they refused to worship the idols of gold and silver, the Latins abandoned them to their fate, and to the ravages of the Mahometan arms.

The strangest part of this system is the length of time sometimes required to elapse before the event can be sufficiently forgotten to allow of its being mistaken for a fulfilment. Hyrcanus, who lived through the persecution of Antiochus, could describe it in no language more suitable than the words of the prophecy of Daniel. Polycarp, having received, as angel of Smyrna, the promise of a crown, delays the fire by thanking God for the fulfilment. But the reign of Diocletian had to be steeped in a thousand years of forgetfulness, before any one could take it for the opening of the sixth seal; the peaceful reign of Constantine required fourteen centuries, before it could be taken for that great day of the wrath of the Lamb. Others, indeed, find fulfilments in the events of their own lifetime: but these fulfilments seldom survive their discoverers. Luther thought it safe enough that the little horn was the Turks: Melancthon was equally confident.* Sud-

* Melancthon on Daniel vii. "What is this kingdom, rising close upon the decline of the Roman monarchy, propounding a doctrine openly contumelious to the Son of God, openly abolishing the Scriptures of prophets and apostles, which by arms compels other nations to embrace a new, lying, and impious doctrine, and in power excels all kingdoms? The thing speaks for itself, that it is the Mahomedan kingdom."

denly Calvin decides that all are wrong, and the little horn must be Julius Cæsar. Then, as the papacy declines, and people form a confused idea of what it was at its worst, they make the little horn the Pope.

De Lyra finds the Witnesses in Sylverius and Menna. The other characters of the vision he distributes among their cotemporaries; as for the beast from the bottomless pit, that obolus he bestows upon Belisarius. Soon their cloudy chariot has to ascend with Huss and Jerome; at another time with Luther and Zwingle, or with the Old and New Testaments. And, to crown all, it has to return for half the Antichristian rabble of the middle ages: for the arrogant Sergius, who boasts himself the Good Shepherd; and for the Orleanists, who refuse to believe in the Incarnation, because they were not present when it took place. None of these can be said, even figuratively, to have shut heaven, except the Paulikians and Orleanists, who suppressed the greater part of the Bible.

At the basis of the historical method there seems to lie an assumption that the events foretold cannot possibly happen as they are described. Daniel's king of Græcia may indeed have been a king of Græcia; but that St. John's witnesses should turn out to be two individual men, working miracles and breathing out fire,—this seems impossible. It appears more prudent, and less likely to compromise the honour of the prophecy, to style any Antichristian sectaries "the witnesses," than to suppose that the prophet means literally what he says. But should we once hear that two men are at this moment preaching in Judea, turning water to blood, and shutting heaven by the year together, no doubt thousands would at once begin to believe literally the eleventh chapter of the Apocalypse. Show us — now that we intend to walk by sight — show us the thing in a newspaper : otherwise we cannot believe it; the most noble Festus would think us mad.

Who will venture to talk of improbability in matters of prophecy, after reading the promises fulfilled in Mary the Virgin, in Sarah the barren, and in Elizabeth so well stricken in years? Let none think to mend matters by starting difficulties, seeing how little Zacharias profited by that method. Whereby shall I know this? he asks. "Thou shalt be dumb," answers the angel: thou shalt ask no more unbelieving questions.

The ancients look through one end of the telescope, we the other. Where they magnify, we love to diminish: where they strive to let no word of the prophecy fall to the ground, we consign whole predictions to the history of events, which, if the prophets thought worth foretelling, the Church has not found worth remembering. "On Sunday," says Mr. Fysh, "July the 13th, 1788," the first angel poured out his vial upon France.* That is, four years before the Revolution; but who now has the faintest recollection of what happened in France upon that Sunday? What, then, means that prelude to the vials which John heard sung in heaven: "Who shall not fear thee, O Lord, for thy judgments are made manifest?" not "made manifest" to one single person, but "to all nations." Therefore, though expositors continue to cry out, century after century, We are

* Fysh's Beast and his Image, p. 149.

now in the sixth vial; or, We are now in the first droppings of the seventh; — no one is called upon to believe them, till they can show in history the preceding five, as agreed upon among themselves, — or rather, as proclaimed, without their help, by the voice of those nations whose wailing and dismay will constitute a large portion of the fulfilment.

The historical system, when it takes possession of a man, sends him forth to wander through the history of Europe, in search of the seals and the trumpets, the vials and the angels, of the Apocalypse. Like a hard master, it would reap where none has sown: its votary is not suffered to complain that no suitable events can be discovered, or that the Church cannot be brought to recognise his scheme of fulfilment. No such agreement is now required. Long ago, indeed, it was thought needful to be like-minded, to walk by the same rule, and to speak the same thing; but now, if he is to have any success, he must aim at being original: he must learn not to covet his neighbour's interpretation. For, as he quickly discovers, there is room for many to differ, even when applying the same prophecy to the same event: if one has made the sun-like angel to be Luther, another may try Leo; and, for the sixth seal, if Diocletian be already engaged, Constantine is still to let.

His labours will not be unrewarded. Having fixed upon a new and original date of the end, he will enjoy the honours of a prophet. If prudent, he will, by deferring the time, provide against a speedy refutation: if of warmer temperament, he will stake his credit upon an alarming proximity of the end. But he knows not, for he neglects to profit by the experience of his predecessors, that with this honour comes anxiety. The lapse of time, that brings the literalist so much nearer to the object of his expectation, to the disciple of the historical school brings misgivings: each year sounds the knell of some rival system, suggesting gloomy forebodings of the fate of his own. And when the sad hour has arrived, and his own "year of the end" has passed away, in all things like other years (save that to him its December sets in darker), let him expect no pity, attempt by no second calculation to retrieve his credit. Enough that he is not worse off than his neighbours; nor shall they that follow him flourish longer: time, that has consigned his system to oblivion, is even now at the door, and will soon carry theirs out also.

And now we may stay no longer at the threshold, while the Apostles are calling to us from the inner courts. From ephemeral speculations, utterly repugnant to the permanent character of prophecy, we turn to the bulwarks of our faith, — proofs of divine foreknowledge, plain enough to madden a Porphyry, and to cause a Gibbon to stultify himself — testimonies to the inspiration of prophecy engraved in the hard rock of unbelief itself. Even now there are rebels for whom this rock must be made to yield water.

But before entering upon the Christian interpretation, we must turn over a few pages in the history of our elder brother. For a certain man had two sons: while the elder remained at home, we were wandering in a far country. To the Jew were given the adoption and the covenants, the law and the prophets;

with him, therefore, the study of the prophets must begin. But, when we reach the time of the prodigal's return, we shall leave the elder son to stand without by himself: we can no longer keep him company at the door, but must go in, where the music is heard, where they are singing the new song, and where many nations are joining in harmonious measure, forgetting that there is either Jew or Greek, Barbarian or Scythian, bond or free.

CHAPTER I.

THE INTERPRETATION OF PROPHECY BY THE JEWISH CHURCH.

"The books which Daniel left in writing are read amongst us to this day, and from them we conclude certainly that Daniel held intercourse with God. For he not only, like other prophets, declared what was to be, but even laid down the time at which it was to happen."—JOSEPHUS.

THE earliest recorded attempt to expound the prophecies of Daniel belongs to the time of Alexander the Great. About 332 years before Christ, the high priest Jaddus gathered from that prophet that the kingdom of Persia, then in possession of the world, was destined to give place to the kingdom of the Greeks. There is no difficulty in finding the passage from which this inference might be drawn: "The ram having two horns are the kings of Media and Persia; and the rough goat is the king of Grecia; and the great horn that is between his eyes is the first king."

It was the moment of transition from the second to the third empire. The Babylonish monarchy had long since passed away, and the victorious Persians had fixed their seat of government at Susa and Persepolis. But they had meanwhile felt the power of the Greeks at Salamis and Marathon, and were about to receive their death-blow at the Granicus, Issus, and Arbela.

Alexander, when he had gained his first victory over Darius, assumed the air of a conqueror, and demanded supplies from the Jews. But Jaddus, grateful for the favours of former monarchs, returned answer that he was in league with Darius, and was resolved to maintain his good faith. Alexander was at the moment occupied with the siege of Tyre; so that, being unwilling to abandon that enterprise, he was forced to content himself with the threat of chastising Jaddus, promising through him to teach a lesson to the world at large with what sort of persons it was proper to keep treaties. Upon the fall of Tyre, he marched straight for Judæa.

The visit has been slightly sketched by the heathen Justin: " He went into Syria, where he was met by many kings of the East with mitres."* Who were these " kings of the East," and how they met the conqueror, is better told by their countryman Josephus.

On approaching the temple, Alexander was met by a procession of priests, and soon recognised in Jaddus a person who had appeared to him in a dream. The high priest and the warrior embraced; and, in a happy moment, Jaddus produced the book of Daniel. Alexander, who had forced half the oracles of Asia to declare in his favour, obtained without violence a favourable response from Daniel:

" There was shown to him the book of Daniel, in which it is foretold that one of the Greeks must destroy the Persian Empire; and he, supposing himself to be the person intended, in his joy dismissed the people: but next day he called them back, and bid them ask whatever they wished. Upon this the high priest begged that they might retain the laws of their ancestors, and that the seventh year might be free from tribute. All this he granted."†

* Justini Historia, lib. xi. cap. 10.
† Josephus, Ant. Jud., lib. xi. cap. 8. The propriety of the goat

Justin's phrase, "the kings of the East with mitres," reminds us of the contemporary expression, "that the way of the kings of the East might be prepared." The heathen appears to mean either Jewish nobles accompanied by priests, or the priests themselves in the capacity of rulers. The pseudo-Esdras, living at the same time, seems to understand, by St. John's expression, the ten lost tribes.*

B. C. 280.

"How many volumes are there in our library?" asked King Ptolemy of his librarian. "Two hundred thousand," answered Demetrius; "and I hope soon to make it half a million, for I hear that the Jews have many valuable works in their own language. But those works," continued the librarian, who was as great a bibliomaniac as his master — "those works, being difficult to read, will require translation." Upon this, Philadelphus set on foot the version of the Bible known by the name of the Septuagint.†

So runs the story, the credit of which, during the last two centuries, has been repeatedly attacked. But Philo, himself an Alexandrian Jew, reports that in his own time the Jews of Alexandria continued to hold an annual festival in remembrance of the trans-

---

as a Macedonian symbol may have struck Alexander. His ancestor, Caranus, when seeking a home in Macedonia, was warned by the oracle to "Seek empire with goats for guides." This remained an enigma, till, by following a flock of goats, he entered Edessa under cover of a storm. From that time his army, when marching, drove goats before the standards.—Justin. Hist.

* 2. Esdras, chap. 13.
† Josephus, Antiq. Jud., lib. xiii. cap. 2.

lation made under Philadelphus.* Moreover, all antiquity agrees in quoting by the name of Septuagint this Greek version of the Old Testament Scriptures. That all the world should have been altogether mistaken, and that the mistake should be discovered at the distance of nearly two thousand years, cannot reasonably be supposed: yet from some discrepancies in the story, backed by internal evidence of no small weight, there is reason to believe that the so-called Seventy were not so much the translators, as the authorisers of the work: in a word, that the translation is the production of five or six individuals, each of whom submitted his labours to the Alexandrian Sanhedrim, consisting of seventy, or probably seventy-two, elders of the Jews.

The version, it appears, was not executed all at one time. Ptolemy received from the Jews no more than the law of Moses.† The book of Esther, according to its subscription, was translated "in the fourth year of Ptolemy and Cleopatra." The prophets are said to be much later than the Pentateuch; yet the version of Daniel is repeatedly copied from in the first book of the Maccabees, and, from its openly mentioning the *Romans*, appears to have been executed before their power suggested any fear of a collision with the Jews.

In many places the Seventy paraphrased the original, so as to show their own idea of the sense. This practice, freely resorted to in the book of Daniel, may have given rise to the saying of their injudicious admirers, that "they were not only translators, but

---

* Philo Judæus de Vitâ Mosis, lib. ii.
† Josephus, preface to the Antiquities.

also prophets."* The Septuagint Daniel was soon rejected both by Jews and Christians; a proceeding so strongly at variance with the excessive reverence paid to the rest of the version, as to demand a short review of the ascertained facts bearing upon the case.

First, the translators of Daniel, in addition to great inaccuracies, took undue liberties with the sacred text: thus, in the prophecy of the seventy weeks they inserted the words "of years." This reading, which fixed the time of the Messiah's cutting off, could not fail to displease the later Jews. Next, the version disappeared from general circulation about the beginning of the third century, soon after being collated by Origen. "I give the reader notice," says Jerome in the beginning of the fifth, " that the Churches now read Daniel, not according to the Seventy, but from Theodotion, who, though living after the coming of Christ, was an unbeliever."† Further, Theodotion's " Daniel " is to this day published as part of the Septuagint Old Testament. Lastly, the true Septuagint Daniel, so long lost, has been lately discovered, and has already passed through five editions. ‡

This Septuagint Daniel bears strong internal evidence to its own antiquity. On one occasion, while attempting to improve on the text, the Seventy

---

* Philo de Vitâ Mosis, lib. ii. The saying was eagerly caught up by the Christians, who reckoned the version quoted by the Apostles good enough for all practical purposes afterwards.

† Jerome's preface to his Commentary on Daniel.

‡ Besides these should be noticed the Syriac version of the Septuagint Daniel, executed in 928 by the Abbot Mar Paulus. It was published at Milan, 1788. The Greek itself first appeared in Rome, 1772.

showed themselves not indeed prophets, but mis-translators. "The daughter of the southern king," says Daniel, "shall go in to the king of the North." This princess was the daughter of that Ptolemy, who, according to the usual account, promoted the translation of the Scriptures. But, as the daughter of Zion, or of Babylon, sometimes means Zion or Babylon itself, the Seventy took upon themselves to omit all mention of the daughter, and to make "the king of Egypt" go in to "the kingdom of the North." In this they are opposed by the plain sense of the Hebrew, and by all other versions of Daniel ever made. The reason, as it seems, is simple enough; the other versions were made after the event: the Seventy translated the prophecy while unfulfilled.

They perceived that the scene lay in Egypt, but they despaired of seeing the king of Egypt bestow his daughter on his deadliest foe. The infidel may here be disposed to object, that the prophecy ought to have been so worded as to allow of no mistake, and to require no subsequent history to fix the sense. But prophecy does not profess to tell every thing. Allowing for a moment the reading of the Seventy, Daniel still foretels the intentions and alliance of Ptolemy. For the minutiæ we may go to the Pagan Athenæus: "The second king of Egypt, surnamed Philadelphus, having given his daughter Berenice to Antiochus king of Syria, took care to supply her with water from the Nile, that his child might drink of the water of that river only."*

Where Daniel says (ch. xi.), "Ships shall come from

---

* Athenæus, Deipnosophistæ, lib. ii. cap. vi.

Chittim," the Seventy, dropping all prophetic reserve, write in the broadest way, " And the Romans shall come." It was probably this prophecy that Caiaphas afterwards twisted to his own impious purpose: "All men will believe on him, and the Romans shall come." But the coming of the Romans there intended took place in the time of Antiochus. On such occasions the Seventy become expositors, and, to their credit, it must be told that their renderings are for the most part supported by New Testament authority. Among these may be noticed the *whale* for *fish* in Jonah, afterwards confirmed by our Lord. In close translation they were equally successful: their saying in Malachi, " the priest is the *angel* of the Lord," is carried out in the titles of the seven Asiatic bishops; while Diabolus, their version of Satan, is reckoned in the Apocalypse among the proper names of the ancient serpent. And later in that book, when heaven is opened, John hears its courts resounding with the words of the Seventy, " Lord God Almighty," or "Pantocrat"*; an expression not found elsewhere in the New Testament, and never, in the Old Testament, in the Hebrew.

For Nebuchadnezzar's seven *times* they write seven *years;* also, in the prophecy of the seventy weeks, they have inserted, after much blundering, " of years." With equal confidence they make the four great kings of Dan. vii. " four great kingdoms:" which is obviously the true sense of the passage, since the fourth beast is explained to be the fourth kingdom. The Hebrew text of Jeremiah justifies them in styling Jerusalem " the city the great." (Jerem. xxii. 8.)

---

* Occurring in the Septuagint throughout the minor prophets.

Moreover the phrase, with the double Greek article, is copied into Apoc. xvi. 19.; and, with the casual omission of one article, into ch. xi. 8.

This version of Daniel remained in general use, probably till the end of the first century. At that time there appeared the rival translation of Theodotion, better executed, and less free in its attempts at paraphrase. Of all their amendments he retains but one: " the four beasts are four *kingdoms*:" he neither commits himself to weeks of years, nor does he tear off the disguise from the men of Chittim.

The Daniel of the Seventy, so often appealed to by the Apostles, has since been cast aside. But the lesson which it teaches still remains as fresh and as important as ever: — that the veil of prophetic style was at the first much thinner than we are now accustomed to consider it, being so far transparent as often to allow of being seen through with clearness, and even with certainty, before the fulfilment.

B. C. circ. 160.

Of the persecution raised by Antiochus, but one original history now remains, the first book of the Maccabees, attributed to Hyrcanus. This writer, an eye-witness of what he relates, recognises so evidently the fulfilment of Daniel's prophecies, as often to describe events in the very words which Daniel uses to foretel them. It is a fault in Hyrcanus, though one for which he will readily be forgiven, that he sometimes sinks the historian in the commentator; and here the second book of the Maccabees, though of inferior credit, becomes of value. Where Hyrcanus almost leaves us to guess his meaning in the abomination of desolation, Jason helps us to discover that it was a statue of Olympian Jove.

To obtain the full benefit of this history as a comment upon Daniel, we should study it by the light of the Gospels and the Apocalypse. We shall then, while allowing a primary fulfilment by Antiochus, be in no danger of forgetting that abomination which is to precede "immediately" the second advent: we shall be saved from the supposition that the three years and a half were fulfilled by the Seleucid, when we find that period spoken of as still future by St. John, even after the destruction of Jerusalem by Titus.

With this precaution, we may safely collate the records of the Greek historian with the forebodings of the Hebrew prophet.

DANIEL.	FIRST BOOK OF MACCABEES.
The great horn that is between his eyes is the first king. Now that being broken, whereas four stood up for it, four kingdoms shall stand up out of the nation, but not in his power. And in the latter time of their kingdom, when the transgressors are come to the full, a king of fierce countenance and understanding dark sentences, shall stand up. . . . . And out of one of them came forth a little horn. (Ch. viii.)	Alexander reigned twelve years, and then died. And his servants reigned each in his place. And after his death they all put diadems upon themselves, also their sons after them for many years; and evils were multiplied in the earth. And there came out of them a sinful root, Antiochus Epiphanes.
The place of his sanctuary was cast down, and an host was given him against the daily sacrifice. (Ch. viii.)	Antiochus went up against Jerusalem with a great multitude, and entered proudly into the sanctuary, and took away the golden altar.

DANIEL.	FIRST BOOK OF MACCABEES.
He shall have intelligence with them that forsake the holy covenant. (Ch. xi.)	They went to the king (Antiochus,) who gave them leave to follow the customs of the Gentiles . . . . and they forsook the holy covenant.
They shall place the abominaation that maketh desolation. Ch. xi.)	They built an abomination of desolation upon the altar.
Then shall the sanctuary be cleansed. (Ch. viii.)	They cleansed the sanctuary, and carried out the stones of defilement into an unclean place.

Hyrcanus makes no attempt to account for either the 1260 days, or the 1150. (2300 evenings and mornings.) He is satisfied with noticing that the sanctuary was cleansed on the third anniversary of its defilement: for, being polluted on the 25th Casleu, 145, Anno Seleucidarum, it was purified the 25th Casleu, 148.

B. C. circ. 100.

A reference to Elijah's return is found in the book of Ecclesiasticus. The passage forms a connecting link between the prophecy of Malachi and the saying of the scribes, " That Elias must first come."

Of Elijah this Ben-Sirach writes: " Who was ordained for reproofs for times, to pacify the wrath before the indignation, and to turn the heart of the father to the son, and to restore the tribes of Jacob." (Eccles. xlviii. 10.)

A. D. 35.

The works of Philo disappoint us, from containing no direct reference to the prophecies. To judge from this specimen of the Alexandrian Jews, they must have lost much by their residence in the metropolis of science. Philo seems to know of no future, no Messiah, no restoration of his people to their land. Though living through the lifetime of Jesus, he knows nothing even of His name. Yet the works of Philo must ever be valued by the Christian; for, writing in the same dialect with the Evangelists, he quotes the same Scriptures, and sometimes employs the very same expressions. As an instance, may be quoted his simile of the untrodden field of virtue, and the few that go thereby. And it throws a certain historical light upon the opening of St. John's Gospel, to find in Philo this sentence: "God's Image is the Word, by which all the world was made."*

A. D. circ. 70.

From Josephus we learn the standard Jewish interpretation of the four empires, the ram and he-goat, and the *times* of Nebuchadnezzar's exile.

He thus paraphrases Daniel's account of the metallic statue:—

"It seemed to thee that thou sawest a great image standing. Its head was of gold, its shoulders and arms of silver, its belly and thighs of brass, and its legs and feet of iron. Then thou sawest that a stone, torn from a mountain, smote and felled the image, breaking it till no part was left whole. Then the gold, the silver, the iron, and the brass, became lighter than flour, and by the force of a mighty wind were blown away and scattered; but the stone increased, till the whole earth seemed filled by it.

"Such was the dream that thou sawest, and in this manner is it to be explained: The head of gold represents both thee

---

* Philonis Judæi de Monarchiâ, lib. ii. For some extracts from Philo, see under Irenæus, on the serpent of Dan.

and the kings of Babylon before thee. The two hands and the shoulders signify that this your empire will be overthrown by two kings; but theirs will be destroyed by another, coming from the West, sheathed in brass. And this power shall be brought to an end by another resembling iron, which shall amalgamate them into a whole; according to the nature of iron, which is harder than gold, or silver, or brass.

"Moreover Daniel explained to the king about the stone. But this I see no necessity for repeating, since it is my business to tell of things past, not future."*

The two kings who overturned the Babylonish Empire are afterwards explained to be Cyrus and Darius. The "coming from the West" is borrowed from the Macedonian goat in the next chapter.

The history of Nebuchadnezzar's abasement is told by Josephus, professedly from Daniel; but where Daniel says seven times, Josephus, following the Seventy, reads seven years.

"Soon afterwards the king saw in his sleep another vision: that falling from his empire he should feed with the beasts, and, after seven years passed in solitude, should again receive the kingdom. . . . Having spent in solitude the predicted time, no one during the seven years venturing to assume the management of affairs, he prayed to God that he might again receive the kingdom, and was once more restored to it. And let none blame me for this, that I tell every thing in writing as I find it in the ancient books. For in the very beginning of my history, I guarded myself against all who were disposed either to ask questions, or to criticise, saying that I should do no more than paraphrase and explain in Greek the books of the Hebrews, neither taking from them, nor adding anything of my own."

If Josephus here betrays a feeling of embarrassment, it must be remembered that he is for the first

---

* Antiq. Jud., lib. x. cap. 10.

time delivering to the Roman world the marvellous narratives till then locked up in the sacred volume. But his courage rises as he proceeds, till in the sequel he finds himself in a condition to give a home-thrust at the Epicureans of his day:—

"The great horn in the forehead of the goat is the first king; and by the sprouting up of the four upon its fall, and by their pointing to the four quarters of the earth, are represented those who will succeed upon his death. There is shown also the division of the kingdom among those who are neither his children nor his kinsmen, as well as their governing the world during many years.

"And out of these will arise a king, who will make war upon the nation and their laws, taking from them their constitution; who will ravage the temple, and suffer no sacrifice to be offered during three years. These very things did our nation suffer under Antiochus Epiphanes, even as Daniel had foreseen, having written down, many years before, what was to happen.

"In like manner Daniel wrote about the empire of the Romans, and the desolation that they would inflict. All this he left in writing; God having declared it to him, that they who read, and behold it coming to pass, may wonder at the honour which God bestowed upon Daniel; also that they may detect the error of the Epicureans, who exclude Providence from life, and suppose that the affairs of men are not cared for by God. . . . From these predictions of Daniel, then, I gather, that they are utterly mistaken when they maintain that God takes no oversight of the concerns of men; for if the world were left to be governed by chance, we should not see every thing happening according to God's prophecy."

In this version of Josephus we miss the 2300 evenings and mornings: in one place they are paraphrased by 1296 days; in another by three years. In the reckoning of this period great confusion has ever prevailed, probably owing to an attempt to correct the calculation by the addition of intercalary months, to correspond with the three years of the cessation of the sacrifice. Two things, however, are certain: that Antiochus interrupted the morning and evening sacrifices for three years precisely; and that the early Asiatics were unanimous in understanding, by 2300 evenings and mornings, about half that number of days.

The principle of this calculation seems obvious. The question, asked in reference to an evening and a morning sacrifice, is supposed to have been answered in terms of the same: That the offering of two thousand three hundred lambs should be hindered, and for that number of evenings and mornings the appointed communication between God and His church should be suspended. But the ancients, especially as time passed on, attempted further explanations. Thus the Syrian Polychronius: "Even now, those magistrates that decree banishment do, according to the law, reckon time by counting the night as a day."* Also the Syrian Ephrem: "He adds the nights to the days, and doubles the number of the days."† Chrysostom goes further: "He reduces the years to days; and that their number may seem formidable, he reckons not days only, but also nights; and to strike the more terror, he dwells upon the tragedy to be enacted by Antiochus."‡ And to conclude with Apollinarius: " It does not say, The vision of the days, but of the evening and the morning; showing that in the rec-

---

* Mai, Coll. Vet. Script., t. i. p. 133. (part 2.)
† Ephrem Syrus, Syriac Comment on Daniel.
‡ Chrysostom on Daniel.

koning of the years, he means both the days and the nights to be counted."*

The calculations of the ancients will be best expressed in a tabular form. The Maccabæan author, though he works out, with some exultation, the precise period of three years, makes no allusion to the prophecy. The rest paraphrase the 2300 mornings and evenings as follows:—

Josephus - - -	3 years, or 1296 days.
and in various readings	1266, 1066, and 1275.
Clement of Alexandria -	6 years and 4 months, or 2300 days.
Hippolytus † - - -	3 years and a half, or 1300 days.
Ephrem Syrus - -	1150 days.
Apollinarius - - -	1150 days.
Chrysostom - - -	1150 days.
Jerome - - - -	6 years and 3 months, or 2300 days.
Polychronius the Syrian -	1150 days.
Theodoret - - -	6 years and 6 months, or 2300 days.

From the time of Theodoret, all agree in reckoning 2300 days, till quite lately, when some have begun to count 2300 years.

Josephus, though capable of saying so much about the fourth empire, generally avoids the subject; for he was writing in Rome, and at that time in high favour with the emperor. Titus even affixed his own signature to a copy of the "Jewish War," placing it in his library as a true record of the campaign. Josephus is equally cautious about the future: the stone cut out without hands he thinks to be no business of his. The subject was dangerous either way: the Christians had successfully applied the figure to their Saviour; while it would be thought treasonable

---

* Mai's Scriptores, t. i. part 2. p. 210.
† Roman ed. of Septuagint Daniel, p. 103.

to repeat the Jewish explanation, that the stone signified Israel's triumph in the end of the world.

Besides the Jewish works of ascertained date, there is a mass of floating commentary known by the name of the Targums, reduced to writing during the first ages of Christianity. Their uncertainty of date scarcely affects their value, since they are acknowledged to represent the opinions of the scribes before the dispersion by Titus.

A few passages bear upon the four empires and the time of Antichrist:—

I. The Targum of the pseudo-Jonathan:—

"Habakkuk, iii. 17.: Although the fig-tree shall not blossom. Although the kingdom of Babel shall no longer flourish, neither exercise dominion over Israel; the kings of Media shall be slaughtered, and the strong ones of Greece shall not prosper; the Romans shall be blotted out, and shall receive no more tribute from Jerusalem: yet for the sign and the redemption which Thou wilt give by thy Christ, even to the residue of thy people, they that remain shall confess it with words."

"Zechariah, i. 18.: I saw, and behold four horns; and I lifted up my eyes and saw, and behold four kingdoms; and I said to the angel who was speaking with me, What are these? And he said to me, These are the kingdoms which have scattered Judah and Israel, and the inhabitants of Jerusalem."

"Isaiah, xi. 4.: With the word of His mouth He will smite the sinners of the earth, and with the speech of His lips He will slay the wicked Armillus."[*]

Armillus is the Jewish name of Antichrist; its

---

[*] Walton's polyglot, in loco. The current Rabbinical stories about Armillus have been collected by Buxtorf; "Synagoga Judaica," cap. 36. He is to be the offspring, they pretend, of a marble statue in Rome. The author of this volume feels bound to state that he is dependent on Greek and Latin versions of the Hebrew, Armenian, and Syriac writers.

derivation is unknown. To some such name there seems to be an allusion in Apoc. ix. 11.: "Whose name is in the Hebrew tongue Abaddon." Armillus has not been traced farther back than this Targum.

II. Rabbi Jochanan:—

"It is written, the fourth beast shall be the fourth kingdom upon earth. This is Rome, worthy to be overthrown: she pervades the whole earth."*

III. Chaldee Paraphrase on Canticles. In the absence of any commentary upon Daniel, the following passage displays the Jewish idea of Michael's office in the time of Antichrist:—

"'We have a little sister.'—At that time shall the angels of heaven say one to another, We have a single nation upon earth, and her deserts are small: she has no kings nor rulers to go forth to battle against the army of Gog. What shall we do for our sister in the day when she shall be spoken against by the nations, and when they shall go up to fight against her? Then Michael, the prince of Israel, shall say: Though she stood as a foundation among the people, and gave silver to possess the name of sole sovereign of the world, yet will I and you, together with her scribes, be about her as walls of silver."†

This attempt to defraud the Gentiles of their future rights illustrates well the elder brother's envy in the parable of the prodigal son.

* Bartoloccius, Bibl. Rabbinica, t. iii. p. 610.

† Walton's polyglot, in loco. The Seventy's translation of Dan. xii. 1. should be compared: "And through that region shall pass Michael the great angel, he who stands for the children of thy people. That will be the day of trouble, such as was not since men have been, until that day. And in that day shall the people be exalted, all that shall be found inscribed in the book." In Deut. xxxii. 8., the Seventy read; "He hath placed the bounds of the nations according to the number of the angels of God."

IV. Aben-Ezra, who flourished about 1160 *:—

"It was said by our honourable master Saadias that those weeks are weeks of years. In proof of this may be quoted the saying of Daniel: Dan. x. 2. 'I Daniel was mourning,' &c., to 'three weeks *of days*.' Now Saadias expounds correctly and well. . . . Know also that in holy Scripture days are always days, and never years. Yet it is possible that the word *days* may mean an entire year, since the repetition of the days produces a return of the year; as when it is said, Ex. 13. 10., from days to days, that is, from year to year; *days* meaning a complete year. But when the number is stated, as two days, three days, it cannot mean years, but must be days, as it stands. Therefore it is said in Lev. xxv. 8., 'Thou shalt number to thee seven sevens of years.' For the same reason I said that the 1290 days are half of the week before mentioned."

The early Jewish code of interpretation may now be summed up: —

The four empires of Daniel are the Babylonian, Medo-Persian, Grecian, and Roman.

The ram and the he-goat refer to the ancient wars between the Greeks and Persians. The great horn is Alexander the Great; the four secondary horns express the division of his empire among his successors, according to the four points of the compass; the little horn arising from one of them is Antiochus Epiphanes.

A time in Daniel means a year; and all periods in the prophecies are literally fulfilled, a day by a day, and a year by a year. The 2300 evenings and mornings are about half that number of days.

The abomination of desolation is the setting up a pagan idol upon the altar of God's temple.

* This passage is preserved in the Pugio Fidei of Martini, part iii. dist. 3. chap. 16.

Elijah is reserved to appear again before the great day of the Lord. A certain head of the wicked will be in existence at the time of Messiah's glorious Advent, and will be slain by the breath of His mouth.

This system was slightly amended by our Lord. In His teaching it was explained that an abomination of desolation was yet to come, and that although the scribes were right in saying that Elias must first come and restore all things, yet no objection could thence be drawn to the truth of His own mission: for an Elias to the first Advent had already appeared in John the Baptist; and though John denied being the Elias, yet he came in the spirit and power of Elias, doing for Christ's first coming what Elias himself will do for the second.

The New Testament bears honourable witness to the knowledge of prophecy possessed by the scribes: they erred, not through ignorance, but against knowledge. It was by their abject renunciation of the national hope, saying, We have no king but Cæsar; by their efforts to suppress the miracles of Christ, both his own Resurrection and that of Lazarus; and, above all, by the desperate attempt to explain them on the principle of Satanic power;— it was by these things, and not through ignorance of the prophecies, that they came to ruin. They were right when they told Herod that Christ should be born in Bethlehem; right when they reminded Nicodemus that no prophet was promised from Galilee; and to the question, What think ye of Christ, they answered rightly, He is the Son of David. Even the seventh chapter of Daniel was, in part at least, understood. When, to the question, Art thou the Son of the Blessed, the

Saviour answered that they should see the Son of man coming in the clouds of heaven, the chief priest and the elders well knew the passage referred to: "One like the Son of man came with the clouds of heaven." It was to them as plain as if He had said, "I am the Son of the Blessed."

On that occasion their knowledge did but increase their guilt: had they been blind, they would have had no sin. But, as far as the understanding of prophecy is concerned, these Jewish scribes might teach a lesson to some modern Christians, who, with Grotius, expound Daniel's coming of the Son of man as the coming of the Romans to subdue the Greeks. For the Son of man who comes with clouds is the Son of the Blessed; not Mummius and Flaminius; no, nor yet Titus and Vespasian.

Not less honour does St. Paul put upon their interpretation of Isaiah xi., where the Targum makes Antichrist to be that Wicked one, whom the Lord will slay with the breath of His mouth: for St. Paul does the same, saying of the Man of Sin, "That Wicked one, whom the Lord shall consume with the spirit of His mouth."

The Jewish interpretation of the four beasts and metals is the groundwork of that system upon which the Apostles and their followers explained the prophecies. In its support, pens many and triumphant have been wielded; for the fulfilment of these visions has been stamped upon the face of history, and acknowledged by almost universal acclamation. In this world of sin and blindness, prophecy is accustomed to extort no higher homage from our rebel race; nor can it, without forestalling the triumph reserved for a day still future, when " All flesh shall see it together, for the mouth of the Lord hath spoken it."

To avoid repetition, the current exposition of the four empires is here amalgamated into a continuous form; and, as most of the paraphrase is the common property of many writers, both Christian and Jewish, the names of authors are omitted, except where any have made the subject peculiarly their own.

And first, for the repetition of the prophecy, and the different aspects under which the same empires are revealed to king and prophet. The conqueror and the captive, beholding the same objects from opposite points of view, require to be taught different lessons. To the one it must be shown that what seems brightest shall fade: to the other, that what is most proud and cruel shall yet be subdued. But on this subject the men of old shall show forth wisdom:

" To the monarch, deluded with the unsubstantial image of the world, and admiring the beauty of things visible, as the colours of a painting spread before him, — to this monarch there is fitly shown, under the figure of a great image, the universal history of man: but the prophet, in a great sea, beholds the great and manifold tossings of human life. Again, to the monarch, admiring that which is precious in the sight of men, — the gold, the silver, the brass, and the iron, — there are shown, under the figure of these metals, the empires successively dominant in the history of man: but to the prophet, the same kingdoms appear in the shape of beasts corresponding to their imperial style.

"Lastly, to the monarch, thinking, as it appears, great things of himself, and proudly boasting his ancestral sway, there is shown a change in the state of things, and the end of earthly rule: and this, to bring down his pride, and to teach him that nothing among men shall stand securely, save only

God's final and universal kingdom. . . . These four empires, and these only, were shown to the king as well as to the prophet; I suppose because the Jewish nation was to be enslaved by those only, from the prophet's time downwards." — Eusebius.*

I. The kingdom of Babylon represented by Nebuchadnezzar its head: Thou art this head of gold; "that is," says Theodoret, "thy kingdom." And this point he argues well: "For after Nebuchadnezzar's decease Evil-Merodach reigned in Babylon, and after him Belshazzar. If, then, we make the individual king to be the head of gold, how shall we take this: — after thee shall arise another kingdom, inferior to thee? for this means, not the kingdom of his sons, but of the Persians. Therefore the head of gold is not Nebuchadnezzar himself, but the entire kingdom of the Assyrians or Babylonians."† Eudoxius makes a stand for the verbal sense: "The head represents the Assyrians, especially the Assyrians' noblest king."

And who so golden, so superb as he, who, in the extravagance of Oriental splendour, raised a statue of gold ninety feet in height? "Thy greatness," says Daniel, "reacheth unto heaven, and thy dominion to the end of the earth." In the second vision the gold is replaced by a royal compound‡ of beast and bird:

---

* This passage, lost for fourteen centuries, has been recovered by Mai. It was quoted from Eusebius by Apollinarius, and from his work copied again into the Greek chain on Daniel. — Mai's Vet. Script., t. i. p. 173.

† Theodoret in Danielem, in locum.

‡ So Chrysostom: "Two royal emblems." And Polychronius: "The most royal of beasts." Also Eudoxius: "The most royal of quadrupeds; the swiftest and most royal of birds."

— a lion with eagle's wings. But, while Daniel looks on, a cloud obscures his master's splendour: the eagle's wings are plucked. The monarch is seven years (Septuagint) among the beasts; his fit place, for a beast's heart is given to him.

And as Daniel watches, he beholds once more in vision what he had before witnessed in history, the beast is set upon its feet as a man, and a man's heart is given to it. No longer seeking heaven on wings of pride, he knows himself to be but man,—with barbaric mouth he honours and extols the God of heaven, no longer foolish and ignorant, and as a beast before Him.

In this way, during some eighteen centuries, the Church has by conjecture expounded the symbol; but now, so late in history, the key has been brought to light. A British traveller, scouring the Assyrian plains, lights upon the palaces of heroes and the monuments of kings. Among these is found a colossal sculpture;—a lion with eagle's wings, and a man's head has been given to it.*

Thus, while the basis of the ancient explanation is confirmed, some of the work needs to be done over

---

* Layard's Nineveh, vol. i. p. 68. 70.: "I ascertained by the end of March (1845), the existence of a second pair of winged human-headed lions."— See at p. 70, first edition, a drawing of the bas-relief.

So complete had been the break up of the Oriental world, that even Nisibenus, living on the borders of the Assyrian empire, knew nothing of its earlier customs. Being thus forced to seek the explanation within the prophecy itself, he turned to the parallel passage in chap. ii. Finding that Nebuchadnezzar was there styled ruler of beasts and birds, he thought this a sufficient explanation of the king of beasts and the king of birds, composing the symbol.— Sermon 5.

again. We must study the emblem afresh: first becoming, like Daniel, familiar with the Assyrian hieroglyphic. We shall have then to decide, whether or not the vision expresses simply this: that the national winged lion was converted into a man by the process of plucking its wings, causing it to stand up on its hind legs, setting it on its feet as a man, and giving it the disposition and the heart of a man. Further, whether Daniel and the sculptor might not be each aiming at the same thing, each embodying some popular and well-known story belonging to the Assyrian kings: only that the sculptor, having no better means of expressing a human heart, was driven to the natural resource of designing a human head.

II. The Medo-Persian. "After thee shall arise another kingdom inferior to thee." To Belshazzar, in Babylon, succeed Ahasuerus in Shushan, and Xerxes in Persepolis. The seat of empire is changed, and the law of the Medes and Persians is now the law of the world. Both Daniel and the sacred historians reckon the beginning of the Medo-Persian empire from the death of Belshazzar: "Thy kingdom is divided, and given to the Medes and Persians." "They were servants to Nebuchadnezzar and his sons until the reign of the kingdom of Persia," 2 Chron. xxxvi. 20. Also in Jeremiah li.: "The Lord hath raised up the spirit of the kings of the Medes, for his device is against Babylon to destroy it."

The empire now consisted of three elements,— Medes, Persians, and Babylonians: moreover the bear has in its mouth the unusual number of three tusks. Of the four beasts, the first and third do not devour; the fourth devours and breaks in pieces; while to the second it is *said* only, " Devour much flesh."* If the intention of the vision be, as Eusebius thinks, to describe these empires in relation to their dealings with the Jews only, there is but one known event that corresponds with this saying. To the Persians it was said, first by Haman, and next by the messengers of the king, that they should destroy, kill, and cause to perish — all Jews in one day. It was said, Devour much flesh (Jerome): but the *saying* never came to *doing:* it was unsaid in haste, from India to Ethiopia; and Mordecai ascended, not fifty cubits in Haman's garden, but to the second post of honour in the kingdom.

Thus far Daniel has worked his way, half prophet and half historian: he now quits the present, and launches out with equal boldness upon the unseen future. The transition to unmixed prophecy is noticed by Hippolytus: " Thou didst prophesy of the lion in Babylon, for that was the home of thy captivity: thou didst reveal the future history of the bear, for still thou wast in the world, and didst see it fulfilled. Now thou tellest me of the pard: but how knowest thou of this, having already fallen asleep? Who taught thee to say these things, unless it were He that formed thee from the birth? God, thou sayest, for thou didst speak the truth. The pard arose; the he-goat came: he smote the ram: he broke his horns: he trampled him under foot: he was exalted in his fall; the four horns arose after him. Rejoice then,

---

* The voice seems to be like that which said to the Apostle, "Rise, Peter; kill and eat." In that case it was *said* only. The Seventy make the bear address itself: "It said thus, Arise."

blessed Daniel: thou wast not deceived, for all these things have come to pass."*

III. Alexander and the Greeks. Says Josephus: "Another will come from the West, sheathed in brass." The sound recalls Homer and his brass-clad heroes. This brazen kingdom was to bear rule over all the earth; and so, in the usual way of speaking, it did. For it is affirmed, upon authority not to be despised in what concerns ordinary modes of speech, even a nursery tale, supported by a *consensus* of babes and sucklings, that Alexander, when he had conquered all the world, sat down and wept. As Hyrcanus words it, "The earth was still before him."

The third kingdom is also, like the rest, compared to a beast. "He desires," says Chrysostom, "to show something rapid, unrestrained, and destructive; therefore he calls up a pard." The leopard is used in comparisons on account of its swiftness: "Their horses," it is said, "are swifter than leopards." Moreover, to make this leopard swifter, it has four wings: for in twelve years Alexander rose from the government of a province to universal empire. In the next vision, therefore, the king of Grecia comes from the West, not touching the ground. History has something to say of this also.

A young Roman once shed tears before the statue of Alexander, when he remembered that at an age when he himself had done nothing, the Macedonian had conquered the world. And yet that young Roman is no sluggard in conquest, for it is early manhood with him yet: he will one day write home to the senate that he also came, and saw, and conquered.

* Hippolyti opera, ed. Fabricius, p. 16.

Alexander's empire has one more mark, the four heads. This is fully explained in the next vision: the first king of Grecia being broken, four kingdoms shall stand up out of the nation; and in another vision, his kingdom is said to be divided towards the four winds of heaven, and not to his posterity.

It fell heavily upon the Christian Greeks, when their empire had been vanquished and disarmed, that they seemed to have lost, with their brass, their place in the prophecy; but Greece, conquered in all besides, still boasted, excepting while Cicero was living, supremacy in eloquence. Now eloquence had been compared, by St. Paul, to sounding brass, as the most resonant and clear-toned of metals. The expositors, therefore, deprived of the substantial character of the metal, fell back upon its sound. Titus Bostrensis first gave out that the brass of the third kingdom represents its eloquence. Eudoxius, also a Greek, remarks that the hard iron of the Romans conquered the precious gold, the resplendent silver, and the sonorous brass.*

IV. The Roman Empire, described as an iron kingdom, and represented by a nameless beast with teeth of iron. This kingdom also was to rule the whole earth: so the Cæsars begin by issuing a decree that all the world shall be taxed. Yet their "whole earth" was limited: they never ruled beyond the Euphrates.

The interpretation of the fourth kingdom gradually passed through a complete history of its own. At first, Josephus confines his exposition to the iron, the clay finding no counterpart in the kingdom of Vespasian.

* Greek chain on Daniel. Mai, t. i. in locum.

Hippolytus stops short at the teeth of iron, exclaiming, "This we ourselves have seen, and we give God the glory." Thus far the clay had been lying dormant. Eusebius shows himself no wiser about it than his predecessors. Apollinarius, Jerome's master, recognizes the iron, but has nothing to say about the clay. His pupil knew better: under the tuition of the Goths, the Church had made rapid progress in mastering that part of the vision. Sulpitius found the incongruous mixture abundantly plain: Theodoret was but too happy to discover that the mixture would remain, and that the iron would not altogether disappear. Eudoxius next proposes to use the condition of the empire as a measure of the times: "The weaker you see the Roman Empire, the nearer you may suppose the end." In this state the interpretation still remains.

Next in order comes the mysterious stone, which Josephus leaves untouched, as if conscious that to him it must prove a stone of stumbling and a rock of offence; but the Christians gladly accept the subject, hailing that stone as the Headstone of the corner. And, for the mystery, "cut out, yet without hands," since Josephus is silent, Victor of Antioch shall speak: "The being born of a virgin was above nature; the union of substance, a paradox. It is therefore called a mystery, not as unknown, but as incomprehensible. For the plan of the Cross exceeds all human understanding: how the Sufferer achieved salvation, and how the Dying rose; how the Dishonoured conferred glory, and how the Crucified removed the curse."*

* This Victor of Antioch, a Greek writer, flourished about 380. Mai, vol. i. p. 177.

The Jews, while the darkness lasted, pored over the passages of sacred prophecy: at sun-rise they closed the book. They had now enough to do in evading the consequences of their literal system; for the sixty and two sevens had expired, the sceptre had departed from Judah, and Shiloh must have come. A connected account of their further proceedings is beside the purpose of this work: it would indeed furnish but a melancholy history, the elder brother still standing without, desperate of the future, careless of the present, and driven to console himself with visions of the glories once the birthright of the elder son. As one who has no future, he begins to dream of the past: " My ancestors," says the Rabbi Eleazar, " kept goats on the mount of Mihvor, and they grew fat upon the smell of the incense wafted from the temple."*

* Babylon Talmud, Codex Tamid, cap. 3.

CHAPTER II.

THE CHRISTIAN INTERPRETATION OF PROPHECY IN THE PRIMITIVE AGE.

"I have heard some say, Unless I can find it in the ancients, I will not believe it in the Gospel. And when I have said, It is written ———, they have answered me, That remains to be shown. But *my* antiquity is Jesus Christ: His cross, His death and resurrection, and the faith that is by Him, these are an Antiquity that defies age."— IGNATIUS, A.D. 107.

As new wine is put into new bottles, so the new revelation was committed to a new Church. And both were preserved; for as, down to the time of Constantine, the Church withstood the utmost assaults of Satan, so on the other hand, no particle of the prophetic creed was lost. During that golden age of Christianity, one system of prophetic interpretation was everywhere received: which system, gathered from writers of the whole period throughout the world, may be reduced to the following form:

The four beasts and four metals represent alike four empires, the Babylonish, Medo-Persian, Grecian, and Roman. The last of these is to give place to the kingdom of Antichrist, embracing the four.

All prophetic times are fulfilled literally: the 2300 evenings and mornings, expressing half that number of days, were fulfilled by Antiochus. The sixty-ninth land-week of Daniel expired at the death of Christ: the seventieth probably refers to the time of Anti-

H

christ, which will occupy its latter half, or three years and a half.

The city of Rome, as existing from the Apostles' time to that of Antichrist, is shown under the figure of Babylon: Rome will be destroyed, about or before the beginning of Antichrist's reign, by the ten kings in league with him.

The Status Romanus, or Roman order of government, is the appointed means of *letting* or withholding the coming of Antichrist: in its fall, and consequent division among ten kings, there will be accomplished the removal of "him that letteth." These ten kings, typified by the ten horns both of Daniel's fourth beast and of St. John's scarlet beast, are to precede the appearance of Antichrist, to give him their power, to destroy Rome, and finally to be slain in the great battle with the King of kings.

The contents of the sealed book correspond with the substance of the prophecy delivered on the mount of Olives. The seals represent *,

 I. Christ's triumph through Gospel-preaching.
 II. Wars ⎫ These are the beginning of the
 III. Famines ⎬ sorrows, (that is, of the
 IV. Pestilences ⎭ birth-pangs of the end.)
 V. Martyrs, chiefly under Antichrist.
 VI. Precursors of the second Advent: and,
 VII. The Sabbatical silence in heaven.

* The earliest extant expositors of the seals are these:—

		DATE.
1st seal,	Irenæus - - - - -	180.
2, 3, and 4.	Victorinus - - - - -	290.
5.	Tertullian - - - - -	200.
6.	Anonymous - - - - -	257.
7	Victorinus - - - - -	290.

The trumpets, though not explained in detail, were supposed by some to represent the plagues inflicted by the witnesses, briefly noticed in the history of the witnesses themselves. The vials (perhaps the concluding climax to the trumpet-plagues) are the final judgments poured out upon the Antichristians.

The great red dragon is the Devil; the woman clothed with the sun, the Church. (The birth of the man-child was not clearly understood.) The casting down of the dragon to earth marks the beginning of Antichrist, and of Satan's renewed supernatural power over men. The woman's flight to the wilderness corresponds with the flight of the Church from Judea to the mountains, there to be miraculously sustained during the three years and a half.

The personal Antichrist, though possessed by a devil, will be a real and individual man, — a false Christ raised up by Satan. That power, and seat, and great authority which Satan will have to offer, Antichrist will accept, being suffered to reign for three years and a half, to tyrannize over the whole earth, and to wear out the saints. He will lay claim to divine honours; and, in language supremely blasphemous and insulting to God, will set up himself above all that passes by the name of God, or that is made an object of worship.

Though head of the last form of universal empire, Antichrist will probably be a Jew, the serpent of the tribe of Dan. Of that tribe, as St. John shows, none will be sealed in the final apostacy. Antichrist is the person described in prophecy as the little horn; the vile person; a false Christ; the man of sin; also as the beast which has two origins, from the sea and from the bottomless pit. He rises from the sea as man, possessed of temporal power; from the bottomless pit as of demon origin, and possessed by a devil.

The proper name of Antichrist is concealed in an enigma, probably not meant to be decyphered till after the rise of the ten kings. As the Greek letters of the name of Jesus make 888, so those of Antichrist's name will make 666: for eight is the number of the Lord's day, and of the eighth millennium, the beginning of the eternal state; whereas six is the number of the days of the world and of the thousands of years of sin.

As Christ came in His Father's name, and was rejected by the Jews, so Antichrist will come in his own name, and will be received by them. All the world, excepting the elect, will worship him: for he will work great miracles, which, whether true or false, will appear to be real. By divine grace and a knowledge of prophecy, the elect will be enabled to see through the delusion, according to the saying of our Lord: Behold, I have told you before.

This Antichrist will set up his throne in Jerusalem, appearing to realise the ancient hopes of the Jewish nation. He will also cause his image to be set up in the temple, which will be restored, probably when Elias comes to restore all things, in the first half of the seventieth week. In this temple Antichrist himself will sit: and either he or his image (the image of the Beast) is the abomination of desolation spoken of by Daniel the prophet. This abomination, says Daniel, will last 1290 days; and the sight of it, standing in the holy place of the temple, is to be the signal for flight to the churches of Judea. By diabolical power, this image will be made to speak, and all who refuse to worship it will be put to death.

The time of Antichrist is limited, for the sake of the elect then living, to three years and a half: being 1290 days of ancient Jewish, and 1260 of ancient Gentile reckoning. This time coincides with the days shortened for the elect's sake, with the short time which remains to the Devil when cast down to earth, and with the speedy avenging of the elect: probably, also, with the last half week of Daniel, with the short space of the seventh head's continuance, and with the little season during which the white-robed martyrs are instructed to wait. This is the time of the great tribulation, such as was not since the beginning of the world, and which will consist of two parts: the persecution of the Church by Antichrist; and the judgments divinely inflicted upon his followers.

St. Paul's theory of Antichrist was thus understood. His coming, though effected by the operation of Satan, will be God's judgment upon the world for its rejection of Christ. For God's great truth is the Word made manifest in the flesh: whoever opposes this truth is an antichrist: whoever denies it, a liar. But the great opposition and the great lie will be Satan's Contra-Christ, who will be received by the generation then living. Thus will that whole race of unbelievers be found inexcusable; for, rejecting Him to whom all the prophets bore favourable witness, they receive one whom many prophets have denounced as a blasphemer and an enemy to God.

Before this, Elias shall come first, and restore all things: possibly being employed to confirm the covenant during the first half of the seventieth week. Elias, and perhaps Enoch, will preach against Antichrist during three years and a half, exercising the miraculous powers of Moses and Elijah. In the end they will be slain by Antichrist, and their bodies will lie for three days and a half in the streets of Jerusalem: but on the fourth day they will rise again, and, in sight of their enemies, will go up to heaven in a cloud.

When Antichrist's power is at its height, his pretensions will be suddenly destroyed by the appearance of the true Christ, who will be known by His own test:—Every Christ that henceforward comes from among men is a false Christ: he that comes from heaven as the lightning is the true. Yet Antichrist, blinded by Satanic influence, will lead on the kings of the earth to oppose his heavenly foe: he and his false prophet will be cast into the lake of fire, while the kings and their armies will be slain.

The scarlet beast is in some way connected with the red Dragon,— possibly as the demon-empire, or the system of idolatrous devil-worship: it will reascend from the bottomless pit in the days of Antichrist.

[The greater part of the mystery of the scarlet beast cannot be gathered from the primitive writings now extant; yet this principle appears to have been recognised:— that the seven heads of the Apocalyptic beasts, when surmounted by a city, signify hills; when crowned, they stand for kings; and, when one of them is seen to be wounded, they are likewise meant to express kings.]

The six thousand years of the world's duration having passed away, the seventh thousand (reckoning loosely, for none can know the times or seasons of the end) will be the sabbatical state. Before this the saints will arise, those who have not received the mark of the beast, whether martyrs or not. Many will come from the East and from the West, and will sit down with Abraham, Isaac, and Jacob, at the marriage supper of the Lamb. To this state will succeed the eighth or eternal age, typified by the first day of the new week, the eighth of the old: before this the earth will be purified, and cleansed from all sin.

The New Testament writers, even when delivering fresh predictions, sometimes take occasion to expound Old Testament prophecies. These inspired expositions, being the basis of all true understanding of the subject, must be first examined.

A.D. 29.

The phrase, "the abomination of desolation," though several times paraphrased in the Septuagint Daniel, occurs in that precise form twice only: once in chap. xi. 31., and again in chap. xii. : "The abomination of the desolation shall be given for 1290 days." From our Lord's manner of quoting Daniel, "the abomination of the desolation, *the* spoken of by Daniel," (Gr.), it appears that all these abominations are one, though admitting of a secondary fulfilment. This calamity, as it appears from Dan. xii., will befal the Jewish nation in the end of the world: the Saviour's exposition makes the certainty doubly sure; for thus speaks He who hath the key of David : "When ye shall see the abomination of desolation, spoken of by Daniel the prophet, then let them which be in Judea flee to the mountains;" and as for the period at which this is to happen, it is added, that "immediately" after that tribulation, the sun shall be darkened, and then shall all the tribes of the earth mourn, and they shall see the Son of man coming in the clouds of heaven.

This abomination is to stand "in the holy place," and, "where it ought not." These expressions, though plain enough to a Jew, throw us back upon Daniel for explanation. In the ninth chapter, according to the Seventy, it stands thus: "In the *temple* shall be the abomination of desolations." (v. 27.)

St. Luke reports another saying having reference to the same event: " When ye shall see Jerusalem compassed with armies." This siege is described at length in Zechariah xiv.: " I will gather all nations against Jerusalem to battle, and the city shall be taken, and the houses rifled." A comparison of the two passages shows that the New Testament prediction, though capable of a passing application to Titus or Adrian, refers to the siege in Zechariah. For, after it, says the Jewish prophet, the Lord shall go forth to fight with those nations: after that tribulation, says the Divine Teacher, shall the Son of man be seen. And, for the *times* of the Gentiles (left indefinite in St. Luke), we have to consult the Apocalypse, where it is said that the Gentiles shall tread under foot the holy city forty and two months. From this point the collation of the prophecies runs on smoothly: the standing on the mount of Olives, the great earthquake, and the mourning of the tribes, all these, when read by the New Testament light, become plain in their order and connection.

A.D. circ. 50.

The famous conversation in Thessalonica, from the casual manner in which it is referred to, seems to have been an exposition of old prophecies rather than a formal delivery of new. If we take as the text the version of the Seventy, the passages commented on will appear to be the following:—

OLD TESTAMENT.	ST. PAUL.
He shall have intelligence with them, because they have forsaken the holy covenant. (Dan. xii.)	There shall come first the apostacy.
And behold, eyes like man's eyes. (Dan. vii.)	That Man of Sin shall be revealed.
And the other king shall arise after them. (Dan. vii.)	
He shall speak words against the Most High. (Ch. vii.) And the king shall be exalted above every god. (Ch. xi.)	Who opposeth and exalteth himself above all that is called God.
He shall pitch his tent upon the mountain of the will of the Holy One. (Ch. xi.) In the temple shall be the abomination of desolation. (Ch. ix.)	So that he sitteth in the temple of God.
The fourth kingdom ... and ten kings shall arise ... and after them the other. (Ch. vii.)	And now ye know what withholdeth.
He shall smite the earth with the word of his mouth, and with the spirit of his lips he shall destroy that Wicked One. (Isaiah xi.)	And then shall that Wicked One be revealed, whom the Lord shall consume with the spirit of his mouth.*

* Noticed by Severianus: "This is that smiting the Wicked One spoken of by Isaiah." He quotes both that passage in Isaiah and the last words of Malachi: "Lest I come and smite the earth." — Cramer's Greek Chain on 2 Thess.

A.D. 64.

At this time Rome is first called Babylon by St. Peter, who thus prepares his readers for the coming transfer of Old Testament prophecies in the Apocalypse. This use of the name is so entirely in conformity with the usual style of Rabbinical disguise, that the Apostle's meaning was never doubted till the fifteenth century.

A.D. circ. 80.

About this time the name Antichrist began to be applied to the man of Sin. From St. John's method of introducing the word, it seems to have been already familiar to the Church: "Ye have heard that the Antichrist shall come." St. Paul's word, *Antikeimenos*, is the nearest approach to it in older writings.

The Apostles, as it cannot fail to be remarked by the most hasty reader, uniformly describe the day of the Lord as close at hand; but, let any one misunderstand them, so as to *reckon* upon it coming in a few years, or within any given time, and at once they hasten to correct the mistake, and to explain their true meaning. Happily for *our* instruction, they were, even during their own lifetime, so far misunderstood by some, as to find it needful to lay down the principles of a more sober calculation:—That God's reckoning differs from man's in the proportion of a day to a thousand years; that what some men call slackness is with Him long-suffering: and yet that the last day, when it does come, shall come quickly, that is, suddenly, and like a thief in the night. Where the Saviour reveals one obstacle to His speedy coming, St. Paul adds two besides: not only must the gospel be preached everywhere, but the letting power must be first removed, and the Mân of Sin must next appear. Moreover, adds the Apostle, let none tell you, as if he had learnt it from me, that the last day is at hand; let none think that I meant it in my epistle; let no man deceive you by any means.

Thus the Apostles, secure in the infallibility of their inspiration, so treated the subject as to convey precisely the same impression that their Master had left before them: for He, who said "Surely I come quickly," said also, "The end is not yet." To all, therefore, they say, Be ready; to the over-anxious, Be not troubled. Let no fond and frustrated hopes give a handle to the scoffer; but, above all, let no unexpected arrival of death or of judgment peril your eternal safety.

A.D. 96.

A year to be much remembered by the Church, for the publication of a book which so far exceeds all other prophecies in fulness and clearness as to merit the exclusive title of "The Revelation." Its date is fixed by the testimony of Irenæus, who talked with those that had talked with St. John; for the Apostle lived several years after his return from Patmos.

The Apocalypse is found to be chiefly an arrangement of earlier prophecies and emblems: in it we recognise the tree of life from Paradise, Eve's ancient serpent, Enoch's ten thousand saints, Judah's Lion, the Song of Moses, Job's accuser, David's Prosperous Rider, Isaiah's Dragon, Jeremiah's Babylon, Ezekiel's four sore judgments, Daniel's three times and a half, together with his lion, leopard, bear, and ten horns; nor are there wanting Zechariah's great earthquake, Joel's darkened luminaries, Malachi's Elijah, Jeremiah's "great city," Isaiah's spiritual Sodom, the great tribulation of the Gospels, the Western Babylon of St. Peter, and the Sabbatism of St. Paul. All these are here so collected and arranged, that the Apocalypse becomes a guide to all prophecy: an index placed at the end of the sacred volume, both marking its completion and facilitating the study of its contents.

The book itself, as may be gathered from its opening chapter, was addressed as a circular epistle to seven Asiatic churches. Before long it was remarked by the heretical Alogi, that the church of Thyatira, spoken of as infested by "that woman Jezebel, which calleth herself a prophetess," was not then in existence. From this they inferred that the book was fallible, and therefore uninspired.

Within sixty years from the date of the Apocalypse a church was founded in Thyatira, and was actually troubled by three false prophetesses, Priscilla, Maximilla, and Quintilla. Epiphanius, therefore, in reply to the Alogi, grants the premises of their argument, but draws his own conclusion:—

John spoke of a church and a false prophetess in Thyatira:

But that church and false prophetess did not exist till long afterwards:

Therefore John must have written in the spirit of prophecy.*

Thus much for the inspired expositors in person

---

* Epiphanius contra Alogos, c. 33.

Here ends implicit faith : here begins caution, with the need to prove all things, and to hold fast that only which Scripture declares to be good.

It had been foretold to Daniel that knowledge should be increased : and now the promise was fulfilled ; the Lamb had opened the seals, and had given to His servants that revelation which God gave to Him. From the prophecy delivered on the mount of Olives, down to the Apocalypse itself, fresh lights had continued to dawn upon the future, till the path of the Church, as far as was needful for her to see, was clearly revealed. With what measure of steadfastness she followed that light, given her to rule the night in the absence of the Day-star, will appear in the course of this history.

To become learners in the Apostles' school we must seek them where they taught; and as they were sent into all the world, round the world we must follow them. Confining ourselves to the time before Constantine, and starting from the centre of the Apocalyptic earth, we shall visit Barnabas in Cyprus, Polycarp at Smyrna, and Papias not far from Laodicea. Reluctantly we pass by Sardis, for Melito's commentary on the Apocalypse is lost. We have, however, Methodius in Tyre, Lactantius in Nicomedia, and Justin Martyr in Sichem. Victorinus next calls us northward to Austria, while Irenæus beckons from the western Lyons. Crossing the Alps, we find Hermes and the Pseudo-sibyl among the seven hills; Porto has its martyr Hippolytus, and Carthage is by no means to be erased from our map, yielding Cyprian and Tertullian. Returning to the Apocalyptic home, we pass through Alexandria, where Origen and the younger Clement hold their school.

A.D. 70.

Jerusalem is now about to be surrounded with an army; the Jews of Jericho have already fled to the mountains*; will the Christians of Jerusalem follow them? Upon their conduct hangs the answer to this question, Did they understand, by the approach of Vespasian, the abomination of desolation spoken of by Daniel? They did not; for, instead of fleeing from Judea to the mountains, they fled from Jerusalem to another city of Judea. A special revelation, as it seems, authorised them to flee to Pella, where they remained till their return to Jerusalem.

For this statement there are two authorities, though neither of them very ancient.

I. Eusebius (in 320.): "The church which was in Jerusalem, by an oracle given by Revelation to fit persons among them before the war, were ordered to leave the city, and to inhabit a town named Pella, beyond Jordan."†

II. Epiphanius (in 380.): "When the city was about to be taken by the Romans, all the disciples were warned by an angel to depart from it, since it was to be totally destroyed; and they, emigrating, dwelt in the city of Pella beyond Jordan."‡

This Pella, so far from being in the mountains, is one of ten cities grouped in a plain, and thence named Decapolis.

* Josephus, Bell. Jud., iv. 8.
† Euseb. Hist. Eccles., lib. iii. c. 5.
‡ Epiphanius, De Mensuris et Ponderibus, cap. 15.

A.D. circ. 75.

The Catholic Epistle of St. Barnabas,—a work that was universally received as genuine, though not inspired,—bears evidence of having been written soon after the year 70. It notices the destruction of the temple as recent, and makes no reference to the Apocalypse, even when treating of the millennium. Also, when describing the little horn, Barnabas makes no use of the word Antichrist, which first appears in St. John's Epistles after the year 80.

Of Barnabas it is recorded that he was "a good man, and full of the Holy Ghost and of faith." (Acts xi. 24.) Therefore his Epistle deserves every attention short of that implicit faith which is due to inspiration alone.

Part of the early chapters being lost in the original Greek, we are sometimes dependent upon the ancient Latin version:—

Chap. iii., iv.: "To all of us God has shown these things beforehand, that we may not run, as proselytes, to their law. Therefore, closely examining into the future, I must needs write that which will be for our safety.

"Let us flee every evil work, and hate the error of the present time, that we may find favour hereafter: let us give our soul no licence to hold intercourse with the wicked and the sinner, lest at any time we become like them.

"For the consummate trial, as it is written, and as Daniel says, draws near: for the Lord has cut short the times and the days, that His beloved may hasten to His inheritance.

"Thus saith the prophet, Ten kingdoms shall reign on the earth, and after them shall arise a little one, who shall subdue three at once. So also of their kingdoms.

"Of this one Daniel says again, And I saw the fourth beast, wicked and strong, and fiercer than the other marine beasts, and on it there appeared ten horns. And there came up in the midst of them another short horn, which cast down three of the greater horns. We ought therefore to understand.* Furthermore I beg of you, as one of yourselves, loving you all above mine own soul, that you take heed to yourselves, and become not like those who heap up their sins, and say, that their Testament is also ours. Yet ours it is, for that which Moses received they lost for ever."

Barnabas is almost the only primitive writer on prophecy who notices the destruction of Jerusalem, to which, as very recent, he twice refers as an argument against the Jews.

" Chap. iv. : Beware lest after being called we fall asleep and slumber in our sins, and the Wicked one, receiving power over us, awaken us and shut us out from the kingdom of the Lord. And now, especially, understand this, having seen such signs and fearful things in the Jewish nation, and how the Lord has abandoned them."

" Chap. xvi. : Again he says, Behold, they that have destroyed this temple shall themselves build it. And so it is; for because of their going to war, it was destroyed by their enemies, and now the very servants of their enemies shall rebuild it.† Moreover it was shown how the city and temple and people of Israel were to be delivered up: for the Scripture says, And it shall come to pass in the last days, that the Lord will deliver up the sheep of the pasture, their sheepfold and their tower to destruction. And, as the Lord said, so it has happened."

From the passages now quoted we gather these opinions of Barnabas :

The great tribulation is connected with the little horn of the fourth Beast, and not with the destruction of Jerusalem.

---

* " He that readeth (Daniel) let him understand."

† Spiritually, as appears from the context: through the Gentiles being chosen to form the Christian church.

In the time of Barnabas, the ten horns were expected to come next: showing that the fourth Beast was considered to be the Roman Empire then existing.

The vile person of Dan. xi. is the same as the little horn, and his power is to be cut short, that Christ's coming may be hastened.

The antichristian apostacy will be closely connected with the Jewish opposition to Christianity.

But the "son of consolation" has better news in store for the Church: he is the first to tell of the thousand years of the coming kingdom. The promise of a sabbatical period had been already given by St. Paul, who, after an appeal to the history of the Jews and of the creation, declares that there remains a sabbatism ($\sigma\alpha\beta\beta\alpha\tau\iota\sigma\mu\grave{o}\varsigma$) to the people of God. But Barnabas, Paul's companion in travel, defines it more exactly:

"Chap. xv.: Observe, my children, why it says, He ended in six days. This means that the Lord God will finish all things in six thousand years: for with Him a day is a thousand years, as he testifies, saying, Behold, to-day shall be as a thousand years.

"Therefore, my children, in six days, that is, in the six thousand years, all things shall be finished. And he rested on the seventh day: this means, When his Son shall come, and shall abolish the time of the Wicked one*, and shall judge the ungodly, and shall change the sun and moon and stars; then shall He rest gloriously on the seventh day.

"He says moreover, Thou shalt hallow it with pure hands and a pure heart. If, then, that day which God has hal-

---

* The Anomos, St. Paul's name for Antichrist. — This account of the millennium derives great importance from its date. Had Barnabas conveyed a false impression, doubtless that impression would have been contradicted, not supported, by the Apocalypse, twenty years afterwards.

lowed, can now be kept holy by any one, unless he be altogether pure in heart, I am mistaken. See therefore; He truly will hallow it, resting honourably, when we ourselves shall be enabled to work righteousness, having received the promise; when iniquity shall no more exist, and all things shall be made new by the Lord. Then shall we be able to hallow it, having been first made holy ourselves.

"Furthermore He says to them, Your new moons and your sabbaths I cannot endure. Observe how He speaks; The present sabbaths are not acceptable to me, but those which I have made. In which sabbath, having ended all things, I will make the beginning of an eighth day, that is, the beginning of another world. Therefore we keep with gladness the eighth day, on which Jesus both rose from the dead, and, after showing himself openly, went up into heaven."

Barnabas and Peter both quote the ninetieth Psalm, though for a different purpose: the one to prove that God's reckoning of time differs from ours; the other to establish the principle, that each day of the world's creation typifies a thousand years in its history. As far as the seventh day is concerned, Barnabas is supported by St. John; he seems therefore to be justified in the general sense which he puts upon the words of the Psalm. If so, the saying of Moses may be understood as a comment upon his own history of the six days' work, a first sketch of the great plan of the seven thousand years.

Yet this calculation must not be taken in too strict a sense; for the day and hour of Christ's second coming, and of its precursory troubles, no man knows, — not even the Son, but the Father; and though the loss of the true chronology may account for *human* ignorance, it will scarcely explain that of the angels or of the Son.

A. D. circ. 100.

The first Christian writer after the appearance of the Apocalypse is Hermes of Rome. His name occurs in the Epistle to the Romans: "Salute Asyncritus, Phlegon, Hermas, Patrobas, HERMES." The "Shepherd" of this author, a work of undoubted genuineness, contains some imitations of the Apocalypse, showing him to have written after 96. His advanced age is alluded to in one of the visions, which was deferred on account of his infirmities: after seeing it he felt younger.

By this work the English reader will be strongly reminded of the "Pilgrim's Progress;" a comparison which will enable him at once to enter into the intention of the pretended visions. Hermes is taken, in his dream, to the tower of the Church, built upon the Rock of ages: here he is left in charge of four damsels, named Faith, Abstinence, Power, and Patience. In the morning his guide inquires, "Upon what didst thou sup, Hermes?" "I supped all night on the word of the Lord."* Though the style of Hermes is simple almost to childishness, there are, throughout his artless effusions, gushes of penitence and hope and joy, that show him to be no novice in the religion of the heart.

Where St. Paul's Epistle found him, there he remained, as may be learnt from his references to the Tiber and the Via Campana. The fourth vision, "concerning the trial and tribulation to come upon mankind," will be made clear by first noticing the chain of inspired declarations on the subject:—

* Lib. iii. similitudo 9.

Dan. xii.: "There shall be a time of trouble such as never was since there was a nation . . . . . and many of them that sleep in the dust of the earth shall awake."

Matt. xxiv.: "There shall be great tribulation, such as was not since the beginning of the world . . . . . and immediately after that tribulation shall the sun be darkened . . . . and they shall see the Son of man coming."

Luke xxi.: "Pray always, that ye may be accounted worthy to escape all these things that shall come to pass, and to stand before the Son of man."

Revelation iii.: "I will keep thee from the hour of temptation, which shall come upon all the world."

Revelation vii.: "A great multitude which no man could number, of all nations and kindreds . . . . . These are they which came out of the great tribulation."

Revelation ix.: "It was commanded them (the locusts from the bottomless pit) that they should hurt only those men which have not the seal of God in their foreheads."

Of this great tribulation, affecting all nations, kindreds, and tongues, a certain portion, represented by the stings of the fiery locusts, may be escaped. But how? On this momentous subject Hermes undertakes to admonish his brethren.

His vision is styled "a figure of the tribulation to come." The scene lies in the Via Campana, ten furlongs out of Rome. The emblem of the tribulation is compounded of the dragon and the locusts of the Apocalypse; for, like the Roman Christians in general, Hermes appears to consider a dragon and a whale as synonymous*:—

"I walked a little further, when suddenly I saw a cloud of dust mounting to the sky. I began to say to myself,

* Throughout the whole school of ancient Christian art, a dragon, instead of a whale, is seen to swallow Jonah. This idea is probably founded upon the words, "He will slay the dragon that is in the sea."

Can this be cattle raising the dust? It was about a furlong distant, and still I saw it rising more and more, till I suspected something supernatural. And now there was a gleam of sunshine, when, behold, I saw a great beast like a whale, with fiery locusts coming out of its mouth. Its height was about a hundred feet, and its head was shaped like an urn. I began to weep, and to call upon the Lord to deliver me from it. Then I remembered the saying that I had heard — 'Hermes, doubt not.'

"And now, my brethren, putting on the faith of God, and remembering who had taught me great things, I boldly presented myself to the beast, which was coming on as if with one blow it would demolish a city. I came close up to it; — and that beast, so great, stretched itself upon the ground, and moved nothing but its tongue: it lay quite still until I had passed by it."

Hermes now meets a noble virgin, coming forth as from the wedding chamber: —

"From former visions I knew that she was the Church, and I felt glad. Saluting me, she said, 'Hail, O man!' And I said in return, 'Hail, lady!' She said to me, 'Have you met with nothing?' I answered, 'There met me, lady, a beast capable of devouring a nation, but through God's power and special mercy I escaped it.' 'You have well escaped,' she said, 'casting your solitude and your care upon the Lord, and opening your heart to Him, — believing that by none other could you be saved than by His great and glorious Name. Therefore the Lord sent His angel who is over the beast whose name is Hegrin (or, over the beast whose name is the Wicked one*), and stopped its mouth that it might not hurt you. Through your faith, and through not fearing that beast, you have escaped the great tribulation. Go then, and tell the elect of God His great doings: tell them that this beast is the figure of the tribulation to come. If therefore you are found prepared,

---

* The Greek is here lost; the reference is probably to Apoc. xii.: "The dragon, called the Devil."

you shall escape the operation of the Wicked one, if your heart be pure and without spot.'"

Hermes now asks the meaning of the four colours upon the head of the Beast: the black, he is told, is the present world; the fiery and blood-colour show that the age is to perish by fire and blood. The gold represents those who escape its influence; the white is the age to come, the habitation of the elect.

"'Cease not,' continues his guide, 'to speak these things in the ears of the saints. You have a figure of the great tribulation to come: if you choose, it shall be as nothing. Bear in mind that which is written.' When she had finished speaking, she departed; and I did not see which way she went, for there was a noise, and I turned round in fear, thinking that the beast was coming."*

Hermes follows St. John in making the apostacy of Antichrist to consist in the denial of the Father and the Son:—

"Blessed will he be, that will support the great tribulation to come, and will not deny his life: for the Lord has sworn by His Son, that whoever shall deny His Son and Himself, promising themselves His life, the same shall also deny Him in the coming days."†

He also understands literally the new heavens and the new earth. The Church, represented by an aged woman, reads from a book the destiny of the righteous:—

"Unrolling the book, she read in a manner glorious, magnificent, and wonderful, things which I was not able to remember: for they were terrible words, which a man could not endure. Yet the last words I remembered, for they were few and useful to ourselves: 'Behold, the Lord of hosts, who by His invisible power and great wisdom has founded the world, and in His glorious purpose has sur-

* Lib. i. visio 4. † Visio 2.

IN THE PRIMITIVE AGE. 119

rounded His creation with beauty; who by His mighty word has built the heavens, and established the earth upon the waters; who with His mighty power hath built up His holy Church, and blessed it: behold, He will change the heavens and the mountains, the hills and the seas, and will make all things plain for His elect, that He may give them the promise which He has promised, with much honour and joy, if in stedfast faith they keep the commandments of God, which they have received.'" *

A. D. circ. 100–105.

The so-called second book of Esdras, if we may judge from the period at which its predictions break down, appeared about this time; for the Roman Empire of this pretended prophet flourishes under the twelve Cæsars, but, after Nerva, falls into confusion. As the twelfth Cæsar died in 96, the date of the book must be about, or a little after, the year 100.

The credit of this anonymous writer is much lowered by his endeavour to pass off his work as a genuine prophecy of Ezra. This attempt, though clumsily carried out, is not the less calculated to injure the authority of the sacred books themselves. That he was a Christian is proved by these words: " My Son Jesus shall be revealed with those that are with him, and they that remain shall rejoice within four hundred years." His knowledge of the Apocalypse appears in many passages, especially the account of the palm-bearing multitude: " I, Esdras, saw upon the mount Zion a great people, whom I could not number . . . so I asked the angel, and said, Sir, what are these?" &c.

According to the system of this writer, a year in

* Visio 1.

prophecy signifies a natural year. The declaration that Jesus would be revealed after four hundred years refers to the time from Ezra to Christ; apparently an imitation of the seventy weeks of Daniel, allowing for the interval between Daniel and Ezra. Another instance occurs elsewhere: "Whereas she said to thee that she hath been thirty years barren, those are the thirty years wherein there was no offering made in her."

Esdras is the earliest Christian expositor of the fourth Beast; for, though he avoids the Roman name, he describes plainly enough the twelve Cæsars, of whom the second (Augustus) reigned longest, and was the first regularly appointed emperor of Rome:—

"The eagle which thou sawest ascending from the sea, this is the kingdom which was shown in vision to thy brother Daniel; but it was not explained to him, therefore I now explain it to thee. Behold, the days come, that a kingdom shall arise upon the earth, more terrible than all the kingdoms before it; and over it twelve kings shall reign, one after another; for the second shall begin to reign, and shall reign longest of the twelve."

When, in the visions of the Apocalypse, the sixth angel has poured out his vial upon the Euphrates, its waters are dried up to afford a passage for the kings of the East. Esdras attempts an easy and natural explanation of this prediction:—the miraculous drying of the Euphrates to facilitate the return of the ten tribes. This is to be at the time of the end, when the nations rise up against Jerusalem. His history of the ten tribes is worthy the attention of all who concern themselves about the fate of that exiled people.

A. D. circ. 110.

Early in this century lived Papias of Hierapolis, who devoted himself to the task of collecting information about Christ and the Apostles. In the preface to his work, the only part now extant, he describes his object: —

"Whatever I have learned and remembered from the elders, I will labour to set forth and explain, that thereby I may confirm the truth: for, unlike the many, I have delighted to follow, not great talkers, but true teachers; not those that repeat strange precepts, but those that declare the articles of faith given by the Lord, and flowing from the Truth itself. Therefore, when I saw any who had followed the elders, I asked what those elders had said: what Andrew, what Peter had said; what Philip, Thomas, or James; what John, Matthew, or any other of the Lord's disciples; what Aristion or John the Presbyter (both disciples of the Lord) had said."*

Eusebius appears to quote this passage, solely for the sake of the two Johns; for from it he proceeds to argue that the Apostle John may not have been the real author of the Apocalypse. He would rather believe that the other John wrote it, and that the whole Church has been mistaken in the authorship, than allow the inspiration of a book which promises a millennium. But Eusebius, belonging to the fourth century, must not be allowed to disturb the unanimity of these early times.

The millennial hope is the only portion of apostolic teaching which has come down to us through Papias. Unfortunately, we must here read Papias through the glasses of Eusebius, who is bent upon running down both the millennium and its supporters: —

* Eusebii Hist. Eccles., lib. iii. c. 39.

"Papias also declared other things as having come to him through unwritten tradition; certain strange parables and doctrines of the Saviour, and other things more like fable. Among these, that there will be a certain thousand years after the resurrection from the dead, during which the kingdom of Christ will be bodily established upon the earth. This, I suppose, came from his misunderstanding the teaching of the Apostles, and not allowing for what they said mystically and in figures: for he seems to have possessed very little judgment, as may be gathered from his books."

Papias is as far superior to Eusebius in faith as beneath him in learning; the one is a semi-Arian, the other makes it the business of his life to hear about Jesus. But Papias injures his cause when he paints, in hyperbolical language, the fertility of the millennial age: "Every vine," he says, "will bear ten thousand stems; every stem ten thousand branches; every branch ten thousand twigs;" and so forth. This passage, preserved by Irenæus, appears to be a fanciful amplification of the words, "There shall be a thousand vines at a thousand silverlings." For want of better arguments, these words of Papias are still often cited, to throw discredit upon the doctrine of the millennium.

Most of the writers who have flourished hitherto may be classed together, as far as personal intercourse is concerned, as the school of St. Paul: for Barnabas was his fellow-traveller, and Hermes his Roman disciple; Clement, who writes simply of the Advent, was that fellow-labourer Clement whose name was in the book of life. We now approach what may be called, in the same limited sense, the school of St. John: including Ignatius and Polycarp his disciples, Irenæus their pupil, and Hippolytus, said to have learnt under Irenæus. True it is that the uniformity of apostolic teaching leaves no room for any to style himself " of Paul or of Cephas :" nor was any such distinction allowed for a moment to be entertained*; yet St. John and his immediate followers, living in later times and among new dangers, are remarkable for the prominence which they give to this principle, that the apostacy of Antichrist will impugn the doctrines of the Trinity and the Incarnation.

The Church, having been told every thing else about Antichrist, was not left to herself to guess the road that led to him. Scripture decided, once for all, whether the danger would lie in believing too much or too little, — in explaining away these doctrines, or in holding them too grossly and too literally. The spirit that *confesses not*, the spirit that *denies*, that is the spirit of Antichrist.

It was these heresies that drew forth St. John's catholic Epistle. Being sinners, he argues, we need an atonement; that atonement we have in Christ Jesus. But to this conclusion two premises are necessary: that Jesus was a true Son of God, and that He became truly man.

The position, commanding as it did the very citadel of Satan, was attacked on either side: first, by Jews, Simonians, and Pagans, who treated Jesus as an impostor; and, secondly, as well as more danger-

---

* It must not be supposed that the Apostles had so negligently conducted themselves as to induce their followers to form parties, under pretence of following some Apostle in particular. It was others who had become the leaders of sects; but, rather than perpetuate their names in the sacred record, St. Paul puts the case as if it lay between himself, and Apollos, and Peter: — "These things I have in a figure transferred to myself and to Apollos for your sakes: that ye might learn *in us* not to think of men above that which is written."

ously, by Gnostics and Nicolaitanes, who contended that the Incarnation had been fictitious. For the first class, the Apostle fulminant (remembering late in life his title of Boanerges) could find no milder name than liars: they denied the Truth of truths. The second he calls the many antichrists who precede the coming of the Arch-Antichrist.

Early church history is loaded with the sayings and the doings of these men. Of the first class was Simon Magus, who after his rebuke by St. Peter went to yet greater lengths, saying in his work: " I am the word of God, I am the Excellent, I am the Paraclete, I am the Almighty, I am all things of God."* Of the second class was Valentine, from whose Epistle to Agathopus this sentence has been preserved: " Jesus, having endured all things, and having attained to perfect continence, wrought out His own Divinity: He ate and drank in a manner peculiar to Himself, not assimilating His food."†

A. D. 107.

In opposing these doctrines, St. John's disciples were not less zealous than himself. It was the last care of Ignatius, while on his way to martyrdom, to fortify the Church against the many antichrists. To the Church of Trallis he writes:—

" Shut your ears when any one speaks to you without Jesus Christ, who came of the race of David and of Mary; who was in very deed born, did eat and drink, did truly suffer under Pontius Pilate, was truly crucified, and did die, in the sight of those in heaven, and on earth, and under the earth; who was also truly raised from the dead by the power

* Hieron. in Matt. xxiv.
† Clem. Alexand. Stromatum, lib. iii.

of His Father, who will in like manner raise up us also in Christ Jesus, without whom we have no true life.

"But if, as some say, being atheists, that is, unbelievers, He *seemed* only to suffer, then they themselves seem only to exist. And if so, why am I bound, why longing to fight with the beasts? Do I then die for nothing? or am I bearing false witness for the Lord?

"Flee, therefore, these evil growths, which bear a fruit so deadly, that whoever tastes it, dies. These are no planting of the Father: for, if they were, we should see shoots of the Cross, and their fruit would be incorruptible."

From the custom of appealing to the Crucifixion in proof of Christ's true humanity, the cross itself began to assume a new force and meaning. Already it had been to the Jews a stumbling-block, contradicting their notions of a glorious Messiah: it had been to the Greeks foolishness, for their pride and subtlety rebelled against it. Now, in the second century, it was to be wielded as a weapon against the Antichristians: to these it was fatal, for it proclaimed a true humanity and a true atonement.

Therefore, with the necessities of the age, the customary mode of speaking of the cross changes also. When self-indulgence is the temptation, the command is given to take up the cross; when there is a question of being ashamed of a suffering Christ, one, and he a standard-bearer, talks of glorying in the cross; when letting go the atonement is proposed, we hear of being nailed to the cross. This flaming sword, it was found, could be turned every way, and on all sides the tree of life was guarded. Ignatius writes to the Church of Smyrna: "I know that you are fixed in stedfast faith, as it were nailed, body and spirit, to the cross of Jesus Christ our Lord; being established in love, through the blood of Christ, and fully persuaded concerning our Lord that He is truly of the race of David according to the flesh, God's Son according to the will and power of God."*

Polycarp showed himself a zealous disciple of the same school. A little before his martyrdom he wrote to the Philippians: " Whoever confesses not that Jesus Christ has come in the flesh, is an antichrist; whoever confesses not the witness of the cross, is of the Devil; whoever twists the words of the Lord to his own wishes, saying that there is neither resurrection nor judgment, he is the first born of Satan."†

A. D. circ. 130.

A little before the middle of this century, the world was surprised by the appearance of a work entitled Sibylline Oracles. In spite of its title, a Greek poem embodying a paraphrase of much of the Apocalypse was not likely to go down with the heathen as the work of their own prophetess. Accordingly they assigned it to a Christian author, and took no further notice of its contents.‡ But the Christians were less sagacious: blinded by their wishes, they hailed it as a tribute from Paganism to the truth of their own religion. The forgery cannot be defended: all that can be attempted is to state the motives that probably led to it.

The Christians, hard pressed by their enemies, possessed a means of retaliating, not at first brought into play. They knew that the Roman Empire, far from being eternal, was certainly destined to perish; that Rome herself, the boasted queen of cities, was to

---

* Ad Smyrnæos, cap. 1. † Ad Philippenses, cap. 7.
‡ Celsus (apud Origenem, lib. vii.): " You have inserted many blasphemies in the Sibyl's writings."

be miserably ravaged and burnt. This knowledge, it might seem to them, if properly applied, would strike terror into their foes, and cause their enemies no more to triumph over them: but this knowledge the inspired writers had concealed in figures, for the Church was not needlessly to be exposed to the suspicion of inculcating treason. At length, some member of the suffering community, more zealous than scrupulous, discovered a plausible expedient: the denunciations of the Apocalypse were to be put into the mouth of a Pagan prophet. Thus the Pagans were to receive them without suspicion; while the Church, in no way committed by the effusions of a sibyl, might securely look on, and profit by the result.

In this work, all disguise was to be dropped: there were to be no mysterious hints about the mouth of the lion, about him that letteth, about a wicked kingdom, or a nameless beast: every where it was to be plain Rome and the Roman Empire. But the poet's ingenuity was ill rewarded; the new oracles were traced to their true source, and that within the lifetime of their author: for the Christians were called Sibyllists, first by Celsus.

With great simplicity and perfect truth, Lactantius remarks that some people took these things for the fictions of the poets, not knowing whence the poets derived them*: for he supposes that the poets had learnt them from primæval tradition, together with the story of Deucalion and the custom of propitiatory sacrifice. And truly it was well for the Church that the heathen did not trouble themselves to inquire into the source of the new Sibyl's

---

* Institutions, lib. vii. cap. 22.

inspiration. It would have been impossible to deny that the figure of Rome, as a woman, adorned with gold, wooed by many lovers, clothed in purple, seated on seven hills, and destined to be burned with fire, was taken from an authentic Christian work. This Clavis Apocalyptica would have let the Pagans into the most secret recesses of the prophetic mysteries; and it is certain that, had they read the handwriting, and heard the interpretation, the interpreter would neither have been clothed in scarlet, nor made the third ruler in the kingdom.

The pseudo-Sibyl, professing to write long before the Christian era, begins by declaring that the Son of God will come to earth, and that the letters composing His human name will contain eight tens, eight units, and eight hundreds: for the letters of the Greek name of Jesus make 888.

The second book begins with the tenth age of the world, an expression probably familiar to the Romans. The miseries of that time are made to open with the "beginning of sorrows," war, famine, and pestilence:—

"At length there shall arrive the tenth age of the world, when the Shaker of all things, He who wields the lightning, will destroy the worship of idols, and will shake the nation. Then shall perish the great wealth of seven-hilled Rome, overwhelmed with much fire by Vulcanic flame: Then shall sanguinary times be sent from heaven: the whole race of men shall be maddened to mutual slaughter, and in the tumult God will send, upon those who live without law and justice, pestilences, famines, and thunders."

The poet makes the first attempt on record to explain the sign of the Son of man: his idea is apparently borrowed from the star of Bethlehem:—

"Then will God display a great sign. There shall appear, like a glittering crown, a bright and resplendent star, sparkling in heaven for many days. From heaven shall be displayed the victor's wreath for those who have striven in the race. Then shall be established the great age which brings in the heavenly city — an age which shall embrace the world, and shall possess the lustre of immortality." (Lib. ii.)

Antichrist is described under the name of his prime mover and master, Satan. His connection with the Jews and with the great tribulation is well set forth; nor is the "strong delusion" passed over: —

"There shall come certain false prophets, prophesying upon the earth. Belial also will come, and will do many wonders among men. Then shall be the restoration of holy men, elect and faithful; but the ruin of these Hebrews, for great wrath shall come upon them. * * *

"Then the Most High, who dwells in heaven and beholds all things, shall cause a sleep to fall upon men, and shall blind their eyes. Blessed will be those servants whom their Lord, when he comes, will find watching. Let all be wakeful, ever waiting with unclosed eyes: for he may come in the morning, or in the evening, or at mid-day. * * *

"In a heavenly chariot shall the avenging Tishbite descend from heaven to earth, and shall show to all the world three signs in the destruction of food. Woe to those that shall then expect offspring: woe to those that shall be burdened with the support of infants."

The three signs here attributed to Elijah are probably the shutting heaven, calling down fire, and smiting the earth with plagues: for all these will affect the means of subsistence, and are to be inflicted by the witnesses during the three years and a half.

Next follows the darkening of the sun and moon, taken either from the Gospel or from the sixth seal. The stars fall from heaven, and men gnash their teeth with anguish. The resurrection and the judgment succeed; and Abraham, Isaac, and Jacob come from afar to receive the eternal kingdom.

The ruin of Rome, the great burden of the poem, is principally copied from the Apocalypse and the Old Testament prophets. From the latter is borrowed the idea of describing Rome as the daughter of Rome:—

"Then shalt thou lament the broad purple of thy rulers, stripped of thy brightness, and clothed with sorrow. O boastful sovereign, progeny of Latian Rome, there shall be heard no more the glory of thy boasting: miserably shalt thou be abased, and shalt be no more exalted, and the glory of thine eagle-bearing legions shall fail. Where then thy power? what country will then be thine ally, foully enslaved by thy vain arts? For then shall all the inhabitants of the earth be shaken, when the Almighty Himself shall come with thrones, to judge the souls of quick and dead throughout the world." (Lib. viii.)

The origin of Antichrist and consequent destruction of Rome, are attributed to Satan, under the figure of the Dragon:—

"When the great and fiery Dragon shall come upon the waves, and shall feed thy children during the time of famine and civil war, then the end of the world and the last day are at hand, with the judgment of the immortal God, for the faithful and elect. But first there shall come inexorable wrath upon the Romans, a time of blood and a life of misery. Woe, woe, to thee, Italy, great and barbarous nation; dost thou not recall the day when naked and dishonoured thou camest forth to the light of the sun, that naked thou mayest return to the same place? Thou who didst commit injustice, when with giant hands alone controlling the world,—thou thyself shalt in the end be brought to judgment. Descending from on high, thou shalt dwell beneath the earth; with naphtha and pitch, with sulphur and much fire shalt thou disappear, and shalt be as ashes burning for ever. And he who looks on thee shall hear a groaning as the great wailing of hell, and a gnashing of teeth."

The pseudo-Sibyl distinctly connects the destruction of Rome with the coming of Antichrist from the East: —

"The destroyer of nations shall come to the united tribes of the Hebrews; then shall war repel war. He shall destroy the proud boasting of the Romans; then shall perish the now-flourishing empire of Rome, the ancient queen of surrounding cities. No more shalt thou possess the fertile plain of Rome, when the strong one shall come in arms from Asia." (Book viii.)

The Asiatic empire of Antichrist seems to be alluded to in the third book, where it is said that, as Rome once received tribute from Asia, she shall one day pay it back to Asia threefold. Rome is also described as a woman courted by many lovers; but, owing to the absence of historical fulfilment in that age, the poet makes little of this part of his subject. Yet his prediction, being in the main founded on Scripture, now seems in a fair way for being realized: "O virgin daughter of Latian Rome, delicate and rich in gold, oftentimes intoxicated with much-courted marriages, then a slave, thou shalt no more wed with any in this world." (Book iii.)

The Sibyl is the earliest of the very few Christian writers who express a belief in Nero's return. Although the tyrant's name does not occur in the poem, there are frequent allusions to the matricide emperor whose name begins with N, who will return and declare himself equal with God. The Pagans are the true authors of this superstition; for such it must be judged, not being supported by any of those who had personal intercourse with the Apostles.

For the world, though glad to be rid of Nero, soon betrayed a strange anxiety to see him brought back. It was reported that he would soon be restored, and the expectation was kept alive by various impostors. In describing this state of things, Suetonius grows almost pathetic: —

"There were not wanting those who for a long time decked his grave with spring and summer flowers, and set up in the rostrum, at one time his images dressed in robes, at another time his edicts, as if he were still living, and soon to return, to the great discomfiture of his foes. Moreover, Vologesus, king of the Parthians, when proposing to the senate a renewal of friendship, begged earnestly that the memory of Nero might be cherished. Lastly, about twenty years later, during my youth, there was a man of unknown origin, who boasted that he was Nero; and so popular was that name among the Parthians, that he was supported with enthusiasm, and with difficulty reduced to submission."

Dio mentions another false Nero; Tacitus a third: —

"A slave from Pontus, or, as others have it, a freedman from Italy, whose skill in lute-playing and singing, as well as his personal likeness, favoured the deception. . . . . Whoever he was, he was killed; and his body, remarkable for the eyes and hair, as well as for the fierceness of its countenance, was carried to Asia, and thence to Rome." *

During Nero's lifetime it had been given out by St. Paul that the mystery of iniquity was already working. Some, taking the word *mystery* in its Apocalyptic sense, supposed that Nero was thus held up as a type of Antichrist; one or two, misled by

* Suetonius in Neronem, c. 57. Dio, lib. 63. (Otho). Tacitus, Historiarum, lib. ii.

the Pagan superstition, and remembering Nero's death-wound with the dagger, took him to be that head whose deadly wound is to be healed: the beast that was and is not, and is to ascend from the bottomless pit.

A.D. 135.

The Jews, returning to their city after its destruction by Titus, presently recovered their former spirit and power. There soon appeared among them a false Messiah, whose pretensions and ultimate ruin correspond so closely with much that is said of Antichrist, as materially to aid our conceptions of that archapostate.

This miniature precursor of the little horn was originally a vile person, of a fierce and rapacious disposition. Too ignorant to support his own pretensions by an appeal to Scripture, he secured the services of a false prophet, the eminent Rabbi Akiba. That perverter of the law, taking advantage of the name of Barchochebas, which signifies the son of a star, applied to him the prophecy of Balaam, "There shall come a star out of Jacob." Once, seeing Barchochebas pass by, Akiba exclaimed, Behold the King, the Messiah! and from that time the imposture flourished apace.

The Jews readily gave credit to the deceiver, when, with bold and savage eloquence, he dwelt upon their degraded state, and the heaven which he had left for their deliverance; but, as Justin Martyr is careful to remind Antonine, the Christians resisted his pretensions, and no tortures could force them to deny Christ or to confess Barchochebas. According to a Jewish writer, the more resolute of his followers had a mark of their own: 200,000 cut off one finger in token of their constancy.*

Events seemed to conspire together to deprive the Jews of all political excuse for their rejection of Christ. On first hearing of the impostor's success, the Romans did not come, nor did they show any disposition to take away the place and nation of the Jews; but when, as Dio relates, the Jews allured other nations to join in the revolt, so that the whole world seemed about to rise in arms against the Romans, Adrian bestirred himself to meet the danger.

So desperate was the valour of the Jews, that the Romans did not venture to attack their main body, but preferred to cut them off in detail. In the end, Barchochebas was slain, 580,000 of the Jews were killed in battle, and a great number perished by famine and pestilence. The slaughter was greatest in Beth-thera: the Jews say that the blood ran down to the sea, a distance of thirty-two furlongs, and that in one place horses sunk in it to the mouth. The Jews cannot be suspected of copying this from the Apocalypse, though the words of Ezekiel may have suggested the addition, that the dried blood sufficed to manure the neighbouring vineyards for seven years. The whole event has in it something of a judicial character: Galatinus notices a report that, in the sale of the captive Jews, thirty might be bought for one piece of silver.

There are extant, histories of this war by Jews,

---

* Galatinus found this stated by R. Jochanan, in a commentary upon the words "The hands are the hands of Esau."

Pagans, and Christians. The Romans look upon the affair solely in a military point of view, noticing the battles and the sieges, the number of the slain, and, most of all, Adrian's dispatch, in which he was forced by his losses to omit the usual salutation:—" If you and your children are well, it is well; I and the army are well."

The Romans, having had enough of the Jews and their fighting Messiahs, took measures for putting down the whole system. Jerusalem was rebuilt as a Roman colony, and its name, in honour of Adrian, changed to Ælia. Over the Bethlehem gate was set up a marble sow, in which some modern interpreters have thought to trace the abomination spoken of by Daniel. By a decree of Adrian, the Jews were banished from Judea, and forbidden to behold, even from a distance, the land of their fathers. In their exile they changed the name of their deceiver, who to this day is known among them as Barcosbam: for by that name was expressed the true parentage of the Star-begotten, " The son of a lie."

Few events have supplied so much work for the interpreters as the Barcosbam revolt. To the Christians all this was an argument in favour of their own religion: for it was now clear, as Tertullian remarked, that the sceptre had completely departed from Judah, and there was no congregated nation of the Jews to welcome a Messiah. There was now no people to be scattered if they should reject him; but, on the contrary, a people evidently scattered for a previous rejection. The Jews, reckoning the war to have lasted three years and a half, applied it to the elucidation of Daniel's last half week. Jerome has preserved an outline of their scheme: —

136 THE CHRISTIAN INTERPRETATION OF PROPHECY

" Some of the Jews say that the one week, of which it is written, He will confirm the covenant with many for one week, is divided between Vespasian and Adrian; and that, according to Josephus, Vespasian and Titus made peace with the Jews for three years and a half. Three years and a half are also reckoned under Adrian, when Jerusalem was utterly destroyed, and the Jews were slain in heaps. The remainder were also banished from Judea. These things the Jews maintain, not much caring that the time from the first year of Darius King of Persia, down to the final destruction under Adrian, is 174 Olympiads, that is, 696 years, which make 99 Hebrew weeks and three years over."*

A.D. circ. 150.

As the Pagan philosophers began to form some acquaintance with Christianity, those that remained unconvinced began to attack what seemed to them its weakest points. Among other things, Celsus imagined the warnings against a coming Antichrist peculiarly open to ridicule. That a true Christ should foretel the coming of an impostor, who would appear to equal Him in miraculous powers, and would far exceed Him in success among the Jews — this,

* Jerome on Daniel viii. Eusebius, Hist. Eccles., iv. 6.; also in his Chronicon. Dio, under Adrian. Tertullian, Adversus Judæos, cap. 13. Justin Martyr, Apologia ad Antoninum. Galatinus de Arcanis Catholicæ Veritatis, lib. iv. cap. 21. Galatinus quotes much from the Jewish history entitled Echa-Rabbethi: among other stories is the following: — "Adrian besieged Bitter (Beththera) during three years and a half; when the city was taken, Barcosbam was slain, and his head was brought to Adrian. 'Who killed this man?' asked the Emperor. 'I,' said a soldier, 'I killed this man.' 'Go and fetch me his body,' said Adrian. He went, and found a serpent coiled round the neck of it; Adrian, seeing this, said, 'Unless his God had slain him, who could have prevailed against him?' for of such it is written in Deut. xxxii., Unless their God had sold them, and their Lord had shut them up.'

said Celsus, argues a sense of failure on the part of Christ. His words, full of the very spirit of infidelity, are these:—

"Therefore the Son of God is vanquished by the devil; and, being Himself worsted, He bids us also despise his assaults, declaring that Satan himself will also appear in like manner, showing great and wonderful works, and usurping the glory due to God; and that to those works all who desire to resist him are to give no heed, but to believe in Himself alone. This is evidently the scheme of an impostor, labouring and guarding beforehand against those who may contradict and oppose him."*

The accuracy with which Celsus describes the coming of Antichrist, and the true way of resisting his delusion, is equalled only by his malice in scorning the mercy which forewarns us against the danger. The reply of Origen will appear in the history of the third century.

A.D. circ. 150.

The defence of Christianity was next taken up by Justin the Martyr. A point at issue between Jews and Christians was the Millennium, on which subject Justin thus states the belief of the Church:—

"With all perfectly orthodox Christians, I acknowledge the future resurrection of the flesh. Now the thousand years in Jerusalem, when it shall be built up, adorned, and enlarged, are declared by the prophets Ezekiel, Esaias, and others. For thus did Esaias speak of that thousand years: There shall be a new heaven and a new earth, and the former shall not be remembered, nor come into mind, &c. . . . . .

"We know also the saying, that a day of the Lord is as a thousand years. Moreover, one of our own people,

---

* Origen against Celsus, lib. vi.

named John, an Apostle of Christ, prophesied in the Apocalypse that for those who believe in our Christ there will be a thousand years in Jerusalem; and afterwards there will come the catholic, or universal and simultaneous, resurrection and judgment of all men."*

In this matter of the millennium the Jews and the Christians appear to have changed sides: for the doctrine, first maintained by the Church against the Jews, was soon discarded by the Church as a fiction of Jewish origin. The following slight sketch of the controversy will illustrate the change: —

A.D.

75. Barnabas teaches the millennium.

96. St. John also.

150. Justin Martyr supports it against the Jews.

400. Jerome styles it a Jewish fiction.

450. Ammonius launches out against the Jews for expecting another Christ to bring about their millennium: "Vainly do they imagine that they will reign with Antichrist a thousand years: he will not flourish longer than three and a half." †

1000. The book Zohar teaches the millennium; also most of the Rabbinical works.

To return to Justin. The Jews on one occasion departed from their custom of interpreting a time as a year: of this he complains: —

"He who will utter blasphemies and insults against the Most High, even he is at the door: whose duration Daniel fixes at a time, times, and half a time. But you, not knowing how long he is to continue, think differently: for you take a time to mean a hundred years. If it be so, the Man of Sin

---

* Dial. cum Tryphone Judæo.

† Mai, Vet. Script., t. i. Greek Chain on Daniel.

must reign at the least 350 years, supposing that by Daniel's *times*, we understand no more than two."

Justin next takes occasion to discuss the future coming of Elias: —

"*Trypho.* — We all expect that Christ will be a man, born of men, and that Elias will come to anoint him. Now, if this man (Jesus) is to be esteemed the Christ, we ought to know by all means that he is man, born of men. Moreover, I do not think that he is the Christ, because Elias is not yet come.

"*Justin.* — Does not the word given by Malachi say that Elias will come before that great and terrible day of the Lord?

"*Trypho.* — Certainly.

"*Justin.* — Since the word forces us to confess that two advents of Christ are foretold, — one in which He will appear suffering, dishonoured, and inglorious; the other in which He will be illustrious, and the Judge of all, as I have already proved at length — must not we suppose the word of God to mean that Elias will be the precursor of that great and terrible day, that is, of His second coming?

"*Trypho.* — Certainly.

"*Justin.* — Our Lord also, said I, declared the same thing in His teaching, that Elias is to come. And this we know will take place when the Lord Jesus Christ is about to be revealed from heaven in glory, whose first coming was heralded by the Spirit of God, which was in Elias in the person of John, a prophet of your nation; after whom no other prophet appeared among you."

The Scriptures referring to the second coming of Elias are these: —

1. The prophecy in Malachi: "I will send you Elijah the prophet before the coming of the great and dreadful day of the Lord."

2. John's mission: "To go before Him in the spirit and power of Elias;" apparently the spirit and power of Elijah's second coming, for John's office

bore no evident resemblance to the first mission of Elijah.

3. John's denial: "Art thou Elias? And he saith, I am not."

4. The statement that Elias had shut heaven for three years and six months, found nowhere in the Old Testament, but twice in the New.

5. The declaration that "Elias truly shall first come and restore all things," made after the disciples had seen Elias upon the mount, though applied in a secondary sense to John the Baptist.

6. The two witnesses are said to repeat several of the miracles peculiar to Elijah, and for the same space of time, three years and six months.

While everything points to Elijah as one of the Witnesses, Scripture leaves us in uncertainty respecting the name of the other. Following Ben-Sirach and the scribes, the Pseudo-sibyl, Justin, and Origen speak of Elias alone; Tertullian and Hippolytus add Enoch. Lactantius speaks of one only. Victorinus suggests Jeremiah as a second. The Pseudo-Hippolytus is disposed to make *three* tabernacles, — one for John, one for Enoch, and one for Elias.

For the office of second witness three principal candidates have been proposed: Enoch, Moses, and John the Apostle. The reasons adduced in favour of each are, for the most part, more curious than weighty.

For *Enoch.* — 1. Like Elias, he was translated. If Enoch and Elias are yet to die, it will be true of all, (excepting those that are alive and remain) that it is appointed to men once to die. 2. He prophesied of Christ's second coming as near at hand, as if in anticipation of his future office.

For *Moses*. — 1. That Michael contended with Satan for his body. 2. That he appeared with Elias on the mount, and can therefore testify to having seen Christ in the flesh. 3. Moses and Elias spoke of Christ's death at Jerusalem: to this conversation there may be an allusion in the words, " Where also their Lord was crucified," &c. 4. The witnesses enjoy the miraculous powers of Moses, tunning water to blood, and inflicting plagues. 5. Christ appeals to Moses as His witness against the Jews: " Had ye believed Moses, ye would have believed me, for he wrote of me."

For *St. John*. — 1. There be some standing here, &c. (unless this refers to the Transfiguration only). 2. Thou must prophesy again before many peoples, &c. 3. Ye shall indeed drink of my cup; but John has not yet been martyred. 4. If I will that he tarry till I come*, &c. 5. John is the only witness of the true death of Christ: he saw the water and the blood, and he saw and bare witness.

Where Scripture holds no torch, we must be content to remain in darkness; nevertheless, most of the ancients have recorded their sentences in favour of Enoch.

A. D. 168.

In this year occurred the persecution at Smyrna, an accomplishment of prophecy too signal to be passed over in silence.

The angel of Smyrna, addressed in the Apocalypse,

---

* Some of these reasons are beside the mark, for the second witness is to be killed, and does not tarry till Christ comes; he also tastes of death, &c. It has been suggested that John *did* tarry, till Christ came to him in Patmos.

was none other than John's disciple Polycarp, whose pupil Irenæus tells us that "he was appointed by the Apostles bishop of the Church in Smyrna."* His work was now well ended: he had been eighty-six years a Christian, and of these not less than seventy-two waiting for his crown; but now after lying, as it were, so long becalmed, while others were sailing past him, a sudden blast of persecution sped him to the desired haven. Nor does he, even at the stake, forget to return thanks for the fulfilment of the promise: "Thou hast both foreshown and fulfilled, O God of truth, who canst not lie!"

Immediately after the persecution, the Smyrniotes dispatched to the neighbouring churches an account of the martyrdoms. We have thus the epistle general *from* Smyrna†, as well as the epistle *to* Smyrna: in which epistles, as if the one were a supplement to the other, we read of the blasphemy of the Jews, and of their eagerness to gather faggots for the pile of Polycarp; of the injunction given him, not to fear his sufferings, and of his contempt of that fire which burns but for an hour. We read of the ten days' tribulation predicted, and of the sufferings of the Church during the April games: we read that some were to be tried; in which trial Quintus was found wanting, being terrified by the beasts,—while Germanicus faced them boldly, and obtained his crown. Also, how Polycarp proved faithful unto death, for

---

* Adv. Hæreses, lib. iii. cap. 3. Angel is a Septuagint word for priest; as in Haggai i. 13.: "Then Haggai the Lord's angel spoke to the people among the angels of the Lord."

† Published entire by Ussher: the greater part is also preserved by Eusebius, Hist. Eccles., lib. iv.

the "Amen" of his last prayer was the signal for firing the pile. All this, and much more, was written by the believers of Smyrna, that it might be transferred to the records of the Church's experience, teaching her to trust the plain sense of the Apocalypse, and strengthening her faith against the yet greater tribulations foretold in that book.

The persecution lasted during the April games; whether nine days or ten, is uncertain. In Rome, says Bulengerus, the Megalesian games of April occupied nine days.* According to the same authority, the Roman games, in general, "at first lasted one day, afterwards two days, and latterly nine." † Yet these games are sometimes spoken of as occupying ten: Cicero speaks of ten days' games appointed by the augurs to avert a threatened calamity. ‡ From the details of the persecution it can only be gathered that more than five days elapsed from the beginning to the end. §

---

* Bulengerus de Circo Romano, in Grævii Thesauro, t. ix. col. 612.

† Ibidem.

‡ Cicero in Catilinam, iii. cap. 4.: "Ludi decem per dies facti sunt."

§ The fulfilment of this prophecy has not attracted so much attention as might be expected. The ancients took these things as a matter of course: Andreas simply remarks, "It is for ten days only, and not long." Berengaud, "He shows how long the worst part of the persecution would last." Dionysius also supposes that the worst was limited to ten days. Daubuz is more precise: "The persecution lasted not long, perhaps not more than ten days." Grotius hazards a rash assertion: "After ten days the Christians of Smyrna were released from prison." Foxe is too good a Martyrologist for this: he notices the martyrdom of Polycarp and the accompanying persecution; also La Haye. Pareus likewise refers to Polycarp: "I suppose, with Andreas, that ten days are mentioned

A.D. 178.

A comparison drawn by the Lyonnese, between a persecution which they had just suffered and that which is to come in the days of Antichrist, is too instructive to be omitted. The torments of their martyrs had been among the most severe on record. The slave-girl Blandina, after being tortured for a whole day, was hung upon a cross to be torn by beasts; the Bishop Pothinus, upwards of ninety years old, died of his wounds in prison; and Attalus expired honourably, having sustained more torments than can be related in a few words. When all was over, the survivors wrote an account of the persecution, which had helped them to form an idea of the times of Antichrist. "The adversary," they say, "bore down upon us with his full strength, giving us already a prelude to that coming in which he will be unrestrained; keeping his servants practised at all points, and exercising them before-hand against the servants of God."*

This vivid conception of the future tribulation, rising above and casting into shade the horrors so lately witnessed, bespeaks the existence of a flourishing school of prophecy in Lyons. Could there be in that city any pupil of the disciples of John? some

to show the shortness of the time." Says Aretius, "It will not be long; its severity will be ended in ten days' space." And to conclude with a name of our own time, Dean Woodhouse supposes that the persecution was "only of ten days, and was fulfilled in that generation." For a similar use of "ten days," also in reference to the duration of the games, see *Cicero de Oratore*, lib. iii. c. i.

* Epistle from Lyons and Vienne, preserved by Eusebius, lib. v. cap. 1.

IN THE PRIMITIVE AGE. 145

one deeply impressed by those words which cast so strong and lurid a light upon the days of the end :—
"*Here* is the patience and the faith of the saints?" The salutation of the epistle explains everything: Irenæus was present throughout the persecution, evidently as a leading character, since he was elected bishop in the room of the martyred Pothinus. To Irenæus then we turn, for he has much to say about the days of Antichrist.

A. D. 180–190.

In his work "against the heresies,"* after describing the many antichrists of his own time, he goes on to the last great heresy, the apostacy of the Arch-Antichrist. There is no single commentator upon the Apocalypse of equal historical importance with Irenæus; for, while second to none in zeal and knowledge of the Scriptures, he possesses an advantage over all his successors, in having learned from a pupil of St. John himself. Against those who had altered the number of the Beast's name, he could bring this conclusive argument: "They that have seen John face to face say otherwise." Hence the value of his declaration, that the Apocalypse was written by the Apostle John in the end of Domitian's reign.

Hitherto we have met with *teaching* only on the

---

* The Latin version of this work seems equally original with the Greek, being at once too good and too bad for a translation: too good, from its close and vigorous rendering of the sense; and too bad, from the number of Greek words used in it by way of Latin. Both Greek and Latin were spoken in Lyons during the persecution.

L

subject of prophecy; we have now to weigh the doubts and the conjectures of inquirers like ourselves. Through Irenæus we discover that many persons had been employed in this study, and that even in his time false interpretations and presumptuous guesses were not unknown. Some had changed the Beast's number to 616; a mistake which he supposes to have begun with the copyists, and to have been kept up by "vainglorious" attempts to support some names that agreed with 616. All this tampering with the number he regards in the most serious light; "for," he says, " there is no light penalty denounced against those who add to, or take from, the Scripture."*

He advises that all positive conclusions regarding the Beast's name be reserved till the appearance of the eleventh king. In support of the established reading, 666, he adduces three arguments: first, it is found in all the old and approved copies of the Apocalypse; secondly, those who have seen St. John adopt it; and, thirdly, the three sixes, he remarks, are an essential part of the meaning; for Antichrist will sum up the sins of the six thousand years, typified by the six days of the world. Whether Irenæus learnt this from St. John, or from his own meditations, he does not say. Elsewhere he remarks that the name of Jesus contains 888.

The mischief liable to be produced by hasty conclusions is well set forth: —

"Great will be the danger of those who falsely presume

---

* Irenæus adv. Hæreses, lib. v. cap. 30. The fifth book contains nearly all that he says about Antichrist: the exceptions will be marked by special references.

upon the knowledge of Antichrist's name; for if, while they are thinking it to be one, he comes under another, they will easily be deceived, supposing that he against whom they are to watch has not yet come. Let such persons, therefore, take a lesson, and come back to the true number of the name, lest they be ranked among false prophets: but, after learning the genuine number as declared by Scripture, namely, 666, let them first wait for the division of the empire among the ten; and afterwards, when those ten are reigning, and beginning to settle their affairs, and to increase their kingdom—and another comes suddenly, usurping empire, and terrifying the said ten, and having a name containing the predicted number —then let them know that this is truly the abomination of desolation."

The last expression is used by Irenæus in a broad sense: the ancients sometimes apply it to the image of the Beast set up in the temple, sometimes to Antichrist himself set up as God, and sometimes to the defilement of the holy city and temple by his presence and blasphemies.

For his account of the political designs of the horns, Irenæus may find support in the Septuagint. In place of the words, "I considered the horns," the Seventy render, "Many counsels were in the horns," which the Syriac Septuagint takes to be "great thoughts." To these counsels St. John seems to refer when he describes the designs of the ten kings in reference to Rome. Of these same kings, as it appears, David also wrote, that they will take counsel together, how they may break the bonds of the Lord, and cast away His cords from them. A later writer, ingeniously fitting together these passages, undertakes to unravel the whole plot:—The ten kings, finding Rome an easy prey, and knowing nothing of the divine counsel, argue from the fall of the ecclesiastical city, the falsehood of Christianity itself. Upon this, joining with Antichrist, they will labour to extirpate both the faith and its followers throughout the world.*

Irenæus proceeds, with a fresh caution against rash conclusions, to communicate the result of his own labours: —

" Many names may be found having the predicted number, and yet the question remains as it was; for, if many names are found, we still have to inquire which of them will belong to the coming man.

" I speak thus, not from any want of suitable names, but from fear of God, and from zeal for the truth. Euanthas does indeed contain the required number, but of this I will affirm nothing. Lateinos also contains 666; and this is a very likely name, since the last kingdom bears it; for they are Latins who now reign: yet of this solution I will not boast. But Teitan, having its first syllable written with the two Greek vowels *e* and *i*, is the most likely of all the names that have been discovered among us. * * *

" Yet about this name (Teitan) I will make no rash assertion, nor declare positively that he will bear it; for this we know, that if his name were meant to be openly published at the present time, it would doubtless have been declared by him who saw the Apocalypse: for that was revealed, not long ago, but almost in our own age, about the end of Domitian's reign."

Time, the great refuter of human systems, has done nothing to shake the monument of prudence and sagacity raised by Irenæus. The question remains as he left it, and doubtless for the reason which he assigns. Happily, he was not entrapped into hasty conclusions, even by the word Latinus, tempting as it seemed while Roman emperors were patronising false prophets, and seating themselves as divine in the temples of the gods. The judgment of nine-

* Abbot Joachim, A.D. 1195.

tenths of the Church has approved his caution, and not without obvious cause; for Latinus, if used in the sense of Romanus, is altogether beside the purpose. Under the name Romanus St. Paul was glad to shelter his Gospel and himself, at once a free-born Roman and a citizen of the Jerusalem above. But, when Irenæus suggested the word Latinus, it was evidently with the idea of its acquiring some new signification in aftertimes.

It now seems most unlikely that a mere geographical name should ever obtain a meaning that will ensure the eternal ruin of all who receive it. Both history and Scripture lead us to expect something more closely corresponding to "the number of a man:" perhaps some proper name, like that of Antiochians, given to the Jews by Antiochus (2 Macc. iv. 9.); perhaps some name of pride or blasphemy; perhaps some watchword expressing the leading principle of Antichrist's apostacy.*

Of the many names which later commentators have proposed, "I deny" (ἀρνοῦμαι), found by Hippolytus, is almost the only one supported by the analogy of Scripture; for, that Antichrist should be so candid as

* This subject has been dexterously handled in a series of tracts very lately published. "This is the clue to the mark of the name of the idol Messiah. At his first appearance he will be hailed with acclamations and hosannas, as the Redeemer of Israel, another Judas Maccabæus; and, either from the initials of his name, or from the initial letters of some scriptural motto adopted by him, an artificial name will be formed, a cypher of his real name. And that abbreviated name or cypher will be ostentatiously displayed, as their badge, their watchword, their shibboleth, their 'Maccabi,' by all his adherents. This artificial name, this mark or symbol of the real name, will be equal, by Gematria, to 666."— Jewish Missionary, p. 52. (1848.)

to assume the name of "Bad Leader," "Unjust Lamb," "Formerly envious," or the like, is opposed to all that we are taught of his deceivableness of unrighteousness.*

To return to Irenæus: we have from him the earliest connected account of the doings of Antichrist, and of the Scriptures which describe his coming: —

"From what is said of the times of Antichrist, it appears that he, being an apostate and a robber, will desire to be worshipped as God, and though a slave, will seek to be proclaimed a king. Receiving all the power of the Devil, he will come, not as a just and lawful sovereign subject to God, but as impious, unjust, and without law; as an apostate, a wicked one, and a murderer; as a robber, summing up in himself the diabolical apostacy. Putting away idols, to persuade man that he is God, he will set up himself as sole idol, combining in himself the manifold errors of all other idols. * * *

"He will sit in the temple of God, showing himself that he is God. I have proved in the third book that the Apostles call no one God, in His proper person, excepting Him who is God indeed, the Father of our Lord: by whose command, for reasons already given, the temple in Jerusalem was built. In this temple the adversary will sit, striving to show himself to be the Christ; as also the Lord says, When ye shall see the abomination of desolation spoken of by Daniel the prophet, standing in the holy place," &c. * * *

---

* Some curious discoveries have been made on this subject: Maometis contains the number; also Saxoneios, proposed by Bellarmine, merely "for the satisfaction of Luther." Alcassar finds that not only is 666 "the pride of life," but 555 is the "lust of the flesh." Besides these attempts to penetrate the mystery by fair means, the number, for its obstinate refusal to give up its secret, has been tortured in every conceivable manner. Forced into the shape of a repeating decimal, its second digit mutilated, and its square root unskilfully extracted, it is at last dispatched without remorse, as the illegitimate offspring of a transcriber's fancy.

"Concerning the last time and those ten kings which belong to it, among whom the empire now ruling is to be divided, the Lord's disciple John has declared more fully in the Apocalypse, explaining the ten horns which Daniel saw. For thus it was said to him: The ten horns which thou sawest are ten kings, which have received no kingdom as yet, &c. It is therefore clear that the coming one will kill three of these and subjugate the rest, and become the eighth among them; and they shall desolate Babylon and burn her with fire, and give their kingdom to the Beast, and put to flight the Church: afterwards they themselves will be destroyed by the coming of our Lord. * * *

"They shall believe, it says, in the False one, that all may be condemned who believed not the truth, but had pleasure in unrighteousness. His coming John thus describes in the Apocalypse: The beast which I saw was like unto a pard, &c. And afterwards of his armour-bearer, whom he calls also the false prophet, He spake, it says, like a dragon, and he exercised all the power of the first beast before him, &c. This is said that all may know his miracles to be done, not by divine power, but by magic art; and no marvel if, having demons and apostate spirits to help him, he through them performs miracles by which he deceives those that dwell on the earth. He will also command them to make an image to the beast." (Cap. 28.)

Whether the second Beast represents an individual false prophet only, or, as some have thought, the entire college of false prophets, inclusive of their head, matters little to the understanding of the history.* As Jannes and Jambres were to Pharaoh, as Balaam to Balak, as Akiba to Barchochebas, so will be the second Beast to the first. But even in the midst of that judicial delusion God will not leave Himself

---

* In the case of Thyatira, the false prophetess Jezebel appears to have stood for Priscilla, Quintilla, and Maximilla. Epiphan. adv. Alogos.

without witness: there will be an Elijah to withstand that Ahab, a Moses and an Aaron to defy the Jannes and the Jambres of the city spiritually called Egypt: there will be once more waters turned to blood, and the earth smitten with all plagues. This subject is but slightly touched upon by Irenæus, who makes no mention of the witnesses by name: "If any one will observe carefully what is said by the prophets concerning the end, and what John, the Lord's disciple, saw in the Apocalypse, he will find that the nations universally will suffer the same plagues that then fell upon Egypt in particular."*

Irenæus continues:—

"The Lord said to those who did not believe in Him, I am come in my Father's name, and ye received me not: when another shall come in his own name, him ye will receive. He calls Antichrist another, because he is alien from the Lord.† He is also that unjust judge spoken of by the Lord, who feared not God, neither regarded man; to whom flies the widow forgotten of God, that is, the earthly Jerusalem, to be avenged of her enemy. And this he will do in the time of his kingdom: he will translate the empire to that city, and will sit in the temple of God, deceiving those who worship him, as if he were the Christ. Therefore Daniel says again, And the sanctuary shall be desolate; and there was given a transgression for a sacrifice, and righteousness was cast down to the ground: and he practised and prospered." (Cap. 25.)

To place in the most favourable light this explanation of the unjust judge, the seventeenth and eighteenth chapters of St. Luke should be read consecutively. It will then be seen that the Lord, while

* Lib. iv. cap. 30.
† Compared with the saying, "I and my Father are one."

describing the times of the end, touches upon the false kingdoms and the false Christs which will perplex unstable souls. Then follows a reference to the great tribulation; for the warning about coming down from the housetop occurs also in St. Mark, in connection with the flight from Judæa: and lest, in that time of unparalleled trouble, men should despair and cease to pray, a parable is given to encourage them.

At this point Irenæus diverges from the common track, being followed by Hippolytus only. He supposes the illustration to be taken from that time to which the body of the discourse refers; as if it had been said; — Lest in the great tribulation the elect should cease to cry day and night, let them take courage from the answer which, by mere importunity, the Jews will extort from Antichrist: if he, so unjust a ruler, will be moved to take the part of that perseveringly clamorous nation, much more will the righteous God avenge His own elect, for whose sake He has shortened those days; for, though it be His character to bear long, yet in this instance He will avenge them speedily. (Gr. $\dot{\epsilon}\nu$ $\tau\acute{\alpha}\chi\epsilon\iota$, commonly used to express the quickness of Christ's second coming.) Nevertheless, continues the Saviour, speedy as will be the avenging, and short the trial of your faith (even three years and a half), shall I, when I come at the end of it, find your faith still kept alive upon the earth?

This passage of Irenæus is the most ancient in which Antichrist is identified with him that is to come in his own name. On this point primitive writers were unanimous, though the modern translations of the Gospel leave it doubtful whether the case is not merely hypothetical. But there are three declarations of our Lord, all expressed in the same form: If I be lifted up — If I go and prepare a place — If another shall come in his own name. In all these places, the primitive Greek Christians (who must be supposed to know best the meaning of their own language) understand the ἐάν as *when;* making what follows, not doubtful, but merely indefinite in time: as if it were said, When I shall be lifted up — When I go to prepare a place — When another shall come in his own name.

Irenæus now hastens on to the closing scene:—

" And when this Antichrist shall have laid waste all things in the world, reigning three years and six months, and sitting in the temple of Jerusalem; then the Lord shall come from heaven in clouds, in the glory of the Father: and casting him and those that obey him into the lake of fire, will bring about to the just the times of the kingdom; that is, the rest, even the seventh day made holy. And He will restore to Abraham the promise of the inheritance; in which kingdom, saith the Lord, many shall come from the East and from the West, and shall sit down with Abraham, with Isaac, and with Jacob." (Cap. 30.)

Irenæus supposes the sealed book to contain those things of which Christ said, " All things are delivered to me by my Father;" thus seeming to identify it with the Apocalypse itself, which is entitled, "The Revelation of Jesus Christ, which God gave to him." The first seal he expounds as Christ's triumph: As Jacob wrestled and conquered, " so was Christ also born to conquer, the type of whose going forth Jacob displayed. And John also says of Him in the Apo-

calypse, He went forth conquering and to conquer." *
He supports also the doctrine of the millennium, though adding little to what Barnabas had said before.

The Jewish origin of Antichrist was a question much studied by the ancients. To avoid repetition, its whole history shall be collected together in this place.

The patriarch Jacob, when telling his sons what should befall them in the last days, declared that two of them would bear rule in Israel, — one as a lion, the other as a serpent. The Apocalypse, which identifies Judah's lion with Christ, seems to point out Dan's serpent as Antichrist: for, in the sealing which takes place during or before the time of Antichrist, none of Dan's tribe are sealed; and Jacob, as if allowed a glimpse of the time of trouble, and of the crying of the elect, interrupts his prophecy with this exclamation, — "I have waited for thy salvation, O Lord."

This serpent had from the beginning so unpleasant an appearance, that the Jews laboured hard to explain it away. First, Philo attempted to connect it with the brazen serpent, with us a type of the Messiah :—

"From one serpent Moses would have fled, but another serpent he made of brass, symbolising temperance; that he who was bitten by pleasure might look upon temperance, and live the true life. Such a serpent Jacob prays that Dan may become, saying, Dan shall judge his people as one tribe of Israel; and, Let Dan become a serpent in the way . . . Let him sit in the path. And what means this? The field of virtue is not trodden, for few go thereby: but the way of vice is trodden. He persuades him, therefore, to sit, and to occupy in ambush the trodden way of malice and concupiscence." †

* Irenæus adv. Hæreses, lib. iv. c. 37, 38.
† Allegoriarum, lib. ii.

Philo makes another attempt in favour of Dan; but the more he labours, the worse his cause becomes. In the treatise upon agriculture, Dan passes from a serpent to a dragon. " Dan is interpreted judgment: that power of the mind which examines, discerns, and judges all things, is compared to a dragon; for it is an animal possessed of great agility, singularly crafty, and prone to violence."

Dan's biting the horse's heel might seem to refer to the prophecy given to the serpent, " Thou shalt bruise his heel." Philo raises a slender objection: " Thou shalt bruise his heel — but Dan's serpent, of which we are now speaking, bites the heel, not of the man, but of the horse."

It was noticed by Onkelos, who lived about the first or second century, that Samson had come of the tribe of Dan, and that he had for a time ruled the tribes of Israel. The difficulty was to make Samson and the serpent agree in their history: the serpent being crafty and concealing itself in ambush, while Samson did everything by brute force. Dan's serpent bites the horse and throws the rider; while Samson never fought with chariots or horsemen, but confined himself to massacres of the Philistine infantry.

Onkelos thus paraphrases the words of Jacob:—

" A man shall be chosen, and shall arise from the house of Dan, whose fear shall be upon the people. He shall smite the Philistines strongly, like a snake, — like an asp shall he lie in ambush in the path. He shall kill the strong ones of the Philistines, both horse and foot: he shall hamstring the horses and the chariots, and shall cast down their riders backward. I wait for thy salvation, O Lord ! " *

---

* Targum of Onkelos; Walton's Polyglot, in loco.

Onkelos is followed, with little variation, by Jonathan Ben Uzziel, supposed to have been his pupil. Another explanation was afterwards sought in the burning of Laish by the men of Dan (Judges xviii.*); an event still more insignificant, though more in accordance with the serpent's character. But the Christians, rejecting all such interpretations as evasive, considered the omission of Dan, in the sealing of the tribes, as decisive of the question. This event, taking place about the time of Antichrist, answers well to the "last days" of Jacob's prophecy.

At this point comes in Irenæus, the earliest Christian expositor of Dan: —

"Jeremiah not only describes his sudden coming, but even the tribe from which he will spring, saying, Out of Dan shall we hear the sound of the swiftness of his horses; the whole land shall be moved by the neighing of his horses: he shall come and shall devour the earth with its fulness; the city, and them that dwell therein. (Jeremiah viii.) And for this reason that tribe is not numbered in the Apocalypse among those that are saved." (Cap. 30.)

The Jews, now exasperated, endeavoured to write up the serpent, wandering as far from the plain sense as Dan itself from Beersheba. About the seventh century the Jerusalem Targum thus expounds the passage: —

"There shall arise a Redeemer, who will be strong and lifted up above all kingdoms. And he shall be like the serpent that lieth in the way, like the basilisk that lieth in ambush at the meeting of the ways: which biteth the horse in his hoof, and through fear of him the rider thinketh to turn back. And this is Samson, the son of Manoah, whose

---

* Theodoret, Quest. in Genesin. (Theod. rejects it for himself.)

fear was upon all his enemies, and the dread of him upon those that hated him. For he killed both kings and princes."*

Theodoret, writing about 430, well expresses the general opinion of the Christians: —

"I suppose that the Divine Spirit, having by the patriarch spoken of our Saviour, does in this prophecy speak of Antichrist: for what is written closely agrees with him. Dan, it says, shall judge his people, even as one tribe in Israel; that is, in like manner as our Lord and Saviour, springing from the tribe of Judah, shall save the world, — so also shall a destroying serpent come out of the tribe of Dan; for he says, Let Dan be a serpent in the way."†

A close parallel may be drawn between the twelve tribes and the twelve Apostles: the same city that has on its gates the names of the tribes, has on its foundations the names of the Apostles. To the latter, also, it was said: "Ye shall sit upon twelve thrones, judging the twelve tribes of Israel." And, if Dan's serpent be the true cause why that tribe is not to be sealed, the parallel may be carried out to the two sons of perdition, and to the election of a new twelfth to fill the gap occasioned by the defection of each.

"I have chosen you twelve," said the Saviour, "and one of you is a devil." Jacob also begat twelve, and one of them was to be a serpent. Of the whole human race two alone are styled sons of perdition, Judas and Antichrist. And, as after the sop Satan entered into Judas, and he went to his own place, — so will Antichrist's coming be after the operation of Satan, and he also will go into perdition. But the enemy will not

---

* Walton's Polyglot.
† Theodoret in Genesin, quæst. 110.

be suffered finally to mar the perfection of either twelve: as a new Apostle filled the bishoprick of Judas, so one of Jóseph's sons is to supply the place of Dan. By the partition of Joseph's tribe Manasseh is made a twelfth, leaving Ephraim to represent his father: thus Joseph's blessing shall prevail above the blessings of his brethren, for 24,000 of his tribe will be sealed.

A. D. circ. 190–200.

Hitherto, if we except the anonymous revelations of the pseudo-Sibyl, expositors had been careful to make no pointed allusions to Rome or the empire. But this system is abandoned by Tertullian, who, scorning such caution, seems to think that the sooner the Romans know their fate, the better. By his impetuous genius the position of parties is suddenly reversed: where others had implored, he threatens; where others had seen a captive at the stake, he points to one of heaven's favoured ones, by his supplications averting from the threatened empire the bolts of an offended God.

Yet, when he has told the worst, he draws from it, in favour of Christianity, an argument of more peaceful spirit. Since the existence of the Roman empire restrains the coming of the great tribulation, how earnestly must the Christian pray for the welfare of that empire! After Rome, Antichrist: who, then, so averse to change as the Christian? For Tertullian, being by profession a special pleader, does not chose to spoil his argument by adding — after Antichrist, our eternal kingdom.

That argument he employs twice: once to the governor Scapula: — " A Christian is no man's enemy, least of all the emperor's; for, knowing him to be appointed by God, he must of necessity love, reverence, honour, and wish him safe, together with the whole Roman empire, as long as the age stands: for so long will the empire stand." * And more pointedly in the Apology : " We have even greater need to pray for the emperors, and for every condition of the empire, and for the affairs of Rome; knowing that by the safeguard of the Roman Empire, there is kept back that time of extreme violence which hangs over all the world, even the very end of the age, which threatens horrible calamities." †

Tertullian is the first to explain, by the analogy of Scripture, the transfer of the names Babylon and Sodom to Rome and Jerusalem: —

"It is no new thing with the Creator to employ by a figure a transfer of names, implying a comparison of crimes; He calls the rulers of the Jews rulers of Sodom, and the people itself a people of Gomorrah; also, in another place, Thy father was an Amorite, and thy mother Cethea, from their resemblance in wickedness. Yet He had formerly called them His children, saying, I have nourished and brought up children. In the same sense, also, is to be understood Egypt, and sometimes the whole world, being used by Him to express superstition and an accursed way. So, also, with our own John, Babylon is a figure of the city Rome; which is great and proud in her kingdom, and hostile to the saints of God." ‡

Hitherto, no expositor had touched upon the past destruction of Jerusalem as a partial fulfilment of the prophecy recorded in Luke xxi. Tertullian first assigns to that event a place in the prediction: —

* Ad. Scapulam, cap. 2.   † Apol. cap. 32.
‡ Adv. Marcionem, lib. iii. cap. 13.; also Adv. Judæos.

"Being asked by the disciples when those things should happen, which have since come to pass in the ruin of the temple, He lays down the course of the times: first the Jewish, down to the destruction of Jerusalem; and afterwards those common to all, down to the end of the age.

"For He says, Afterwards Jerusalem shall be trodden down by the Gentiles, until there be fulfilled the times of the nations; that is, of those nations which are to be chosen by God, and to be gathered together with the remnant of Israel. After this He prophesies against the world and the age, in accordance with Joel, Daniel, and the whole council of the prophets; saying that there will be signs in the sun, and moon, and stars, and distress of nations with perplexity. The sea sounding: men's hearts chilled with terror." *

St. Paul noticed certain heretics who said that the resurrection was past already: this heresy was not extinct in the time of Tertullian. There were still some who reckoned themselves already partakers of the resurrection, already living and reigning with Christ. To these thorough-going præterists Tertullian shows no mercy: —

" Who," he asks, "forestalling the Father, has yet placed Christ's enemies (as David promises) beneath His feet, while all this mob is still shouting, ' The Christians to the lion?' Who has yet seen Jesus coming down from heaven, (according to the saying of the angels,) in like manner as the Apostles saw Him go up? To this day no tribes have mourned apart, smiting their breasts, and beholding Him whom they pierced. No man has yet welcomed Elias; none yet fled from Antichrist; none wept Babylon's ruin. And who is there that has risen, but the heretic himself? Truly he has quitted the body's sepulchre, being still liable to wounds and diseases! He indeed has trodden down his enemies, being still doomed to struggle with the strong ones of the world! And he for-

---

* De Resurrectione Carnis, cap. 22.

sooth is reigning, still forced to render to Cæsar the things that are Cæsar's." (Ibid.)*

From Tertullian we have the earliest connected exposition of 2. Thess. ii. The custom of interweaving with the text a continuous gloss or scholia was first introduced about his time: —

"Let no man deceive you by any means; for, — except there come first a falling away (undoubtedly of this kingdom), and the Man of Sin be revealed, — that is, Antichrist, the son of perdition, who opposes and exalts himself above all that is called God or religion: so that he will sit in the temple of God, declaring that he is God. Remember ye not that when I was with you, I told you these things?

"And now ye know what keeps him back, so that he should be revealed in his own time: for the secret of iniquity already works, only he who now holds, may hold, till he be out of the midst: — who, but the Roman state? The breaking up and dispersion of this among ten kings will bring on Antichrist, and then shall be revealed that wicked one whom the Lord Jesus shall slay with the spirit of His mouth, and shall destroy by His appearance.

"Also in the Apocalypse of John there is laid down the course of the times, during which the souls of the martyrs beneath the altar, demanding vengeance and judgment, are instructed to wait. First, the earth must drink in its plagues from the vials of the angels, and that harlot city suffer merited destruction by the ten kings, and the beast Antichrist, with his false prophet, make war upon the Church of God; and then, the Devil being banished for a season to the bottomless pit, the privilege of the first resurrection will be adjudged from the thrones, and afterwards, fire having been sent down, the sentence belonging to the universal resurrection will be pronounced from the books."†

---

* The argument was afterwards inverted by Tychonius: "We have no right to doubt of the eternal kingdom, since even in the present world the saints are reigning." For Tychonius was an anti-millenarian, and lived after Constantine.

† De Res. Carnis, cap. 25.

The African apologist zealously supports the literal millennium: —

"We confess that a kingdom is promised us upon earth, but before heaven, and in another state, even for a thousand years after the resurrection; in the city of divine workmanship, the Jerusalem brought down from heaven, which the Apostle styles our Mother who is above. And, by declaring that our citizenship, that is, our municipality, is in heaven, he certainly traces it to some heavenly city. This city Ezekiel knew, and the apostle John beheld." *

The Gnostics, thinking the endurance of martyrdom a needless tax upon their self-denial, endeavoured to stigmatise the sacrifice, as savouring rather of rashness than of devotion. Tertullian knew well where to find an answer; "satis de Apocalypsi instructus." Enumerating the blessings described in the early chapters of the Apocalypse, he vindicates the martyr's claim to their possession: —

"Those conquerors so blessed, who are they but the martyrs in particular? For *theirs* is the victory whose was the fight; theirs the fight, whose the bloodshed. But meanwhile the souls of the martyrs rest tranquilly beneath the altar, and, in the confidence of being avenged, wear the white robe of brightness, till the others also shall fill up the companionship of their glory.

"And now they are seen once more, an innumerable multitude, clothed in white and ennobled with the victor's palm, triumphant over Antichrist. For thus said one of the elders, These are they that came out of that great tribulation, and have washed their robes, and made them white in the blood of the Lamb." †

The expression, "*that* great tribulation" (illa pres-

---

* Adv. Marcionem, lib. iii. cap. 23. † Scorpiace, cap. 12.

sura magna), accurately conveys the force of the Greek, — "the tribulation the great." This passage contains the earliest identification of the fifth-seal-martyrs with those who suffer under Antichrist.

By the white robes then given to them, they are afterwards recognised when standing before the throne, reinforced by fresh martyrs, till they form a multitude which no one can number: — no one, says Bernardine, save He who numbereth the stars, and calleth them all by their names. Of this entire white-robed company it is said, that they came out of that great tribulation: they are, as Tertullian words it, "De Antichristo triumphales:" there has been decreed to them, and they are actually celebrating, a triumph "concerning Antichrist." For Antichrist, thinks the fiery Roman, must be triumphed over as well as conquered.

Not content with standing in arms single-handed against the nations, "Tertullianus adversus Gentes," the apologist must needs attack in succession Jews and heretics, and at last even the Catholic Church. Some heretics had denied that the flesh of our bodies will rise with the souls. Tertullian, while arguing against them, introduces a reference to the times of Antichrist : —

"O my people, enter into thy closets for a little season, until my wrath be past. The graves will be those closets, in which they who in the end of the world and in the last indignation shall suffer by the violence of Antichrist, will have to rest a little season. . . . Until my indignation, which shall extinguish Antichrist, shall be past. After that indignation He shows that the flesh shall come out of that sepulchre in which before the indignation it had been laid. For out of closets nothing can be taken but what was before put in, and after the extirpation of Antichrist will follow the resurrection."*

He says little about the first seal; the Rider he styles "the Angel of Victory, crowned, and going forth upon a white horse, to conquer." † But in another place he expounds the prosperous Rider of the 45th Psalm, as if identical with the Rider of the first seal.

Tertullian is the first to break the long silence concerning the second witness: —

"Enoch and Elias are translated; their death is not found, being delayed. Yet they are reserved to die, that with their blood they may extinguish Antichrist."‡

A. D. 203.

The sixty-nine weeks of Daniel, according to the reckoning of both Jews and Christians, had long since expired; the seventieth was not so easily disposed of. While the Jews imagined it to have been fulfilled by the desolations of their temple under Titus and Adrian, the Christians were still looking for the abomination spoken of by Daniel. At this time a writer named Judas, abandoning the argument founded upon the cutting off of the Messiah in the sixty-ninth week, proposed a calculation, so contrived as to bring the end of the seventieth to his own time. On this plan Antichrist was to come in 204.

In spite of the warnings against declaring the times, a few were found willing to believe in Judas. In the year 203, a violent persecution was raised by Severus.

* De Res. Carnis, cap. 27.   † De Coronâ Militum, cap. 15.
‡ Tertull de Animâ, cap. 50.

The false prophet now enjoyed a short-lived celebrity, for some persons were thrown into alarm, expecting nothing less than the immediate coming of Antichrist.*

The seventieth week was next taken in hand by Clement of Alexandria, the first Christian who attempted to apply it to past events. " During half a week," he remarked, " Nero reigned, and set up the abomination in the holy city Jerusalem; and in the half week he was taken away, with Otho, Galba, and Vitellius. Then Vespasian reigned, destroying Jerusalem and desolating the holy place." † The attempt can scarcely be termed successful.

A. D. 220.

About this time the martyr-list was swelled by the name of Hippolytus, bishop of Ostia, the port of Rome, and for that reason mistaken by the Greeks for Rome itself. The bishop, it is reported, was torn to pieces by a wild horse, and his remains, in part at least, were afterwards collected by his friends. Strangely enough, a similar fate has befallen his works; of which, for a long time, nothing could be found excepting his " Oration upon Antichrist," partly spurious and containing evident traces of Ephrem Syrus and the fourth century. For Hippolytus is made a prophet as well as an expositor when the saying is put into his mouth, that in the times of Antichrist monks will seek the things of the world; for when he wrote, the monks were not in being. The body of

---

* Eusebius, Hist. Eccles., lib. vi. cap. 6.
† Stromatum, lib. i.

this work, free from all such difficulties, was afterwards recovered by Fabricius; next came to light the commentary on Daniel, lately published together with the Septuagint version of the prophet; and lastly, some remaining fragments rewarded the diligence of the unwearied Mai.

The spurious oration contains two statements, both opposed to the tenor of the genuine works. The first, that John will return in company with Enoch and Elias; the other, that Antichrist will be the Devil incarnate.

Hippolytus, though with more caution than Tertullian, points out Rome's place in prophecy: "Tell me, blessed John, apostle and disciple of the Lord, what hast thou seen and heard concerning Babylon? Awake and speak, for she also sent thee into exile."* For John, according to Tertullian, was banished from Rome to Patmos.†

Of the seventy weeks, Hippolytus gives a short connected sketch, making the last week to belong to the times of the end; "When the sixty-two weeks," he says, "have been fulfilled, and Christ has come, and the Gospel has been preached in every place, and the times have run out, there will remain one week — the last, in which Enoch and Elias will come. And in the midst of that week there will appear the abomination of desolation, until Antichrist announces desolation to the world." ‡

* Opera, a Fabricio edita, p. 18.
† De Præscript. Hæret., c. 36.
‡ Roman edition of the Septuagint Daniel, p. 110. The Roman editor suggests, "even Antichrist, who announces." He appears to be printing from a single MS.

Nor should we pass over his testimony to the millennium, contained in the same commentary on Daniel:—
" The six thousand years must needs be fulfilled, that the Sabbath may come,— even the Rest, that holy day on which God rested from all his works. The Sabbath, then, is a type and image of the future kingdom of the saints, when they shall reign with Christ after his coming down from heaven, as John declares in the Apocalypse, For a day of the Lord is as a thousand years." *

Like Irenæus, our bishop knows many names that make the number of the Beast, but of these he will say nothing positive. He prefers the word " I deny," doubtless from the predicted denial of Christ's having come in the flesh : —

" Perhaps the seal will be written Arnoumai, I deny. For in former times the adversary did by his servants, that is, by idolaters, persuade the martyrs of Christ, saying, Deny thy God, the crucified. Such will be the mark of that wicked one ; I deny the Creator of heaven and earth ; I deny my baptism ; I deny Him worship. To thee I adhere, in thee believe.

" And this the prophets Enoch and Elias will declare, saying, Believe not the coming enemy, for he is an adversary and destroyer and son of perdition; he will deceive you and bring you to ruin. But the sword shall smite them."

Unfortunately for this theory, the word requires to be mis-spelt to make the required number. The bishop treads on surer ground when he descants upon the glory of the future confessors : " Blessed they," he exclaims, " who will then conquer the tyrant ; they will take rank above former martyrs, as more exalted

---

* Roman edition of the Septuagint Daniel, p. 100.

and more glorious. For those vanquished Satan's satellites only, but these, overcoming the Devil himself, the son of perdition, will be indeed conquerors. With what praises and crowns will they not be adorned by Jesus Christ our King!"*

One more extract, and that from the genuine oration given by Fabricius, must suffice for Hippolytus. The following is by seventy years the earliest account of the sun-clothed woman:—

"By the woman clothed with the sun is signified most clearly the Church, clothed with the Word of the Father, that outshines the sun. And, by the moon beneath her feet, she is shown to be adorned with heavenly glory like the moon; and when it says, Upon her head a crown of twelve stars, it means the twelve Apostles by whom the Church was founded.

"And she being with child, cried, pained to be delivered. For the Church will never cease bringing forth, from her heart, the Word, which, when it is in the world, is persecuted by the unbelieving. And she brought forth, it says, a man child, who shall rule all nations. For the Church teaches all nations, evermore bringing forth that male and perfect offspring, Christ, the Son of God, declared to be both God and man. And the saying, that her child was caught up to God and His throne, shows that He whom she continually brings forth is no earthly, but a heavenly king, as David also cried of old, The Lord said to my Lord, Sit thou on my right hand, till I make thy foes thy footstool.

"And the Dragon, it says, beheld; and he persecuted the woman that brought forth the man child. And there were given her the two wings of that great Eagle, that she should flee to the desert, where she is nourished for a time, times,

---

* This extract, as well as the preceding, is from the doubtful oration. Capp. 28—30. The identity of Satan with Antichrist is rejected in the authentic works.

and half a time, from the face of the serpent. These are the 1260 days, even the half week during which the tyrant will rule, persecuting the Church, as she flees from city to city. And she will lie hid in solitude in the mountains, having with her nothing besides the two wings of that great Eagle, even the faith of Jesus Christ."*

At this time flourished the chronologist Julius Africanus, who attempted to correct the calculation of the seventy weeks. Eusebius, who gives the rest of his system, has omitted his account of the seventieth.†

A. D. circ. 225.

Still the calumnies of Celsus had remained unanswered; but now the challenge was to be accepted, and that Philistine to fall by the hand of the youthful Origen. It was every way needful that some champion of the faith should enter the lists, for Celsus, not content with ridiculing the prophecies about Antichrist, had gone on to propose the wars of the Titans as a model for the imitation of Christian prophets.

Origen makes short work with the proud Pagan. Celsus, he remarks, has not read Daniel. It was as much a part of God's revealed will that the little horn should prevail, as that the Stone should smite the image. It was no after-thought of a baffled would-be Messiah, that another shall plant his tabernacle on the glorious and holy mountain.

"To what is thrown out concerning Antichrist by Celsus, who has read neither what is said about him by Daniel, nor by Paul, nor what is prophesied about his coming in the Gospels by the Saviour, a few words must be said in reply.

* Opera, ed. Fabricii, p. 30.
† Eusebii Demonstratio Evangelica, lib. viii.

"Through the assistance of his father the Devil, that wicked one will perform miracles, and signs and wonders of a lie. For, as wonders were wrought by magicians through the help of those demons who seduced man into wickedness, so this man will receive from the Devil himself power to do yet greater wonders, to deceive the human race. And concerning the so-called Antichrist Paul speaks, teaching us, though with some reserve, the manner, the time, and the cause of his visiting the human race. And now see if Paul has not spoken on this subject in a manner most grave, and not deserving even the slightest ridicule, 'We beseech you, brethren, by the coming of the Lord,' &c. 2 Thess. ii.

"To explain the whole of this is not our present business. But there is in Daniel a prophecy about this same Antichrist, which cannot but excite the admiration of any one who will read it with common sense and candour. For there, in words truly divine and prophetic, are described the kingdoms that were to come, beginning from the time of Daniel down to the destruction of the world. And this prophecy may be read of all men.* Now see if Antichrist is not spoken of there also, in these words, In the end of their kingdom, when their transgressions are filled up, there shall rise a king impudent of face and understanding problems, &c.

"And that which I have already quoted from the words of Paul, that he will sit in the temple of God, showing himself that he is God — even this also is said by Daniel, and in this manner, In the temple shall be the abomination of desolations; and until the end of the time shall a consummation be given against the desolation."†

The poets, when they wish to make their hero invincible, have his armour forged upon the same anvil with the bolts of Jove. Origen does better: his weapons are the same that the Captain of his salvation had wielded before him. For Christ Himself, instead

---

* Probably referring to the Greek versions, especially the Septuagint.

† Origen against Celsus, lib. vi. cap. 45.

of uttering new prophecies about Antichrist, refers to that which was before spoken by Daniel the prophet: it being His purpose not to bear witness to Himself, but to support His own mission by the witness of His Father's prophets. The rejection of that witness, according to the primitive belief, will increase the condemnation of the Jews, and in the end bring Antichrist upon them: God will send them strong delusion, that, as they rejected Christ in spite of their own Daniel, so they may receive Antichrist in spite of Daniel also.

Celsus was not able to decide whether the Scriptures represented Antichrist as a " Devil-demon, or an impostor man-adversary." Origen remarks that the latter expression was the more correct.

Thus Origen identified the time of Antichrist with the latter half of the seventieth week. By the abomination standing in the holy place he understood Antichrist sitting in the temple of Jerusalem. As for his partial opposition to the millennium*, it was provoked by the excesses of the Cerinthians, who expected fresh marriages during the thousand years. But in the resurrection, as Origen remarked, they neither marry nor are given in marriage. He expects, though doubtingly, the literal return of Elias:—

" The vision upon the mountain, in which Elias was seen, did not appear to agree with what the scribes had said: for Elias, it seemed, came not before Jesus, but after Him. They asked the question therefore, supposing that the scribes had

---

* Origen never speaks against the thousand years. He applies the epithet Judaizing to those who take literally the prophecies of Isaiah, especially the predictions of a restored Jerusalem, and the birth of children in the coming age.

misled them. But to this the Saviour answers, not contradicting the tradition about Elias, but declaring that there was another coming of Elias, before Christ, which had been unknown to the scribes."*

A. D. circ. 250.

For some time the Church had been threatened with a controversy about the millennium. The doctrine, grossly misapplied by Cerinthus, was now vindicated by Nepos. His book gave occasion to a controversy, conducted by Dionysius, according to his own account, with great moderation. Yet the story holds badly together: for, when the readers of Nepos are charged with not suffering their brethren to think of the second advent, or of the resurrection from the dead, it is clear that the real point at issue was far removed from the Apocalypse and the millennium. Dionysius next attacked the Apostolic authorship of the Apocalypse itself, endeavouring to prove that it contained " not a syllable " in common with the Gospel and Epistles of St. John: for Dionysius, when it came to a question of language, was one of those bat's-eyed critics whose main difficulty in seeing arises from the clearness of the light. In the opening of the Gospel he found these words:—" In the beginning was the Word." The Epistle also resembles it: " That which was from the beginning." Now Dionysius seems to have taken up an idea, that if two works of an author begin alike, the same expression must needs be repeated in the third: therefore, finding these words missing in the beginning of the Apo-

---

* Origen in Matth., tom. xiii. cap. 1.

calypse, he concluded it to be no production of the Apostle John.

Had he looked further, he would have found that Christ, who is there styled "the Word of God," announces Himself as the "Beginning and the Ending." He would also in that case have noticed the ascription, "To Him that loved us, and washed us from our sins in His own blood:" which would have led him to spare the remark that the Apocalypse contains nothing about the forgiveness of sins, and God's love to us. Finally, when Eusebius repeats with approval, that Dionysius could find in the Apocalypse nothing against the Devil or Antichrist, he shows to what lengths good and learned men may be suffered to go, when they set up their own reason against the inspired Word.*

A. D. 255.

This year produces the earliest direct notice of the sixth seal. A Latin writer, whose name is now lost, is commenting upon the judgment of the little horn in Daniel: "I saw thrones: John also speaks more plainly concerning both the day of judgment and the end of the world, saying, And when he had opened the sixth seal."†

A. D. 252–258.

The Church had lately received an important accession in Cæcilius Cyprian, formerly professor of rhe-

---

* Eusebii Hist. Eccles., lib. vii. cap. 24. The book of Dionysius is lost: Jerome styles it " an elegant work, ridiculing the fable of the thousand years."

† Anonymus ad Novatianum. Galland's Fathers, t. iii. p. 375.

toric in Carthage. In a few months (for the years are scarcely enough to be reckoned) Cyprian rose to the primacy of all Africa; and even now, at this distance of time, he appears like one standing alone in his generation, for all that we know of the Cyprianic age of Christianity is but the background to the history of Cyprian himself.

Persecution left the bishop no time for writing systematic treatises upon prophecy: yet his thoughts were filled with the expectation of Antichrist's coming; for the sufferings of his own time were then reckoned but a foretaste of the great tribulation to come. Under the guidance of their martyr-bishop, the Carthaginians felt themselves to be skirmishing with the advanced guard of Antichrist's army: "You have conquered a pioneer of Antichrist," wrote Lucian to a brother-confessor in Rome.

In Cyprian's "Exhortation to Martyrdom," there occur some sentences relative to the future:—

Chap. xi. "The first seven days, by the Divine appointment, contain seven thousand years." Cyprian must therefore be reckoned a millenarian.

"That most hostile King Antiochus, yea, Antichrist expressed in Antiochus."

The first resurrection is explained as including not martyrs only, but all who are undefiled by the worship of Antichrist:—

"It is said in the Apocalypse, And I saw the souls of them that had been slain for the name of Jesus, and for the word of God. Having placed in the first rank those who were slain, he adds, And those that had not worshipped the image of the beast, nor received his inscription on their forehead, or in their hand. All these, being seen by him at once, and in the same place, he joins together, saying, They lived and reigned with Christ. He says that all lived and reigned with Christ, not only those who were slain, but all who, persisting in steadfast faith, and in the fear of God, did not worship the image of the beast, nor obey his fatal and impious decrees."*

During his banishment, Cyprian dreamed that he was brought before the proconsul, and sentenced to immediate execution. In his dream, he begged for a short respite, if only for a day, that he might set his affairs in order. The proconsul, he fancied, made a note of the demand, and through the gestures of a youth who overlooked the writing, Cyprian learned that his request had been granted.

The event proved still better than the dream, for he was not apprehended till a whole year afterwards: and even at the time of his condemnation, the execution was unexpectedly deferred for a day. His biographer Pontius, resolved to make the most of the vision, considers both the year and the day as distinct fulfilments, the one exact, the other by excess:—

" This one day signified that year which he was to pass in the world after the vision: for, as I shall tell at length, he was crowned on the first anniversary of the day on which he had seen it. Now a *day* of the Lord, though we do not read in Scripture that it is a year, we yet take to be the very time set apart for promises of the future. Therefore it matters not, even if by the expression, *a day*, there be meant one

---

* Exhortatio ad Martyrium, cap. xii. Where St. Paul speaks of " them that are Christ's," St. John mentions none but the elect of Antichrist's time. The explanation seems to be this:— that St. John is speaking of that generation only. Of these, all that resist Antichrist will arise, whether martyrs or not: all the rest must await the end of the thousand years.

year only, for the greater the occasion, the fuller may be the meaning."*

A year after the vision, Cyprian was surprised by a party of soldiers; if, says Pontius, any thing may be called a surprise to one who was always prepared. The martyrdom was then unexpectedly deferred till the next day: for, says Pontius, "that *next day*, which the divine condescension had foretold a year before, was to be truly the *next day*."

The story of Pontius is worth repeating in this place, if only as showing that the year-day interpretation was as yet unknown in the Church.

A. D. circ. 290.

After long waiting for a continuous commentary on the Apocalypse, we come to the earliest now extant, from the pen of Victorinus Martyr. Throughout Church history there is scarcely to be found a writer so unlearned as Victorinus: "Great in thoughts," says Jerome, "but unable to express himself in words." Nevertheless his merits were universally acknowledged: the Church preserved and valued his work; while the heathen marked him out for one of the first victims of the Diocletian massacre. But we have first to inquire how far his commentary may be supposed to represent the teaching of the Apostles on subjects not noticed by older expositors.

From the earliest times there had appeared successive commentaries on the Apocalypse, now lost. One of these was written by Melito, bishop of Sardis, who outlived Polycarp by three years only, and

---

* Pontius, in Vitâ Cypriani.

may have been one of those "few names in Sardis which had not defiled their garments." Hippolytus also wrote on the Apocalypse; while Nepos defended its literal meaning in a "Refutation of the Allegorists." Through these works it was then possible to obtain a traditional interpretation of the Trumpets, the Dragon, and the scarlet Beast, subjects not fully explained in any earlier commentary now extant.

But with these works Victorinus was little acquainted, as may be learnt from his remarking that all the ancients expected Jeremiah as the second witness: for of this opinion there is no earlier trace, except once in the Maccabees, and once in the saying of the Jews, that Christ might be "Jeremias, or one of the prophets."[*] He also falls into the error of expecting Nero's return: a supposition not countenanced by any other writer of credit, still less by any hearer of the Apostles. As bishop of Pettau in Austria, he was cut off from intercourse with the world of civilisation, and cannot therefore be relied upon as always representing with accuracy the substance of the apostolic traditions.

The copyists have much injured the text of this author. Jerome afterwards endeavoured to rectify their mistakes, adding, that the entire passage opposing the millennium is a forgery. For Victorinus, as became a martyr and a primitive bishop, was a millenarian: he looked forward to that thousand years during which he is yet to reign with Christ.

---

[*] The idea is taken from Jeremiah i. 5.: "I ordained thee a prophet unto the nations." But Jeremiah, as it seems, has hitherto prophesied in person to the Jews only. It is next noticed by Hilary, Comment. in Matth. xx. See 2 Maccabees, xv. 14.

One clause has escaped the vigilance of the anti-millenarian copyists: "Judea, where all the saints will assemble, and worship their Lord."*

Victorinus has much to say upon the glories ascribed to Christ; who was, long before He was born of the Virgin; who is, abiding ever; and who is to come, to be our judge. The sealed book he takes to be the book of the Old Testament which Moses sprinkled with blood. It was sealed till the death of the Testator; being of no force till He was dead: but now the Lamb had been slain, the Testator had died and returned to life; and, having conquered death, had been appointed by His Father heir of all things. Therefore He is worthy to open the seals, and to take away the veil from the reader's heart. The book which contains the results of this opening is called an Unveiling or Revelation.

When the Christ of the New Testament prevails to open the mysteries of the Old, the unity of the two dispensations is shown forth: —

"The preaching of the Old Testament, combined with the New, displays the Christian people singing a new song, that is, publicly confessing their belief. And a new thing it is for the Son of God to become man; a new thing to go up bodily into heaven. It is a new thing that remission of sins should be given to men; new that they should be sealed with the Holy Spirit. It is new to receive a priesthood of holy ordinance; new, to expect a kingdom of boundless reward."

If, as Victorinus supposes, the sealed book contains the substance of the old Testament prophecies, we

---

* Victorinus in Apoc. cap. i. Published in most editions of the Bib. Patrum Maxima; also, with some variation, by Galland.

ought to see something relative to those prophecies when its seals are opened. And this proves to be the case: the opened seals display the emblems before dimly set forth by the older prophets. In the first we have David's Prosperous Rider: in the next three, Ezekiel's four sore judgments; (the "beasts of the earth" not having a seal to themselves). The fifth displays the victims to Daniel's little horn: the sixth, the day of the Lord foretold by Joel.

The living creatures prepare the Apostle for what is to follow the opening of each seal: — Come and see. The words of this invitation have been made the subject of many refinements, as if the repetition implied some mystical and latent meaning. Upon ordinary occasions, indeed, this reasoning might hold good; for the Apostle, though somewhat bewildered by the greatness of the sights, is neither so dazzled by the glory, nor so stunned by the thunder, as to require to be told, each moment, where to stand, and which way to look. But here the case is peculiar; for, as each seal flies before the touch of the Lamb, there bursts forth a mounted warrior; and the Seer is by these words prepared for the moment at which each will sweep past him, since it is his office to sing the arms and the man, the colour of the horse, and the mission of its rider.

Victorinus finds no difficulty in expounding the seals, for he uses the primitive Clavis Apocalyptica, "Ait enim Dominus in Evangelio." In Matt. xxiv. he finds the writing to which these pictures belong. On this system, the first six seals are a pictorial illustration of that prophecy, teaching us, as we would teach children, by a picture-book, about the progress of the Gospel, the wars, famines, and pestilences, the great tribulation, and the darkening of the sun and moon. By the silence of the seventh seal, he understands the unchangeableness of the eternal state: but the silence is limited to half an hour, for this reason, "that, had it been made perpetual, this would have been the end of the vision."

"On the opening of the first seal, he says that he saw a white horse and a crowned horseman, having a bow. For this was done first; after the Lord had gone up into heaven, and had opened all things, He sent forth His Spirit, the words of whose preaching are like arrows, penetrating to the hearts of men, to conquer their unbelief. The crown upon His head is that which is promised to preachers by the Holy Spirit.

"The other three horses, as it plainly shows, are the wars, famines, and pestilences, foretold by the Lord in the Gospel. Now, it adds that one of the animals said (for they are all one)* 'Come, and see.' To him who is invited to believe, it is said, 'Come': to him who sees not, 'See.' The white horse, therefore, is the Word of preaching, with the Holy Spirit sent forth into the world. For the Lord says, 'This Gospel must be preached throughout all the world for a witness before the nations, and then shall the end come.'

"The red horse, and his sword-bearing rider, represent those wars which are predicted, of which we read in the Gospel: — 'Nation shall rise against nation, and kingdom against kingdom, and there shall be great earthquakes.' This is the red horse.

"The black horse means famine, for the Lord says, 'There

---

* According to the parallel passage in Ezekiel, where each living creature is described as having the faces of these four. The introduction of those symbols seems to confirm the belief that the Old Testament prophecies are here referred to. Irenæus takes the living creatures to be the fourfold aspect of Christ in the four Gospels: in Matthew as the man, in Mark as the eagle, in Luke as the sacrificial calf, and in John as the lion. Victorinus follows him, but exchanges the places of Mark and John, thus restoring the order of Ezekiel. — Iren., lib. iii. c. xi.

shall be famines in divers places.' Now this saying properly extends to the time of Antichrist, when there will be a great famine, by which all men shall suffer."*

This is the famine which will be caused by the witnesses withholding the rain during their time of prophesying. At this point Victorinus grows vague; yet he explains the pale horse as the pestilence described in the Gospel, and the souls under the altar as those of martyrs in the separate state. The sixth seal he also takes to be a symbolic representation of the troubles under Antichrist.

The seals still present some minor difficulties. The second, third, and fourth, are plain enough, being interpreted in the text: their horsemen have power to kill with sword, with hunger, and with death, and with the beasts of the earth. These seals, therefore, seem to correspond with the prophecy of Ezekiel, "When I send my four sore judgments upon Jerusalem, the sword, and the famine, and the noisome beast, and the pestilence." The Gospel, omitting the beasts, adds earthquakes; these are found in the Apocalypse, in the sixth seal, which opens with a great earthquake.

These wars, famines, and pestilences, are they the immediate precursors of Antichrist, or are they ordinary judgments sent throughout the dispensation? The Gospels do not conclusively settle this question, unless, by the " beginning of sorrows," we understand, the beginning of the throes of Antichrist's bringing forth. And this sense is fully borne out by the

* With regard to the severity of the famine under this seal :— a day's wages will be required to pay for the day's allowance of corn. It is impossible, at such prices, to feed and clothe a family.

Greek, which is paraphrased by Jerome, "conceptus adventûs Antichristi." Cyprian translates it, "the beginning of the childbirth."*

If Ezekiel and St. John refer to the same events, it appears that these judgments will ravage a fourth part of the earth, including Jerusalem; and that, although Noah, Daniel, and Job were living at the time, they would be able to save neither son nor daughter from the calamities foretold.

The fifth seal presents no difficulty, if we allow the white-robed martyrs to fix it as belonging to the great tribulation. Yet, from the third century downwards, this explanation has been generally abandoned.

The precise meaning of the sixth seal has not been found so clear as might have been supposed. For although, until the twelfth century, it was applied by all to the precursors of Christ's second coming, yet there was a question, whether it represents the literal darkening of the sun and moon foretold in the Gospels, or a general state of the world symbolised by these figures? To this question three answers have been given:

I. The other seals being symbolical, this must be taken as symbolical also: implying a certain disruption of the frame-work of society, corresponding to St. Luke's "distress of nations with perplexity." Men's hearts will then fail them for fear; and, while looking for those things which are coming upon the earth, they will gather the near approach of that great day of the wrath of the Lamb.

II. It has been supposed that though most of

---

* Exhortatio ad Martyrium, cap. xi.

the seals are symbolical, yet the sixth, referring to an event more easily dramatised than symbolised, is a literal representation of the coming times. That the earthquake is copied from Zechariah, the darkness from Joel, the taking refuge in caves and rocks from Isaiah, and the calling to the mountains to fall, from the days of the Dry Tree, foretold on the road to Calvary: that Isaiah supplies the fugitive heaven, the blasted stars, and the shaken fig-tree: and, if any one would learn further particulars, he must accept Tertullian's summary reference to " the whole council of the prophets."

III. Some have thought to make all sure, by including, in the literal, a figurative fulfilment also. While they expect the sun to be darkened, they look for a mist of unbelief which shall obscure the sight of the Sun of Righteousness: while the moon becomes as blood, the Church is again to be crimsoned with the blood of martyrs. This scheme, from its comprehensiveness, was popular with the monks and the schoolmen. *

* Under this head may be classed the refinement of the Roman senator Cassiodorus. The literal earth, he says, is figuratively declared to be shaken, as by an earthquake. The darkening of the sun and moon he takes to be literal. Complexiones in Apoc., cap. vi.

To complete the subject, the Jewish account must be added. " The sun shall be turned into darkness, and the moon into blood. (Joel ii.) But, after thirty days, God will restore to the sun its accustomed brightness, as it is written, They shall be gathered together as prisoners in the pit, and after many days they shall be visited. (Isaiah xxiv. 22.) Upon this the Christians shall be struck with terror, and, being covered with shame, shall confess that this has been done for the sake of the people of Israel. Then many of them shall embrace the faith of the Jews." — Buxtorf, Synagoga Judaica, cap. xxxvi.

Victorinus, the earliest expositor of the trumpets, takes them to be the judgments inflicted by the witnesses, who will have power to smite the earth with all plagues. The vials he supposes to be a second history of the trumpet-plagues; a theory which still has many supporters, owing to a partial resemblance between the vials and the trumpets. But the trumpets, apparently, sound throughout the three years and a half, while the vials are the last plagues, filling up the wrath of God. The vials, therefore, would appear to be a concluding and more intense effusion of the trumpet-plagues.

Victorinus sums up in these words his brief notice of the plagues:—

"The trumpet is the word of power; and though there is a repetition in the vials, it is not that the thing will be twice done, but because that which God decrees to happen once, is spoken twice.* Whatever, then, is slightly touched upon in the trumpets is more fully described in the vials.

"Nor are we to be tied down by the order of the words; for oftentimes the Holy Spirit, having travelled onwards to the end of the last times, returns to the same point, and supplies what had been slightly expressed. In the Apocalypse, therefore, not the order, but the sense, is to be sought for.

"Let us follow the prophet himself. In the trumpets and vials there are described, the execution wrought by the plagues sent upon the world, the madness of Antichrist himself, the blasphemy of the people, the variety of their plagues, the hope in the kingdom of the saints, the fall of the cities, and the fall of that great city, Babylon, that is, Rome."

In the history of the two witnesses, he follows Hippolytus in dividing seven years between their

---

* Compare the doubling of Pharaoh's dream, indicating certainty of fulfilment. Also the psalm: "Twice have I heard this."

prophesying and the reign of Antichrist. "By him, as the Apocalypse shows, they will be slain; and they will rise again, but on the fourth day, that no one may be found equal to the Lord.* He calls Jerusalem, Sodom and Egypt: for that persecutor of the people will make it such."

The birth of the man-child, already taken in hand by Hippolytus, is now expounded by two other martyr-bishops, Victorinus and Methodius. These last, however, differ on one point: the former makes the birth of Christ literal, the other, like Hippolytus, mystical, in His members. Victorinus, therefore, places a gap between the resurrection of Christ and the coming of Antichrist: —

"The woman clothed with the sun, having the moon under her feet, and a crown of twelve stars; she that is travailing in pain: — this is the ancient Church of the fathers, and of the prophets, and of the holy Apostles. For she had groans and torments of desire, until she saw, of her people according to the flesh, the fruit so long promised her, Christ clothed in a body taken from that very nation. * * *

"The crown of twelve stars signifies the chorus of the Fathers" (the twelve Patriarchs) "according to the flesh of the Nativity. For from them Christ was to take a body. The red dragon, who stands and waits for her to bring forth, that he may devour her son, is the Devil, that vagabond angel, who supposed that every man's destruction might be equally effected by death. But He who was not born of mortal father, owed nothing to death; for which reason the

---

* The ancients attached great importance to the third day's resurrection, quoting from Hosea, "After two days he will revive us," &c. So Chrysologus: "I venture to say that if Lazarus had risen from the dead on the third day, he would have forestalled the whole mystery of the Lord's resurrection. But Christ returns on the third day as the Lord; on the fourth, Lazarus is called back as the servant." Sermo 63. cap. iv.

dragon could not devour Him, that is, hold Him in death: for on the third day He rose again.

"Also, before He was made manifest, the Devil approached to tempt Him, as man: but not finding Him to be such a one as he thought, he departed from Him, it says, for a season. And He was snatched up to God's throne: even as we read in the Acts of the Apostles, that while talking with His disciples, He was taken up into heaven."

This description includes the scarlet beast, which he identifies with the Devil, calling it "Imago Diaboli." Elsewhere he supposes that the beast will reappear as Nero, or Antichrist, his deadly wound being healed.

Irenæus had hinted at the woman's flight to the wilderness, saying of Antichrist and his allied kings, "They will put to flight the Church." Victorinus enters upon the subject more fully:—

"In the woman's flight to the wilderness, by the wings of a great eagle, that is, by the gift of the prophets, there is represented the state of the Catholic Church, of which, in the last times, 144,000 will believe on Elias. (It here shows, also, that other people will be found alive at the coming of the Lord.) So, also, the Lord says in the Gospel, 'Then let them which be in Judea flee to the mountains;' that is, let as many as are gathered together in Judea go to that place which is prepared for them, and be nourished there for three years and six months from the face of the Devil.

"The two great wings are the two prophets, Elias, and that prophet who will be with him. The water, which the serpent casts out of his mouth, represents the army which he will send in pursuit of her: by the earth opening its mouth and swallowing the waters, is shown the vengeance that will be inflicted at the moment.

"Now, though she is here shown to us, both before the birth, and again, as flying, after the birth, the two events do not take place in connection. For some time has now elapsed since Christ was born; but that flight from the face of the serpent is still future.

"It follows, 'And there was war in heaven; Michael and his angels. And their place was no more found in heaven. And the Dragon, that old serpent, was cast out into the earth.' This is the beginning of Antichrist."

When we compare the flight of the Israelites under Moses and Aaron with that of the Church in the time of the two witnesses, the submersion of Pharoah's host with the swallowing up of the serpent's flood, and the miraculous sustenance of the Jews in the wilderness, with that promised to the mystic woman, — we shall not wonder that the Jerusalem from which the Church is to be driven out should be called, spiritually, Egypt. Although, as Tertullian remarks, transferred names occur often in Scripture, yet in the Apocalypse they are never used without a warning against being understood literally: the one city is "spiritually" called Sodom and Egypt: the other has a name before which is written "a mystery": that is, according to the usual Apocalyptic sense, a type or figure of something else. No such qualification is prefixed to the Euphrates, Armageddon, or the land of the sixteen hundred furlongs.

With the rest of the ancients, Victorinus explains the woman Babylon as the city of Rome: "I saw the woman drunk with the blood of the saints, by that decree of consummated wickedness, when she issued to all nations an edict against the preaching of the faith. The red and murderous beast upon which she sits, is an image of the devil." And again, "The seven heads are seven mountains, upon which sits the woman, that is, the city of Rome."

With equal closeness he follows Scripture in the matter of the city of the Crucifixion. He doubts whether Antichrist will originally come from the East, or be sent out from Rome: —

"The false prophet will cause a golden image to be set up to Antichrist in the temple of Jerusalem; and into this image the vagabond angel will enter, emitting voices and oracles. He will also cause both bond and free to receive a mark in their foreheads, or on their right hands, even the number of his name, that none may buy or sell without it.

"Now Daniel had foretold this abomination and provocation, saying, 'He will set up his temple in Samaria,'" (or, between the seas, *inter maria*, as suggested by Malvenda)* "upon the glorious and holy mountain; that is, he will then set up in Jerusalem an image, such as Nebuchadnezzar made. This the Lord explains, admonishing His churches against the last times and dangers; saying, 'When ye shall see the abomination spoken of by Daniel the prophet, standing in the holy place.'"

A. D. circ. 290.

Methodius, martyr, and bishop of Tyre, will detain us but a short time: like Victorinus, he fell in the beginning of the Diocletian persecution. In his "Banquet of the ten Virgins," Thecla, one of the ten, is made to expound the vision of the red dragon and the man-child: —

"The woman seen in heaven, clothed with the sun, and adorned with a crown of twelve stars, having her feet resting on the moon; she who is travailing and pained to be delivered, is, in the highest and strictest sense, our mother. She is, O virgins, a certain power existing by herself, apart from her children: and the prophets, considering what is spoken of her, call her Jerusalem; at other times the Bride, the mount Sion, the temple and the tabernacle of God.

---

* Malvenda de Antichristo, lib. v. cap. 22.

"To this power the prophet cries, inviting her by the voice of the Spirit, and saying, Shine, Shine, O Jerusalem! for thy light is come, and the glory of the Lord is risen upon thee! For darkness shall cover the earth, &c. This power is the Church. * * *

"Raise your thoughts therefore, and behold this illustrious woman, as a virgin prepared for the marriage. Behold her, glittering in perfect beauty, altogether pure and spotless, and in no way inferior to the lustre of the heavenly lights. See her, clothed with light itself as with a garment; and by way of jewels and precious stones, her head adorned with sparkling stars. For what a garment is to us, light is to her; and, what gold and transparent stones are to us, she possesses in the stars. Stars, not such as lie scattered on the heavenly plain, but so much more bright and dazzling, as to deserve that those which are seen in heaven, should be but *their* types and shadows."

Thecla proceeds to the man-child:—

"It would teach you nothing, if I were to explain this to mean the natural birth of Christ; for the mystery of the Word's Incarnation was completed long before the Apocalypse was written, and John prophesies about things that are, and that are to come. And Christ, born long before, was not snatched up to God's throne, as soon as brought forth, lest He should be devoured by the serpent; but He was born, and came down from the throne of His Father, for this very purpose, that He might roughly handle the dragon, and give him battle in the flesh.

"You must allow, therefore, that this woman is the Church, travailing with, and bringing forth, her ransomed ones. As also the Spirit says by Isaiah, 'Before she travailed she brought forth, before her pain came, she fled, and brought forth a male.' (Septuagint.)"

Methodius seems to have forgotten that these promises were made originally, not to the Christian, but to the Jewish Church.

Thecla pursues her discourse in the mystical style. The red dragon is said to make war upon the newly-converted, that he may destroy the image of Christ conceived in them. But he is thrown off the scent; his prey is snatched from him, and the regenerate one is raised aloft in heart and soul, even to the throne of God. This is among the oldest specimens of the mystical style: that it is opposed to the method observed in the fulfilment of other prophecies, and generally destructive of the historical sense, must be evident.

Andreas has preserved a fragment from Methodius, more in accordance with the Apostolic system:—

"It does not please me to hear it said that everything will be utterly destroyed, and that earth, air, and heaven will no longer exist. The whole world shall indeed be deluged with fire, but for its purification and renewal, not for its destruction and utter ruin. This, also, Paul clearly shows, when he says, 'The earnest expectation of the creature waiteth for the revelation of the sons of God.'"*

A.D. circ. 300.

About this time died Porphyry the Apostate, once a pupil of the great Longinus, and afterwards a formidable opponent of the primitive church. His history is melancholy enough: having been worsted in a quarrel with his fellow-believers, he took revenge by renouncing Christianity. In its place he framed a sort of Pantheism, made up of Judaism, Paganism, and a little Christianity. Living when he did, his pantheon contained no more divinities than Jehovah, Jove, and Lord: his followers have since enriched the catalogue with Mahomet and Voltaire.

* Andreas in Apoc. sub fine, quoted from a sermon of Methodius on the Resurrection, now lost. In this application of the passage he had been forestalled by Irenæus.

Porphyry suffered much uneasiness from the constancy of his wife Marcella. At length, in hopes of drawing her after him, he applied to the Delphic oracle: but Apollo, now taught by experience, declined the unequal contest with the God of gods. His kingdom, he saw too plainly, "was, and is not." "What God," asked Porphyry, "shall I endeavour to appease?" "You may write upon water," answered the oracle, "you may fly with the wings of a bird; but hope not to recover the soul of this impious and polluted wife." *

The philosopher was not to be discouraged: he addressed to Marcella a showy treatise, hoping to dazzle her with the beauties of his new system. "Even when speaking of things indifferent," he enjoins her, "let your heart still mentally turn to God. Then, through the light of the God of truth, will your very speech become divine, shining, and eloquent. For the knowledge of God gives fluency of speech; but, where forgetfulness of God has entered in, there the evil spirit is sure to dwell." †

The infidel directed his main strength against the book of Daniel: he perceived, doubtless, that if this pillar of the faith could be shaken, the whole structure must also tremble. For the times and emblems of that book are the very foundation of the Apocalypse; and still more, if Daniel can be shown to be false,

---

* Augustini Civitas Dei, lib. xix. c. 23.

† Angelo Mai, Porphyrii Fragmenta. Milan, 1816. Had Porphyry said "*seven* evil spirits," he would not have betrayed more plainly the source of his information. Yet his reserve shall not deprive us of this lesson: — that a parable, now reckoned among the most mysterious and obscure, once bore a sense so plain, as to be realised without difficulty by one of the very persons at whom it had been aimed.

Christ Himself, the faithful and the true, is proved to bear witness to an impostor. For our Lord, on the mount of Olives, quoted, as the words of Daniel, the very prophecy objected to as forged. But, besides this motive, which is rather left to be inferred, than stated in so many words, Porphyry was driven on to the attack of Daniel by the vexatious satisfaction of Jews and Christians, who agreed in pointing to the fulfilment of the prophecies as a conclusive argument against the heathen. For it has been agreed, from Josephus downwards, that no other prophet was so signally honoured of God as Daniel: the precision of his descriptions still excites amazement; and, if Daniel himself was astonished for one hour, he has kept the Church in astonishment for two thousand years. So Porphyry must needs confute Daniel.

His line of attack was so well chosen, as to leave his successors no room for improvement. These prophecies, he maintained, were written, not by Daniel, but by some one who lived in Judea in the time of Antiochus, and who wrote, in the future tense, a history of past events. Moreover, this pretended Daniel wrote, not in Hebrew, but in Greek. Also, that the history is accurate down to a certain point, at which point it suddenly becomes misty and confused.

In the original story of Susanna and the Elders, Porphyry noticed two expressions seeming to favour his theory. Daniel, in addressing the elders, is there made to play upon the names of the trees under which they pretended to have found Susanna. As if they had said, Under a clove-tree, or, Under a yew-tree: to which Daniel answers, "The angel of the Lord shall cleave," or, "shall hew, thee in pieces." These allusions, Porphyry argued, are natural enough, if the Greek be the original: ἀπὸ τοῦ σχίνου σχίσαι, καὶ ἀπὸ τοῦ πρίνου πρίσαι· but cannot be translated from another language without changing the trees, or at least the sense. Consequently, he argued, the book of Daniel was originally written in Greek.*

Porphyry was answered both by Eusebius and by Apollinarius. The story of Susanna, they said, is not part of the Hebrew book of Daniel, but a spurious Greek addition. Jerome afterwards paid so high a compliment to the critical skill of Porphyry, as to offer to receive the story of Susanna, if any one could show him in the Hebrew, idioms corresponding to those found in the Greek.

The book was next attacked on the ground of its historical character: it was too accurate for a prophecy, and must, therefore, have been written after the events. But alas for the wisdom of Porphyry and his school! The book itself, as all antiquity agreed, had been translated into Greek by the father of the princess mentioned in the beginning of the eleventh chapter. Perhaps the objector anticipated this answer, since he took care not to quote the Septuagint, but to use the later version of Theodotion.

The better to support his objections, Porphyry composed an elaborate exposition of Daniel, founded upon a new arrangement of the beasts and metals; for it would have availed him little to get rid of the

* Jerome's preface to Daniel: also his preface to the Commentary on Daniel. The objection was first advanced by Africanus, about 220; he thought the answer of the Pseudo-Daniel savoured too much of the buffoon in the mimes. It was next taken up by Porphyry, and then by a certain Jew, who repeated it to Jerome.

prophecies about Antiochus, while he had, staring him in the face, a history of the Roman empire down to the end of the world. He therefore made the fourth beast to be the Post-Alexandrine kingdoms.

There now remain few original histories of the Seleucidæ: but Porphyry, having consulted nine *, was well qualified to decide which parts of Daniel had been already fulfilled. It is therefore a matter of importance to know how far he continues his testimony to the accuracy of the descriptions. This testimony goes no further than the reign of Antiochus Epiphanes: for, as soon as Daniel begins to look onward from Antiochus to Antichrist, Porphyry grows abusive, and cries out about the mistakes of Daniel. Where the Church makes a transition from the type to the antitype, the infidel makes a transition from Daniel the historian, to Daniel the would-be prophet. In this way he helps to fix the point at which a worse than Antiochus emerges from the shadow of the Northern king.

The example of Porphyry shows the mischief of the spiritualising system, by which an infidel may plausibly explain the prophecies, when to believe their literal sense requires faith. Having expounded the eleventh of Daniel in reference to Antiochus, he was met by no less a difficulty than the resurrection of the dead, following close upon the great tribulation. By ingenious mysticising he contrived not only to escape the difficulty in this place, but even to convince some unstable Christians that no literal resur-

* These were Suctorius, Callinicus, Diodorus, Hieronymus, Polybius, Posidonius, Claudius, Theon, and Alypius. (Jerome's preface to his Commentary on Daniel.)

rection of the dead is foretold in Scripture. For this Pantheist, coming upon the resurrection of the dead, neither mocks, nor proposes to hear again of that matter: he at once undertakes to explain the history, and to vindicate the propriety of the figure. There was indeed a time of trouble such as never was since the beginning of the world: but in due season Antiochus dies, and then the people of Israel are delivered, every one that is found written in the book; that is, every one who had boldly defended the book of the law. Then they that slept, as in the dust of the earth, did awake: that is, continues the pupil of Longinus, men who had been buried under the weight of ills, and, as it were, entombed in sepulchres of woe, rose from the dust to unexpected triumph. From the ground they raised their heads, and came forth; some, the keepers of the law, to everlasting life; others, its transgressors, to everlasting contempt. They that had fled to the desert, and had lain concealed in caverns and rocks, now enjoyed a figurative resurrection; doctors and teachers who were wise in the law now shone as the firmament, and they that had exhorted the many to the observance of ceremonial righteousness, as the stars for ever and ever.*

* Let us confront the infidel with a Christian. In the thirteenth century, Albertus Magnus thus expounds the passage: "At that time, that is, after that time, shall thy people be saved, even the people of the Jews. For so it is written in Isaiah x., Though the number of the children of Israel were as the sand of the sea, yet shall a remnant of them return. For then, seeing that they have been deceived in Antichrist, they will all turn to the faith. And this is the meaning of what follows: Every one that shall be found written in the book, that is, God's book. But who are written in the book? Those of whom God has foreordained that He will give them grace here, and glory hereafter." — In Dan. xii.

Jerome laments that this work of Porphyry had beguiled "some unskilful ones of our own people."* Some trace of its effects still remains. In a fragment lately found in the Vatican there has been discovered the exposition of Daniel written by Polychronius, one of Porphyry's Christian admirers. At the beginning of the twelfth chapter the expositor remarks: "I know that some people apply this passage to the resurrection of the dead. But it is my business to follow, not the multitude, but the truth." He likewise copies Porphyry in making the three horns to have been plucked up by Antiochus; adding these words: "I wonder that Apollinarius, in the face of so plain a history, forces this passage to the coming of Antichrist." To which is subjoined an ancient Greek note: "Eudoxius says, This interpretation of thine, O Polychronius, belongs to that mad Porphyry."†

A. D. circ. 300.

Lactantius, though he wrote his Christian Institutes before the Diocletian persecution, lived to present the work to Constantine in time of peace. Being a layman, and writing mostly for heathen, he imitates rather St. Paul preaching on Areopagus than St. Paul writing to the Churches.

To give the heathen a complete idea of Christianity, he thinks it needful to set before them an outline of the revealed future. Without going much into theology, he lays down the history of Western

* Jerome on Daniel xi.
† Angelo Mai, Vet. Script., tom. i. part ii. p. 126. Polychronius was bishop of Apamea, in the year 430.

Babylon, Asiatic Antichrist, the coming of Christ, and the millennial reign of the Church. The fall of the Roman Empire, corresponding to the removal of "him that letteth," is enlarged upon with a minuteness that must have excited both the fears and the anger of the imperial court. Taking the prophetic vials and trumpets literally, he directs the heathen to expect once more miraculous plagues like those which formerly desolated Egypt. But, before these things, great political changes must occur: —

"That desolation and confusion will be thus caused: the Roman name, by which the world is now governed (I tremble to say it, but speak I must, for it will take place), the Roman name will be taken from the earth, and empire will revert to Asia. Once more the East shall rule, and the West obey. * * *

"For the works of mortals are mortal; and other kingdoms, though they flourished long, yet not the less came to ruin. The world, as history tells us, has been governed by Egyptians, Persians, Greeks, and Assyrians; and, after their fall, the Romans succeeded to the primacy. And this kingdom, in proportion as it excels all other kingdoms, shall fall with the greater crash: for that which stands the highest ever falls most heavily. * * *

"And, lest any one should think this incredible, I will explain how it is to come about. First, the empire will be subdivided, and the powers of government, being frittered away and shared among many, will be undermined. Then will follow continued civil discords; and there will be no respite from destructive wars, till ten kings arise at once, dividing the world among themselves, to consume rather than to govern it. Levying boundless armies and leaving the lands uncultivated (the beginning of the confusion and the slaughter), they will scatter all things, desolating and devouring on all sides.

"Then suddenly there will arise against them a most powerful enemy, from the extreme borders of the north:

and this man, sweeping away three of those then reigning in Asia, will be taken into league by the rest, and appointed chief of all. With insupportable dominion he will harass the world, will confound things human and divine, and will form designs unspeakable as well as execrable."*

In this treatise, the darkening of the sun and moon is understood literally, as well as the fall of the stars. These events, he says, will be altogether distinct from what occasionally happens in the course of nature. But he still fears that he has not made his bad news sufficiently clear: —

"I will explain still more distinctly how this will come about. When the end of the times draws near, God will send a great prophet who will convert men to the knowledge of Himself, and will receive power to work miracles. Wherever men refuse to listen to him, he will shut heaven and withhold the showers; he will turn water to blood, will torment men with hunger and thirst; and whoever attempts to hurt him will be devoured by the fire that proceeds out of his mouth.

" By these miracles and powers he will turn many to the worship of God; and, when his works are finished†, another king shall arise out of Syria, begotten of an evil spirit, to the ruin and perdition of the human race; and he will blot out altogether the remains of that former wicked one.

" He will fight against God's prophet, and conquer and slay him, causing his body to lie unburied. But after the third day he will rise again; and, while all are looking on and wondering, he will be snatched up into heaven."

Not knowing the name of the second witness, Lactantius follows Malachi in speaking of Elijah only.

* Lactantius, Institutiones, lib. vii. cap. 15, 16. Owing to a repetition in the story, it is uncertain whether Lactantius takes this king to be a precursor of the horn, or the very Antichrist: his own " Epitome " makes the former almost certain.

† Paraphrased from Apoc. xi. : " And when they shall have finished their testimony, the beast that ascendeth out of the bottomess pit shall make war against them."

A similar variation is found in Scripture in the case of Moses and Aaron, who are sometimes spoken of together, and at other times as doing the same things under the name of Moses only.

The fire called down by Antichrist he takes to be real fire, called down from above; the image of the beast, a real statue. At that time also he places the great tribulation and the flight of the Church to the wilderness. "All who believe in and join him will be marked by him as cattle; but those that refuse his mark will either flee to the mountains, or being taken, will be despatched with cruel torments. Just men he will wrap up in the writings of the prophets, and so set fire to them: and it shall be given him to desolate the world during forty and two months." (Cap. xvii.)

In foretelling the destiny of Rome, Lactantius shelters himself under the authority of the Sibyl: "That this will happen shortly, the prophecies declare, though under the disguise of other names, lest they should be easily understood. But the Sibyls say plainly that Rome is to be destroyed, and by the judgment of God, because she has hated His name, and, being opposed to righteousness, has slaughtered the people that are born of the truth." (Cap. xv.)

Tacitus, speaking politically, had styled Christianity a destructive religion; Lactantius, therefore, labours to display it as eminently conservative:—

"It is evident from the state of affairs that the end of all things would not be distant, save only that while Rome is safe there seems no room to fear. But when that head of the world shall fall, and begin, as the Sibyls say, to be a ruin, who does not see that the end of human affairs, yea, of the world itself, will have arrived?

"For it is this city which still supports every thing: and it is our business to supplicate and beg of the God of heaven, that His will and pleasure may be yet postponed, and that we may not behold, even sooner than we expect, the coming of that abominable tyrant, who meditates nothing less than the extinction of that Eye through the loss of which the world will stumble and fall.

"And now to consider what will follow these things. I said lately, that, in the beginning of the holy kingdom, the prince of the demons will be bound by God. But towards the end of the thousand years' reign, that is, of the seven thousand years, he will once more be loosed, and will go forth out of his prison."* (Cap. 25, 26.)

Before dismissing the primitive writers, we should notice accurately the amount of agreement prevailing among them in reference to, 1st., the thousand years of St. John, and 2nd, the last half week of Daniel.

Those who have recorded their opinion for or against the Millennium may thus be classed:—

FOR.	AGAINST.
St. Barnabas.	
Papias.	
Justin.	
Irenæus.	
Tertullian.	
Hippolytus.	
Nepos.	
	Origen.
Cyprian.	
	Dionysius.
Victorinus.	
Lactantius.	

* Lactantius has given offence to many by the following words: "Those who are then living in the body will not die; but will,

But on which side shall we range St. John? Were he uninspired, nothing could be more decisive than his statement:—"They lived and reigned with Christ a thousand years." Have we at length come to this, that because we reckon him inspired, the plain sense of his words is to go for nothing?

The two writers who appear in opposition to the doctrine, are not altogether unexceptionable. The system by which Origen contrived to get rid of the millennium was soon branded with the name of Origenism, having been found to interfere with the belief in the literal resurrection of the flesh. Nor can Dionysius be justified in his method of dealing with the Apocalypse: for, not daring to revile it in his own name, he repeats with satisfaction the saying of "certain persons," that the book itself is devoid of sense and reason: also, that its title is utterly false, since it is neither written by St. John, nor does it, covered as it is with a thick and dense veil of ignorance, deserve the title of a Revelation.*

Regarding the latter half of the seventieth week, the primitive writers were not entirely agreed. It was applied by

Irenæus	to	Antichrist.
Tertullian	,,	Vespasian.
Judas	,,	Antichrist.
Clement of Alexandria	,,	Vespasian.
Hippolytus	,,	Antichrist.
Origen	,,	Antichrist.
Victorinus	,,	Antichrist.

during the same thousand years, bring forth a countless multitude, and their offspring shall be holy, and beloved of God." (lib. vii. c. 24.) Imitated from Isaiah: for he does not say that the *risen ones* will bring forth children.

* Eusebius, lib. vii. c. 25.

The majority, therefore, make that half week identical with the three years and a half of Antichrist. In their favour may be urged: —

First, The precise agreement of the time; the weeks being land weeks, or weeks of years.

Secondly, The identity of the events assigned to each: for everything said of the half week is repeated in the prophecies relating to Antichrist. These things are, the cessation of the daily sacrifice, the setting up of the abomination, the desolation thereby occasioned, the consummation of God's mystery, and the pouring out of the vials upon the Desolator.

Thirdly, The events of the half week are continued till the consummation: apparently the sounding of the seventh trumpet, when the mystery of God shall be finished.

According to the primitive scheme, the sense of the whole passage amounts to this:—

Seventy sevens of years are fixed in the history of the Jews and of Jerusalem. In these will be accomplished the summing up of iniquity, the work of atonement, the winding up of all prophecy, and the anointing of the Christ.

Between the edict to rebuild Jerusalem and the mission of Christ there will elapse two periods, seven sevens, and sixty-two sevens, of years. In the course of the first, the city will be rebuilt; and at the end of the second the Messiah will be put to death.

Afterwards the Romans under Vespasian will destroy both city and temple, sweeping them away as with a flood; and, until the end of God's warfare with His people (or, after the end of the Roman war*),

---

* So the Vulgate, "post finem belli, statuta desolatio."

it is determined that the desolation of the city and of the temple shall continue.

But God will renew His covenant with many of His chosen people, during a certain seven years, the remaining week of the seventy; (probably by means of Elias, who will come and restore all things). But, throughout the latter half of this week, that is, for three years and a half, the daily sacrifice will be taken away; and, on account of the abomination set up by Antichrist, the temple will be made desolate: to remain so, till the consummation of the mystery, and till the end of the plagues that will be poured upon Antichrist the Desolator.

Later commentators, far from making the passage clearer, have increased its difficulties by the numberless alterations proposed in the text. In this state of uncertainty we are forced to fall back upon that sense which was at first admitted as the basis of the argument between Jews and Christians;—that after sixty-two sabbatical years an Anointed one should be cut off. This is the plain, *working* sense of the passage: unlike its modern and fantastic rivals, it has borne the burden and the heat of the day.* This sense it was thought vain to deny, much

---

* Nisibenus reserves this argument for his last thrust at the Jew. " You say thus :— Christ has not yet come. It is, indeed, written that He will come, that the Gentiles will trust in His coming, and believe upon Him. But I hear from the Gentiles that He is still to come. Now if, in anticipation of that coming, I believe on Him, and through Him worship the God of Israel, perhaps, when He comes, he will rebuke me for having forestalled the time, and believed on Him before He came. But, foolish and ignorant one, the prophets utterly forbid you to say that Christ has not yet come. For Daniel refutes you in that saying of his, — After sixty and two weeks Christ will come and will die, and at His coming the city of the sanctuary will be destroyed." — Sermo xvi.

as its admission cost the Jews. But how, allowing it, could they escape becoming Christians?

The argument was variously evaded. Some made the Anointed one to be Agrippa; some, Joshua the high priest. Others applied the words to the succession of high priests, the anointed ones, spoken of as one.* Under Titus this anointed one was cut off: for to this day the nation have been without him. And this indeed may be a part of the true meaning: for by Christ's death the succession of high priests was abolished, and He, having summed up the series, sat down on the right hand of the Throne till His foes should be made His footstool.

The prophecies relative to the first Advent are not included in the design of this work. It has been agreed, by the Church in all ages, that what the New Testament writers apply to Christ, was spoken with a distinct reference to His life and actions. On this subject there is no room to doubt, without incurring the blame of open rebellion against the Lord of the prophets. The question has been decided once for all: it is enough to have once heard the rebuke, "O fools and slow of heart to believe all that the prophets have spoken! Ought not Christ to have suffered these things, and to enter into His glory?"

---

* Galatinus, de Arcanis, lib. iv. cap. 17.

CHAPTER III.

THE INTERPRETATION OF PROPHECY IN THE PATRISTIC AGE.

(From Constantine to Gregory the Great.)

" The Jews believe that Jerusalem will be restored to them, golden and jewelled, and that there will be once more victims and sacrifices, the marriage of the saints, and the kingdom of the Lord and Saviour upon earth. All which, though I do not support, yet I am not able to condemn, since many churchmen and martyrs have said the same. Therefore, let every one be fully persuaded in his own mind, and let all things be reserved for the decision of the Lord." — JEROME on Jeremiah, chap. xx.

THE fourth century opens with a new class of expositors, the old having been, for the most part, disposed of by Diocletian. The patristic period, if we can agree to understand by that name the fourth and two following centuries, witnessed several changes in prophetic belief.

First, the Church in general abandoned the millennium; and soon afterwards the identity of Antichrist's time with the last half week of Daniel. In the fifth century it was made an open question whether Babylon meant Rome; also it was reckoned doubtful whether the temple of Jerusalem would be rebuilt, so that Antichrist should sit in it. Lastly, it was believed by many that most of the prophecies were to receive a double fulfilment: one indefinite, lasting throughout the dispensation, the other literal, and belonging to the time of the end.

The history of this age opens badly: Eusebius is a semi-Arian, a rationalist, and almost a præterist. In prophecy he can believe nothing but what he sees: he must be shown a fulfilment either in history or in passing events. But let none, following his example, think to find history a safer guide than the Bible: for Eusebius, neglecting the infallible, and trusting to what seemed to him more secure, became the sport of circumstances, being forced to change his belief with the changes of his eventful time. At first he received the Apocalypse: since he explained the seven seals as the obscurities of the Old Testament prophecies, which Christ, the Lion of the tribe of Judah, now opens.* Afterwards, the establishment of Christianity seemed to interfere with the literal millennium; and then Eusebius must needs reject both Apocalypse and millennium. Lastly, Constantine begins to rebuild Jerusalem as a Christian city: and now the Apocalypse seems to be thought of again, for this may be, perhaps, the beginning of the new Jerusalem. But the great event of the day was the emperor's episcopal dinner.

The twentieth anniversary of Constantine's accession was hailed with general rejoicings throughout the world. Since the Augustan age, so long a cessation from bloodshed had not been known. "Throughout the whole kingdom," says Eusebius, "the sword of justice hung idle; and men and nations obeyed rather from filial affection than by means of force."†

* Demonstratio Evangelica, lib. vii. Perhaps it was at that early period that he wrote the prophetic Eclogues (edited by Dean Gaisford): also the passages contained in Mai's Chain.

† De Vitâ Constantini, lib. iii. c. 1.

The heathen rejoiced scarcely less than the Church: it was clear that no rod of iron was as yet to be swayed by the triumphant faith. Therefore, on the twentieth anniversary, the people set apart a day for feasting; and Constantine, improving upon the popular idea, invited the bishops of the whole empire to dine with him. All who came received presents; to those who were unable to attend, the emperor sent letters of friendly greeting.

That dinner turned the head of Eusebius. "It surpassed," he says, "all power of description. The cuirassiers and spearmen, drawn up in a circle, guarded with naked swords the entrance to the palace; and, through the midst, walked fearlessly the men of God, on their way to the inner chambers. There, some reclined beside the emperor, while others occupied couches ranged on either side. The whole seemed to shadow forth an image of the kingdom of Christ, being more like a dream than a reality."*

A great change for Eusebius, who had lived in the days when the sword grew blunt, and the lictor weary, in the massacre of Christians. For it was not so much as hinted in prophecy that the Iron kingdom would become a nursing father to the Church: it was strange, therefore, to see Constantine circulating, at the imperial expense, costly editions of the Scriptures, and stranger still to see the bishops drinking wine with the representative of the fourth beast;— now no longer stamping and blaspheming, but uttering words of piety and praise. For thus spoke the autocrat of East and West: "Now that the Dragon is removed from the administration of affairs, through

* De Vitâ Constantini, lib. iii. c. 15. See also c. i.

the providence of the supreme God and by my instrumentality, I imagine that the divine power has been made clear to all men."*

By this Dragon, Constantine meant the Devil: and in order to advertise more publicly his religious intentions, he caused an allegorical painting to be set up before the gate of his palace. In this picture, executed in wax, in the encaustic manner, Constantine was the principal figure: above his head shone the cross, and beneath his feet, skulking in the depths of the sea, writhed the Dragon, "that adverse and hostile beast, who, through the tyranny of atheist monarchs, had aforetime ravaged the church of God." To heighten the effect, Constantine was made to hold a dart, the point of which was buried in the body of the Dragon. In illustration, Eusebius quotes from Isaiah xxvii.: "He shall smite the Dragon that fugitive serpent, and shall slay the Dragon that is in the sea."† (Septuagint.)

We are tempted to wonder that Constantine, but just escaped from hereditary paganism, should at once succeed in striking out that scheme of political relationship with the Church, which experience has since proved to be the best calculated to spread the Gospel, and to confirm its conquests. But we cease to wonder, though not to admire, when we find him diligent in promoting the circulation of that volume which tells of a Solomon and a Josiah, a Hezekiah and a David. Doubtless, the same pages that he loved to adorn with the gold and the purple, had

---

* De Vitâ Constantini, lib. ii. c. 46.
† Ibid. lib. iii. c. 3.

taught him in return the royal lesson, how to smooth the way for the performance of a duty not always easy to the jealous worshipper;—to divide rightly between God's and Cæsar's; at once to fear the One, and to honour, in his due place and degree, the other.

By these marvellous doings the prophetic school was shaken to its centre: for half a century the expositors were almost silent. Eusebius still handled the prophecies, explaining them, as much as possible, in reference to things past; and, when that was impracticable, neglecting them altogether. His most signal failure was in the last half week of Daniel, which he referred to a supposed three years and a half occurring between Christ's resurrection and ascension; during which, on forty different days, He appeared to his disciples.* In like manner he expounds the abomination of desolation in reference to Titus only, though he does not profess to explain how, immediately after the tribulation of those days, the sun was darkened, and the tribes of the earth mourned on seeing the Son of man coming in the clouds of heaven.

We have no means of knowing whether the Church then attempted to identify her existing state with any condition described in prophecy. Probably not; for few seemed willing to trouble themselves with the prophecies in that period of profound repose. But on this enchanted ground the Church was not suffered to wander long: a stern message was sent to remind her that this was not her rest, and that she had mistaken an earthly home for the city with the golden

* Demonstratio Evangelica, lib. viii.

street and the crystal towers. To her hour of highest hope succeeded her most disastrous fall: she found Arius a bad exchange for Diocletian. For that bold gainsayer would have taken away her Lord, leaving her but a shadow of Deity, impotent to redeem, and unworthy to be worshipped. This denial of the Father and the Son was styled by Athanasius, "Christ's enemy, Antichrist's forerunner:"* but it does not appear that any one mistook Arianism for actual Antichristianity. The controversies then raging served to prolong the silence of the prophetic school.

A.D. 350.

First from the deadly strife emerges Hilary, second only to Athanasius in the ranks of Trinitarian orthodoxy. This Hilary, bishop of Poictiers in Gaul, found leisure to write an exposition of St. Matthew's Gospel, which necessarily brought him to the subject of Antichrist.

"Matth. xxiv. When ye shall see the abomination. Now follows the sign of the future Advent. When they shall see the abomination of desolation standing in the holy place, then let them understand the return of daylight. And on this subject, after what the blessed Daniel and Paul have written, I think it needless for me to speak: for this refers to the time of Antichrist.

"He is called an abomination, because, coming in opposition to God, he will arrogate to himself Divine honour: and, of desolation, because he will wickedly desolate the earth with war and slaughter. He will also be received by the Jews into the holy place; and, where God has been invoked by the prayers of the saints, there will Antichrist, received by the faithless, be worshipped with Divine honour.

"And as this will be an error especially Jewish (for they

---

* Athanasii Apol. contra Arianos.

who rejected the truth will receive the lie), He warns them to quit Judea and to flee to the mountains: lest, by admixture with those that believe in Antichrist, they should suffer violence or imbibe contagion; for, to the faithful then living, the mountainous deserts will be safer than the thickly-peopled Judea."*

The Church, now fairly roused and restored to her senses, returned afresh to the study of prophecy. The danger had not ceased to threaten, for Arian emperors still employed every art to subvert the apostolic faith. Once, by elaborate frauds and unscrupulous cruelty, an œcumenical council was entrapped into signing what proved to be an Arian confession: and, as Jerome has expressed it, "The world groaned to find itself Arian." But the fields of Rimini afforded no solid triumph to the gates of hell: the spirit of Arianism had displayed itself too openly, and henceforth the Church was to be free from that form of infidelity in her high places. Meanwhile, the expositors addressed themselves to the prophecies with a diligence never since equalled.

A. D. 360.

The first complete set of lectures on the Creed was published by the elder Cyril, bishop of Jerusalem. These *catecheses*, his only remaining work, were delivered to persons preparing for baptism or for confirmation. Our business is with the fifteenth, which explains the clause, "He shall come with glory to judge both the quick and the dead."

---

* Commentary upon St. Matthew. In expounding chap. xx., he states his belief that Moses and Elias are to be the two witnesses.

After the late confusion, Cyril attempts, by noting the signs of the times, to fix the place of his own age in prophecy. To do this, he enumerates the signs which are to precede Christ's second coming, marking them off as either fulfilled or still future. His list might have been written yesterday, so little have fifteen centuries advanced the fulfilment:—

I. Many shall come, saying, I am Christ. Partly fulfilled in Simon Magus and Menander.

II. Wars, and rumours of wars. Now going on.

III. Famines, pestilences, and earthquakes. Already fulfilled.

IV. Do we churchmen seek a sign within the Church? Many shall be offended, and the love of many shall wax cold. Too much seen now.

V. The Gospel preached throughout all the world. Almost fulfilled.

VI. The abomination spoken of by Daniel, standing in the holy place. This is Antichrist, not yet come. But Satan, adds Cyril, is even now preparing schisms, that the coming man may find a better reception.

VII. The falling away first. Partly seen in Arianism and other heresies.

The appearance of Antichrist, therefore, remained as the sole event that must necessarily stand between that age and the coming of Christ. In his account of the man of sin, Cyril paraphrases the "power of Satan" in the usual manner, by magic and sorcery:—

" When the true Christ is about to come the second time, the Adversary, taking advantage of the expectation of simple persons, especially those of the circumcision, will produce a certain magician, deeply skilled in the treacherous and wicked arts of spells and incantations. This man will usurp the government of the Roman empire, and will falsely call himself the Christ. By this title he will deceive the Jews, who still expect the anointed one; while, by his magic arts and delusions, he will draw after him the Gentiles."

The four empires are next explained as the Assyrian, Medo-Persian, Grecian, and Roman. Like Barnabas, he dwells upon the Jewish character of Antichrist's apostacy, and the shortening of the days of his reign. He then devotes some space to the case of his own congregation, for he was preaching in Jerusalem. To those who would be living in the time of the Beast, the question would arise, whether to resist or to flee. To the weak in faith he holds out the permission, "Let them that be in Judea flee to the mountains." He recommends them to flee from city to city, adding this consolation, that the time will be short, even three years and six months; and that, perhaps, they may not have gone over the cities of Israel before the Son of man be come. "Antichrist," he adds, "will sit in the temple of God. But what temple? That of the Jews, which has been destroyed; for God forbid that it should be that in which we now are."

"Who will then be so blessed as piously to bear witness for Christ? I say that those martyrs will be above all former martyrs. For they that have suffered hitherto have striven with men only, but the martyrs, under Antichrist, will contend hand to hand with Satan. The kings, who persecuted formerly, could do nothing but put to death; they could neither pretend to raise the dead, nor show a semblance of miracles and signs. But here will be the persuasiveness both of terror and deceit, so as to seduce, if it were possible, even the elect.

"In that day let it enter into no man's heart to ask, What has Christ done more than this? Or by what power does this man perform these things? for, unless God approved of him, He would not suffer him. The Apostle warns you beforehand:—For this cause God shall send them strong delusion. Now that word, *shall send*, is put for, *shall suffer to exist*. Not that they might be excused, but that they might be condemned. And why? Because, believing not the truth, that is, the true Christ, they approved unrighteousness, that is, Antichrist. * * *

"Fortify thyself therefore, O man: thou hast been told the marks of Antichrist; be not content with knowing them for thyself only, but without envy teach them to others. Hast thou a son after the flesh? Teach him these things. Hast thou, through sponsorship, become father to any one? Forewarn him also, lest he mistake a false Christ for the True. For the mystery of iniquity doth already work. I fear the wars of the nations; I am terrified by the dissensions of the churches: the discord of the brethren alarms me. I say these things that we may not be taken by surprise: yet God forbid that they should be fulfilled in our own time."

A. D. circ. 370.

In the growing expectation of Christ's speedy coming, the precautions against surprise by Antichrist were redoubled. Under the protection of the state, the prophecies could now be expounded in a more public and popular manner: so that the reader, who has hitherto been supplied with extracts from elaborate treatises or cautiously worded epistles, will now be taken to hear sermons, and to learn from catechisms and expositions about Antichrist in the vulgar tongue. And first comes the easy catechism written for Prince Antiochus, containing "things needful to be known by all Christian people."

This Greek catechism once bore the honoured name of Athanasius, but is now attributed to some unknown writer of his time.

"*Question* 108. What sign should one bear in mind, so as not to be deceived into following Antichrist under the idea that he is the Christ?

"*Answer.* The same sign that the Lord gave us when He said, As the lightning goeth out of the East and shineth into the West, so shall be the second advent of the Son of God. Hence we learn, that every Christ who may come, and who will not be discovered at the same moment by the whole world, — that man is undoubtedly an Antichrist: for at Christ's second coming the whole race of men will be gathered together, and Christ, being in the midst of them, will be seen by all.

" Q. Is it true that Antichrist will come out of Egypt, and that he will have a certain mark in one hand, or in one eye?

" *A.* All these are old women's myths: Antichrist will have no such mark. He will come out of Galilee, whence Christ came; as the Scripture says, Dan is a lion's whelp, he shall leap from Bashan. This Bashan is now Scythopolis.

" Q. Some say that Antichrist will not be able to raise the dead, though he may perform all other miracles.

"*A.* The Apostle's words concerning Antichrist, 'in *all* miracles and powers of deceivableness,' show plainly that he will seem to raise the dead, not in reality, but in appearance."*

A. D. 370.

About this time flourished, or rather mourned, the Syrian Ephrem, deacon of Edessa. Upon his mind, always disposed to sad and penitential subjects, the prospect of Antichrist's coming weighed deeply; his whole soul seemed to respond to the declaration, "Then shall be great tribulation, such as was not since the beginning of the world."

Ephrem's sermon on Antichrist was preached, or at least, published, in Greek: —

* Questions for Prince Antiochus. Inter Opera Athanasii.

"Let me declare in sorrow, and tell with sighing, the approaching end of the world. Let me speak of that shameless and terrible Dragon, who will trample down all beneath the sky, and will plant terror, profaneness, and horrible unbelief, in the hearts of men. He will do signs, and miracles, and fearful things, to seduce, if it were possible, even the elect, and to deceive all men by his lying wonders and unreal miracles: for, by permission of the Holy God, he will receive power to deceive the world, because its impiety is filled up, and evil of all sorts is every where committed."

Ephrem takes little care to distinguish between the Dragon and the Beast, probably because the second wields the power and fills the throne of the first. In what follows, the mention of the Beast's name is not needed, as the Dragon himself is said to persecute the woman and to cause her to fly to the wilderness:—

"Who then will have a soul so adamantine as to bear unmoved the shock of all these scandals? Tell me, I say, who that man will be, that all angels may call him blessed. As for me, my Christ-loving and perfect brethren, I tremble at the very thought of that Dragon; reflecting on the tribulation that is to come upon mankind. How cruel will that Dragon prove, not only to our race at large, but in particular to those holy ones who will be enabled to resist his delusions! For there are many (as it will then be discovered) pleasing in God's sight, who will find safety in mountains and in desert places, in many prayers and in boundless tears: and the holy God, beholding their unspeakable anguish and steadfast faith, will, as a compassionate father, have mercy upon them, and will preserve them in that their hiding-place. But the wicked one will not cease to make inquisition for the saints by land and by sea, reckoning that, but for them, he reigns over the whole earth and governs all men. And he expects to stand his ground even in that tremendous hour when the Lord shall come from heaven, miserably ignorant of his own weakness and presumption, which have been his ruin."

It was promised to the Philadelphians that they should be saved from the hour of temptation which shall come upon all the earth. This promise seems to refer to the saying of our Lord, "Pray always, that ye may be accounted worthy to escape all these things that shall come to pass." It is thus amplified by Ephrem: "Is any of you master of tears and prayers? let him ask of the Lord that we may escape the tribulation that is to come upon the earth; that he himself may by no means behold that Beast, nor hear of its fearful doings."

Ephrem continues, drawing largely from the Apocalypse:—

"All who receive the mark of Antichrist, or who worship him as the good God, shall have no part in the kingdom of Christ, but shall be cast into hell with the Dragon. Blessed he who shall be found altogether holy and faithful, having his heart steadfastly fixed upon God: fearlessly will that man repel all the wiles of Antichrist, despising alike his torments and his snares.

"But, before these things, the merciful Lord will send Elijah the Tishbite, and with him Enoch, to teach religion to the human race; and they shall preach boldly to all men the knowledge of God, exhorting them not to believe in the tyrant through fear. They shall cry out and say, 'This is a deceiver, O ye men! Let none of you in any way believe him, or obey one who is an enemy to God. Let none fear him: for in a little while he will be utterly abolished. Behold! the Lord, the Holy One, is coming from heaven, to judge all who shall believe in these miracles.' But few will choose to obey or believe the preaching of those prophets."*

Ephrem gives the length of Antichrist's reign as three times and a half: as a Syrian, he probably

---

* Many of these sentences are closely imitated, and even copied, by the Pseudo-Hippolytus.

thought that this required no explanation. Like Cyril, he reckons the precursory signs fulfilled, excepting the fall of the Roman Empire: "All else that is written is fulfilled; the predicted signs are accomplished. Nothing now remains but what concerns our enemy Antichrist: for, when the Roman Empire ends, all things must be fulfilled."*

A. D. 380.

The primitive teaching is next supported by Ambrose, almost the latest of what may be called the Athanasian phalanx.

His commentary on St. Luke brings him to the subject of Antichrist:—

"When ye shall see Jerusalem compassed with armies.— Truly Jerusalem has been compassed by an army, and stormed by a Roman general: whence the Jews thought that the abomination of desolation was set up, when the Romans, mocking the Jewish ceremonial, threw a pig's head into the temple. With which I am not so mad as to agree; for the abomination of desolation is the abominable advent of Antichrist, who with disastrous sacrilege will defile the inner chambers of men's minds, and will moreover sit literally in the temple, usurping the throne of divine power."†

---

* Sermo de Vitâ Religiosâ.

† Ambrose does the Jews no injustice in quoting the story of the pig's head. Bartoloccius gives another from the Rabbis, told with the usual suppression of the Roman name: "Now in the days of the wicked kingdom, the Jews were accustomed to let down to the —— two baskets of gold, and the —— sent them up in return two kids. On one occasion, when they had let down by the chain the two baskets of gold, the —— sent them up two pigs. Before the pigs came halfway up the wall, there was an earthquake, and one pig, being excited, sprang out of the land of Israel, a distance of forty leagues. In that hour the transgressions were finished, the daily sacrifice ceased, and the house was overthrown." — Bibliotheca Rabbinica, tom. ii. p. 353.

Noticing Arius and Sabellius as forms of Antichrist, Ambrose adds this caution against negligence: — that of those times the Lord has condescended to express Himself as if in doubt, whether, when He comes again, He shall find faith still surviving upon the earth.

A few names of less note may be briefly despatched. Apollinarius, in a commentary on Daniel, broached a new theory of the seventy weeks; dating from the birth of Christ, and dividing the last week between the preaching of Elias and the reign of Antichrist, whose statue, set up in the Jewish temple, will be the abomination of desolation.* Remains of this work are contained in the Chain on Daniel, published by Mai: all trace of his volume in support of the millennium is lost.

Gregory of Nazianzen gives the same explanation of the temple of God, which he expects to be rebuilt in the end of the world, that Antichrist may sit in it as the abomination of desolation.† He wrote some iambics, meant to be used as a catechism in verse: in these he draws upon the Apocalypse, styling Antichrist the Beast.‡

Ruffinus wrote an exposition of the creed; introducing the subject of Antichrist at the clause, "He shall come with glory." He follows the primitive track, making Antichrist the abomination of desolation. (Published in the Appendix to Jerome.)

Gaudentius of Brixia, in his tenth tract, supports the millennium. "We expect," he says, "that truly sacred day, the seventh thousand of years."

* Apud Hieronymum, in Daniel ix.
† Oration 47.   ‡ Iambic 15.

The poet Prudentius introduces the subject of the Apocalyptic visions, in his hymn, written for " Before sleep." The purport of that book he takes to be the coming of the true Christ to destroy the Antichrist. These passages should not be overlooked by those who collect ancient testimonies to the inspiration of the Apocalypse.

A. D. 390.

And now back to the eastern world, to hear the sweet strains of the Byzantine Patriarch, John of the Golden Mouth. For Chrysostom, though he adds little to their knowledge, exhausts the subject of Antichrist for the eastern church. What he says, he says so well, that none ventures to alter or to add to it. There being in the Greek Church no Pope and no Popery, there was no need to change the exposition of Scripture in compliance with the demands of an ever-changing creed.

Chrysostom's, therefore, is the latest original Greek commentary on 2 Thess. ii.

"And now ye know what withholdeth. Here any one may well ask, first, What is that which withholdeth? and next, For what possible reason does Paul allude to it so obscurely? What then is that which withholds, that is, which hinders, the revelation of Antichrist.

" Some say, the grace of the Spirit; others, the empire of the Romans; with these last I fully agree. And why? Because, had he meant the Spirit, he would have said, not obscurely, but openly, — The grace, that is, the gifts of the Spirit, keeps him back. Besides, if the coming of Antichrist were to follow the cessation of the gifts, he must have come already, for the gifts have long since ceased.

" But speaking here of the Roman empire, he does so, and with good reason, enigmatically and obscurely. For he had no wish to provoke needless hostility, or to incur superfluous risk. And, had he said that the Roman empire would soon be overturned, they would presently have dispatched him as a pestilent fellow, and with him all the faithful, as persons living and fighting for that end. Therefore he does not say that this will happen, or that it will happen soon, although he says what amounts to the same thing. And what does he say? That he should be revealed in his own time; for the mystery of iniquity doth already work, meaning Nero, who was a type of Antichrist, for he wished to be reckoned a god."*

Chrysostom here uses the word mystery in the sense in which it is used in the Apocalypse; "the mystery of the seven stars"—"a mystery, Babylon the great:"—something that helps us to realise another thing yet future or unseen. The idea that Antichrist was typified by Nero, had become common in the patristic church. But Theodore expounds it differently: "The Devil, though he does not as yet openly bring about the apostacy, does even now, in mystery, accomplish much of it." †

The Archbishop proceeds:—

"He is called a son of perdition, because he himself will perish. And who is he? Satan? By no means; but a certain man, receiving all the operation of Satan. There shall be revealed, it says, the man, who will be extolled above all that is called God, or that is made an object of worship. For he will not incite men to worship idols, but will be himself an Antitheos. He will put down all gods, and will command men to worship him as the very God. And he will sit in the temple of God; not only that which is in Jerusalem, but in the churches everywhere." ‡

Chrysostom now enters upon what may be called

---

* Chrysost. in Epist. ii. ad Thess. (Homily 4. on the Chapter.)
† Catena Græca in Epist. ed. Cramer, p. 389.
‡ Homily 3. on the Chapter.

the theory of Antichrist, the place which his coming occupies in the Divine plan. This subject he treats in his own golden manner: —

"What advantage, say they, in the coming of Antichrist? That they who perish may be struck dumb. And how? Because, even if Antichrist did not come, still they would not have believed in Christ. He comes therefore to reprove them, to prevent their having this excuse: — Christ said that He Himself was God, not perhaps openly in person, yet by His preachers after Him; therefore we did not believe in Him, having heard that there is one God, through whom are all things. And for that reason we did not believe in Him.

"This excuse of theirs Antichrist will destroy. For when he comes, though he does nothing good, but every thing against the law, they will believe in him solely upon the strength of his lying miracles. And so their mouths will be stopped. For, if you believe not in Christ, much less should you believe in Antichrist. The One said that He was sent by the Father, the other the contrary. Therefore said Christ, I am come in my Father's name, and ye receive me not: if another shall come in his own name, him ye will receive.

"But, they will say, we saw miracles. True, but Christ also did many and great miracles: much more then should you have believed on Him. For of Antichrist many things have been declared, — that he will be the lawless one, the son of perdition, and that his coming will be after the working of Satan; but of Christ the contrary, — that He would be a Saviour, and that He would bring with Him countless blessings. That they all might be condemned who believe not the truth. Condemned, he says, not punished. For even *without* this they were to be punished, but *by* this they are proved guilty."

In this way the ancients rejoiced to vindicate God's justice in permitting the coming of Antichrist. The man of sin ruins no one: those who are already hardened in unbelief he will ensnare to their own confusion. He will place the rejection of Christ upon its true footing, a repugnance, not to the miraculous, but to the good; for, where purity with miracles has repelled, sin with miracles will attract.

To those who believe in Christ, Chrysostom holds out a consolation: —

"But fear not ye: he will have power, it says, in those that perish. And Elias also will come to confirm the faithful, even as Christ declares: — Elias will come, and will restore all things. For this reason it is said of John, In the spirit and power of Elias: for he did neither miracles nor wonders, as Elias did. John, they said, did no miracles, but all things that John spake of this man were true. How then did John come in the spirit and power of Elias? By receiving the same ministry: for, as the one was forerunner of the first coming, so will the other be forerunner of the second coming in glory. And for that purpose he is reserved."

In expounding Matthew xxiv. Chrysostom makes two greatest tribulations, one of the Jews under Titus, the other of the whole world under Antichrist. He places the transition at these words, — If any man shall say unto you, Lo! here is Christ: —

"Immediately after the tribulation of those days shall the sun be darkened. The tribulation of what days? Of Antichrist and the false prophets. The deceivers being so many, the tribulation will be great; but it will not last long. For, if the Jewish war was shortened for the elect's sake, much more will this trial be shortened for their sake also. Therefore it does not say, after the tribulation, but, immediately after the tribulation of those days, shall the sun be darkened; for all these things will be done almost at once. As soon as the false prophets and the false Christs grow tumultuous, then He will straightway appear."

Chrysostom finds a difficulty in the expression, "*This* generation shall not pass away till all be fulfilled." To escape it, he explains the generation to be "the generation of those that seek the Lord." In opposition to the general sense of the Church, he arrives at this meaning:—The generation of the faithful shall not be brought to a premature end by any of the calamities here foretold. On this plan the spiritual seed is literally "counted for a generation."

The difficulty appears not to have been felt by the primitive writers, probably because they understood the αὕτη in the sense which it sometimes bears, "*this*, of which I am speaking." It is so used in Luke xvii. 34. "In this night there shall be two in one bed;" meaning, not this coming night, but, this night of which I have been speaking:—To avoid confusion, our translators have rendered it *that* night; they might also have rendered this passage, *that* generation. This would make the sense easy, and in perfect accordance with the context. When these things begin to come to pass, when the fig-tree begins to bud, the end is close at hand, even within the lifetime of the same generation.

In Chrysostom's commentary on Daniel, not long ago discovered, the usual account of the beasts and metals is repeated. In addition to internal evidence, its authenticity is confirmed by the Greek chain on Daniel lately published by Mai, compiled about the sixth century.

A. D. 400.

The fifth century opens with Jerome, and "incipit feliciter," for he entered upon the study of prophecy in a spirit well suited to the greatness of the subject.

The attack of Porphyry had produced in the minds of some believers a doubt of Daniel's real meaning, so that one of the chief supports of Christianity seemed to be shaken. To vindicate the honour of Divine truth was now the object of Jerome, and if, he argued, to those who stand before the tribunal of a persecutor, there are promised a mouth and wisdom irresistible, equally may that promise be claimed by those who stand up against the blasphemer and the infidel.

Jerome's exposition of Daniel may be styled the last that has been written. He has left nothing to his successors but to comment upon his commentary. The work, moreover, is marked by a spirit of moderation and mildness which his friends would have rejoiced to see sustained throughout his writings.

The four beasts and metals were expounded by Jerome in the usual way. Some of his expressions have been treasured up with peculiar fondness, such as the description of Alexander under the figure of the pard, "Præceps fertur ad sanguinem, et saltu in mortem ruit." He is the first writer who notices the admixture of the clay with the strength of the Roman iron:—

"Ch. ii. Now the fourth kingdom, clearly that of the Romans, is of iron, which breaks in pieces and subdues all things. But its feet and toes are partly iron and partly earthenware, which at the present time is most distinctly verified. For as, in the beginning, nothing was stronger and harder than the Roman empire, so in the end of things nothing is weaker, since both in civil wars, and against foreign nations, we require the aid of other and barbarous people.

"But, in the end of all these kingdoms, the gold, the silver, the brass, and the iron, there is cut out a stone, the Lord and Saviour; without hands, that is, without human father, being born of a Virgin out of the course of nature. And, breaking in pieces all these kingdoms, it becomes a great mountain, and has filled the whole earth. But the Jews, together with the impious Porphyry, misapply this to the people of Israel, which will, they say, in the end of the world, become very strong, breaking up all other kingdoms, and reigning for ever."

From this commentary it will be sufficient to extract a few passages: —

" The fourth beast. I am not a little surprised, that after representing the other kingdoms by a lioness, a bear, and a pard, he should have likened the Roman to no individual beast. Unless, perhaps, to make it appear more formidable, he conceals its name; so that whatever we think fiercest in beasts, we should suppose to belong to the Romans. But the Jews imagine that what is here passed over in silence, is told in the Psalm : — The boar out of the wood has laid it waste, and the unique beast has devoured it. But the Hebrew has it thus : — All the beasts of the field have devoured it. For, in the single empire of the Romans, we recognise together all the other kingdoms, which in former times were separate."

The concluding statement is liable to an exception, for the Romans have never possessed the principal site of the Babylonish empire. Perhaps Jerome refers especially to the time of Antichrist, into whose kingdom the lion will enter as a constituent part.

" I considered the horns. Let me now repeat what all church writers have handed down. In the end of the world, when the kingdom of the Romans is to be destroyed, there will arise ten kings, who will divide among them the Roman world. And an eleventh will arise, a little king, who will conquer three of the ten, that is, the kings of Egypt, Africa, and Ethiopia, as I shall explain more fully in the sequel. These being killed, the other seven will also bow their necks to the victor.

" And behold, he says, in this horn were eyes like the eyes of a man. That we should not, like some persons, suppose that he will be either the Devil or a demon; but one from among men, in whom all Satan will dwell bodily. And a mouth speaking great things. For he is the man of sin, the son of perdition, who will presume to sit in the temple of God, making himself to be God."*

That a time signified a year was so well known, that even Porphyry did not think it open to cavil: —

"The time, times, and a half, Porphyry expounds as three years and a half, which I do not deny to be according to the idiom of holy Scripture. For we read above that seven times passed over Nebuchadnezzar, that is, the seven years of his dwelling with the beasts." (Cap. xii.)

The Jews, continuing to grow more Antichristian in their expositions, maintained that the "little help" was the assistance given them by the apostate Julian.† Porphyry, with more show of reason, applied it to the aid rendered by Matthias in the Maccabean war.

We now come to the most original part of

* The human eyes of the horn have been generally understood to signify the human nature of Antichrist. "He is not then a demon," says Jerome; "no," add some later writers, "nor a God, as he would have men believe." This passage in Daniel first fixes Antichrist's humanity; before, it was uncertain whether he might not be a tribe, a fallen spirit, or an empire.

† The Jews were not unreasonable in expecting the Romans to rebuild their temple. According to the Seventy, it was said by Isaiah (xlix. 17.) "Thou shalt soon be rebuilt by them that have destroyed thee." Barnabas, as we have seen, thought it needful to explain this passage in reference to the restoration of the spiritual Zion under the Romans.

The failure of Julian's attempt is thus accounted for by the heathen Ammianus: "Alypius and the governor of the province laboured at the work; but terrible balls of fire, bursting out near the foundations with frequent eruptions, repeatedly scorched the workmen, and prevented their approach to the place." Lib. xxiii. cap. 1.

Jerome's work, his defence of the transition from Antiochus to Antichrist:—

"Dan. xi. 21. And in his estate there shall stand up a vile person. Down to this point the historical order is preserved, and there is no difference of opinion between Porphyry and our own people. But all that follows, down to the end of the book, he applies personally to Antiochus Epiphanes, brother of Seleucus, and son of Antiochus the Great. For, after Seleucus, he reigned eleven years in Syria, and possessed Judea; also in his reign there occurred the persecution about the law of God, and the wars of the Maccabees. But our people consider all these things to be spoken of Antichrist, who is to come in the last time.

"And whereas they seem open to this objection,—Why does the prophecy pass over so many between Seleucus and the end of the world? they answer, That in the earlier part of the history, when the Persian kings are spoken of, four only are reckoned after Cyrus; for, passing over many between, it comes suddenly to Alexander, king of Macedon. Also, that it is the custom of Holy Scripture, not to detail every thing, but to explain what seems of most importance. Yet, since much that we shall afterwards read and expound agrees with Antiochus in person, they consider that he is a type of Antichrist, and that, what Antiochus has already done in part, Antichrist will completely fulfil.

"Also, that it is the custom of Holy Scripture, to anticipate in types the reality of things to come. For so is our Lord and Saviour spoken of in the 72nd Psalm, which is entitled a Psalm of Solomon: and yet all that is there said cannot be applied to Solomon. For Solomon did not endure for ever, as the sun, nor from generation to generation, as the moon. Nor did he possess dominion from sea to sea, and from the river to the end of the earth. No more can it be said that all nations served him, and that his name endured beyond the sun. And all tribes of the earth were not blessed in him, neither did all nations call him blessed.

"But in part, and as in a shadow and image of the truth, these things are foretold of Solomon, to be more perfectly fulfilled in our Lord and Saviour. As then, in Solomon and other saints, the Saviour has types of His coming, so Antichrist is believed to have for his type that wicked king Antiochus, who persecuted the saints and defiled the temple.

" Let me now pursue the course of the exposition, briefly noting down, according to each system, both what is said by our opponents, and what by our own people."

A happy state of unity in prophetic study: Christians think this, — infidels the other. But Jerome was not aware of (or perhaps at the moment forgot) two Christians who had followed Porphyry; Nisibenus, who wrote in Armenian, and Ephrem, whose exposition of Daniel is in Syriac.* Omitting these stragglers, the whole body of the Church agreed with Jerome. But first for the scheme of Porphyry: —

" Now Antiochus, sparing the youth, and pretending friendship, goes up to Memphis, and there, in the usual form, is invested with the government of Egypt. Then, professing to act as guardian for the youth, with a little people he subdues all Egypt, and enters into many and very rich cities. Thus he did what neither his fathers, nor his fathers' fathers, had done; for no king of Syria had so wasted Egypt, or scattered all their wealth: and none had been so crafty as by fraud to subvert the wise counsels of the generals of the youth.

" All that I have here abridged, Porphyry sets forth most elaborately, borrowing from Suctorius.† But our people interpret more correctly, that Antichrist will do these things in the end of the world; that he will arise from a little people, namely, the Jews; and that he will be so mean and vile, that royal honour will not be given him, but he will obtain the kingdom by stratagem and fraud: and the arms of the fighting one, that is, of the Roman people, will be overthrown by him, and will be broken.

* For an account of the followers of Porphyry, see the Appendix, Section I.

† A historian whose work is now lost.

"And this he will do, under pretence of being the leader of the covenant,—that is, of the law and the testament of God. And he will enter into the richest cities, and will do that which neither his fathers, nor his fathers' fathers have done; for no Jew besides Antichrist will have reigned over the whole world. And against the most steadfast thoughts of the saints he will take counsel, and will do all these things for a season, even as long as God's will shall suffer him."

Having professed to repeat what the Church had said before him, Jerome exceeds his promise, anticipating all that it has to say after him. "To this exposition," writes Malvenda, in 1604, "nothing has yet been added;" for, of the required fulfilment, the Church has been satisfied to receive an instalment at the hand of Antiochus — an earnest of what must be accomplished by history, when, in the end of the world, it shall hastily work up the arrears due to its inflexible taskmaster, Divine prophecy. For this is certain, that when the prediction and the history part company, it is not that the Divine forekowledge flags in the race, but that the prophecy, though content for a time to measure steps with history, suddenly expands the wings till then folded, and shoots forward to the end of time. It is not that the prophet did not see so far, but that he saw so much farther.

The difficulty usually felt in this prophecy may be thus stated: we are shown a picture representing, with an accuracy that defies criticism, the history of the Greeks from Alexander to Antiochus. Suddenly, and without warning, this picture grows faint, the likenesses vanish, the figures fade from the canvas; but, out of the dissolving shadows, there springs a new creation: in place of Epiphanes stalks Antichrist; and in the distance, seen through the glare and havoc of the great tribulation, are the deserted sepulchres and the eternal blessedness of the risen saints.

On examination, this turns out to be but one of a series of similar prophecies. Jerome's instance of Solomon is strictly in point: where, though the Psalmist professes to celebrate the son of Bathsheba, he has not gone far before the "greater than Solomon" stands revealed : for, to the glory of this hero, not even Solomon, with all his glory, can be said to have attained.

All nations, it is said, shall call him blessed. But how many of the nations heard even the name of Solomon? Plutarch, Strabo, and Tacitus, all writing about the Jews, knew nothing of him. Justin, who, for a Pagan, dived deeply into Hebrew history, so as to discover that Abraham and Israel were kings of Damascus, and that Moses was the father of Aaron— this laborious Justin had not heard of Solomon. And this, not because the Jewish monarch lived so long ago, — for they tell of Semiramis and Seostris, Belus and Memnon,—but because the acts and the glory of Solomon were preserved only in the records of his own subjects: they were written nowhere but in the chronicles of the kings of Israel.

To quote another instance. It was told Ahaz that a sign should be given him : a virgin should bear a son; and, before the child should be able to speak plainly, both Syria and Israel should lose their kings. The child's name was to be Emmanuel; the King of Assyria was to fill the breadth of his land. Yet who does not see that the child is two, and that the Virgin is not so much the prophetess as her antitype Mary? for none ventures to seek in the wife of Isaiah the fulfilment of the promise, The Lord himself shall give you a sign: nor can *her* child be truly named Emmanuel, which is, being interpreted, " God with us."

Jerome's commentary on Daniel gave less satisfaction than might have been supposed. For this he had to blame, not his work, but his own hasty temper, which had created him many enemies. Some censured him for not expressing an opinion about the seventy weeks; others, for speaking too plainly of the clay that had entered into the structure of the Iron empire. The truth of this exposition was self-evident; the only question was its safety. This objection he condescends to notice: " If, in expounding the feet and toes of the statue, I have explained the discordant iron and clay in reference to the Roman empire, which the Scripture describes as being at first strong and afterwards weak; let them lay that, not to my account, but the prophet's. For the truth of holy Scripture is not to be neglected in compliment to princes." *

Jerome wrote no commentary on the Apocalypse, apparently deterred by the difficulty of the millennium; for he was well aware that his own opinion was opposed to that of the primitive church. Of the book itself he says, that all praise is beneath it; also, that it contains as many mysteries as words. A few passages of his writings may be brought to bear upon its contents.

In his epistle to Dardanus, the breadth of the Holy

* Præfatio in Isaiæ cap. xxxvi.

Land is stated at "scarcely 160,000 paces from Dan to Beersheba." The Olympic furlong, measuring 600 feet, was estimated at 100 Greek paces: this brings the 160,000 paces to 1600 furlongs, Greek measure. This seems to be the principle on which some writers have estimated the Roman mile at ten, instead of eight Greek furlongs, so that 160 miles also may agree with the 1600 furlongs of St. John.*

By the spiritual Sodom and Egypt Jerome understands Jerusalem: "Read in the Apocalypse of John how the place in which the Lord was crucified is spiritually called Sodom and Egypt. If, then, Jerusalem, in which the Lord was crucified, is spiritually called Sodom and Egypt, &c."† Elsewhere he compares the Jews, when rejecting Christ, to those youths who mocked Elisha: but out of the Roman wood came two wild bears, Vespasian and Titus, and destroyed them. "From that time," he continues, "Jerusalem is not called the holy city; but, losing its holiness and its ancient name, is spiritually called Sodom and Egypt."‡

Rome, though Christian, he still calls Babylon. Referring to his residence in that city about 370, he writes: "When I dwelt in Babylon, and was an inhabitant of the purple-bearing harlot, and lived after the manner of the Quirites, I was desirous of attempting something upon the subject of the Holy Spirit,

---

* Mitford (History of Greece) makes it doubtful: "Twelve hundred Grecian stadia, at eight to the mile, would be 150 miles; at ten stadia, 120 miles." Vol. ii. p. 101., note. See Aulus Gellius, lib. i. c. 1.

† Comment. in Zephaniæ cap. ii.

‡ Epistle to Hebidia, question 8.

and of dedicating the work to the pontiff of that city. .... But the said Pontiff Damasus already sleeps in Christ." *

While applying to Rome the name and character of Babylon, Jerome does justice to her recent confession of the Trinitarian faith. He allows that she had thus wiped off the blasphemy written on her forehead: by which he means, not the title of Babylon, but, as he tells Algasia, the proud and rebellious name of eternal Rome. He goes so far as to invite Rome to fresh repentance, in the hope that she may yet escape the doom still hanging over her: "I will speak to thee, who, by the confession of Christ, hast wiped out the blasphemy written on thy forehead. ..... The curse with which the Saviour hath threatened thee in the Apocalypse, thou mayest escape by repentance; thou hast the example of the Ninevites." †

A. D. 400–410.

While the fourth century glories in its era of martyrs, the fifth must be content to boast its era of matrons;—a short period during which the treasures of sacred learning were shared, in almost equal proportion, between the sexes. Our present inquiry takes us among these honourable women, whose intimate acquaintance with Scripture proves that no jealousy of lay and female Bible-reading had as yet infected the Church.

* Preface to Didymus on the Holy Spirit.

† Adv. Joviniaum, lib. ii. in fine. In commenting upon Isaiah xlvi., he notices an opinion that the "daughter of Babylon" is Rome, the *Babylon junior* of the Apocalypse.

Of these learned ladies, Algasia and Hebidia lived in Gaul, Marcella in Rome, Paula and Eustochium at Bethlehem; others wandered from place to place, either flying from Gothic invaders, or drawn to Palestine as to the geographical centre of all that interests a Christian. But this little world revolved round a sun of its own: whatever subject was discussed, whether proposals of marriage, or corruptions of the Hebrew text; the education of a daughter, or the prospects of a trembling empire, — every difficulty was alike referred to the great man of his age, — at once the most irascible and the most humble, the dirtiest and the most sublime, — the presbyter Jerome.

For the purpose of studying Hebrew at headquarters, Jerome took up his residence at Bethlehem. The little village soon teemed with versions and commentaries, transcribers and grammarians; and, becoming the metropolis of sacred learning, was visited by scholars from all parts of the world. Jerome had many friends among the Italian matrons, and, before he had been long established, Paula and her daughter decided upon leaving Rome, and joining him at Bethlehem. Pleased with the change, they soon endeavoured to bring Marcella after them, hoping to tempt her by the peaceful seclusion of the country, contrasted with the dissipation of a life in Rome. "We are there," they complain, "either receiving visitors, and so there is an end of privacy; or, we see nobody, and are accused of being proud. Sometimes, in the course of returning visits, we approach lofty doors, and have to cross gilded thresholds, amidst the insolent remarks of servants." Remarks probably provoked by their reduced style of dress and equipage, a species of self-mortification which they carried to an extreme. "Once," says Jerome, "silk was too coarse for them: now they sweep the floor, and light their own fire."

"But here, in the village of Christ, all is simplicity: the silence is broken only by psalms. Turn where you will, the husbandman, as he follows the plough, sings Hallelujah; the weary reaper refreshes himself with a psalm; while the vine-dresser, as with crooked sickle he lops the shoots, sings something from David. . . . I think this place is more holy than the Tarpeian rock, which, being repeatedly blasted by the bolts of heaven, is shown to be displeasing to the Lord."*

To induce Marcella to follow them, the authors of this famous epistle left no argument untried; and with reason, for Marcella's company, as they knew by long experience, was well worth having. When Jerome, little more than a boy, had been sent to Rome to study, it was at her house that he had found assistance and advice; though it was with difficulty that he, a poor country youth, could be persuaded to join the illustrious society of Marcella, whose refusal of the Consul Cerealis had thrown a crowd of suitors into despair. Her advancing years now qualified her to advise young persons of either sex: moreover by the habit of noting down scriptural difficulties in the hope of an opportunity of propounding them, she had attained to an unusual knowledge of the Bible. This useful life in Rome she had no wish to exchange for a state of dreamy contemplation in the East; nor, indeed, was she con-

---

* Ep. Paulæ et Eustochii ad Marcellam, inter opera Hieronymi, ep. 44. ed. Bened.

vinced of the intrinsic holiness of the land of Judea. Her reply was drawn from the Apocalypse:—

" The great city in which the Lord was crucified is none other than Jerusalem.
" But where the Lord was crucified is spiritually called Sodom and Egypt.
" Therefore Jerusalem is the Sodom and Egypt in which the Lord was crucified." *

Against this attack the temper of her Bethlehem friends was scarcely proof. Their elaborate answer contains this argument:— Scripture cannot contradict itself; Jerusalem has just before been called the holy city; therefore it cannot here in the same sense be called Sodom and Egypt. In short, Jerusalem, when styled Sodom, must be a figure of something else, doubtless the world.

This argument may be refuted from St. Matthew, who twice calls Jerusalem the holy city, while our Lord styles it the slayer of the prophets, and its people an adulterous generation. It is remarked by Paula and Eustochium that Jerusalem is never called Egypt elsewhere throughout the Bible†; a fact not to be ascertained without much labour, when Bibles were in manuscript, and concordances unknown. Jerome appears to have had no hand in the composition of this letter; first, because he wrote another on the same occasion ‡; and, secondly,

---

* Repeated in the same epistle.
† For the Old Testament passages connected with Apoc. xi. 8., see the beginning of the next chapter.
‡ Ep. 45. ad Marcellam. In this letter he fully confirms his friends' account of Roman idleness: " The second hour of reading finds us yawning; then we rub our faces and have had enough,

because in two places, already quoted, he calls Jerusalem Sodom and Egypt.

After abundantly displaying their learning, the Bethlehem ladies fall back upon the great argument which they have been keeping in reserve — Read in the Apocalypse about Babylon.

Marcella, living in Rome, had not been altogether prudent in quoting the Apocalypse against Jerusalem; for in her time the title of Babylon was still applied to Rome, in its Christian as well as in its Pagan state. Her friends therefore now retort upon her: —

"Read the Apocalypse of John, and see what is there prophesied about the woman in purple, and the blasphemy on her forehead, the seven hills, and the many waters, and the destruction of Babylon. 'Come out of her, my people,' says the Lord, 'that ye be not partakers of her sins, nor receive of her plagues.' And then turn back to Jeremiah, and see what is there written: 'Flee out of the midst of Babylon, and deliver every man his soul,' &c.

"There is in her, indeed, a holy Church: there are trophies of the Apostles and the martyrs: there is the true confession of Christ: there is the faith preached by an Apostle: and in her, upon the ruins of Gentilism, does the Christian name exalt itself day by day: — but the very ambition, power, and greatness of the city, the seeing and the being seen, the salutations, the compliments, and the slander, both the talking and the listening, and the meeting, though unwillingly, so great a crowd of persons, — all this is opposed to quiet, and to the intention of a monastic life."

Marcella still remained immovable, perhaps thinking that the time for fleeing out of Babylon had not yet come. In vain her friends expressed a hope some

and after such severe labour must return to the things of the world. I say nothing about the dinners."

day to receive the message, " Marcella is come to Palestine:" in vain they hoped to visit, hand in hand with her, the Manger and the Sepulchre, and thence, making their way to the Mount of Olives, in heart and soul to ascend with their ascending Lord. Marcella, deaf to the voice of these charmers, continued in Rome till the day of her death. But though, as will presently be seen, her resolution cost her her life, the prophetic belief of that age was too well established to allow of any false inference from its eventful history.

A.D. 391.

In her letters to Jerome, Marcella put questions more easily asked than answered. It is appointed unto men, she observed, once to die; and that so rigidly, that not only must Christ die, but even Enoch and Elias, though once translated, must also die as the two Witnesses. But how can those be said to die who are to be caught up to meet the Lord in the air? Jerome, in his reply, makes very little of the subject; but cautions her, for he was then young, and an admirer of Origen, against taking the Apocalypse too literally.

At some later time he maintained the second coming of Elias, as while expounding Matth. xi.:—

" If ye choose to receive it, this is Elias. Now, that this is mystical and requires discernment, is shown by the Lord's subsequent words: ' He that hath ears to hear, let him hear.' For if the sense were plain, and the meaning free from obscurity, what need to prepare us for the understanding of it? John, therefore, is called Elias, not in the sense of the foolish philosophers, and of some heretics, who introduce a metempsychosis, but because, according to another passage of the Gospel, he came in the spirit and power of Elias. . . . . Some think that John is called Elias because, as in the Saviour's second Advent, according to Malachi, Elias is to go before and to announce the coming Judge, so did John announce the first Advent. Thus each becomes a herald,—the one of the first, the other of the second Advent of the Lord.

"Ch. xvii.: Elias is come already: He who at the Saviour's second Advent is to appear in bodily reality, has now in power and in spirit come by John."

A.D. 407.

In this year Jerome was gratified by the receipt of a letter from Gaul, containing eleven questions on Scriptural difficulties. The writer was Algasia, a lady not personally known to him, but so deeply impressed with the report of his learning, that she also, like the rest, must needs know what "St. Hierome saith." Her questions had but one fault: they were entirely on New Testament subjects; which looked, said Jerome, as if she did not sufficiently study the Old Testament, or perceive its exceeding difficulty. Perhaps some questions on the prophets would have done more credit to his knowledge of Hebrew. Still, as the letter passed by Rome on its way to Bethlehem, he was flattered by the compliment, and compared his correspondent to the Queen of Sheba, who came from the end of the earth to hear the wisdom of Solomon. Not that I am Solomon, he modestly adds: "Non quidem ego Solomon."

The fourth and eleventh questions were about prophecy:—

"Question 4. What means the declaration, 'Woe to them that are with child,' &c.?

"Answer. In those days. In what days? When the

abomination of desolation shall stand in the holy place. That this is spoken literally of the coming of Antichrist, nobody doubts; for then the severity of the persecution will compel men to take flight, and they that are with child, and nursing infants, will hinder escape. Some, however, suppose that this refers to the war of Titus and Vespasian against the Jews, and especially to the siege of Jerusalem." *

Algasia's eleventh question concerned the letting power. In his answer, Jerome takes the falling away to be the political dissolution of the Roman world, and prefers understanding by the temple of God, the Church in general: —

"Unless, he says, the Roman empire shall be first destroyed, and Antichrist precede, Christ will not come; since He comes for the special purpose of destroying Antichrist. 'Remember ye not,' he says, 'that when I was with you, I told you by word of mouth these very things which I now write to you by letter — and that I said to you that Christ will not come unless Antichrist come first? And now ye know what withholdeth, that he should be revealed in his time; that is, you know perfectly what prevents Antichrist from coming at the present time. He does not choose to say openly that the Roman empire is to be destroyed, because its rulers think it eternal †: wherefore, according to the Apocalypse of John, there is written on the forehead of the purple-bearing harlot a name of blasphemy, Eternal Rome. For, had he said openly and boldly, Antichrist will not come, unless the Roman empire be first destroyed, this might have seemed to furnish just cause for persecuting the Church, then in its infancy.

"It follows, For the mystery of iniquity doth already work, &c.; and the meaning is this: By the many evils and crimes with which Nero, most impure of Cæsars, oppresses the world, the coming of Antichrist is prepared; and that which Antichrist will do afterwards, is in part fulfilled in

---

* Quæstiones ad Algasiam.

† According to the promise which Virgil puts into the mouth of Jove: "Imperium sine fine dedi."

Nero. Only let the Roman Empire, which now restrains all nations, depart and be out of the midst, and then Antichrist will come; a fountain of iniquity, whom the Lord Jesus will slay with the spirit of His mouth; that is, by divine power, and by the empire of His majesty, with whom to command is to ensure performance. And that, not by the multitude of an army, not by the strength of soldiery, no, nor by the help of angels — but instantly, as He appears, Antichrist will be slain; and as the shadows flee at the rising of the sun, so, by the brightness of His coming, will the Lord destroy and blot him out.

"For his works are the works of Satan; and as in Christ there dwelt bodily the fulness of the Godhead, so also there will be in Antichrist all powers, and signs, and wonders, but all lying. For, as the magicians, by their lies, resisted God's miracles which He wrought by Moses, and Moses's rod swallowed up their rods, so will the Truth of Christ swallow up the lie of Antichrist.

But his falsehood will deceive those who have been already prepared for destruction.

"And since there might arise a question, not indeed expressed in words, why does God suffer him to have all power and signs, and wonders, so as to deceive, if it were possible, even God's elect? — the question is forestalled by an answer, and the objection met before propounded. He will do all these things, it says, not by his own power, but by God's permission, on account of the Jews; because they refused to receive the love of the truth, that is, the Spirit of God through Christ: since the love of God is shed abroad in the hearts of them that believe in Him.

"He says also of Himself, I am the Truth; and it is written of Him in the Psalm, Truth has sprung out of the earth. To those, then, who received not the love and the truth, that by receiving a Saviour they might be saved, — to them God will send, not the worker, but the working itself, that is, a fountain of error, that they may believe a lie: for he is a liar, and his father. For, if Antichrist had been born of a virgin, and had come first into the world, the Jews might have an excuse, saying, that they took *him* for the truth, and therefore received a lie instead of the truth; but now they are to be judged, yea doubtless, to be condemned, because, having despised the truth of Christ, they will afterwards receive a lie, — that is, Antichrist."

A. D. 409.

The events of this period are closely connected with the history of prophetic interpretation. At this point the old and new worlds touch; the flood of Goths may be compared to a deluge, by which the old iron race was swept away, to be succeeded by another, part of iron and part of clay. The students of prophecy were not slow to mark the signs of their time.

In 409 Rome suffered a fresh invasion. At that inauspicious moment the young widow Ageruchia was discussing with Jerome the project of a second marriage. So great was the confusion, that the empire itself seemed to have fallen; for the Romans, stripped of their wealth and abandoning all thought of fighting, were glad to ransom their lives with the furniture of their houses.

In his letter to Ageruchia, Jerome draws a picture of her proposed wedding: the bridesmaids, if any, in tears; the Fescennines performed on the hoarse trumpet that calls to arms. Her husband, is he to fight, or to run away? a pointed question to a Roman matron. "But what am I doing?" he asks; "the ship is wrecked, and I am disputing about the fare. He who withheld is now taken out of the midst, and we do not perceive that Antichrist is at hand, whom the Lord Jesus will consume with the spirit of His mouth. Woe unto them that are with child, and to them that give suck, in those days."*

But Jerome was in too great haste with his favourite text:—"Væ prægnantibus et nutrientibus:" the empire still remained unbroken, and the younger Theodosius soon proceeded to remodel the laws of the civilised world by the publication of that code which bears his name.

The invaders, in search of plunder, entered the house of Marcella. But her treasure was laid up where the Goths could not find it: her worldly wealth had long been exhausted in charity, so that their hopes were mocked by empty coffers and a dismantled house. After beating her in the hope of extorting money, they prepared to separate her from her god-daughter Principia; but, moved by her sudden distress, they so far relented as to drag both the ladies to the asylum of a church: there Marcella, after offering up her thanksgivings, died of the injuries which she had received.

For two years Jerome was inconsolable: at length he summoned resolution to comply with the request of her god-daughter, that he would attempt to record her worth. To Principia, therefore, is dedicated the tract in which this history is preserved,—" Marcella's Epitaph."

A. D. 410–420.

The scene now changes to Africa. To the golden age of theological learning suddenly succeeds a state of deep ignorance and frantic superstition. The study of prophecy suffers in proportion; the most puerile

---

* Hieronymi Epist. 91. ad Ageruchiam.

mistakes, the shallowest conceits, incessantly demand from Augustine refutation or reproof. In the Getæ and Massagetæ some persons thought to have discovered the Gog and Magog of the Apocalypse; a supposition which, on the plan of a spiritual millennium, invested those northern invaders with preternatural terror: for now, it seemed, Satan was about to be loosed out of his prison.* Others called the man of sin *Antechrist*, as coming *before* Christ. It is not so spelt, it is not so pronounced, explains Augustine; but *Antichrist*, that is, contrary to Christ.†

The Donatists exceeded all bounds in the extravagance of their interpretations. From the proclamation uttered under the fifth seal they gathered that, to hasten the blessedness of the martyrs under the altar, there was needed a continual succession of fresh sufferers. To support this standing army of martyrs, the Donatists practised suicide, throwing themselves from precipices, or even rushing into fire and water. Augustine tells them that there will be martyrs enough under Antichrist, even though there should be none till then; at the same time reminding them who it was that influenced that boy in the Gospel, casting him ofttimes into the fire and into the water to destroy him. Also who it was that sent the swine down the steep place; and who bid the Saviour cast Himself from the pinnacle of the temple.‡ The last argument was followed up by Chrysologus a few years later: " Cast thyself down. He delights in falls, he

---

* To the " Getæ and Massagetæ " succeeded " Gothi and Mauri," noticed by Prosper. B. P. M. t. viii. p. 48.

† In Epist. Johan., tract iii.

‡ Aug. contra Gaudentium, lib. i. cap. 27.

enjoins headlong ruin; and by such advice he makes martyrs throughout Africa, suggesting noiselessly,—If thou wilt be a martyr, cast thyself down."*

By the labours of Augustine many of these Donatists were restored to the Church, and among them Tychonius, author of a commentary on the Apocalypse. By this means there was introduced among churchmen a new and fanciful set of interpretations: for the Donatists seem to have mysticised whatever they thought unlikely to be fulfilled literally. They show little or no respect to primitive tradition: for Tychonius revives the Jewish theory rejected by Justin, that a *time* may signify a century. To these he adds some conceits altogether new, such as the making the "hour, and day, and month, and year," to be three years and a half.† By such methods he attempts to fix even the time of the end: "A day sometimes means a hundred years, as it is written of the Church, They shall lie in the city where their Lord was crucified, for three days and a half."‡

Of the many novelties introduced by Tychonius, one at least still holds its ground: for the reclaimed Donatist is author presumptive of the theory, that a day in some parts of prophecy means a year. In the three and a half days of the witnesses' death, he professes to find the three and a half years of Antichrist's reign. For this bold and novel deviation

---

* Chrysologus, Sermo 13.

† This accommodating method pervades the Donatists' entire system. They attempted to prove that the true Church lay in Africa, because the bridegroom "maketh his flock to rest at noon," that is, in the South. Augustine, Sermo 138. adv. Donatistas.

‡ Tychonius, de septem regulis, regula v. Galland's Fathers, vol. viii.

from the universal custom of Scripture he attempts an excuse:—

"How can the inhabitants of the earth rejoice over the death of two men, if they die in one city? Or how send gifts to each other, if, in three days' time, they that rejoice over the death will be grieved by the resurrection? Or what sort of feasting or pleasure can there be, while in the streets there are human bodies infecting the banquet with the effluvium of a three days' putrefaction? From which may the Lord vouchsafe to deliver us! Amen."*

Tychonius seems to have forgotten the case of those Parthians, Medes, and Elamites, who heard the Apostles speaking with tongues, not on the third day, but before the third hour of the day, of the Pentecostal effusion. The present case is similar: for St. John does not say that *all*, but *some* † of the nations and tribes shall see the dead bodies of the witnesses. The news also might travel far before that of their resurrection overtook it; and though on the fourth day the great earthquake must end the world's rejoicing, the rapidity of modern communication destroys the force of this objection to the literal sense. Before long, if we may judge by the progress of practical science, the objection itself will be treasured up as a reminiscence of another and more tardy age. As for the corruption of the bodies, it is not probable that those whom God will so soon miraculously raise up should be suffered to see corruption.

Excepting the three years and a half of Antichrist, Tychonius unsettles almost every thing that had been fixed by inspired interpretation. With him

* Tychonii Homiliæ, inter Op. Augustini.
† For the meaning of the Greek, let us consult a Greek. Says Aretas: "Of the tribes:—the Jews out of every tribe, who will be deceived by Antichrist."

Babylon is no longer Rome, but the world: there is no millennium beyond the present state; and even the blessedness of God's wiping away all tears from men's eyes is applied to the present life of a Christian. This idea, calculated to undermine the believer's hope of the future, was too mischievous to pass without censure: Augustine charges it with "excessive impudence."*

In this general darkness a ray of light falls upon the historian's path. Some anonymous bishop, while lecturing to his catechumens, has occasion to expound the twelfth chapter of the Apocalypse: "that the Dragon is the Devil," he remarks, "not one of you is ignorant." It may be hoped that these young Africans deserved the compliment; for here even Tychonius follows Scripture. This bishop, till lately supposed to be Augustine himself, interprets the sun-clothed woman as the Church, seen under the figure of the Virgin Mary.† But Augustine takes her to be that Sion of whom glorious things are spoken, seen as the mother of Christ: "clothed with the light of Him with whose flesh she travails."‡

While all around were bent upon innovation, Augustine was not able entirely to resist the stream. Sometimes he makes Babylon to be but a figure of the world, though in three places he interprets it as Rome, "the Western Babylon, during whose rule

---

* De Civit. Dei, xx. 17. "Impudentiæ nimiæ mihi videtur."

† Sermo alius, de Symbolo, ad Catechumenos, inter Op. Augustini. The idea of connecting the Virgin Mary with the sun-clothed woman may be traced to Epiphanius. Noticing the uncertainty of her later history, he remarks, that for anything known to the contrary, she may be that woman flying to the wilderness. Lib. iii. t. ii. c xi.

‡ Exposition of Psalm cxlii.

Christ was to come."* He was also unsettled in the matter of the ten kings, doubting whether that precise number would be found at once in the Roman world:—" I confess my fear that perhaps we are mistaken in the matter of those ten Kings, which, as it seems, Antichrist will find as ten actual men, and that so he may come unexpectedly, when there are not so many kings in the Roman world. For what if the number ten should mean simply the whole body of kings existing before his appearance?"†

Augustine, though in doubt, prefers the primitive explanation of the letting powers. He divides persecutions into three classes: Pagan, heretical and antichristian: " The first was marked by violence; for, by proscriptions, tortures, and massacres, Christians were forced to sacrifice. The second is fraudulent, now carried on by heretics and by false brethren. The third is future, under Antichrist: this will be the most dangerous of all, being at once both violent and crafty. He will possess power by his empire, craft by his miracles." ‡ The four empires, the times of Antichrist, and the infidel character of the apostacy, are explained in the usual manner.

The bishop, when he entered upon office, was a millenarian. " The eighth day," he remarks, " signifies the new life in the end of the world: the seventh, the future rest of the saints upon this earth. For on the earth, as the Scripture says, the Lord will reign with His saints, and will here preserve the Church so that no evil one shall enter it."§ But

---

* De Civit. Dei, lib. xviii. cap. 2. 22. and 27.
† Lib. xx. cap. 23.
‡ Comment. on Psalm ix. v. 27. § Sermo 259.

this doctrine he afterwards thought fit to abandon:—

"Apoc. xx. A thousand years. They who from these words infer that the first resurrection will be corporeal, are, among other things, chiefly influenced by the number of the thousand years; as if it were necessary that there should be, in holy things, a Sabbatism of that length. That is, a holy vacation after the labours of the 6000 years, dating from the time when man was created, and, on account of that great transgression, banished from the bliss of paradise to the toils of this mortal state.

"That, as it is written, One day is with the Lord as a thousand years, and a thousand years as one day, so when the six thousand years have been fulfilled, to correspond to the six days, there should succeed, as it were, a seventh day of sabbath in the last thousand years, to celebrate which sabbath the saints will arise. Now this opinion would be in a certain degree tolerable, if they would allow, in that sabbath, some spiritual delights procured to the saints by the presence of the Lord. For I myself was once of the same opinion. But, when they describe those who have risen, as doing nothing but pass their time in most immoderate carnal banquets, in which the quantity of food and drink will exceed, not only all decency, but even all power of belief, they will find none but carnal persons to believe them."*

Augustine must be allowed to speak for himself in support of his new scheme. The following passage embodies the opinion current in the Church during the next twelve centuries:—

"Our Lord Jesus Christ says Himself, No man can enter into the strong man's house and spoil his goods, except he first bind the strong man. By the strong man He means the Devil, who had succeeded in holding captive the human race; and by the goods of which Christ was about to spoil him, those who were to believe in Christ, and whom Satan then detained in various sins and states of guilt.

* Civitas Dei, lib. xx. c. 7.

"And because this strong one was then bound, the Apostle sees in the Apocalypse an angel coming down from heaven, having the key of the bottomless pit, and a chain in his hand. And he laid hold of the Dragon, that old Serpent, called the Devil and Satan, and bound him a thousand years; that is, he restrained and curtailed his power to deceive and to possess those who were to be set free."

The thousand years are next explained as a round number, put for the undetermined time between the first and second Advents. On this principle Antichrist is made to come at the end of the millennium; but the millennium, according to St. John, begins with the resurrection of those who have resisted Antichrist, — who have not worshipped the beast and his image. Augustine confesses the difficulty. "It is," he says, "a subject for diligent inquiry what that beast can mean." He is reduced to explain it as Satan's empire generally, perhaps meaning that form of the scarlet beast which "was and is not," before the time of St. John. There still remains the difficulty of worshipping the image of the beast, an image not made till after its deadly wound is healed in the time of Antichrist.

A. D. 419.

In this year Augustine was drawn into correspondence with a certain bishop named Hesychius, a diligent student of prophecy, though gifted with more zeal than judgment. From an anxious examination of the signs of the times, Hesychius thought himself justified in announcing the near approach of Christ's second coming. Not content with hoping and wishing, he set about proving; and with the help of a bad translation of Daniel, and some verbal criticisms of an ingenious character, he soon worked himself into a high state of confidence and excitement. At length he fancied himself in a condition to attack Augustine upon the subject; but, while he marshalled his forces and counted his ten thousand, he forgot that his adversary might be able to oppose him with twenty thousand.

Because the seventy sevens were not completely fulfilled in the first coming, Hesychius would refer them altogether to the second. This would bring the advent to the year 490: but the days are to be shortened for the elect's sake, therefore Christ may be expected at any time between 419 and 490.

This plan of reckoning the weeks had been invented by Judas in the third century, supported by Apollinarius in the fourth, and was now revived by Hesychius in the fifth. It had been resolutely opposed by the mass of the Church, as destructive of a principal argument against the Jews. A dangerous opinion, said Jerome; rash, adds Augustine, and contrary to all that is said of the Messiah being cut off. But neither Jerome nor Augustine professed to understand the single week, nor to be satisfied with any known method of disposing of it.

The difficulty was but newly felt. The primitive writers separated the seventieth week from the sixty-ninth, placing in the interval the whole history of the Prince of the coming Romans, and the course of the first desolation. Irenæus and Hippolytus would probably have been able to satisfy the doubts of the later expositors.

The first letter of Hesychius is lost. In answer, Augustine enclosed part of Jerome's commentary, as the best that had been written on Daniel. In that work Jerome gave no opinion of his own, except to condemn the scheme now revived by Hesychius.

Augustine continues : —

"That passage of Daniel about the weeks I understand as referring to the past. For concerning the Saviour's coming, expected in the end, I dare not calculate the times; nor do I suppose that any prophet has laid down in this matter the number of the years. But the case, I take it, stands as the Lord Himself put it, — No man can know the times, which the Father hath put in his own power. But what He says in another place, — Of that day and hour knoweth no man; — some take to mean, that though no man can know the exact day and hour, yet they may be able to calculate the times.

"Now I need not say that it is the custom of the Scriptures to put *day* and *hour* for *time;* for, without doubt, this is most clearly said of our not knowing the times. For, when the Lord was asked that question by His disciples, He answered, — No one can know the times, which the Father hath placed in His own power. He does not say the day or the hour, but the times, a word not commonly used of a short time like a day or an hour; especially if we consider the expression in the Greek, from which language that book was translated into our own. But this cannot well be expressed in Latin, for the Greek has times or seasons, both which words we render alike by *tempora.*"*

Hesychius mistook the modesty of his correspondent for ignorance or indifference. In reply he made some smart allusions to that wicked servant who said in his heart, My Lord delayeth His coming, and whose Lord nevertheless did come, at an hour when least expected. Nor did he forget the case of those hypocrites who could discern the face of the sky, but not the signs of the times. Finally, after complaining of Jerome's indecision, and summing up the signs

* Augustine, Ep. 197. Ad Hesychium.

which appeared to him already fulfilled, he returns to his original position: —

"*I* believe what the Lord said: Heaven and earth shall pass away, but one iota or one apex shall not pass from the law until all things be fulfilled. How then the mystery of the weeks could be fulfilled down to the birth and passion of Christ, I wonder; for, in the midst of the week, says the prophet, shall my sacrifice be taken away, and the supplication; a destruction of desolations, and an abomination for a sacrifice. But if this abomination had been already fulfilled, why does the Lord say, — When ye shall see the abomination of desolation, spoken of by Daniel the prophet?"*

Augustine, now better acquainted with the character of his correspondent, bestirs himself in reply. And first he repels the insinuation so unjustly thrown out: —

"The Apostles themselves were told by the Lord, — It is not yours to know the times. They knew therefore no more than we know, (I speak for myself and my companions in ignorance). And yet those very persons to whom it was not given to know the times, they loved His appearing. *They* gave to their fellow-servants meat in due season; *they* neither smote, nor lorded it over any; nor did they riot with the lovers of this world, saying, My Lord delayeth his coming.

"Therefore, not to know the times is one thing; to live negligently and in the love of sin, is another. When Paul said also, be not disturbed in mind, nor terrified, as if the day of the Lord were at hand, he certainly did not wish them to believe that the Lord's coming was to follow immediately, nor yet to say with that servant, My Lord delayeth His coming."†

Augustine professed to have no expectation of improving upon the Apostles: where they knew nothing, he was content to remain in ignorance.

* Ep. Hesychii; numbered 198 of Augustine.
† Ep. 199, de Fine Sæculi.

Answering in detail his correspondent's arguments, he comes to the basis of the scheme, which, among other absurdities, involves a contradiction between Christ and Daniel. For the prophecy of the weeks professes to be exact to half a year; but, if the time be afterwards cut short for the elect's sake, Daniel's calculation is contradicted and annulled: —

"Moreover, what you quote from Daniel about the beast being slain, and about the kingdom of the other beasts, and in the midst of this the Son of man coming with the clouds of heaven; — this, you say, is clear to those that understand the Scriptures. But had you condescended to explain what this has to do with our knowing the chronology of the Saviour's coming, so that its date may be calculated beyond a doubt, I also would confess with deep gratitude, that the Lord's saying, It is not *yours* to know the times, refers to the Apostles only, and not to those better informed persons that were to come after them."

To repeat a fourth part of what Augustine urged on the occasion would exceed all reasonable limits. Enough to say that he exhausted the subject, as far as concerns the power of fixing the time of the end. For this knowledge is divinely represented as unattainable until the beginning of the great tribulation, when the redemption may be certainly pronounced to be very near. Hesychius wisely attempted no reply; nor, until the last fifteen years, has his scheme again been heard of.

The story is not yet ended. It still has to be told, that Africa, now degraded and trampled on, once produced the man that wrote these words: —

"He who gives out that the Lord will come very soon, speaks pleasantly, but may be mistaken dangerously. I wish that his saying may come true, for, if false, it will prove mischievous. But he who says that the Lord will be longer in coming, and yet believes in, hopes for, and loves His appearing, such a one, if mistaken in the nearness, is mistaken on the right side. If it be as he says, greater patience will be his lot; if otherwise, greater joy. Those, therefore, that love the Lord's appearing, while they listen to the one with more pleasure, trust to the other with more safety. But he who confesses himself unable to decide between them, longs for the one and submits to the other; in neither case mistaken, having declared for neither opinion. And, for being of this number, I pray you, despise me not."*

A. D. circ. 420.

The division of power among so many sovereigns was noticed by Sulpitius as a fulfilment of the predicted mixture of iron and clay; but none yet thought of seeking in history the ten toes or the ten horns. Sulpitius paraphrases the dream of Nebuchadnezzar by the aid of passing events: —

"The legs of iron are understood to be the fourth empire, that is, the Roman, stronger than all former kingdoms. By the feet, part of iron and part of clay, it is shown that the Roman empire is to be divided, so as never to unite again. This also has been fulfilled; for now the Roman constitution is administered by several emperors, always at issue among themselves by war or intrigue.

"Lastly, by the mixture of iron and clay, things never able to amalgamate together, there is represented a mixture of the human race, unaccompanied by real union. And in this way we now see the Roman soil occupied by foreign nations; some obtaining possession by open rebellion, others by treaty, under pretext of peace. So also in our armies, our cities, and our provinces, we see an admixture of barbarous nations, especially Jews, who live among us, but without conforming to our customs. Now these times the prophets declare to be the last.

"Also, in the stone cut out without hands, which broke in

---

* End of Augustine's Epistle.

pieces the gold, the silver, the iron, and the clay, there is seen a figure of Christ, who was produced by no human operation, being born, not of the will of man, but of God. And He will bring to nothing this world, in which are the kingdoms of earth, setting up another kingdom incorruptible and eternal, that is, the future age, prepared for the saints. But about this kingdom some people still doubt, it being their maxim not to believe in the future, although convinced about the past."*

The confusion prevailing in the West brought about a partial expectation of Nero's return. This idea, once taken up by the extravagant Martin†, was soon communicated to Sulpitius, to whom its marvellous character was recommendation enough. Augustine could see in it nothing so marvellous as the presumption of those that started it.‡

A. D. 430.

A salve was now to be applied to the wounded dignity of the Eastern empire. Daniel had indeed spoken of clay to be introduced into the fourth kingdom, but he had never said that the iron would altogether disappear. Theodoret, therefore, now reminded the world, that down to the end of this empire, there was to be iron as well as clay. With this understanding the Byzantine Cæsars might monopolise the whole honour of the iron, leaving the baseness and the brittleness of the clay to Eugenius or Augustulus in the West.

The acute Theodoret first detected a danger al-

---

* S. Severi Sacræ Historiæ, lib. ii. c. 4. The concluding sentence appears to favour the millennium.
† Severi Dialogni, lib. ii. c. 16.
‡ Civit. Dei, xx. 19.

ready menacing the Christian interpretation. The course of time might throw doubts upon the propriety of classing together, as a single kingdom, the Roman empires of Italy and Byzantium. Although one in succession and in name, they might seem so widely different in character as to excite a doubt whether prophecy could possibly include in one empire elements so discordant. But for this difficulty, the Byzantine Hooker, if such a title may be allowed him, is well prepared: —

"Thou sawest the feet and toes, part of iron and part of clay. He describes this part as distinct, not in race, but in quality of power: for, had he meant another kingdom, distinct in race, he would have numbered it fifth, as he had called the others third and fourth. But, foreseeing that the end of the iron kingdom would be weak, he reckons it distinct as to weakness, and with excellent reason. For he had described it above as very strong, and such at first it was.

"Yet he does not say that its end will be altogether weak, for there will be in it of the root of the iron, and the toes are part of iron and part of clay. Now this needs no interpretation of mine, for the prophet himself expounds it, saying, Part of the kingdom shall be strong, and part broken. To this he adds, Because thou sawest the iron mixed with the miry clay, they shall mingle themselves with the seed of men; which shows especially that this is no new kingdom distinct from the iron, but the same grown weaker."*

The cautious Greek next perceives an omission in the usual explanation of the miraculous stone, which Justin and the rest had been satisfied to apply to the first Advent only, not carrying out the exposition to the destruction of the earthly kingdoms.

* Theodoret on Daniel, in locum.

This subject brings Theodoret once more into contact with the politicians: —

"That heavenly kingdom shall stand for ever. And if any one kicks at this, and will not have it to be so, let him show me something human that is eternal, or some kingdom of man's that shall not come to an end. . . . . And if they say that the Lord's first coming is here intended, let them show in what sense the Roman empire was destroyed as soon as He appeared. For it happened altogether otherwise; since the empire was not destroyed, but consolidated, at the moment of the Saviour's birth.

"For the Lord was born in the reign of Augustus, who ruled second, and subjugated, so to speak, all men : since, as the Gospel tells us, he enrolled the whole world, and caused it to be taxed. Under him, therefore, the Roman empire was established, and it has subsisted down to the present time. If then the Lord's *first* coming did not destroy the Roman empire, we are forced to expound the passage in reference to the second. For the stone, before cut out without hands, and grown into a great mountain, filling the whole earth, this stone shall in the second Advent smite the image upon its feet of clay. That is, He will appear in the end of the iron empire, already grown weak, and, destroying all empires, will consign them to oblivion, preparing, for those that are worthy, His eternal kingdom."

A. D. circ. 440.

In this way Theodoret leaves a gap of some centuries between the first production of the stone and its finally smiting the image. Eudoxius now proposes to fill that gap by inserting a spiritual fulfilment, a gradual triumph of the Gospel, preparatory to the more literal destruction of earthly power in the coming times. And, as the stone first smote the *feet* of the image, even so, remarks Eudoxius, did the Gospel first invade the empire of the *Romans:* then, spreading to the Greek kingdoms of Egypt and Macedon, it travelled over Persia and Babylon, and from all these it is destined to travel to the ends of the earth.* For the Gospel must be preached to all nations, and then shall the end come.

Before taking a final leave of the four empires, let us cast a backward glance at their history, noting how the world, in its own reckoning of its masters, has unconsciously followed the prophet.

First, beneath the walls of Jerusalem they proclaim the title " The great King, the King of Assyria." The next who claims the title of the great king is he who from Shushan sends out his posts to India and Ethiopia. And that his is no empty assumption, we may learn from those demagogues who are labouring with superfluous diligence to inflate the Athenian pride: for he whom they think it distinction enough to style "the king," is ruler, neither of Sparta nor of Macedon, but of the distant Persia.

Once more, the tide of nations ebbs and flows. Upon the shifting sand the sword of the conqueror writes, though in short-lived characters, a new name. At once all the world has become Greek: the Old Testament, if it is to be any longer understood, must be turned into Greek; and Moses, who once refused to be called the son of Pharoah's daughter, is now made known to the world through the fostering care of Egypt's Grecian king.

But beneath the shadow of this empire there springs up another, yet wider and more lasting. Already Cicero talks slightingly of the " Græculi:" already

* Greek Chain on Daniel; Mai, Vet. Script., t. i. p. i. 175.

Cæsar gathers laurels from the utmost Isle. Every where does that beast leave marks of its footsteps: the same fine and close-set " Pavement" that still turns aside the British ploughshare, adorned, under the name of Gabbatha, the Prætorian halls of Pilate. Upon that Pavement stand Hebrews shouting, "We have no king but Cæsar:" their own King is shown to them, mocked with the imperial purple of the Roman. The spear of a Legionary brings forth the water and the blood: the Greek and Hebrew of the Saviour's title is underlined with Latin.*

The Roman times still drag along their weary length of ages. The Byzantine historians, living in Asia and writing in Greek, for twelve centuries styled themselves "the Romans." In the West, the name of Rome still frets the nations: and we, who eyed with terror her earliest Cæsar, must watch, with undisguised suspicion, her latest Pope.

A.D. 440–450.

Omitting a few passages from Orosius, Ammonius †, Isidore, and Cyril of Alexandria ‡, we come to the original and solid work of Prosper, "On the Promises and Prophecies of God." In this treatise, the

---

* In the Apostles' age the whole world seems to be at once both Greek and Roman: the Greeks reign in arts, the Romans in arms. In education and religion the Apostle recognizes no distinction but that of "Jew or Greek;" but the password that takes him through the world is "Roman."

† For what remains of Ammonius and some other Greeks, see Mai, t. i. p. i.

‡ By Isidore the Pelusiot, the four empires are explained in the usual manner. Epist. lib. i. ep. 218. Orosius compares Rome with Babylon in crime, and with Sodom in recent judgments. Lib. i. adversus Paganos. Prosper and Orosius both make the third empire the Punic instead of the Greek. The fourth they make the Roman.

woman Babylon is identified with Rome, obscurely indeed, but as much as can be expected from the secretary of Pope Leo the First. The name of blasphemy is explained to be the name of Eternal: "for, when that which is temporal is called Eternal, surely this is a name of blasphemy." And in another place more distinctly: "After the" (fourth) "beast all these things (described in 2 Thess. ii.), will come to pass: that is, upon the destruction of that empire on which sits the woman drunk with the blood of the saints. Which things we believe, leaving it to posterity to see them fulfilled." *

The Jews, Prosper thinks, will be peculiarly open to delusion from the miracles of Antichrist, it being their custom perversely to "require a sign." The three frogs, not mentioned by any earlier writer, he understands to be three unclean spirits, which will go through Asia, Africa, and Europe, persuading men to believe in Antichrist.

A.D. 448.

This year may be styled the turning point in the history of Christian Rome. Hitherto, under the pressure of enormous calamities, she had been waging war with success against the many Antichrists; for when she was weak, then she was strong: while trampled upon by Alaric and Attila, she stood firm as a pillar of orthodoxy, the support of the wavering faith. But now the object of her ambition is changed: letting go her hold of heaven, she bows her head to receive the crowns of earth: she

* De Dimidio Temporis, cap. 9. in the Bibliotheca Maxima Patrum, t. viii.

must needs reign now by herself, for she cannot wait to live and reign with Christ.

A bold man was Leo, who, with the Goth at his door, and the Apocalypse thundering above his head, conceived the hope of making the seven-hilled city the head and centre of the Christian world. The project was to be carried out by means of two assumptions: the first, that St. Peter had received the right of exercising dominion over the other Apostles; and the second, that he had been made Bishop of Rome*, and had bequeathed to the church of that city the inheritance of his supposed powers.

In a sermon preached on the festival of Sts. Peter and Paul, Leo first gave vent to his aspirations:—

"These are the men that have promoted thee to so great glory, that being a holy nation, a chosen people, a royal and priestly city, and made head of the world through the holy seat of the blessed Peter, thou shouldst rule more widely through divine religion, than before by earthly sway. For great as thou didst become by thy many victories, extending by land and by sea thine imperial rule, the toils of war have won thee less than what Christian peace has placed beneath thy feet."†

This sermon of Leo became in turn a text, upon which his successors loved to dilate. Clement the Eleventh, preaching in 1706, thus hails the fulfilment of Leo's hopes:—

"Rome exults in the most firm foundation of the apostolic rock: so raised to the summit of human affairs, that she now rules more widely through divine religion, than before by earthly sway. * * *

"Henceforth thou shalt be called the city of the Just One,

---

* Irenæus and Eusebius repeatedly affirm that Peter and Paul ordained Linus first bishop of Rome.

† Sermo i. in Natal. SS. Petri et Pauli.

the faithful city, the new Jerusalem; even the same that John saw coming down from heaven, prepared by God as a bride adorned for her husband; by imitation of which other things become fair, by comparison with which, foul. Hear this, you that inhabit the city of the Holy One, the city of the Just One, the faithful city, the new Jerusalem, by imitation of which other things become fair, by comparison with which, foul:—It is monstrous to be in Rome, and not to be holy."*

In the same strain does Arnulphus, in the tenth century, address the "Mother of Harlots:"—"Almighty Rome! Glorious things are spoken of thee, seeing thou art become the city of God."† The Jesuit Baldwin concludes his eulogy with a sudden affectation of surprise: "This city so like heaven, why dwells it an exile upon earth?" ‡

A.D. 450–500.

Leo was not the only man of his day that anticipated the revival of Roman power. What he learnt from the whisper of his own ambition, Andreas gathered from the Apocalypse. But the oracles, though they agreed in this one particular, differed in all the rest. Where Leo promised a blessing, Andreas expected a curse. He thought, that to fulfil the predicted history of Babylon, especially its destruction by Antichrist, Rome might again rise to power, and Constantinople, then the queen of cities, be taken away:—

"Reasoning from the sequel, we understand by Babylon either the universal empire of the earth seen in one body, or the city which will reign till the coming of Antichrist.

---

* Homilies of Clement XI., hom. xvi.
† Baronius in anno 1001.
‡ Aicher Hortus Inscriptionum, p. 42.

For old Rome has long fallen from the power of her kingdom; unless we suppose that her ancient dignity will again return to her. But, if we grant this, the city now ruling must be taken away, for, says the Apocalypse, the woman which thou sawest is that great city that reigneth over the kings of the earth."*

Andreas suggests with great caution this revolution of the world's aspect: he seems fearful of restricting to one city what may be meant to include all cities that persecute and oppose the truth. Moreover, the subject was embarrassed by a difficulty not merely geographical or political. Rome, as if weary of her old residence, had lately absconded from the seven hills: her rulers had transported her to Byzantium, from that time familiarly called new Rome. By this migration she had indeed fled from the Goths: but could she escape also the curse of the Apocalypse? Thus the question became one of prophetic justice; and it may be suggested, in excuse for the doubts of Andreas, that since many prophecies had been transferred from old Babylon to old Rome, the same might possibly be again transferred from old Rome to new Rome.

So strongly did the state of Christendom appear to contradict the plain sense of the Apocalypse, that some persons proposed to explain the woman Babylon as the city of Nebuchadnezzar. Andreas dares not hope it:—

"We might wish indeed that it were so, and that on that city should fall the punishment of proudly raging against Christ and His servants. But to that opinion it must be opposed, that the ancient teachers of the Church consider these things to be

* Andreas in Apocalypsin, cap. xvii.

prophesied against the Babylon of the Romans, because the ten horns belonged to the *fourth* beast, that is, to the Roman empire. And out of that beast grew one horn, which is to root up three, and to subdue the rest, and to become king of the Romans. And this, under pretence of fostering their power; but in truth, to overthrow it utterly. Therefore if any one chooses here to understand a condensed representation of that kingdom which has ruled from the beginning until now, and which has indeed shed the blood of Apostles, prophets, and martyrs, he will not err from the meaning." (Chap. xviii. in fine.)

While thus stating the case between Rome and Constantinople, Andreas feels no difficulty in applying the name of Babylon to a Christian city. Nor does he know anything of those seven hills, which some modern apologists for Rome attribute to the Eastern capital.

Since that time, the Popes, though they have never attempted to *expound* the prophecy about Babylon, have contributed largely to its illustration. In these matters there is usually, if we may so express it, a division of labour: one expounds, another fulfils: by this means the honour of prophecy is vindicated, and no room is left for collusion. For when the expositor undertakes also to fulfil, the fulfilment, to be worth anything, should be in itself miraculous. But in ordinary cases the task is divided: Jaddus expounds, Alexander fulfils: Andreas lays down the sense, the Popes labour to bring it about.

This Andreas, into the middle of whose work the reader has been dragged so abruptly, was a bishop of Cæsarea late in the fifth century. His commentary on the Apocalypse is the oldest to which much importance can be attached in questions of critical difficulty. Writing in Greek, the language of the Apocalypse itself, Andreas is independent of translations; and, possessing the works of Papias, Methodius, and others, now lost, he is still able to gather up some fragments of apostolic tradition.

It will be sufficient for the present purpose to extract from this commentary a few more sentences:—

"Apoc. ch. v. The sealed book may be interpreted as Prophecy; which Christ himself, in the Gospel, declared to have been fulfilled, and the rest of which will be accomplished in the last days."

"Ch. xi. Their bodies shall lie. He will leave their bodies unburied in Jerusalem itself, that ancient and now ruined city, in which also the Lord suffered. For, in that city, as it appears, Antichrist will establish his kingdom, in imitation of David: for thereabouts was born, according to the flesh, the Son, Christ our true God. By this he will persuade men that he is the Christ, apparently fulfilling that prophecy, I will raise up again the tabernacle of David, which is fallen down, and will build up its ruins. Which prophecy the mistaken Jews will apply to his coming." * * *

"When they have lain dead as many days as are equal to the number of the years of their prophesying, they shall rise again, and shall go up to heaven in the cloud, the chariot of the Lord."

Andreas, writing in Greek, is forced to preserve the definite article prefixed to the cloud. He seems to understand an allusion to that cloud which took up Christ, and which now waits upon His witnesses. St. John has been evidently alluding to our Lord's history, as is shown by his late remark, "Where also their Lord was crucified." The pseudo-Sibyl seems to take it as referring to the cloudy chariot of Elijah's former ascent.

"Ch. xiii. The beast which I saw was like a pard. By the pard is meant the empire of the Greeks; by the bear that of the Persians; and by the lion, that of the Babylonians. All these empires Antichrist will possess, coming as king of the Romans; he will destroy, as soon as they appear, the clay toes of the image, by which is represented the weak and fragile state of the Roman empire, divided into ten.

"Ch. xvi. The great city was divided into three parts, and the cities of the Gentiles fell. The great city we understand to be Jerusalem, — not great in the number and size of its buildings, but great, as being the most ancient and exalted in the worship of God. Also great by the sufferings of Christ; and set in opposition to the cities of the Gentiles."

The scarlet beast, hitherto little noticed, now for the first time undergoes a connected examination: —

"Ch. xvii. The beast that thou sawest, was, and is not. This beast is Satan; who, having been slain by the cross of Christ, is said to revive in the end of the world; bringing about, by the signs and lying miracles of Antichrist, the denial of that cross. Therefore, before the crucifixion, he was, and flourished. He is not, being by the saving Passion stripped of his power, and deprived of that influence which, through idolatry, he exercised over the Gentiles.

"And is to come: in the end, as was before said; rising up out of the abyss, or that place to which he has been consigned, and to which the cast-out demons begged of Christ that they might not be sent, but rather into the swine. Or, from the present life; figuratively called an abyss, on account of its depth of sin, being tossed and lashed into waves by the storms of passion.

"From the abyss, Antichrist, bearing in himself Satan, will ascend to the destruction of mankind; he himself going into perdition in the coming age. And they shall wonder. The beast's coming, it says, by means of his lying miracles, shall excite the wonder of those who are not written in the book of the everlastingly living, and who, not being firmly grounded in the prophecies of Christ concerning him, shall speculate how he has recovered his former sway."

A. D. 520.

The senator Cassiodorus, one of the few men of learning left in the old metropolis, now took in hand the Apocalyptic prophecies. As a Roman, he gladly avails himself of any excuse for doubting about Babylon. "That harlot," he writes, "some think to mean the city of Rome, which sits upon seven hills, and exercises sole dominion over the earth. But others take it to be spoken rather of Babylon; supposing that what is said of her situation refers not to mountains, but to arrogance of power. This harlot is to be destroyed by those people over whom she was before seen to rule." *

A. D. 500–550.

The Western school of prophecy was now rapidly settling down into the state in which it continued during the Middle Ages. Primasius did it a bad turn, by inventing a new explanation of Babylon, calculated to satisfy the wishes of Rome, without flatly contradicting Scripture. Babylon was to be interpreted Rome indeed, but Rome, only as a figure of something else:—"The seven heads, he declares, are to be understood as seven mountains, pointing out Rome, which is seated upon seven hills; and because she once governed the world, she is set forth as the figure of its kingdom. So that by the name of Rome there is typified the power of the whole kingdom." †

Primasius makes the witnesses to lie dead as many years as they prophesy. This notion, which partially prevailed during several centuries, was finally exploded

---

* Cassiodori Complexiones in Apoc. cap. xvii.
† Primasius in Apocalypsin; Bibliotheca Maxima Patrum, tom. x. 326.

by the more accurate of the schoolmen. To give an outline of its history, the following table has been drawn up: in the first column are all the expositors (down to the Reformation) that have taken the three and a half days to be days; in the second, those that have explained them as years. Those that have expressed no positive opinion are written across the line.

AS DAYS.	DOUBTFUL.	AS YEARS.
Tertullian. *		
Victorinus.		
Lactantius.		
		Tychonius.
		Prosper.
Andreas.		
Cassiodorus.		
		Primasius.
Aretas.		
		Bede.
		Haymo.
		Ansbert.
Anselm of Laon.		
		Bruno.
		Rupert.
Richard St. Victor.		
Joachim.		
Albertus Magnus.		
Cardinal Hugo.		
	Thomas	Aquinas.
	De	Lyra.
Aureolus.		
De Gorram.		
Oremius.		
Telesphorus.		
	Beren-	-gaud.
	Ber-	nardine.
Dionysius Carthusianus.		
The "Art or Craft to live well."		
John of Kemnitz.		

* Tertullian's opinion is implied in these words:—"With their blood they will extinguish Antichrist."

A. D. 533.

Meanwhile the history of the fourth kingdom had been making progress. The Western Empire was suppressed by Odoacer, in 476; and not till fifty years afterwards was Rome restored to the emperors, through the valour of Belisarius. At that time the Romans placed a deputy in Ravenna, who, under the title of Exarch, governed Rome.

The Western Church was now infested by the followers of Eutyches and Nestorius, who maintained that the Word of God, and the man Christ Jesus, were two. Justinian addressed a letter to the bishop of Rome, bidding him rebuke the supporters of this heresy: "We," said the Cæsar of the East, "do not acknowledge one God the Word, and another Christ, but one and the self-same Person; of the same substance with His Father, according to His Godhead, and of the same substance with us, according to His manhood."[*]

This epistle, which says nothing about persecution, does credit to the zeal and the moderation of Justinian. A few centuries later (according to the best researches of modern times), the Roman jurists inserted in this letter the following words:—"We hasten to unite and to make subject to the seat of your holiness, all the priests of the entire Eastern region," &c.

Those that support the authenticity of this clause (still a numerous body), should be prepared to meet the consequent difficulty:—That pope, emperor, and patriarch, were for years engaged in discussing the

[*] Harduin's Councils, tom. ii. col. 1146.

precedence of the churches, without being aware that so decisive a decree had issued from the imperial pen.

A. D. 590–600.

The bishops of Rome and Constantinople did not long enjoy equal honour, the imperial presence soon turning the scale in favour of the East. Late in the sixth century the Byzantine John assumed the title of universal bishop, in a faint degree anticipating the later pretensions of the Roman pontiffs. This happened during the life of the only pope who ever studied prophecy to any purpose. The first Gregory, fresh from the contemplation of the times of Antichrist, had scarce raised his eyes from the prophetic page, when he beheld the pride and arrogance of John, blazing, like some portentous meteor, in the eastern sky. "A forerunner of Antichrist," exclaimed the expositor.

Gregory first addressed a remonstrance to the Patriarch John. In this letter we shall find a portrait of popery, painted by a pope: —

"The Apostle Paul, hearing some say, 'I am of Paul, and I of Apollos, and I of Cephas,' vehemently deplored this rending of the Lord's body, by which His members joined themselves in a manner to other heads. Was Paul, he exclaimed in horror, crucified for you, or were ye baptized by the name of Paul? If then he would not suffer the members of the Lord's body to be, as it were, made partially subject to individual heads, other than Christ, Apostles though they were, — what, in the reckoning of the last judgment, will you say to Christ, the head of the universal church, when, through the title of universal, you have laboured to subject to yourself all His members? And whom, I ask, in this froward title, do you set before you as your model? None but him, who, despising the legions of angels appointed to be his fellows,

T

strove to force his way to the height of supremacy, that he might appear subject to none, but alone superior to all. * * *

"Long ago cried the Apostle John, Little children, it is the last hour. And as the Truth itself predicted, pestilence and sword now ravage the world, — nations rise against nations, — the world is shaken, and the yawning earth, together with its inhabitants, is swallowed up. All things that have been foretold are accomplished: the king of pride is at hand; and, dreadful to tell, an army of priests is prepared for him. For they who were ordained to take the lead in meekness, are fighting with the neck of pride." *

Gregory might well tremble at the supposed signs of Antichrist's approach, for he had drunk deeply into the spirit of these words, — " There shall be great tribulation, such as was not since the beginning of the world." Of those times he asks : —

"What is it in those torments that will exceed in severity all other torments? Doubtless that which the Truth has by itself declared in the Gospel : — There shall arise false Christs and false prophets, and shall show great signs and wonders, so as to deceive, if it were possible, even the elect. For now our faithful ones, while they *suffer* tortures, perform wonders; but then, the satellites of this Behemoth, even while they *inflict* tortures, will do wonders. Let us consider, then, what temptation will assail the mind of man, when the holy martyr submits his body to torments, and meanwhile the torturer works miracles before his eyes. What man is there whose courage will be proof against the reasonings of his inmost soul, when he who tortures with the scourge will also dazzle with miracles ? " †

A. D. 606.

The Emperor, it seems, took no measures to restrain

---

* Gregorii. Max., lib. v. ep. 18. ad Johannem.

† Gregorii Maximi Moralia in Job, lib. xxxii. cap. 15. For another extract, bearing on the same subject, see the concluding chapter of this volume.

the ambition of the Eastern Patriarchs. But it did not suit Rome's interests that the question should be left in so unsatisfactory a state. A hundred and seventy years later, when the Popes had risen in open rebellion against the Emperors, it was given out in the West, that Phocas had settled the dispute by conferring the precedence upon the church of Rome. The whole story rests upon the evidence of a single writer, — insufficient proof in a case where the frequency of papal forgeries demands unusual caution.

The pretended decree of Phocas, said to have been issued in 606, appears to have been seen by nobody. It is first spoken of in 780, by Paul the deacon: "This Focas, at the request of Pope Boniface, ordained that the see of the Roman and Apostolic Church should be the head of all churches, because the Constantinopolitan Church had entitled itself the first of all churches." *

The words are repeated in the "Additions to Eutropius," once ascribed to Paul the Deacon, but reckoned apocryphal by Bellarmine.

In 860, Anastasius repeats the sentence; but, though librarian to the Popes, and entrusted with the charge of all such documents, he knows nothing of the decree, except from Paul. . "Boniface," he says, "obtained from the Prince Phocas, that the Apostolic seat of the blessed Apostle Peter, that is, the church of Rome, should be the head of all churches, because the church of C. P. had entitled itself the first of all churches." †

---

* De Gestis Longobardorum, lib. iv.

† Anastasius De Vitis Pontificum. Boniface sat one year only, so that, if the transaction took place at all, it happened in 606. It is by this reckoning that the famous date has been obtained.

In 880, Ado repeats the words: " Focas, at the request of Pope Boniface, decreed that the see of Rome should be the head of all churches, because the church of C. P. had entitled itself the first of all churches." *

Thus, parrot-like, the historians repeat a sentence, which they fear to paraphrase, and have no means of verifying. But against the testimony of this servilely-copied passage must be set the profound silence of history for 170 years: the omission of the incident in all the lives of Gregory, including that by John the Deacon, written about 870; also its non-appearance in the histories of Cedrenus, Zonaras, and Theophanes, and probably in the whole range of Byzantine historians. Baronius treats the whole question as of little importance, being a dispute about a name.† And such, indeed, it is: moreover, as far as the priority over Constantinople was concerned, the act would have been a just concession to the rights of the mother-city.

A. D. circ. 650.

The Greek commentary of Aretas, though in most respects a copy from that of Andreas, claims notice from some adaptations of prophecy to passing events. The Saracens here first come upon the stage, appearing in the new character of Babylonians. This proves that Aretas lived after their settlement in Babylon, or, as it has since been named, Bagdad.

Of the Anti-christian beast he says:—

* Ado Viennensis in Chronico.
† Baronius, anno 606 : " Some misinformed people have thought that Phocas granted to the Pope of Rome this privilege of holding the primacy in the Catholic Church."

"The lion's mouth means the Babylonish empire, by which we may undoubtedly understand the Saracens, especially as their capital now is Babylon: and over them, as king of the Romans, Antichrist will reign."*

Rome's last master had been Totila, who left her in a state little answering to St. John's description. Not a soul, it is reported, remained alive in her: not one, through whom she might lift her head from the dust, and groan forth, however feebly and falsely, " I sit a queen." It was therefore natural for Aretas to explain Babylon, chiefly in reference to New Rome, though not exclusively; for " calling her the mother of harlots as often as you will, whether you mean Old Rome, New Rome, or the time of Antichrist's coming, you cannot go wrong." (Ch. xvii.)

The honesty of these Greeks contrasts happily with the evasive spirit of the Western expositors. The Greek would force the prophecy to mean more than it says, rather than that his own metropolis should escape her due share of the threatening. The Latin exhausts his ingenuity to evade the definition, lest his own metropolis should appear to suffer a merited rebuke.

* Aretas in Apoc. cap. xiii.

CHAPTER IV.

THE INTERPRETATION OF PROPHECY IN THE MIDDLE AGES.

(From the Independence of Rome to the Reformation.)

"'He cried with a great voice.' Perhaps *great*, because supported by Scripture: for that is a small voice which Scripture supports not." — ALBERTUS MAGNUS, in Apoc. xix.

THE mediæval school of prophecy consists of two parts: the systematic commentators, who repeated or embellished what they had learnt from the ancients; and an irregular body of observers, who, with the Apocalypse in their hand and Rome before their eyes, recorded from time to time the progress of Babylon's career.

No class of writers has realised better than the monks the truth and importance of prophecy. By the monotonous seclusion of the cloister the unseen world seemed to be brought nearer; and, in proportion as the present faded, the prophetic future grew more distinct and real. Some would sit down to write the life and times of Antichrist; others, condescending to know something also of the past, composed a history of the world from Adam to Antichrist. These last, as far as to their own time, compiled from chronicles; then they took to the Apocalypse, for the rise of the ten Kings and the disruption of the Roman world. Here they begin a new chapter: "Incipit feliciter vita Antichristi:" and now, emerging from the tangled present to a broad and even causeway, the King's own highway of the future, they hold on their steadfast course to the goal of a Christian's hopes. Of these happy enthusiasts, all of whom reckoned themselves to be living in the "beginning of the end," one at least tells of the coming Reformation; while not a few look far enough before them to foresee corruptions and disasters in the history of the Roman Church.

Once more, the popular style of exposition is entirely changed. The first followers of the Apostles had been remarkable for the use of abrupt transitions, for quoting the sense of Scripture rather than the words, and for a masterly grasp of the whole range of passages bearing on their subject. In the patristic age, free and vigorous paraphrase was employed; and this was executed with a dramatic and rhetorical force which goes far to support the popular story, that while Jerome's youthful hands were filled with Cicero, Aristophanes reposed in honour beneath the pillow of Chrysostom. In this way, as they sometimes expressed it, they spoiled the Egyptians. But the monks, increasing in caution with their distance from the sources of inspiration, devised a method of expounding, which, if liable to the charge of servility, was at least, as far as it went, safe.

The Bible, it is acknowledged by all, is written in the fewest words possible (lest the world should be unable to contain, or at least to circulate, its ponderous tomes); and into those words there is compressed as much matter as merely human writers would have expanded into many times the number. With this belief, the monks, in their glosses, retained the actual words of Scripture, which they set, after the manner of precious jewels, in the baser fabric of their own exposition. This method tied them down to the natural sense; though, from their neglect of the sacred languages, they were betrayed into refinements upon the wording of the Latin, altogether without foundation in the inspired text: for, with all their learning, the schoolmen knew little of Greek, and almost nothing of Hebrew.

The style of monkish commentary will appear to advantage in the current exposition of the history of the witnesses' death. The substance of their comments, cleared of some casual and extraneous conceits, may be condensed into the subjoined form:—

Apoc. xi. And when they, that is, Elias and perhaps Enoch, shall have finished the three years and a half of their testimony, declaring Antichrist to be an impostor, and preaching Jesus as the only true Christ, soon to come again in judgment: the beast, Antichrist, that ascends out of the bottomless pit, being raised up by the operation of Satan, and reinforced from the abyss or prison of demons; this beast shall make war upon them, by violence, by miracles, and by controversy; and shall overcome them, speaking after the manner of men, who reckon those vanquished that are slain: for he shall kill them, bodily.

And their dead bodies shall lie, unburied, in order to terrify others, in the street of the great city, Jerusalem: great, once, as the city of the great king; now, in wickedness: great, once, from Christ's miracles and Passion; now, by the confluence of the Gentiles and the residence of Antichrist; which spiritually, that is, not literally, is called Sodom, that is, by interpretation, dumb, even in God's praise; and Egypt, that is, dark. Or Sodom, from its impurity, and in allusion to the words of Isaiah, Ye rulers of Sodom; and Egypt, as the scene of the coming plagues.*

Where also their Lord; He in whose service they are slain; their Lord, by Redemption as well as by Creation; *their* Lord, and the Lord of all, being King of kings and Lord of lords; where their Lord was crucified, referring to Christ's decease, which (as it was said by one, perhaps by both of them,) He must accomplish at Jerusalem. For, though He suffered without the camp, yet the place where Jesus was crucified was nigh unto the city, even Jerusalem that killeth the prophets. Therefore these prophets also shall perish there, for it cannot be that a prophet perish but in Jerusalem.

And they, that is some, or many, of the people and tongues and tribes and nations, that is, both Jews, and the Gentiles then residing in Jerusalem, treading under foot the holy city; shall see their dead bodies lying unburied for three days and a half (which some expound as the entire three years and a half of Antichrist's reign); and shall not suffer their dead bodies to be put into graves.

And they that dwell on the earth, either, they that inhabit the land, that is, Judea; or, they that dwell in heart upon earth, whose names are written in the earth, who desire to have here an abiding city, and whose conversation is not in heaven, shall rejoice

* The monks, who greatly admired the seven rules of Tychonius, did not notice Ezekiel's account of Jerusalem as the Egyptian Aholibah. The rule of Tychonius is thus expressed: "Specific names have always a bad meaning:—Hear the word of the Lord, ye rulers of Sodom, and, spiritually called Sodom and Egypt, where also their Lord was crucified. From that Sodom Lot will go forth; and this will be the departure (discessio) that the man of sin may be revealed."—Regula iv.

over them, seeming to have conquered those that had so long appeared invincible; and shall make merry, promising to themselves lasting indulgence in pleasure: and shall send gifts one to another, in token of peace upon earth, because these two prophets, by evermore warning them of their certain perdition, and enforcing the word with miraculous plagues, tormented those that dwelt upon the earth.

But why does God suffer His witnesses to be thus insulted in the sight of all men? Answer. That their resurrection may be more signal and incontrovertible.

And after three days and a half. Having shown the sufferings of those who will then bear witness for God, it now displays their crowns: for, after three days and a half, the spirit of life, the breath of the resurrection life, not the mortal life before enjoyed by them, entered into them. From God, that is, miraculously and divinely; as opposed to the agency of that Satanic power which was able to give life to the image of the beast, and to heal his deadly wound. And they stood upon their feet, now self-supported and immortal; and great fear fell upon all who saw them: for now it was certain that the eternal ruin denounced by these prophets was no fable, but a true message from God.

And they heard a great voice coming down from heaven, saying to them, and at once executing its own mandate, Come up hither; come up, from the cruelty and the blasphemy of the wicked; hither, to the assembly of the just. And they went up to heaven in the cloud, like their Lord and Master, to whom having been conformed in suffering, and in the scene of their suffering, they are now made like in the glory of their ascension. And it is enough for the disciple that he be as his Master, and the servant as his Lord.

To the city where the Lord was crucified the Apostle gives three names : (v. 8.) one literal, two spiritual. From the addition of the word "spiritually," when compared with 1 Cor. ii. 14., we learn that these names are applied divinely, and in a sense removed from the common use of the words. Let us take the three names in order. It is called, —

I. Literally, "the great city:" a name applied to ancient Jerusalem, Jerem. xxii. 8.; to the new Jerusalem, Rev. xxi. 10.; to Nineveh in Jonah, and to Babylon in the Apocalypse. But the city Jerusalem is indeed great and lifted up to heaven; the city of the great king; the city of which glorious things are spoken; the centre of the earth, Ezek. xxxviii. 12. (umbilicus terræ, Vulgate and Septuagint.) Lastly, great in precedence; "beginning at Jerusalem;" also in judgments, as in Jeremiah xxv. 18.: " To wit, Jerusalem, and the cities of Judah. . . . and Pharaoh, &c." Which order is followed in Apoc. xvi. 19.: " And the great city. . . . and the cities of the Gentiles. . . . and great Babylon, &c."

II. Spiritually, Sodom. In Isaiah i. in the " vision concerning Judah and Jerusalem " it is said, "Hear the word of the Lord, ye rulers of Sodom." Compare "thy sister Sodom," Ezek. xvi. 49. also Jeremiah xxiii. 14.: " They are all of them unto me as Sodom."

III. Spiritually, Egypt. In Ezekiel xxiii. 4.: " Thus were their names: Samaria is Aholah, and Jerusalem Aholibah." These sisters are described as Egyptian courtesans, living, and pursuing their shameful trade, in Egypt. So Calmet in his dictionary: "Aholah and Aholibah are represented as two sisters of Egyptian extraction." Four early Greek expositors (none of whom wrote on the Apocalypse), support this sense.

1. Eusebius. "Ezekiel shows that Israel worshipped idols in Egypt, comparing their metropolitan cities, Samaria and Jerusalem, to two sisters, saying, There were two sisters, and they were corrupted in Egypt in their youth." *

2. Theodoret. "As for their impiety, these sisters had one mother, even Egypt. * * * Having figuratively styled them women, he now gives them the names of certain Egyptian women." (In locum.)

3. Polychronius. "Some say that these women (Aholah and Aholibah), were courtesans in Egypt." †

4. An Anonymous Greek. "These, they say, were celebrated courtesans in Egypt, whose names are now given to Samaria and Jerusalem." This statement of the *names* being Egyptian is probably a mistake, as it is not supported by Jerome or the Jews.

"Their dead bodies shall lie in the *street* of the great city." This street, or broad place, when spoken of in the singular, seems almost characteristic of Jerusalem. It had been promised to Daniel (ch. ix.) that "the street shall be built again." Also, in the new Jerusalem, "the street is of pure gold," while "in the midst of the street is the tree of life."

Thus, in describing the scene of the witnesses' death, the Apostle selects his marks from the four greater prophets of his people. He collects together

---

* Galland's Fathers, t. iv. p. 489. (Euseb. in Resurrect. lib. ii.)

† This passage, with the following, is taken from a Greek MS. Chain, preserved in the Vatican. Extracted by Pradus in Ezek., t. i. p. 282.

" the street " of Daniel ; " the great city " of Jeremiah ; the " Sodom " of Isaiah; the " Egyptian harlot " of Ezekiel. He had before called it the holy city: he yet adds something, and that from his own sad recollections: " Where also their Lord was crucified."

A. D. 700–800.

Thus far the expositors have made little of the resemblance between Rome and mystic Babylon. It was not yet discovered why a city hitherto so fierce and warlike had been compared to a woman strong only in the arts of seduction and deceit. The city of Romulus had still to exchange the sword for the cup, iron for gold, bloodshed for wine. But now these rough places of Scripture were to be made plain: the Wisdom that had dictated the prophecies was to be justified in all its predictions: for, in the eighth century, western Babylon not only returned to her character of an idolatrous city, but at the same time entered upon a new career of intrigue and spiritual corruption. For money or for influence, every thing available was bartered: intercession, forgiveness of sins, and the powers of the priesthood, all were brought into the market. But, as the harlotry of the woman Babylon is the leading feature of her character, so does the idolatry of the Church of Rome stand pre-eminent among its crimes, contributing the most largely to its worldly aggrandisement.

The beginning of the eighth century found Rome a dependent and insignificant portion of the Roman Empire: its end left her free, and in a condition to confer upon her benefactor the crown of the West. This change in her fortunes was brought about by image-worship.

The Roman Empire had been long represented in the West by a viceroy or exarch, resident in Ravenna. The great question of the day concerned the lawfulness of image-worship, which was supported by the Pope, by the western Church, and by part of the eastern; while the emperor, with a few bishops of the East, steadily opposed it. On this occasion Rome and the Roman Empire appear as two.

It may now be seen why, in the Apocalypse, the city of Rome requires a separate figure to itself. After all that Daniel had said of the fourth beast, of the iron, and even of the clay, there still remained one element of Christendom to be described: — Rome detached from the empire. This separation, set on foot by the supporters of idolatry, was completed by the open rebellion of Pope Gregory the Second: for, in 726, the emperor Leo, seconded by his bishop Anastasius, endeavoured to suppress the worship of images: upon this, says the Greek Papist Theophanes, "Gregory, the holy bishop of Rome, condemned Anastasius with his books. He also by letter rebuked Leo as impious, and separated from his empire Rome and the whole of Italy. Upon this the tyrant was enraged, and increased the persecution against the holy images."*

This pretended persecution is described by Anastasius, a papal librarian of the ninth century: —

"After this the emperor decreed that no image of any saint, martyr, or angel, should be suffered in any place whatever, calling them all accursed; adding, that if the Pope would second him in this matter, he should enjoy the imperial

---

* Theophanes, Chronographia, anno 721. Both he and Cedrenus add that Gregory stopped the payment of tribute to the Eastern Cæsar. Vitâ Leonis Isaurici.

favour, but that, if he resisted, he should be deposed from his office.

"Then the pious man, regarding the prince's order as profane, armed himself against the emperor as against an enemy; also, resisting his heresy, he wrote letters in all directions, warning Christians to be on their guard, seeing that such impiety was abroad. Thus all the people of Pentapolis, and the army of the Venetians, were excited to resist the imperial edict, saying that they would never consent to the death of the Pope, but would rather fight manfully in his defence."*

But Rome, thus made independent, found herself unable to defend her rights. Her first enemy was the Lombard Aistulphus, who seized upon Ravenna, ravaged Italy, and threatened the capital itself. Pope Stephen was forced to implore the aid of Pepin, who speedily drove back the invaders. But no sooner had Pepin recrossed the Alps, than Aistulphus returned to the siege of Rome.

In this emergency Stephen devised a stratagem altogether new. The Franks, but just returned to their country, were surprised by the receipt of a letter beginning "Ego Petrus Apostolus," and directed to Pepin, Charles, and Carloman. "Run," said the Apostle, "by the living and true God I exhort and adjure you, — run and help, before the living fountain at which you were consecrated and regenerated be dried up; before the last small spark of that glowing flame from which you received your light, be extinguished."

The Franks, as Stephen well knew, were a simple

---

* Anastasius De Vitis Pontificum, Gregorii II. In the Anglican homily against Peril of Idolatry, part iii., there is a fuller account of these events, though drawn from later sources.

people: the solemn adjuration, the boundless promises, and the threatenings of the pretended Apostle, all this took their rude minds by storm. For the writer of the letter professes to have control over the punishments both of this world and the next:—

"Be not separated from my people of Rome, for so you shall not be separated or cut off from the kingdom of God, and from eternal life. Ask of me what you will, and I will employ my advocacy to gain it for you. Help my Roman people your brethren, fight valiantly, and complete their deliverance. For no man receives a crown, unless he contend lawfully: therefore fight boldly for the freedom of God's holy church, lest you perish everlastingly.

"I conjure you once again, my beloved, by the living God; and in every way I adjure you, by no means to suffer this my city of Rome with its inhabitants to be again torn by the Lombards, lest your bodies and souls be torn and tortured in the eternal and unquenchable fire of hell, with the devil and his pestiferous angels. Let them not again scatter the sheep of the Lord's flock, committed to me by God, even the Roman people, lest the Lord scatter and cast you off, even as the people of Israel were scattered, ...

"If you obey quickly, your reward will be great, even to be helped by my intercession. You shall conquer all your enemies in the present life, shall live long, shall eat the good things of the earth, and shall without doubt enjoy everlasting life. But if, which I do not believe, you make any delay or excuse about executing this my command, and delivering this my city of Rome with its inhabitants, as well as the holy and apostolic church of God committed to me by the Lord, with the bishop set over it,— know that, by the authority of the Holy and undivided Trinity, through the grace of Apostleship committed to me by the Lord Christ, you are, for the neglect of this my injunction, cut off from the kingdom of God, and from eternal life."*

These terrible threats succeeded beyond all hope:

* Labbæi Concilia, tom. vi. col. 1641.

Pepin came to the rescue, Aistulphus was put to the rout. The conqueror, generous with the property of another, bestowed upon the Pope sundry towns belonging to the Roman Empire. In return, Stephen called him "novus Moses," and "præfulgidus David." From that time the Pope possessed the exarchate of Ravenna, with twenty cities of Italy. These he had acquired by selling the blessings of the Gospel, and by brandishing vain threats of eternal damnation. Such an abuse of spiritual gifts seems to be figuratively described by Ezekiel in the case of the Jewish nation: "Thou hast taken thy fair jewels of my gold and of my silver, which I had given thee, and madest to thyself images of men. . . . My meat also which I gave thee, fine flour and oil and honey wherewith I fed thee, thou hast even set it before them for a sweet savour."* And by her manner of doing this she verifies a saying of Aretas about Babylon, (a figure which, he says, "you cannot go wrong" in applying to Rome,) "Her name is written on her forehead, to show that she commits her enormities without a blush."†

A.D. 787.

The Church of Rome, having by the sale of spiritual favours justified the title of harlot, showed next why she is seated on a beast full of names of blasphemy. For that the idolatry, upon which she had now taken her stand, soon rose to downright blasphemy, may be seen in the acts of the second Nicene Council, held under her auspices.

* Ezekiel xvi. 17. 19. † Aretas in Apoc. xvii.

In the fourth session of that Council, there was read aloud with universal applause the following story, from Sophronius: —

"There lived in the Mount of Olives a certain recluse, wrestling zealously: and the demon of uncleanness molested him. One day when vehemently beset, the old man began to lament, and to say to the demon, How long will it be ere you leave me? Depart now, for you have grown old with me. Upon this the demon appeared to him visibly, and said, Swear to tell nobody what I am going to say, and I will molest you no farther. And the old man swore by Him that liveth in the highest, that he would tell nobody. Then said the demon, Cease to worship this image, and I will trouble you no further.

"Now the image was a representation of our Lady the holy Mary the mother of God, carrying in her arms our Lord Jesus Christ. The recluse said therefore to the demon, Allow me to consider of it. The next day he sent for the Abbot Theodore, a Heliot, then living in Laura. When the Abbot came, and had heard all, he said to the recluse, Father, you have indeed been duped, for you have sworn to the Devil. However, you have done well to tell me: for it were better for you to frequent every house of ill-fame in this city, than to refuse to worship in an image Jesus Christ our Lord and God, with His mother. Having confirmed and strengthened him with many words, the Abbot returned home.

"Then the demon appeared again to the recluse, and said, What now, bad old man? Did you not swear to tell nobody, and how is it that you have told every thing to your visitor? I tell you, bad old man, that in the day of judgment you will be reckoned a perjurer. And the recluse answered: What I swore I did indeed swear; but I know that I swore falsely, for in that oath I forswore my Lord and Maker. I will not listen to you.

"Then said Constantine, the most holy bishop of Constance in Cyprus, Like necklaces of gold do our godly Fathers hang together in the worship of the holy images!"*

* Harduin's Councils, tom. iv. col. 208.

Finally, the Council broke out into this exclamation:—

"Anathema to those that apply to the venerable images the words of Holy Scripture against idols. Anathema to those that do not salute the holy and venerable images. Anathema to those that call the holy images idols." *

The connection between the rise of Papal power and the support of image-worship is freely allowed by the great jurist of the fourteenth century, Marsilius of Padua. He thus describes the translation of the Roman empire, which took place in 800:—

"The primary cause of that translation was a quarrel between the Emperor Leo III. and the Church of Rome, about the worship of ecclesiastical images. For Leo said that the images of Christ and of the saints were by no means to be worshipped, as it seemed a sort of idolatry. But Gregory the Third, then bishop of Rome, declared that the images of Christ and of the saints ought to be worshipped. Leo, persisting in his purpose, came from Constantinople to Rome, and carrying away with him to C. P. all the images of Christ and of the saints that he found in Rome, condemned them to be burnt. For which reason Gregory presumed to anathematise Leo, and persuaded all Apulia, Italy, and Spain to revolt from his obedience. And in this he succeeded, to the best of his power, in deed, though not in right. He also solemnly forbade the payment of the tribute to Leo, by what authority I know not, but with what temerity I know well. Then, calling a council in Rome, he confirmed the worship of images, and anathematised those that opposed it." †

A.D. circ. 790.

"By thy sorcery," says the angel, "have all na-

* Harduin's Councils, tom. iv. col. 324.
† De Translatione Imperii, cap. 5. In the Appendix ad Fasciculum Rerum, p. 58.

tions been deceived." Of this φαρμακεία the same black age furnishes another illustration.

So richly had the Church of Rome been endowed by Pepin and Charlemagne, that nothing was left her to desire but a sceptre and a crown. Therefore a crown and sceptre must be obtained: and, if the task seemed difficult, Pope Adrian possessed a talisman to which the purse of the Fortunate man must yield in potency. He had in the Lateran palace a certain "sacred chest," in which were found several things that had never been lost. This chest contained forged title deeds and such like swindling apparatus, which, in an age so dark, and in the hands of a pontiff so ingenious, answered their purpose quite as well as if genuine.

"We possess," said Pope Adrian, "*several* donations, laid up in our sacred chest of the Lateran:"* nevertheless the world was enlightened by the production of one only. By the famous "donation of Constantine" it appeared that about the year 320 Constantine had made over to the Popes, for ever, his sceptre, his purple, and his imperial dignity. Also that, to prevent the possibility of collision between the lay and clerical sovereigns, he had removed his own court to Byzantium. What the modesty of Sylvester had abstained from using, Adrian, being troubled with no such weakness, now demanded of Charlemagne. This pretended donation included the gift of all Italy, and of Rome in particular.

Adrian, having once put on the wishing-cap, pro-

---

* Adrian's letter to Charlemagne, Labb. Concil. vi. 1763.

ceeded to help himself largely. He must have the Emperor's own collar, the cloak off his back, and the crown off his head. Constantine is made to grant —

"The diadem, that is, the crown of our own head, also the triple crown, and the superhumeral, namely that collar which used to encircle the imperial neck, with the purple cloak and the scarlet coat, and all the imperial vestments, even to the dignity of the imperial knights president. We grant him also the imperial sceptres, decorations, and ensigns."

Thus the Pope does not forget the purple and the scarlet of Babylon's array. Guided by the same infallible instinct, he goes on to claim the gold and precious stones marked out in the Apocalypse: — " The crown which we have granted to him off our own head, of purest gold with precious stones."*

The framer of this document, after so long aping the Imperial style, at length betrays himself by breaking out into the cursing and anathema of a pope. "If," continues the pretended emperor, " if, which we do not believe, there should exist any infringer or despiser, let him be involved in everlasting condemnation, and let him feel that God's holy and chief Apostles, Peter and Paul, are opposed to him in the present and in the future life, and let him perish with all the wicked, burning in the lowest hell, in other words, condemned with the devil."

The imposture was completely successful: Charlemagne complied with the Pope's wishes, and was in due time rewarded with the crown of the West. The pretended donation was next quoted as authentic

---

* Constantine's donation. Paramus de Inquisitione, p. 428.; also in Harduin's Councils, t. vi. 936. and in the Fasciculus Rerum.

by Hincmar of Rheims*, and again by Leo IX.† It was first attacked by Valla, (in the fifteenth century,) as a piece of blundering knavery, the production of " some clerical blockhead, venting his folly among his cups."‡

That which nearly cost Valla his life before the Reformation, was done safely by Baronius§ and Pagi after it. For Pagi, though a Franciscan monk, thus rudely denounces the long cherished fiction : " The donation of Constantine," he decides, " is altogether fictitious, as the learned are almost agreed."‖ He attributes the imposture to the noted forger, Isidore Mercator, who lived about the time of Charlemagne.

The Church of Rome now acknowledges the forgery: she almost wonders how any one could have been duped by it. But when will she give up its fruits ? Never, till the ten kings shall make her desolate and naked, and shall eat her flesh and burn her with fire.

A.D. 800.

Charlemagne, having complied with the Pope's request, is now to receive his reward.

In the year 800, he attended mass in Rome on Christmas-day. On rising from his knees, he found himself suddenly crowned by the Pope; and the

* Hincmar, Ad Proceres Regni, cap. 13.

† Harduin's Councils, tom. vi. 936. (anno 1048.)

‡ Laurentius Valla, De Donat. Constant. in the Fasciculus Rerum, p. 149.

§ Baronius thinks that the *Greeks* forged the donation, and is duly shocked at their wickedness. They remind him of Virgil : — " Timeo Danaos, et dona ferentes." Anno 324.

‖ Pagi, critica in Baronium, anno 324. No. xvi.

people, inspired with a reminiscence of their ancient glory, raised the shout, "To Charles, Emperor of the Romans, and Augustus, long life and victory!"* Historians are divided as to the sincerity of his declaration, that, had he known beforehand the Pope's intentions, he would not have entered the church.

This restoration of the Western Roman empire, a further act of rebellion against the Eastern head, was one of a series of intrigues by which the Popes secured the permanent support of the western world. From that time, the Pope and the Emperor have been closely linked together, as the prelate and the sovereign of the Roman empire.

Charlemagne, having thus stumbled upon the empire of half the world, turned his thoughts to the attainment of the rest. For a moment the prize seemed within his reach; his offers of marriage were accepted by the profligate Irene, Empress of the East, and direct successor of Theodosius and Justinian. But her subjects opposed the union, and Irene was thrown into a convent, there to lament the loss of liberty, of empire, and of a royal bridegroom.

* One of the best early authorities is Otto: "In the year of our Lord's Incarnation 801, and from the building of the city 1552, King Charles, in the thirty-third year of his reign, was crowned by the Pope. The name of patrician was taken from him, and all the people exclaimed, ' To Charles Augustus, crowned by God, the great and pacific Emperor of the Romans, life and victory!' He was styled Augustus, and the sixty-ninth emperor from Augustus. From that time the empire of the Romans, which, from the days of Constantine had remained in the royal city, that is, Constantinople, was transferred to the Franks."— Res gestæ ab Origine Mundi, lib. v. cap. 31.

A.D. 730.

The great names of this century are but two, John Damascene in the East, and Bede in our own island: both of these wrote upon the subject of Antichrist.

Bede's commentary on the Apocalypse is remarkable chiefly for its devout tone, and for the happy collation of other Scriptures. It was reckoned a great object to discover some clue to the order of the visions. Bede endeavours to lay down a rule:—

"After describing the four living creatures in the throne of God, together with the twenty-four elders, he sees that the Lamb, by opening the seven seals of the book, discloses the future trials and conflicts of the Church. Here, according to the custom of this book, he preserves the regular order down to the number six, and then, omitting the seventh, recapitulates: he then concludes both narratives with the seventh, as if following the strict order. But this repetition is to be understood according to the place in which it occurs; for he repeats, sometimes from the beginning of the passion, sometimes from the middle of the time, and sometimes from the last tribulation itself, or a little before it. But one rule he observes strictly: to recapitulate from a sixth."*

Bede takes the second, third, and fourth seals to represent the sufferings of the Church, rather than of the world in general. "In the first seal," he says, there "is seen the beauty of the primitive church; in the three that follow, the triple war against it. In the fifth, the glory of those that triumph in that war; in the sixth, the events of the time of Antichrist, with a repetition of matters a little before it. In the seventh John beholds the beginning of the everlasting rest."

* Bede's Preface to the Apocalypse.

In his exposition of the seals these sentences occur: —

"Second seal. To take peace from the earth. Its own peace: for the Church has received eternal peace, which Christ left with it.

"These are they that came out of the great tribulation. Through much tribulation we must enter into the kingdom of God: but who knows not that the tribulation under Antichrist will be greater than the rest?

"A great multitude out of all nations, tribes, and languages. Perhaps, having reckoned the tribes of Israel, to whom the Gospel was first preached, he now intends to celebrate the salvation of Gentiles."

Bede follows the custom of his age, in giving two senses to most of the prophetic times; one literal, the other vague and indefinite. In commenting upon Michael's war with the dragon, at the beginning of Antichrist's reign, he collates the parallel passage of Daniel, describing Michael as standing up at the beginning of the great tribulation.

Bede's Eastern cotemporary was John Damascene, a presbyter of Jerusalem, and therefore peculiarly concerned in the prophecies about Antichrist. "It is needful," he says, "to know that Antichrist must come." The impostor, he tells his people, "will sit in the temple of God, not ours, but the old Jewish temple." *

Living in Jerusalem, where rumours of false Messiahs were continually propagated, Damascenus is careful to warn his people against expecting a second earthly Advent: —

* Joh. Damascenus. Orthodoxæ fidei, lib. iv. cap. 26. The character of this writer is deeply stained by his support of image-worship.

"Antichrist will come with signs and lying wonders, feigned and not true. Those whose minds are baseless and unstable, will be deceived by him, and drawn away from the living God; for, if it were possible, he would deceive even the elect. But Enoch and Elias the Tishbite will be sent, and will turn the hearts of the fathers to the children, that is, the synagogue to our Lord Jesus Christ, and to the teaching of the Apostles; and they shall be slain by Antichrist. And the Lord shall come from heaven, in like mannner as the holy Apostles saw Him go up into heaven, perfect God and perfect man, with power and glory. And with the breath of His mouth He will slay the man of sin, the son of perdition. Let none, therefore, expect the Lord from earth, but from heaven, as He himself has declared."

An instance of delusion had lately occurred. In 713, a Syrian false Christ had appeared, and had deceived the Jews into believing that he was the Son of God.[*] The recent success of Mahomet produced many imitators, by proving that even without miraculous powers it was possible to procure the acknowledgment of the most extravagant claims.

While the East was infested with false Christs, the West suffered no less disturbance from false prophets. The first of these was the woman Thiota, who, in 847, declared that the world would end in the coming year. By promising assistance through her prayers, she not only raised large sums of money, but even procured the support of several priests. She professed to receive her information direct from heaven: but the chronicler does not stop to repeat her arguments or proofs, being in haste to arrive at the moral of the story,—the whipping that she re-

---

[*] Theophanes, Chronographia, sub anno.

ceived, and her consequent abandonment of the speculation.*

A.D. 850–890.

Rome's new resemblance to Babylon was at first beheld by the churches of Europe with an ill-defined feeling of wonder: they scarcely knew whether to be glad or sorry that their sister should be dealt with as a harlot. The monk Freculphus is disposed to be proud of the resemblance; he exults in the greatness of that "Western Babylon, during whose rule Christ was to come." The two Babylons he thus compares: "The one rose in the West, when the other fell in the East. The one, as it were dying, that is, submitting to foreign rule, willed away her inheritance: the other, coming to full age, acknowledged herself the heir, and spurned the limits of her own possessions. Then fell the empire of the East, and that of the West arose. And for this reason Rome is rightly called Babylon by the Apostle (Peter)." †

In 873, the little council of Oveto outdid Freculphus, attempting to derive the supremacy of the Roman Church from her succession to Babylon: "No one doubts," they argue, "that Babylon formerly held the principality of the cities of the world. But when Babylon was destroyed by the Lord, Rome obtained the primacy of the world, and this Rome the blessed Peter received for his share." ‡

---

* Pithœus, Annales Francorum, p. 52. This scarce and anonymous chronicle contains the original of that hackneyed story.

† Freculphi Chronicon, tom. i. lib. iii. c. 17.; also, c. 12. The passage is almost copied from Orosius.

‡ Harduin's Councils, t. vi. col. 134.

In a better spirit was the figure applied by Haymo, who perceived the dangers arising from the secular character of the bishopricks. "Thy merchants:"—he says, expounding Apoc. xviii., "that is, leaders and princes, who make merchandise of their souls to gain earldoms and bishopricks, and the other dignities of this world." *

Ansbert follows the smooth track of Primasius, making Rome the figure of the world. Babylon, therefore, is Rome; but, "under the name of that city is typified the power of the whole earthly kingdom." † The depressed state of Rome seems to have influenced his exposition; for "where," he asks, "is now that Rome, the second Babylon, once exalted above all kingdoms?"‡ Acting up to his definition of Babylon, he identifies together the flight out of Babylon, the flight from Judea to the mountains, and the flight of the woman to the wilderness.

A. D. 954.

As the thousandth year approached, there occurred a fresh panic about Antichrist's coming, and the end of the world. Queen Gerberge, resolved upon procuring the best information, passed by "her excellent chaplain, Dom Roricon," and went straight to the Abbot Adso, one of the few learned men of that "seculum obscurum." "What," she asked, "ought I to believe about Antichrist, his power, his persecutions, and his origin?" The time of his appearing she did

* Haymo in Apocalypsin; a work much read during the middle ages. Its date is about 850.
† Ambrosius Ansbertus in Apoc., B. P. Maxima, t. xiii. p. 590.
‡ Ibid. p. 558.

not inquire, perhaps already cautioned against asking it, for the clergy in general opposed all calculations of the year of the end. *

In answer to these questions, Adso composed a treatise, "De Antichristo." So widely was that tract circulated, that, from being copied into the spare parchment of other works, it has been ascribed in turn to Augustine, to Alcuin, and to Rabanus Maurus; it has been largely borrowed from by Hoveden, and finally has been reprinted by Strype as a recent fragment of Popery. But it is the Abbot Adso who writes thus: —

"All you that desire to know about Antichrist, mark first the meaning of his name. He is called so, because he will be in all things contrary to Christ, and will do the opposite of what Christ did. Christ came lowly, Antichrist will come in pride. Christ came to lift up the humble and to justify sinners: Antichrist will come to cast down the humble, to exalt sinners, and to promote the wicked. Evermore, he will teach those vices that are opposed to virtue, will annul the law of the Gospel, bring back devil-worship into the world, and, seeking vain-glory, will style himself God Almighty.

"Now this Antichrist has in his service many ministers of infidelity, some of whom have already entered the world before him. Of this number were Antiochus, Nero, and Domitian; and even now, in our own time, we know that there are many Antichrists. For every one, whether layman, clerk, or monk, who leads a life opposed to righteousness, sets at nought the rule of his order, and reviles that which is good, even he is an antichrist and a minister of Satan." †

Some new speculations had been broached concerning the origin of Antichrist. Adso finds it needful

---

* Ceillier, Hist. des Auteurs Ecclesiast., t. xix. p. 699.; also, for the letter of Adso, see Duchesne, Script. Franci, t. ii. p. 844.

† Inter Opp. Augustini, Ed. Bened., t. vi. Appendix.

to contradict the report that the man of sin will have no human father; but he approves of the supposition that Babylonia will be his birth-place, and Chorazin or Bethsaida the scene of his education. Thus, it was supposed, will be fulfilled the casting of those cities down to hell, in the same sense in which, by the enjoyment of Christ's presence, they had been exalted to heaven. He notices another new conceit: that the last of the Frank Roman Emperors will lay down his crown and sceptre on the mount of Olives, and will thus end at once the empire of the Romans and of the Christians.

The great point of Adso's treatise is to enforce the Apostolic caution, that the Lord will not come till after the falling away, the removal of the letting power, and the revelation of Antichrist:—

"Lastly, after all the other kingdoms, there came the kingdom of the Romans, which was stronger than all that were before it, and bare rule over all the kingdoms of the earth. For all nations and people submitted to the Romans, and served them under tribute. 'Therefore,' says the Apostle Paul, 'Antichrist shall not come into the world, unless there come first a falling away', that is, unless all kingdoms fall away from the Roman empire, to which they had been subject. But this time has not yet come; for though we now see the Roman empire for the greater part destroyed, yet, while the kings of the Franks endure, whose office it is to hold the Roman empire, its dignity will not altogether perish, but will subsist in its kings."

A. D. 990–1010.

As long as the appearance of Antichrist was expected, many an eye was turned to Rome as the probable scene of his first exploits. The Papal tyranny already provoked a suspicion, either that one of the Popes would turn out to be Antichrist, or that the man of sin, for the furtherance of his own designs, might usurp the Pontifical throne. Something like this idea occurs in the council of Rheims, where bishop Gherbert opposed the Papal claims. This Gherbert, in reporting the acts of the council, puts into the mouth of Arnulph a significant allusion to the absent Pope: —

"Whom, reverend fathers, do you take this man to be, seated on a lofty throne, and radiant with gold and purple? Whom, I say, do you take him to be? Truly, if destitute of charity, and puffed up by knowledge alone, he is an Antichrist, sitting in the temple of God, and showing himself as if he were God. But, if neither based on charity, nor exalted in knowledge, he is in the temple of God as a statue or an idol, from which to seek an answer is to consult stones."*

This speech is professedly made up from scraps, for which reason Gherbert has usually enjoyed the credit of being its author. Baronius divides the palm, noting in the margin, "Horrible blasphemy of Gherbert or of Arnulph."

Gherbert finally rose to the Papacy, taking the name of Sylvester the Second. The Papal historians never forgave his opposition to the spirit of Popery: for, in spite of the favourable testimony of his own age, Stella pretends that "he was made Pope of Rome by the assistance of the Devil; but on this condition, that after death both his body and his soul should belong to him by whose arts he had attained that lofty station." †

* Magdeburgh Centuries, cent. x. cap. 9.
† Stella, De Vitis Pontificum, A. D. 996. For the orignal of this story see William Godell, Bouquet's Historians, x. 260.

The Western Church now presents an uncommon spectacle: the multitude, at other times so slow to expect Christ's coming, now crying out with apprehension; and the students of prophecy, usually the most vigilant on their watch-tower, now labouring to quiet the fears of men, and to persuade them that there is no special reason to expect Christ's immediate return.

If anything might safely have been used as an argument against the nearness of the Advent, it was the very apprehension then generally prevailing. When building and worldly business were neglected through alarm, it could not be said that in that day, as in the days of Lot and of Noah, they planted, they builded: nor, when the multitude were expecting the worst, could that day be said to come as a thief.

Among the earliest of those that opposed the delusion was the Abbot Abbo, whose story is told on a stray leaf of MS. preserved by Baronius:—

"When I was a youth, I heard a sermon preached in church before the people of Paris, about the end of the world. In that sermon it was said that as soon as the thousandth year had ended, Antichrist would come, and soon afterwards the universal judgment. To the best of my power I opposed this preaching, from the Gospels, the Apocalypse, and the book of Daniel." *

Whatever may have been that preacher's text, the motto of his party was this: "When the thousand years are expired, Satan shall be loosed out of his prison." By making the millennium spiritual, and reckoning its beginning from the Incarnation, the

* Baronii Annales, anno 1001. The life of Abbo, including this extract, has been since published by Bouquet, Historians, t. x.

coming of Antichrist seemed fixed for about the year 1000. The inventors of a spiritual millennium took the thousand years as a round number put indefinitely: a supposition needful to their theory, in order to prevent an appearance of fixing the date of the end.

Even ordinary events now assumed an aspect of terror. An eclipse of the sun, that happened about 995, gave rise to a strange panic in Calabria. At noon-day the darkness was so great that the cattle returned to their stalls, and the birds to their nests. But man's guilty conscience suffered him not to rest so peacefully. To the army, then encamped in the district, it seemed that the last judgment was at hand, doubtless from the signs in the sun, so suddenly obscured, and in the stars, now shining at noonday. Happy was he who could secure the asylum of a waggon, a tub, or even an empty wine-cask. The bishop Everaclus, hearing of the panic, rushed in among the ambushed troops: "Bravest of warriors," he began, "you, who in a thousand perils have snatched victory, and have made your names illustrious, rise, I beseech you, and fear nothing!" Their courage returned with the sunshine, and soon they laughed away whatever serious impressions their late terror might have awakened. *

But soon a more important event awakened the fears of prophetic students: Jerusalem was taken and trodden under foot by the Turks. This catastrophe, according to Godell, produced a better effect than the eclipse in Calabria: —

"In the year of our Lord 1009, through God's permission,

* Gesta Leodiensium. Martene, Collectio Amplissima, t. iv. 860.

the land of Judea was invaded by the unclean Turks. Jerusalem was taken, and the glorious sepulchre of Christ our Lord fell into their hands. This happened in the eleventh year of Robert, king of the Franks, when Basil and Constantine were kings of the Greeks, and Henry emperor of the Romans. At that time many of the Jews *barbarized* through fear. In the year following, when these events were reported throughout the world, fear and grief filled the hearts of most people, since they imagined that the end of the world had arrived; and the better disposed, turning the occasion to profit, seriously addressed themselves to the reformation of their lives."*

A. D. 1000–1100.

Through all the terrors of the middle ages, the regular expositors held fast by this great argument, — before Antichrist can come, the Roman empire must be destroyed and the ten kings arise. For they placed themselves by the side of those to whom St. Paul wrote, " That day shall not come, except there come a falling away first; and now ye know what withholdeth." The revival of learning allowed this test to be applied with general effect; and in the eleventh century three great writers opposed the argument of Gherbert, who had contended that Antichrist was probably at hand, because several churches had recently " fallen away" from the Roman communion.

To begin with the nearest home, Lanfranc, Archbishop of Canterbury : — " Only he who now letteth will let. He means the Roman empire, after the destruction of which Antichrist will come."†

---

* Narrative of William Godell, Bouquet's historians, t. x. p. 262.
† Lanfranc in Pauli Epist.

Theophylact was Archbishop of Bulgaria about the same time:—" Only he who now letteth, will let: that is, when the Roman empire is taken away, then he will come. For as long as there is any dread of this empire, no one will readily submit to him; but when it shall be destroyed, he will raise himself upon the anarchy, endeavouring to usurp the empire of God and man."*

Œcumenius also was a Greek, but his diocese or presbytery is unknown:—" Only he who now letteth: that is, when the throne and kingdom of the Romans which now hinders, shall cease to be and shall come to an end, then will be revealed the wicked one, namely, Antichrist."†

The Apocalyptic commentary of Anselm, deacon of Laon, remarkable for its clearness and devotional spirit, is the only other prophetic treatise of this century, now extant.‡ This Anselm was the author of the Interlinear Gloss.

A. D. 1080.

Scarcely three centuries ago we saw Rome a supplicant, first for protection, and next for honours. We have now to behold Rome dominant, Rome insolent, Rome trampling upon the successor of her benefactors, and, under pretence of wielding God's power, imitating the pride and the pretensions of the god of this world.

By a bull dated 1080, Gregory VII. pretended to

* Theophylact in Pauli Epist.
† Œcumenius in Pauli Epist.
‡ Published with the works of Anselm, Archbishop of Canterbury.

depose Henry the Fourth, head of the western Roman empire, appointing in his stead Rodolph, who had been wrongfully elected by rebel princes. This bull was addressed to the Apostles Peter and Paul: —

"Trusting in the judgment and mercy of God, and of His most pious mother, Mary ever Virgin, and supported by your authority, I excommunicate the aforesaid Henry, whom they call king, together with all his abettors, binding them in the bonds of anathema. Also, on the part of Almighty God and of yourselves, I once more deprive him of the Teutonic kingdom and of Italy, take from him all royal power and dignity, and forbid every Christian to obey him as king. Moreover, all who have sworn, or shall swear to him, concerning his government, I absolve from the promise of their oath."*

The friends of Henry called a council, and resolved to excommunicate Hildebrand himself. It was difficult to find a priest bold enough to proclaim the sentence. At length a certain William, under the influence of wine, says the monkish historian, was prevailed upon to "set his mouth against heaven:" and, that he might more thoroughly act out the part of Judas, he afterwards partook of the holy sacrament. But soon he felt an inward burning, like the fire among the thorns, says Hugo; or, as would be said in our days, like the effects of poison. Crying out with the anguish, he fell back upon his seat, and in a little while breathed his last. †

The bull of Gregory threw Europe into amazement. Many years of bloodshed followed; many supporters of the Papacy were shaken in their allegiance; and murmurs against the pretender to these new powers

---

* Harduin's Councils, tom. vi. col. 1591.
† Chronicle of Hugo, in Harduin, t. vi. col. 1593.

were heard on every side. Heriman wrote to Gregory, desiring to have his mind set at rest as to the lawfulness of the proceeding; and Gregory, though professing to see no room for his doubts, condescended to vindicate the act: —

"As for your request that I would by letter fortify and support you against the madness of those who with wicked mouth babble forth that the authority of the holy Apostolic see cannot excommunicate the King Henry, and absolve every one from the oath of fealty to him, he being a despiser of Christian law, a destroyer of churches and of the empire, as well as a favourer and accomplice of heretics; — as for this request, I say, it does not seem to me altogether called for. * * *

"Who does not know that kings and rulers derive their origin from those who, in ignorance of God, have sought by pride, rapine, perfidy, murder, in a word, by almost every crime, at the instigation of the Devil, who is the prince of this world, to reign over mankind, their equals, goaded on by blind lust and intolerable presumption? Such men, when they seek to bend the priests of the Lord to their own footsteps, to whom can they be compared more fitly than to him who is head over all the children of pride? Who, when he tempted the High Priest himself, the head of priests, the Son of the Highest, promised Him all the kingdoms of the world, saying, All these will I give Thee, if Thou wilt fall down and worship me."*

The Church of Rome has no cause to boast of the unchangeableness of her doctrine. From Rome St. Peter once wrote these words, — "Submit yourselves to every ordinance of man for the Lord's sake, whether it be to the king, as supreme:" but Gregory now bids the Church not to submit itself to the king, nor observe its oath of allegiance to him. St. Paul taught

* Gregorii Septimi Epist., lib. viii. ep. 21. in Harduin, t. vi. 1469.

the Romans that the existing powers are ordained of God: Gregory traces them to the Devil. The first Gregory thought it an imitation of the Devil to claim headship over the Church: the seventh Gregory both claims that headship, and reckons those that oppose him as themselves imitators of the Devil. And this is but one way among many in which the Church of Rome has changed from her Apostolic beginnings; one way among many in which the faithful city has become a harlot.

The pride and arrogance of Gregory in some points resembles what is foretold of Antichrist. There is in both the same attempt by superhuman power to crush and master the appointed governments of earth. Happily for the Papal usurper, the comparison fails in one point. Gregory professes to be God's servant and vicar, while Antichrist will set up himself above every god, acknowledging no superior even in heaven.

A. D. 1100–1200.

The twelfth century is not to be so briefly disposed of. Let us first hear what the regular expositors have to say about Babylon; for if, after these doings of Gregory, they do not begin to speak out plainly, they must be suspected of having been themselves drinking deeply of that golden cup.

Bruno of Ast invents a new theory of Babylon:— that it represented Rome Pagan, but has no reference to Rome Christian. "I said that the head of the beast, was Rome, which also was once Babylon. And the beast, having shed the blood of many saints, is seen entirely red and crimson. Because also he followed many superstitions of idols, he is said to be full of names of blasphemy."*

Bruno soon found a follower. Before ten years had elapsed, the Abbot Rupert improved upon his master. He speaks of Rome, " which was once Babylon, but is now a very Zion. She is, I say, according to the faith of the blessed Apostle Peter, the mother of cities, the faithful Zion."†

The Abbot Joachim somewhat redeems the character of the century: —

"I saw the woman drunk with the blood of the saints. As I said before, the city of the reprobate, which is called Babylon, is not to be supposed the city of Rome alone, nor, which God forbid, the city of Rome throughout, but the whole multitude of the wicked, and of those that are born after the flesh. * * *

" And the woman which thou sawest is that great city. Not upon the authority of this book alone, or of this passage, has it been handed down to us by the fathers that Rome is spiritually Babylon, but also from the declaration of Peter, who writes from the city of Rome, — The church which is in Babylon saluteth you. And in this saying there is no small consolation to the people called Roman; for, in the very city which is called Babylon, there dwells as a stranger the city Jerusalem."‡

But though little was said expressly about Babylon, the corruptions of the Church did not escape abundant notice during this age.

A. D. 1106.

In this year Pope Paschal II. had occasion to

* Bruno Astensis in Apoc.; B. P. Maxima, t. xx. 1706.

† De Gloriâ Trinitatis, lib. viii. c. 5.; also, Comment. in Apocalypsin.

‡ Commentarius in Apocalypsin, cap. 17.

travel through Italy. Rumours were afloat that the end of the world was at hand; a comet was visible, and the level of the sea had suddenly changed. All these dangers Paschal boldly faced; but at Florence he was brought to a standstill by the report that Antichrist was coming. The rumour was traced to Fluentius, who, as bishop of that city, had declared on the strength of his own imagination that Antichrist was already born, and would soon appear to the world. A council was forthwith called: Fluentius, faring better than Thiota, was reproved, and Pope Paschal was suffered to pursue his journey in comfort.

But the Pontiff was before long addressed by a voice of warning, neither to be traced to an enthusiast, nor to be contradicted by the progress of events. For some cause not now remembered, he had written to Robert Count of Flanders, ordering him to persecute the clergy of Liege wherever they could be found. This edict drew from them the earliest recorded protest against the Church of Rome, founded on its Babylonish character.

In that epistle they propose to derive the name of Babylon from the character of Papal rather than of Pagan Rome, a remark not less original than important: —

"Peter says in his epistle,—The church that is in Babylon saluteth you. Hitherto this reason has been given for his calling Rome Babylon, that Rome was at that time confounded through idolatry and all uncleanness. But now my grief interprets it thus: that when Peter said, — The church

* Platina in Vitâ Paschal. II. Baronius, anno 1106. Harduin, anno 1105.

which is in Babylon, he foresaw, in the spirit of prophecy, the confusion of discord by which at this day the Church is rent. * * * Esaias says,—Babylon my beloved is become a wonder to me; but I say,—Rome my beloved mother is become a wonder to me; for what so wonderful, yea, what so miserable?"*

A. D. circ. 1130.

The corruptions of the Church, now grown too flagrant to be kept secret even by its friends, were vigorously attacked by the zealous Bernard. He declared repeatedly that its condition was a fit preparation for the coming of Antichrist,—a mode of reproof which had become more usual than a comparison with Babylon; either because the latter was thought too pointed against the Pope, or because the general expectation of Antichrist gave greater effect to a warning drawn from the nearness of his coming.

What most grieves Bernard is that the corruption is universal. "All friends," he exclaims, "yet all enemies; all near of kin, yet all hostile; all servants, yet none at peace; all of one family, yet all seek their own. They are ministers of Christ, yet they serve Antichrist. Enriched with the Lord's possessions, they bring the Lord no honour: hence the meretricious pomp which is daily seen, the theatrical dress, the royal luxury. Hence the gold lavished upon the bridles, the saddles, and the spurs; for the spurs now outshine the altars."†

* Harduin, t. vi. col. 1769. "Nè in hâc tantùm parte," writes the Pope, "sed ubique, cum poteris, Henricum hæreticorum caput, et ejus fautores, pro viribus persequaris."

† Bernardus in Cantica, Sermo 33. Bernard was well supported by his contemporary, the English Aelred. Sermons on Isaiah, xiii.

As Bernard repeats often the same charges, one more extract may suffice: —

"All Christians; yet almost all seek their own, not the things of Jesus Christ. The very offices of church dignity have passed into a matter of filthy lucre, a traffic of darkness; and in them men seek, not the salvation of souls, but the acquisition of wealth. For this they shave their heads, for this they frequent the churches, celebrate masses, and chant the psalms. At this day they shamelessly quarrel for bishopricks and archdeaconries, for abbeys and other dignities, that the revenues of the Church may be wasted in the pursuit of superfluity and pride. It remains that the man of sin be revealed, the son of perdition, the demon, not only of the day, but of the noonday." (English version, the destruction that wasteth at noonday.) "Who not only is transformed into an angel of light, but exalts himself above all that is called God, or that is worshipped. Cruelly, indeed, does he attack the heel of our mother the Church, grieving that by her his head is bruised. This, evidently, will be his worst attack; yet from this even will the Truth deliver the church of the elect, for their sake shortening the days, and with the brightness of His coming destroying the demon of the noonday."*

Bernard was applied to for news of his friend Norbert, who had suddenly disappeared, and was supposed to have started for Jerusalem. "When I asked him," says Bernard, "what he thought about Antichrist, he assured me that he knew most certainly that Antichrist would be revealed within the lifetime of the present generation. On my asking how he had arrived at that certainty, he endeavoured to explain; but, after hearing what he had to say, I did not feel myself called upon to believe it. At length he said positively, that he should not see death till he

* Bernard upon Ps. xci. Sermo 6.

had seen the general persecution raging in the Church."*

The better informed received these speculations with coldness; they felt that it was not theirs to know the times and seasons. But, among the excitable and illiterate, the expectation of Antichrist almost amounted to a mania. The Abbess Hildegarde, who had learnt nothing but the Psalter, attempted a humble Apocalypse of her own: she saw a black pig, representing the impurity of the age. But of this she furnished a more forcible illustration, by inventing an account of Antichrist's mother; a horrible story, which reflects no credit, either on the virgin-abbess, or the nunnery to which she belonged.† Hildegarde did not think that Antichrist was as yet born, but believed that his mother was already prepared, by satanic influence, to become the recipient of hellish power.

A. D. 1145.

A new scheme of interpretation now began to be planned;— an adaptation of history to a part of those prophecies which till then had been applied exclusively to the end. The first part of the Apocalypse so explained was the vision of the seven seals.

Down to the year 1120, every writer that had handled the seals had agreed in the meaning of the first, sixth, and seventh. The first had been taken to mean the Gospel triumph; the sixth the precursors of the last judgment; the seventh the beginning of the eternal rest: and though, in 1120, Rupert applied the sixth to the destruction of Jerusalem, his

* Bernardi Epistola 56.
† Alberti Chronicon. Cent. xii.

innovation met with no favour; nor did he succeed in shaking the Church's confidence in that explanation which had been handed down from the earliest times.

The problem, as it presented itself to the expositor, was this: Given, in the first and sixth seals, the beginning and the end of the dispensation, to find in its intermediate history the intervening four. A solution was first offered by Anselm of Havilsburgh.

The seven seals, according to Anselm, represent seven states of the Christian Church: she is seen, at first white with purity and the lustre of miracles; then red with martyrdom, till the time of Diocletian. She is blackened by heresies from Arius to Nestorius; pale with hypocrisy through the remainder of the dispensation; expectant till her martyrs' recompense be awarded; convulsed under Antichrist and the great tribulation; and, seventhly, she reposes in infinite blessedness in the deep silence of heaven. But this scheme, so simple and attractive, cannot easily be carried out; for few of its supporters can agree in its application. The second, fifth, and even the sixth seals, have been in turn applied to Diocletian: the first, the second, and even the sixth, to Constantine.

In the first and sixth, Anselm follows closely, yet not servilely, the primitive tradition:—

"The white horse is the Church's first state, bright and beautiful with the lustre of miracles: for in that newness all admired and magnified her. And he that sat upon it, having a bow, is Christ, governing the Church with the bow of apostolic teaching, humbling and laying low the proud. And there was given Him a crown: for He went into a far country to receive for Himself a kingdom. And He went forth, conquering, that He might conquer; even as He said to His followers, Be of good cheer, I have overcome the world. Observe, how in that first state of the nascent Church the number of the believers was more and more increased, a multitude both of men and women. So daily did the Church of God shine forth in the lustre of miracles and in the number of its believing members. * * *

"The sixth seal: — That state of the Church in which there is indeed a great earthquake, even that terrible persecution which will come in the time of Antichrist. And great indeed it will be: for the Lord said that then there shall be tribulation such as was not since there began to be a nation. For in other persecutions, though many kinds of torture were employed against Christianity, yet the faith itself was held pure and without doubts. But here both tortures will be employed, and a false faith will be inculcated in the name of Christ: for it will be said, Lo, here is Christ; or, Lo, there; and there will be tribulation, such as never has been; not only in the amount of persecution, but also in the subversion of the faith, for men will not know what to believe or what to cling to."*

A. D. 1150–1180.

The Church of Rome, already secularised in effect by the assumption of temporal power, soon began to proclaim openly that its kingdom was of this world. The Popes now changed the style of the Church, naming it "the court of Rome." The alteration attracted little notice, except from one man, and that a reader of the Apocalypse, who was not slow to perceive its mischievous bearing. Bishop Geroch at once addressed a remonstrance to the Pope, and afterwards, in a second edition of the tract, explained the source of his anxiety: —

* Dialogorum, lib. i. cap. vii.—xiii. In D'Achery's Spicilegium, ed. quarto, tom. 13.

"Ps. cxxxvii. (?): In this Psalm there are described two cities, which, with their citizens, are opposed to each other: these are Jerusalem and Babylon. In a long tract which I wrote during the lifetime of Pope Eugenius, taking this Psalm for my text, I treated both of their admixture and of their distinction. That tract I presented to the Pontiff of blessed memory, with the intention that the court of Rome, which Peter declares to be the Church collected in Babylon (by the name of Babylon figuratively denoting the city of Rome), that their court, I say, should take heed to itself and labour to exhibit both itself and the whole Church, which it ought to govern, distinct from Babylonish confusion, and free from all spot or wrinkle: for in this matter at least she does not appear spotless, that having been called formerly the Church of Rome she is now styled the Court of Rome."*

Geroch quotes largely from the Apocalypse, but with much vagueness, or perhaps caution, as he was writing direct to the Pope.

While Norbert and Hildegarde were stimulating the terrors of the crowd, the regular expositors still plied with effect the counter-argument, drawn from the continued existence of the Roman Empire. Thus Peter Lombard, the "Master of the Sentences:" "He who now holds the Roman Empire may hold, that is, he who now rules may rule, till he be out of the midst, that is, till that power be taken out of the midst of the world."

Otto wrote the world's history from Adam to Antichrist (omitting the Reformation). He reckons that Antichrist's empire will be a last form of the Roman.

Close upon these comes Peter Comestor, the "Master of Scholastic History:" "It had ten horns. This belongs to the end of the world: for then the Roman

---

* Baluze, Miscell. (ed. fol.) t. ii. p. 197.

Empire will be divided into ten kingdoms." Also Hugo Etherianus: " The Roman Empire will suffer ruin from Antichrist, who will be in turn destroyed by Christ, our Lord and Deliverer."*

Hugo notices Michael's office in the time of Antichrist: —

" At that time shall Michael stand up, the great prince that standeth for the children of thy people : for, as the prophet hints in this place, the care of the Jews is delivered to the Archangel Michael, that he may put to flight and to confusion those that oppose them. Therefore, when Antichrist oppresses the Jews, Michael withstands him; as Elias, who will come to announce the advent of the Saviour, that they who believe may obtain the prize of salvation. Then, describing the superabundance of ills which Antichrist will fill up, he adds, And there shall be a time of trouble such as never was since there was a nation." (Cap. xxiii.)

This century produces four continuous commentaries on the Apocalypse. Bruno of Ast follows the earlier monks ; Rupert labours to innovate. His great feat is the transposition of the letters of the Beast's number, from DCLXVI to DIC LVX, for " Dic me esse lucem," Acknowledge me to be the Light. This conceit found some favour with his successors.

Richard St. Victor aims higher: his book displays much of that precision which was afterwards brought to its height by the schoolmen. But these lesser lights of the age fade before the celebrity of Joachim, at once so serious and so extravagant, so opposed to Roman corruption and so obsequious to the Pope ; in a word, so self-contradictory, as to cause the historian

* Peter Lombard on St. Paul's Epistles. Otto Frissengensis, Annales, lib. viii. c. 6. Petrus Comestor, Hist. Scholastica in Danielem, cap. vii. Hugo Etherianus, De Regressu Animæ. Published in the Orthodoxographia, and in the B. P. Maxima, t. xxii.

more embarrassment than all other writers on prophecy put together.

A. D. circ. 1190.

The Abbot Joachim inflicts a lasting injury on the study of prophecy, by uniting in himself two characters till then kept distinct:—the regular expositor, and the rash prognosticator of times and seasons. From that time downwards we shall find men of learning and sincerity, men who ought to be a check upon the credulity of the many, hazarding assertions about dates and years, always mistaken, never profiting by experience, and at last going far to bring the study of prophecy into general disrepute.

Joachim's own history is the best comment upon his commentary. When very young, he travelled to Palestine, and, on reaching Mount Thabor, fasted forty days in a cave. When he came out, he began to write upon the Apocalypse. This romantic preparation so turned his head, that in conversation with the Abbot Adam he declared himself inspired. "God," he said, "who bestowed upon the prophets the spirit of prophecy, has given me the spirit of understanding; so that by God's holy Spirit I understand distinctly all the mysteries of holy Scripture, even as the holy prophets understood them when uttering them in the Spirit of God."

The abbot now asked him the usual question: What do you think about Antichrist? Joachim answered confidently: "He is at this moment a young man." Which opinion, adds the historian, Adam refuted.*

* Bolland's Saints, seventh volume for May, p. 139.

Joachim now began to utter predictions, if possible, still more rash. " There will be," he at first said, "1260 years from the birth of the child Jesus to the birth of Antichrist." At another time he fixed the opening of the sixth seal, and therefore the revelation of the man of sin, for the year 1199. Afterwards he grew more general: " All the time after 1200 I consider dangerous."* When expounding to the crusaders in Palestine, he assured them that Antichrist was already born, and would shortly be raised to the see of Rome.†

Joachim's reputation at length reached the ears of King Richard the First, then on an expedition to the Holy Land. Richard resolved to hear the prophet for himself, and, if we may believe our countryman Roger, even entered the lists with him in prophetic controversy. The Bollandists indignantly reject the whole story; and, considering the circumstances, we shall do wisely to limit our belief to its outline, and to place " Roger of Hoveden" in the same class of historians with Walter of Abbotsford.

Joachim's method of expounding was simple enough: placing himself close upon the end, he adapted the concluding prophecies to the events of his own time. Of any series of seven he makes the sixth present: therefore there is but one more to come. This method, afterwards so often applied to the seals, trumpets, and vials, was not only invented by Joachim, but even made the basis of his commentary. And now, according to Roger, he tries it

* Alberti Chronicon, sub anno 1188. Also Appendix ad Fasciculum Rerum, de Periculo Ecclesiæ, cap. 8., and Oudini Script. Eccles. t. ii. col. 1682.

† Roger Hoveden, anno 1190.

upon our Richard: "There are, it says, seven kings: five are fallen:—Herod, Nero, Constantius, Mahomet, Melsemut; and one is:—Saladin. But Saladin," continues this prophet of good things, "Saladin will soon lose possession of the holy city, and the name of Richard will be exalted above all the kings of the earth. And the seventh will be Antichrist, who, when he cometh, will continue but a short space."

Richard now shows himself as much at home in the Apocalypse as in single combat. Proof against this flattering scheme, he lays down, in opposition, the standard doctrine of the schools:—

"And the king turning to him said, I thought that Antichrist would be born in Antioch or in Babylon, of the tribe of Dan; also that he would reign in the Lord's temple in Jerusalem, and would walk in the land in which Christ walked. That he would reign there for three years and a half, and would dispute with Enoch and Elias, and kill them; that afterwards he is to die; and after his death God will allow sixty days for repentance, that those persons may repent who have erred from the way of truth, and have been deceived by the preaching of Antichrist and of his false prophets."[*]

The clergy who were present supported the king against the Abbot.

In afterlife Joachim grew more sober. The corruptions of the Church, deeply grieving his mind, led him to look forward to some better state of Christianity yet unseen, a "dispensation of the Spirit." Of this change he entertained a vague con-

[*] Roger de Hoveden, in Richard I. Anno 1190. The story seems to have been made up from Joachim's and Adso's works. Roger never knows when to leave off expounding, but, when the story seems quite ended, breaks out afresh: "It follows, And ten horns."

ception, afterwards elaborated by the Franciscans, and, as will appear in the sequel, ultimately ripening into the great Reformation of the sixteenth century. While encumbering the study of prophecy with novel theories, Joachim enforces with great clearness the primitive teaching about Rome. One passage has been already quoted: with one more the abbot of Curacio shall be dismissed:—

"If any man worship the Beast and his image. What the third angel has to say, he says with a great voice, because at that time the tribulation will be great, and the distress such as has never been felt. And how so? Because false Christs and false prophets shall arise, to deceive, if it were possible, even the elect. Also, as was remarked above, the beast that arises out of the earth will cause that whoever will not worship the image of the Beast shall be killed. And when will this take place? Without doubt after the fall of Babylon: for, when the harlot has been delivered into the hands of the Beast and of his ten Kings, the Beast and the false prophet, being ignorant of the Lord's design, will infer that the Roman Empire, once the head of all kingdoms, has been delivered into their power, solely because the Christian religion was false. And thus, triumphing over Babylon, they will attempt to blot out even the Christian name from the earth."*

A. D. 1200–1220.

For some time past the crusades had been carried on with vigour, chiefly through the promise of eternal forgiveness made to those who took up arms. The beginning of this abuse is described by Peter Casinensis:—

* Joachim in Apocalypsin, cap. xiv. This sentiment, which Joachim puts into the mouth of Antichrist, is already repeated by modern semi-infidels, who, in attacking the corruptions of Popery, think to annihilate Christianity itself.

"The movement is said to have begun with the case of some penitents in Gaul, who were not able worthily to do penance among their friends, and were exceedingly ashamed to live without arms where they were known. They therefore received counsel from Pope Urban, of holy memory, a prudent and truly apostolic man, then visiting the country beyond sea, about Church business. By his authority they promised, faithfully and speedily, to set out, to rescue from the hands of infidels the holy place of Christ's sepulchre, for a penance and the forgiveness of their sins. And they were assured that whatever danger or hardship they might undergo would be reckoned by the Lord in the place of penance, provided that for the future they would abstain from their former crimes."*

By this plan the country was cleared of some ruffians, who preferred to have their throats cut in Palestine with the honours of war and martyrdom. Bernard was delighted with the riddance: "Egypt," he exclaims, "was glad at their departure, and the Mount Zion rejoiced in their protection." As for the "truly apostolic" character of the measure, we read nothing of the sort in the Acts or Epistles of the Twelve.

Innocent III. applied a new stimulus to the devotion of the crusaders. He gave out that Mahomet was the man of sin, and that his kingdom would last 666 years. He was not aware that the letters of Maometis make 666, a discovery not made till the revival of Greek learning in the fifteenth century. Nor, indeed, was the name at first spelt in a manner to allow of the adaptation.

The Pontiff, bent rather upon recruiting than expounding, thus addressed the council of the Lateran:—

---

* Chronicon Casinense, lib. iv. cap. 11.

"There has arisen a certain son of perdition, the false prophet Mahomet, who by worldly allurements and carnal pleasures has turned many from the truth; and though his imposture still continues to flourish, yet we trust in the Lord, who has already granted us a sign for good, that the end of this Beast is drawing near; for his number, according to the Apocalypse of John, is limited to 666, and will soon be brought to an end by the operation of the sevenfold Spirit, who, with the flame of charity, will rekindle the hearts of the faithful, now growing cold: for of that number nearly six hundred years are now elapsed."*

Innocent's interpretations were not all equally harmless. On the anniversary of his consecration he boldly declared himself to be the bridegroom of the Roman Church, thus putting himself in the place of Christ, and showing that the Church of Rome acknowledged another husband than her Lord.

Innocent does not scruple to apply to himself what is said expressly of Christ: "He that hath the bride is the bridegroom. Am not I the bridegroom, and every one of you that is willing, the friend of the bridegroom? Certainly I am the bridegroom, since I possess the noble, rich, and lofty, the comely, chaste, and gracious, the sacred and holy Church of Rome, which by God's appointment is the mother and mistress of all the faithful." Nor is he content, even in this sense, to be the "husband of one wife:"† "Have you not read that Abraham had a wife Sarah, who nevertheless brought in to him her maid Agar. In this he committed no crime, but fulfilled an office. In like manner the Roman Pontiff has the Church

---

* Harduin's Councils, t. vii. 3. A. D. 1214.

† A monkish adaptation of the words, suggested by the enforcement of clerical celibacy.

of Rome for his bride, which nevertheless brings in to him the Churches subject to herself."*

A. D. 1215.

In this year Innocent established the Inquisition. Henceforward Rome is seen drunk with the blood of saints; for that, among her innumerable victims, were many of the excellent of the Church, the voice of history declares plainly.

The great historian of the Inquisition, the Inquisitor Paramus, boldly ascribes its establishment to direct inspiration: " the God of glory," he says, " implanted this mind in Innocent." † Before long, Dominic is made Inquisitor-General; and then Paramus finds enough to boast of: —

" Our people seized many of the Albigenses, some of whom were strangled by halters, and others consigned to the flames. These last were so sullenly, obstinately, and pertinaciously lost to all sense, that, though first admonished to consult the safety of their souls, if they wished to escape punishment, they madly hastened to throw themselves headlong into the fire. Beltrand makes their number more than three hundred; but Æmilius makes it four hundred. But one thing I marvel at not a little; that in no history whatever, down to that time, have I read of so celebrated an act of faith, and a spectacle so solemn." ‡

In the same year the annual performance of auricular confession was enjoined upon " every believer of either sex." Those who neglected it were to be

---

* Innocent III. Sermo 3. In Consec. Pont. Max.

† Paramus de S. Inquisitione, p. 94. There is but one edition — that of 1598.

‡ P. 101.

excommunicated, and, in case of death, deprived of Christian burial.*

By this decree Rome forced upon all people the cup of her own mixing. Of the contents of that cup a specimen may still be found in various penitential canons, the character of which secures for them, at this day, a certain degree of obscurity. The history of this much abused ordinance may be sketched in very few words.

In the beginning, the Apostles established a system by which the public offender was separated from communion, lest the Church should be disgraced by the admixture of scandalous characters. In the hands of the first Leo, this ordinance passed into private voluntary confession, followed by private penance. Still later, a system of questioning was adopted by the priest, and voluntarily submitted to by those who desired his guidance. But now, in the 13th century, every member of the Church was forced to undergo an examination, in matters the most revolting, the most minutely detailed, and often the most remotely improbable, that a corrupt and subtle imagination could invent.†

In the present work the confessional will be noticed

* Fourth Lateran Council, canon 21.

† A history of penance has been written by the presbyter Morinus. In his appendix he has collected some penitential rules, which, though not authorised documents of the Roman Church, throw light upon the state of society existing under the system. In those rules it is thus enjoined: —

"Women are to be diligently examined, as I have said; for after they have confessed all their sins, as in the case of men, they are to be asked this also, how many infants they have killed, especially if they are widows or nuns." P. 95.

in no other point of view than as it appears by the light of the Inquisition. The relation thus established between priest and penitent soon produced its too certain consequences, so that, by a bull of Paul the Fourth, the inquisitors were empowered to take the ordinance under their special protection.

First, the woman was enjoined, under peril of the greater excommunication, to report to the inquisitor every suspicious act, word, or deed, on the part of the priest. The subject was beset with difficulties, but through these the inquisitors shaped their course with admirable moderation and skill. The seal of secrecy, till then the priest's safeguard, they declared to belong solely to the strict business of confession: they even defined what might seem indefinable, the precise point at which his advances could be said to begin: "a wicked winking with the eyes,"[*] said Paramus on the authority of Ovid, is enough. The impossibility of procuring witnesses was duly allowed for: and, whereas the woman might be actuated by revengeful feelings against a severe confessor, the liability to this temptation was cautiously weighed against her evidence.

But when the inquisitors had done their best, what

" Dicere debet, in quot personas incidit, hoc est, mulieres : similiter, mulieres in quot viros. Tum qui, Deo juvante, suscipit eorum confessionem, interroget eos quales erant personæ, ordinem secutus differentiarum fornicationum ; hoc est, quot conjugatæ, quot meretrices, quot viduæ, quot ancillæ, quot monachæ magni habitûs, quot sacratæ, nempe Presbyterissæ, et Diaconorum qui in gradu sunt, uxores. Monachæ enim parvi habitus, *et Lectorum uxores, ut meretrices judicantur.*" P.111. A more infamous assault upon the sacred character of marriage has seldom been perpetrated.

[*] Paramus, p. 864.

was the state of the woman under their complicated machinery? What sort of rest in the Church did she enjoy, while Rome's power was at its height, and its institutions in unrestrained operation?

The woman, unless she attended the confessional, was excommunicated, and denied Christian burial: if regular in confessing, she was at the mercy of the priest, whose advances, if listened to, endangered her salvation, and, if repelled, might expose her to a charge of heresy, fatal to her character: "for," says Paramus, "the seizure for heresy defames vehemently." By leaving the solicitation unnoticed, she was in danger of excommunication, being reckoned an accomplice of the priest; by reporting it, she brought herself into the clutches of the inquisitors, a dangerous remedy for the perils of her situation.

Paramus expends his pity on the confessor; for the woman he feels none, unless it be that in the heart of an inquisitor pity turns to gall. Such as it is, his pity is thus expressed: —

"Woman is to man the way of evil, the path of death, the serpent's lesson, the devil's counsellor, the canker of the tree, the fountain of error, the rust of saints, mind's mousetrap, life's robbery; sweet death, a soft blow, delicate destruction, pleasant evil, a savory stab, universal ruin; the head of sin, the devil's arms, loss of paradise, mother of transgression, &c. &c.; the infamy of priests, the confusion of religious orders, destruction of a good name, mother of guilt, root of vices, beginning and end of every ill, leader of the wicked, contriver of crime; and, if any thing worse can be said, woman herself is a heap of wickedness."*

* Paramus de Origine, &c. S. Inquisitionis. Quæstio 10. De Solicitatione ad Libid. in Act. Conf.

A. D. 1240.

A hundred and sixty years after the tyranny of Hildebrand, the anti-social and Anti-Christian tendency of his doctrines was first pointed out. In a speech addressed to the senate of the Roman empire, on the occasion of a feud with the Pope, Archbishop Eberhard employed two principal arguments: first, that Rome was Babylon, and the Pope a wolf in sheep's clothing; secondly, that the end of the world was at hand, and that the Pope, already springing up as the little horn, would merge into the expected Antichrist.*

In maintaining his second, the orator broke down. In vain he appealed to the comets and prodigies, the signs in the sun, moon, and stars, the wars, famines, pestilences, and earthquakes, that had recently been felt. He attempted to prove, for the first time since Daniel wrote, that the ten kingdoms had arisen in the Roman world, and that the Pope was then employed in subjugating three of them, Germany, Italy, and Sicily. This reasoning, though since falsified by history, told powerfully on the fears of the senate; for, at the time, the course of events seemed likely to support his prediction. "The priests of Babylon," he exclaimed, "desire to reign alone, they cannot endure a rival. They will not cease till they have trodden everything under their feet, — till they sit in the temple of God, and are exalted above all that is worshipped."

In addition to this likeness in pride, Hildebrand had introduced a new feature of resemblance to Anti-

---

* Aventinus, Annales Boiorum, lib. vii.

christ, the contempt of appointed governments. This was first noticed by Eberhard: —

They desire us to resist the sovereign majesty appointed by the Supreme God. A hundred and seventy years ago, Hildebrand, under pretence of religion, first laid the foundations of Antichrist's kingdom. He it was that first waged that impious war, which, through his successors, has been carried on till the present day. . . . Trust to experience; they will not desist till they have brought the emperor into submission, destroyed the honour of the Roman empire, oppressed the true pastors that feed the flock, removed those dogs that are able to bark, and have in this manner extinguished and ruined every thing." *

By the wolves in sheep's clothing, Eberhard understands " the scribes and Pharisees of Babylon." The cruellest of these wolves he reckons the Pope.

A. D. 1240–1280.

So strong was now the resemblance between Babylon and the Roman Church, that Matthew Paris, though in communion with that church, was forced to describe it almost in the words of St. John: —

" At that time, by the permission or the contrivance of Pope Gregory, the insatiable covetousness of the Roman Church, confounding right and wrong, reached such a height, that laying aside blushes, like a vulgar and shameless harlot

---

* The resemblance between the doctrine of Hildebrand and the Antichristian principles of the French Revolution has not escaped the notice of the republican Quinet: "I tell you," he exclaims, "that Gregory VII., the man of God, *Vir Dei*, is an ancestor of the French Revolution. In his efforts against the political powers, in his instructions to his spiritual soldiers, a kind of proclamation which precedes the battle, he does not give the royalties of the earth any other foundation than violence, crime, and falsehood." — Christianity, Coxe's translation, p. 61.

(velut meretrix vulgaris et effrons), on sale and exposed to all, she esteemed usury a trifling evil, — simony none at all. So that, with her contagion, she infected the neighbouring countries, even the purity of England."*

In this manner was our nation made to drink of the contents of the golden cup.

Within ten years the subject was taken up by the learned Greathead, bishop of Lincoln. In the guilt of ruining souls he makes the Pope second only to Antichrist: —

" After the sin of Lucifer, which will be repeated in the end of time, in Antichrist, the very son of perdition, whom the Lord Jesus will slay with the spirit of His mouth; — after this, I say, there neither is, nor can be, any other kind of sin so opposite and contrary to the doctrine of the Apostles, so hateful, detestable, and abominable to our Lord Jesus Christ Himself, and so destructive to the human race, as, by the abuse of the pastoral office, to kill and destroy the souls committed to the care and ministry of that office to be quickened and saved." †

Afterwards, when excommunicated by the Pope, Greathead employed his last breath in deploring this merchandize of souls: " Christ," he said, " came into the world to save souls; therefore if any one fears not to destroy souls, is he not rightly to be called an antichrist?" ‡ Here Greathead uses the name in a sense more grammatical than prophetic.

The year 1260, owing to the prediction thrown out by Joachim, excited some alarm. The Paris divines, in a tract on the dangers of the Church, noted the

* Matthew Paris, anno 1241.
† Appendix ad Fasciculum Rerum, p. 401. This epistle was addressed to the Pope.
‡ Matthew Paris, anno 1253.

arrival of that year as a sign of the approaching end. As the destruction of old Babylon followed close upon the appearance of the word Mene, or *number;* so in the new Babylon, even the Church, the completion of the number 1260 must announce a speedy ruin.* Unfortunately for this theory, it is not Christianity, but the abomination, that is to be set up for 1260 days.

The Apocalypse was now taken in hand by four of the great men of the age, Albertus Magnus, Cardinal Hugo, Alexander de Hales, and Thomas Aquinas. But these writers, aiming rather at illustrating what had been said before, than at making any new application of the prophecies, afford little matter for this history. They are almost agreed in rejecting the Tychonian explanation of the three days and a half, which, after the attack made upon it by Albert, never again held up its head.† Albert even attempts to clear the Gloss from the charge of having countenanced it: —

"After three days and a half: the Gloss says, After three years and a half, that is, after the death of Antichrist. But, on the other hand, Antichrist will not reign so long after their death. Answer: They will rise on the fourth day after their death. To what is objected from the Gloss, it may be said that those three years and a half are not reckoned from their death, nor from the death of Antichrist, but from the beginning of their preaching, or of his power. The Gloss, therefore, means, after the three years and a half, either from their preaching, or from his power, which will be ended by his death."

* De Periculis Ecclesiæ, cap. viii. In append. ad Fascic. Rerum. p. 27.
† Alberti Magni Opera, tom. xi. In Apocalypsin. In fine cap. xi.

This Albert had in his school a pupil, in whom, for a time, he seemed doomed to suffer disappointment. The boy, so eager for learning as to have made his escape from the window of the house in which he was confined—this boy, though diligent in his studies, appeared so deficient in talents as to receive from his schoolfellows the name of "Sicilian Ox." A shyness of disposition, taking the form of a morbid anxiety to avoid display, had induced him so far to conceal his real progress, as to submit to receive the assistance of his duller companions. At length Albert, by way of a last resource, ordered him to defend a thesis: the duty of obedience now silenced his scruples, and the character of his performance drew from his master the well-remembered saying, "This Ox will one day roar where all the world will hear him."

The boy's name was Thomas, and he came from the village of Aquino. His real history no man can now pretend to tell; the world then living was too much dazzled by his fame to form a just estimate of his merits. From his writings it may be gathered, that with the simplicity of a child he combined the subtlety of a sophist; and that, as far as the state of mediæval science permitted, he exhausted every subject that he took in hand. To this his contemporaries add, that he was the angelic doctor, that he wrote the Golden Commentary, and compiled the Golden Chain; that he lived almost on his knees, and that his talents were at least equalled by his meekness and humility. But the world was not to enjoy his presence for ever: his friends were early saddened by a vision of mournful import. The monk was seated in his chair of theology, when the Apostle Paul was seen to enter the schools: Thomas rose respectfully, and bowing low to the Teacher of the Gentiles, inquired whether he had succeeded in expressing, in his Commentaries, the Apostle's true meaning. "You have entered into my meaning," answered the Apostle with a smile, "as far as mere man is capable of comprehending it: but now follow me, and you shall know these things more perfectly." Thus his friends learnt that their teacher was soon to be taken from them: and the world, willing to believe anything about Thomas Aquinas, made no difficulty in believing this story also.

The schoolmen, De Hales excepted, say nothing about Rome as Babylon: they spiritualise the millennium, and pay immoderate deference to "the Gloss." The gloss quoted by that name is the "Ordinaria" of Strabus*, not the "Interlinearis" of Anselmus Laudunensis.

In other respects they follow the primitive track. They take the first seal to be Christ's gospel triumph: the sixth, the time of Antichrist. They make Jerusalem the scene of the witnesses' death, as well as the seat of Antichrist's empire. They take the prophetic periods literally, suggesting, at the same time, some mystical adaptations. An innovation is attempted by Thomas, who doubts the precise meaning of the letting power, because the Roman empire

---

* This Glossa Ordinaria, a work of the ninth century, is the earliest and most celebrated of the Latin Catenæ. The next in order was the Catena Aurea of Thomas. The Greeks began to compile chains soon after the sixth century: many of these, still unpublished, contain extracts from early writers now almost unknown.

had changed from temporal to spiritual: (probably meaning the Holy Roman empire:) he thinks therefore that the falling away will be a defection from the spiritual empire, and from the Catholic faith.* But Cardinal Hugo feels no such difficulty: "The little horn," he says, "that is, Antichrist, arose out of the midst of the ten, for he will be born in the time of the Roman empire. And when there comes a falling away from the Roman empire, then he will be revealed."†

The five fallen heads of the scarlet beast defied the ingenuity even of the schoolmen. Thomas supposes a division of the four thousand years into five epochs:—

"The beast that thou sawest, namely, the Devil, beast-like and cruel: was, in great power, before Christ's coming, for then he had great dominion; even he who then had the empire of death, that is, the Devil. (Heb. ii.) And he is not; namely, in possession of that power, since Christ's coming; for, as the Gloss says, on the birth of Christ he lost his power, that is, through the suffering of Christ in the flesh. * * *

"And five have fallen, namely, kings; that is, the rulers of five epochs. They have fallen: he says thus much about the past, down to the time of grace, and thus it is seen that all will pass away. (Eccles. iii.) And one is:—the congregation of the wicked, regnant during the sixth time, the dispensation of grace: those that, while their power lasts, continue to assault the Church. And the other, Antichrist, who will reign in the seventh time, is not yet come: meaning that he was future in St. John's time. And when he cometh, even Antichrist, of whom it was said before that he is not yet come, he must (being governed by the divine will, which has shortened those days, and which cannot be resisted, for

---

* Thomas in Pauli Epistolas, in locum.
† Cardinal Hugo in Apoc

who hath resisted His will?) continue a short space, that is, reign for a short time, even three years and a half."*

A.D. 1280.

To these heroes of the schools the Apocalypse was but one of many branches of theological science: one sheep of the rich man's fold, scarcely to be missed among the number. But to the humble friar whose name stands next on the list, the study of that book was as the poor man's lamb: and so well was his devotion to it rewarded, that from it he learnt more of the subsequent history of the Church than had been foreseen by any student of prophecy since the Apostles' time.

The secret of his success is worth inquiring into. Whence comes it, that when so many go wrong about the future, Peter John of Olivi happens to be right? The answer is easily given. Because he is satisfied with the revealed sense of the prophecies; satisfied to receive as final the interpretations delivered in the Scriptures themselves.

The group of expositors introduced by the friar of Olivi, owed its character to the events of the preceding century. The Abbot Joachim, a man of undoubted genius and originality, had laid down a plan of the future history of the Church, drawn partly from prophecy, and partly from the aspect of his own time. In this plan he had embodied hints of a coming Reformation, and of the appearance of some great preacher in whose time the Church would be sifted, previous to the revelation

* Thomas Aquinas, in Apocalypsin, c. xvii., attributed by some, but apparently without reason, to Thomas Anglicus.

of the man of sin. Within thirty years there came Francis of Assisi, who established a new order of friars, bound them by the strictest rules of poverty, and vigorously opposed the pomp and pride of the Roman clergy. This newly-preached poverty was an element altogether strange to the Roman Church, and not taken into account in the prophetic description of Babylon. Consequently, its history was but short: some followers of Francis rebelled against their founder's rule, and, by appealing to the Pope, obtained leave to hold property in the name of trustees. Upon this, the stricter part of the order styled themselves Spirituals, and protested against the Church of Rome as Babylon.

De Hales, who, though a Franciscan, is better known as the "Irrefragable Doctor" of the schools, first applied these transactions to the explanation of the prophecy:—

"Apoc. xvii. 2. The inhabitants of the earth were made drunk with her wine: that is, with the carnal enjoyment of the pleasures of the world, which so intoxicate both the kings of the earth and the prelates of the Church, that they perceive not the chastisements of the divine wrath. For so it is said in Isaiah xxviii., 'The priest and the prophet have erred through strong drink.' Or thus: The Franciscans dwelling on the earth, that is, loving the things of earth, were made drunk; that is, were turned aside from their right path and station, by the wine of her corruption, that is, of the city of Rome, or of some prelates of the Church. For prelates, by their bad examples, give to others the occasion of sinning and falling." *

The case of the Franciscans was like that of the empire to which they belonged; there was in it of the strength of the iron, but it was mixed with the

* Alexander de Ales, in Apoc.

miry clay. Once attracted to the prophecies, they decided that Joachim's promised Reformer had come in the person of St. Francis. There was not much room for Francis in the Apocalypse: but they found him a niche in the seventh chapter, as the angel from the East: also in the tenth chapter, though in a secondary sense, as the angel whose face is like the sun.

The earliest of these "Spirituals," as well as the most sober, was Peter John of Olivi. His work was referred to a theological commission, by which it was suppressed as blasphemous and heretical. Judging from the passages extracted by them, the key to his reasoning appears to be of this character:—

Rome now numbers among her supporters nearly all the excellent of the earth: but Rome is to be destroyed by Antichrist on account of her opposition to the truth: she must therefore first be seen openly to oppose the Gospel. This will be brought about by a Reformation, which Rome will endeavour to suppress.

The commissioners selected for condemnation these passages among others :—

" From the preceding words we may gather several proofs, that before the temporal destruction of the new Babylon, the truth of the Gospel life will be solemnly impugned and condemned by the reprobate ; while, on the other hand, it will be more fervently defended and maintained by certain spiritual persons who will be raised up. * * *

" Ten things must first happen. First, by God's just judgment, the Church Carnal must be visited as she deserves; also her wickedness must increase, and be carried to the length of attacking the life and spirit of Christ.

" Secondly, the end of the second general state must agree

with the end of the synagogue and of the first general state, which terminated with the condemnation and crucifixion of Christ.

"Thirdly, that spirit which has now grown lukewarm, and is, as it were, extinguished and slumbering in evangelic men, must be revived.

"Fourthly, it is needful that the truth of the evangelic life and rule should be illustrated and exalted, by a strong conflict, before the coming of the great Antichrist.

"Fifthly, these things must take place, so that the subsequent judgment to be executed upon the Church Carnal by the ten kings, may be, and may appear to be, more righteous and more honourable to Christ. For thus it will appear plainly, that not His church, but rather one hostile and persecuting, has been exterminated by them."*

The earlier writers spoke of the church which was *in* Babylon: but since the Papal rebellion in the eighth century, the Church had become Babylon itself. For Babylon, as Peter John knew well, cannot be supposed to mean the mere stones and mortar of the seven-hilled city.

"Sect. 54. The woman here stands for the people and empire of Rome, both as she existed formerly in a state of Paganism, and as she has since existed, holding the faith of Christ, though by many crimes committing harlotry with this world. And therefore she is called a great harlot; for, departing from the faithful worship, the true love and delights of her Bridegroom, even Christ her God, she cleaves to this world, its riches and its delights; yea for their sake she cleaves to the Devil, also to kings, nobles, and prelates, and to all other lovers of this world.

"Sect. 56. She saith in her heart, that is, in her pride, I sit a queen:—I am at rest: I rule over my kingdom with great dominion and glory. And I am no widow:—I am not destitute of glorious bishops and kings."

---

* Baluze, Miscellanea, lib. i. Report against Peter John, cap. xxx.

"Heretical, schismatic, and blasphemous," is the commissioners' remark upon this passage.

The Franciscans applied to the concluding state of Babylon the name of mixed, mystic, or minor, Antichrist. This state they expected to be headed by a false Pope, duly elected, and not an antipope. But in this matter they went beyond Scripture, and, as far as yet appears, against history: for Rome has shown no signs of denying the Father and the Son.

For two centuries the Franciscan school of prophecy continued to flourish. It produced Telesphorus, author of "The great Tribulation:" Ubertinus, who styled Babylon the Church Carnal: and John of Paris, who wrote the Life and Times of Antichrist. All these quoted Joachim as an oracle: after them came Bernardine and John of Kemnitz, who will receive due notice in their proper places.

The mass of the order degenerated into the extravagant sect of the Beguins or Fraticelli, whose existence was cut short by the labours of the Inquisition. Many of the Beguins, when brought before that tribunal, confessed to a vague belief in the lesser, or mystic, Antichrist of Rome: but on this subject their ideas were altogether confused. That confusion excited the surprise of the Inquisitors, and with some reason; for the torture, if any thing, might have been expected to settle all doubts on the subject of a Papal Antichrist.

In 1320 the Inquisitors of heretical pravity examined Bernard of Jacma: the state of his mind occupies much space in their report:—

"He confesses to having believed that the Church of Rome, which he calls the Church Carnal, is that Babylon the great harlot, of which it is said in the Apocalypse, that she sat upon a beast having vii heads and x horns.

"Also, that he believed in two Antichrists, a mystic, and a real: and he was in such uncertainty that he neither believed nor disbelieved that the Lord Pope John XXII. was the mystic Antichrist. And sometimes he believed that the mystic Antichrist and the real were the same person.

"Also, that after the death of Antichrist, the whole world will be so trusty and kind, that a girl, a maiden, may go alone from Rome to St. James's without fear of meeting any one that would harm her.

"Also, that about the year from the Lord's Incarnation 1330, the great Antichrist will have finished his career, and will be dead."*

This Bernard had seen, written in the vulgar tongue, a book "About Antichrist." In it there was the picture of a nun carrying a child: this nun was Antichrist's mother, "et Dyabolus amplexabatur ipsam."

A. D. 1340.

In these wild and untaught notes did the humble Beguins sing the doom of Rome: but soon the strain is taken up by a master, and to him Europe listens, for now " Poeta loquitur." The depravity of the Papal court attracts the notice of Petrarch, and though that court has fled to Avignon, thither does Petrarch pursue it with the reproach and the curse of Babylon. In this he is not strictly in rule: for,

* Limborch's Sentences of the Inquisition, p. 308. The identity is Rome and Babylon, though a subject forbidden by the Inquisition, appears continually in the writings of that age. Thus Ambrose of Camaldula, writing from Rome in 1320: "Commend me, I pray you, to all the brethren, that through their prayers I may soon be set free from the Western Babylon."—Ep. 37. lib. x.; published by Martene.

neglecting the token of the seven hills, he thinks it mark enough of Babylon that the Pope and Cardinals have gone to live there. Therefore the Western Babylon of Petrarch is Avignon, not Rome.

"Thou Babylon, seated on the wild banks of the Rhone, shall I call thee famous or infamous, O harlot, who hast committed harlotry with the kings of the earth? Truly thou art the same that the holy Evangelist saw in spirit, the same, I say, and not another, sitting upon many waters. Either literally, being surrounded by three rivers; or, in the profusion of this world's goods, among which thou sittest wanton and secure, unmindful of eternal riches; or, in the sense laid down by him that beheld thee, that the waters on which the harlot sits are peoples and nations and languages. Recognise thine own features: a woman clothed in purple and scarlet, decked with gold and precious stones and pearls, having a golden cup in her hand, &c. Dost thou not know thyself, O Babylon? Unless perhaps thou art deceived by what is written upon her forehead, Babylon the great, whereas thou art Babylon the little."*

In the same epistle he specifies the evils which the Popes had carried to Avignon: "Suffer not thyself to be overwhelmed by the ruin of the guilty and by the sins of Babylon, of which there is neither limit nor number, measure nor sum. I say nothing of the inheritance of Simon, even that species of heresy, not the least, making merchandise of the gifts of the Holy Spirit. I say nothing of the mother of that sin, even covetousness, which the Apostle calls idolatry, &c." Thus he passes on to the profligacy of the popes and cardinals, of which he draws a picture more befitting the pages of the satirist than of the historian.

In other epistles he does not cease to lament

* Petrarcæ Epist. Rerum Senilium, lib. i. aliàs lib. sine titulo ep. xx., vel. xvi.

the state of "Western Babylon"; "by whom built," he says, "it is uncertain; but by whom inhabited, it is well enough known, even by those from whom most justly it takes that name." *

In this matter Petrarch was a follower of Dante, who had recently noticed the figure of Babylon as a representative of the Papal power. The wrathful Florentine places a pope in the hottest hell, and there, while his feet alone protrude from the burning soil, belabours him with reproaches for his shameless simony: "Were I not withheld by respect for those supreme keys which thou didst hold while living, I would use words still more severe. That your avarice saddens the world, treading down the good, and lifting up the wicked. Of you, O pastors, the Evangelist was thinking, when she who sat upon the waters was seen to him, playing the harlot with kings; she who appeared with the seven heads, and bore the symbol of the ten horns." †

In this state of affairs it was given to another student of prophecy to catch a glimpse not only of the coming corruptions, but even of the secession that would follow them. About 1320, the friar Hervey suggested, as a probable meaning of the "falling away first," a catastrophe, the counterpart of which actually followed. "He who now letteth, will let: perhaps thus; the Pope of Rome, who now holds the churches, may hold them, till he be out of the midst: that is, till the Church of Rome itself, the midst and heart of the churches, shall commit iniquity; on account of which many churches will

* Epistolarum sine titulo liber., ep. xii., vel. viii.
† Inferno, xix. v. 100.

separate from her." * This meaning, though inapplicable to the Apostles' times, Hervey thinks may be supplementary to the original sense: "Only let the Roman empire, which now holds almost all nations, hold them, till it be out of the midst, that is, till this power be taken away from the midst of the world."

A.D. circ. 1360.

If Hervey was almost alone in anticipating how this corruption would end, its existence was generally recognised and deplored. The widow Bridget, though she made no formal application of the prophecies, contributed to the labours of others, supplying to the interpreters of Babylon some forcible descriptions of Romish corruption. What she uttered in the high character of a prophetess, they made bold to repeat as humble commentators: —

"I may say of Rome as the prophet said of Jerusalem;— righteousness once dwelt in her, and her princes were princes of peace: but now she is turned to dross, and her princes are murderers. O Rome, if thou didst know thy day, thou wouldest weep and not rejoice. . . . . Her gates are unguarded and desolate, because their guards and keepers are turned aside to covetousness. Her walls are broken down and unguarded, because they care no longer for the loss of souls, but the clergy and people, whom God has made to be her walls, are scattered abroad to make provision for the flesh. The sacred vessels are sold contemptuously, because God's sacraments are dispensed for money, and for the favour of the world." †

Like most other prophets of her sex, Bridget de-

* Hervæus in Pauli Epist. in locum.   Inter Opp. Anselmi Cantuar.
† Brigittæ Revelationes, lib. iii. cap. 27.

clares the last days to be close at hand. She explains the seven thunders as descriptive of the troubles that are to come upon the Church: not written, lest their severity should altogether banish hope.

It must ever remain a deep reproach to the middle ages, that for several centuries this argument was continually in use: — The age is so bad, that it cannot be made worse, except by Antichrist's coming: therefore Antichrist must be at the door. But none seem to have traced the mischief to its true source, the false and delusive doctrines taught to the people. In the *Golden* Legend of Voragine, named, one might almost fancy, after a certain golden cup, — in this Golden Legend there is seen a fearful picture of the teaching of the age: through all the morals and allegories of that book there seems to rise up a single image: — a monk in his cell; the world shut out, the flesh and the devil within: and, for a motto, the words of the legend itself, "Erat quidam monachus valde lubricus, sed in beatam Mariam valde devotus:"

"There was a certain monk, very profligate, but very much devoted to the blessed Mary. One night, while going out to his accustomed wickedness, he saluted the blessed Virgin as he passed before the altar. On leaving the church, in attempting to cross a river, he fell into the water, and was drowned. As the devils were carrying away his soul, angels came to set it free. To these the devils said, 'Why do you come? you have nothing to do with this soul.' Upon this, straightway the blessed Mary arrived, and asked how they dared to take away his soul. They answered that they found him to have ended his life in wicked works. 'It is false,' she said; 'for I know that whenever he went anywhere he saluted me, and that on coming back he did the same.'"*

---

* Legenda Aurea Sanctorum. De Assumpt. B. V. M.

A. D. 1360–1380.

About this time appeared the treatise of Oremius, "About Antichrist."* The monk, after explaining the boy in Leviticus xxiv. as a likeness of young Antichrist (that boy happening to be of the tribe of Dan), goes on to suggest some serious reflections on the existing state of Rome. The spiritual Sodom and Egypt, though he prefers to consider it as Jerusalem, he thinks may possibly mean Rome; and from the popular report, that Antichrist would be born in Babylonia, he draws this caution: "It is seriously to be inquired, whether Antichrist may not arise from that second Babylon which has succeeded to the first; especially as the prophet Daniel says that from the midst of the ten horns of the *Roman* empire the little horn will arise."

The flight of the Church from Rome to Avignon seemed in some measure to resemble the flight from Jerusalem to Pella. This parallel occurred to Clemangis, who inferred from it the approaching ruin of Rome, an event expected to coincide with the appearance of Antichrist.

This Clemangis, one of the most learned men of his day, was rector of the university of Paris. His treatise "On the Corrupt State of the Church" ranks among the most valuable of those tracts on the times which appeared during the latter part of the middle ages. Far from rejoicing that the head of the Roman Church was established in his own country, he laments the importation of Babylonish crime and guilt:—

"I speak of the temporal power, the glory, and the deli-

* Martene's Collectio Amplissima, t. ix.

cacies, with which the Church has become drunk even to nausea and forgetfulness of herself. Concerning these things it is commanded to the avenging angels, in the condemnation of the harlot, 'How much she hath glorified herself, and lived deliciously, so much torment and sorrow give her.' For, to omit events at a distance, such as the secession of the Greeks, brought about by our own pride and avarice; the now contracted limits of the Catholic religion, once extended over almost the whole breadth of the world; to pass over these, and some other wounds lately inflicted on the Church, there is at least the ruin which we now see befalling the city of Rome, the seat and head of the Church. Does not this ruin declare that the desolation of the Church, as well as of her whole government, is at hand, even as the dispersion of the synagogue and of the Jews followed close upon the destruction of Jerusalem?

"For how can she long endure and flourish, wandering homeless and unstable about the world, her standing destroyed, her head lost, and she herself forced to migrate from place to place, as a pilgrim and a guest in the world? From this she ought to gather certainly that her destruction is at hand; for, quitting the city of Romulus on account of her own hateful corruptions, she has fled to Avignon, where, in proportion to her greater liberty, she has more openly and shamelessly displayed her ways of simony and gain. Her foreign and perverse manners, the forerunners of calamity, she has brought into our Gaul, till that time upright and frugal, as well as restrained by discipline; but now so sunk in prodigious luxury, that it may well be doubted whether the thing itself is more astonishing to hear, or miserable to behold.

"But of Gaul perhaps elsewhere: let me here speak of the Church, which, by some bad bargain, is in the habit of infecting with her own leaven the places in which she settles, becoming to them an occasion of destruction and ruin. But not unrevenged: for Italy has balanced accounts with her, casting her out of her seat stripped and almost spoiled of her patrimony; and Gaul herself, impoverished by her, has begun to pay back her injuries, so as to fulfil the prediction of the prophet, 'Thou shalt be ashamed of Egypt as thou wast ashamed of Assyria.' Also this: ' O daughter of Babylon. wasted with misery, happy shall he be that rewardeth thee as thou hast rewarded us.'" *

Meanwhile the East trembled under the repeated assaults of the Mahomedan power. The empire of the Turks, founded about 1300, soon told with dire effect upon the expositions of prophecy. Within thirty years De Lyra could see little in the Apocalypse but Saracens, Byzantines, and Turks: excepting in the locusts, which he thought to be the Arian Vandals. In expounding Daniel he followed the ancient track, expecting the little horn to appear as Antichrist in the end of the world.† Most of this system was copied from the Franciscan Aureolus, who wrote in 1317.

A. D. circ. 1400.

About this time, without name or date, the Apocalyptic commentary of Berengaud stole into notice. It was first copied from by the Block-book Apocalypse, published soon after 1400, and next quoted by Dionysius the Carthusian, who wrote not later than 1470.

Down to that time every writer on the first seal had explained it in reference to Christ's first triumph through the preaching of the Gospel. But now Berengaud interprets it as Christ striving with the antediluvians: and the idea, too far-fetched to have readily occurred to two persons separately, is presently copied into the Block-book. For there, in the

* Clemangis, de Corrupto Statu Ecclesiæ. In the Appendix ad Fasciculum Rerum, p. 567.

† Nicolas de Lyra, Postilla in libros sacros. For the history of this school, see Appendix, Sect. ii.

wood-cut of the first seal, the living creature displays upon a scroll these words: "Come and see; that is, understand spiritually what thou hast read of as done before the deluge."*

The Abbot Joachim had proposed a double meaning to each seal, seeking a duplicate of the events in the Old Testament history. Berengaud now omitted the New Testament fulfilment as superfluous: in this way he made the seals refer to Jewish history, the sixth describing the breaking up of the synagogue. The city of the witnesses' death he makes the city of the world (like Babylon). It is not Jerusalem, he says, for three reasons: first, that the great city of the Apocalypse is always Babylon; secondly, because the present Jerusalem is not built precisely where the Lord was crucified; and thirdly, because the present city of Jerusalem, being inhabited by Christians, cannot justly be called Sodom and Egypt.†

Having explained away the city in which the Lord was crucified, Berengaud finds no difficulty in getting rid of Babylon. "The harlot," he says, "in some places means in particular Rome, which then persecuted the Church of God: in others it signifies, generally, the city of the Devil, that is, the whole body of the reprobate." (Cap. 17.)

---

* The imitation is equally plain elsewhere, though the order of the seals is not preserved:—

THIRD SEAL OF BERENGAUD.	FOURTH SEAL OF BLOCK-BOOK.
"Veni et vide: id est, intellige spiritualiter Scripturam legis."	"Veni et vide: id est, spiritualiter intellige Scripturam legis." Apoc. Johannis, liber xylographicus.

† Berengaudus in Apoc. inter Op. Ambrosii; also published separately, Paris, 1554.

It often happens, that when a systematic commentator shrinks from the application of this part of the Apocalypse, some other writer makes his appearance at the same time, to supply the omission. Thus, what Berengaud fails to insist upon, is enforced by his contemporary, the Abbot Volkuin. The Abbot's text is appropriate: "An enemy came and sowed tares among the wheat."

"Oh grief and shame! At this day exists the ancient harlot, having in her hand a golden cup full of abomination, filthiness, and uncleanness, with which she wonderfully intoxicates the priests and clergy. It is written of her in the Apocalypse, 'I saw the woman drunk with the blood of men, and with the blood of Christ's martyrs.' Mulierem mollem dicit emollientem luxuriam carnis, ebriam de sanguine suorum scortorum vel scortatorum. This is that leech which sucks the blood of God's ministers and martyrs (or witnesses): who ought to be Christ's martyrs, but have become the Devil's, consuming flesh and blood in his honour and service. 'When I saw her,' he says, 'O ye men, I wondered.' Who would not wonder, and shudder, and be amazed, to see a priest of the Lord, a minister of God, having emptied the cup, and still thirsting to drain even the dregs of the cup of Babylon."*

A. D. 1412.

The famous Vincent of Ferrers now turned his attention to the subject of prophecy. From various signs he concluded that Antichrist was already born, and, from the testimony of some hermits, that he had already attained the age of nine years. At this time he met a certain merchant of Venice, whom he drew into conversation on his favourite subject. The

* Homilia Volkuini Abbatis, in the Appendix ad Fasciculum Rerum, p. 154.

merchant knew how to make himself agreeable: — "Nine years ago," he said, "I was attending vespers in the chapel of a Franciscan convent beyond the sea, when two boys, after long and severe convulsions, exclaimed together, 'At this day and hour Antichrist is born!'" A coincidence so remarkable was forthwith reported to the Pope.*

Vincent, now fairly on the scent, pursued his inquiries with vigour. Being himself an exorcist of some celebrity, he resolved, in his imaginary conflicts with the demon army, to employ stratagem, and to extort from his captives the secrets of their rebel leader. The demons, adjured at the moment of their supposed ejection, confessed the truth of what Vincent had heard, that Antichrist was indeed born, and at the very time specified by the merchant. He next inquired *where* Antichrist was born: but this information they refused to supply. Their silence was fortunate: otherwise the inquisitors would doubtless have stepped in with their fires, and some harmless village might have had to weep a new massacre of Innocents, from nine years old and under.

The story reminds us of Herod, but not of the wise men. In due time Vincent was canonized, and pronounced to be a Vir Apostolicus: a title to which his childlike simplicity formed a large portion of his claim. But the Church of Rome, though, in consideration of his many good qualities, it passed over Vincent's follies, looked coldly upon such speculations, perceiving that they brought unmerited dis-

* These letters of Vincent are published by Malvenda, De Antichristo, lib. i. cap. 38.

grace upon the whole subject of prophecy. In the first council of Milan, held in 1565, it was thus decreed: " Let none give out as certain the time of Antichrist's coming, or of the day of the last judgment, since it is testified by the mouth of Christ our Lord, 'It is not yours to know the times and seasons.'" *

A. D. 1430.

A highly-finished commentary on the Apocalypse does credit to the Scriptural knowledge of the Franciscan Bernardine. He returns to the track which Berengaud had left: his first seal is the Gospel-triumph, his sixth the times of Antichrist. His city of the crucifixion is Jerusalem, and he has something to say even about the Babylonish Church: "In one hour are so great riches come to nought. May not this be applied to certain clergy and prelates of our own time?" †

A. D. circ. 1450.

Before long followed the commentary of Dionysius, a Carthusian monk of great celebrity. Though disposed to make light of Berengaud's reasoning about the city of the crucifixion, he is glad to get rid of both Rome and Jerusalem, interpreting them alike as the city of the wicked world. The motive for giving up Rome is plain enough: perhaps Jerusalem was abandoned to avoid the inconsistency of taking one city literally and the other figuratively. ‡

* Harduin, in Concilio.
† Bernardini Senensis Opera, tom. v., in locum.
‡ Dionysii Carthusiani Enarratio in Apoc., c. x.

The description of Babylon is styled by Dionysius a mystical and difficult passage. The city built upon seven hills, and ruling in the time of the Apostle, perplexes the most accomplished commentator of the age. His contemporary, Gregory of Heimburg, sees farther into this millstone:—

"These prelates and doctors, endowed with knowledge, and shining in eloquence, but perverse in deed, and contradicting their own divine knowledge,— these make up that Church carnal which John, in the seventeenth chapter of the Apocalypse, calls the great harlot, sitting upon many waters. * * * For many years past it has been more allowable to preach about or discuss God's power than the Pope's; for all, drunk with that harlot's wine, and bewitched by her caresses, put a flattering gloss upon the holy Scripture, twisting it to the support of error." *

Could Dionysius have obtained sight of a letter then passing between the Pope and the Grand Turk, he might have found in it a practical illustration of Babylon's spiritual harlotries. Pope Pius the Second, disregarding the rights of his Eastern brethren, offered to secure to Mahomet II. the empire of the East and of the Greeks, on condition of his embracing Christianity, and acknowledging the Pope as Christ's successor upon earth. For this was part of the creed of Pius: "Christ," he tells Mahomet, "transferred the priesthood of the Jews to the Christians, having chosen as His successor Peter, to whom He transferred the high priest's power." †

The arrangement proposed by Pius might have been easily carried into effect: for the forces till then

---

* Confutatio Primatûs Papæ, in the Appendix ad Fasciculum Rerum, p. 117.

† Æneæ Sylvii Epistolæ, ep. 396., op. p. 882.

employed in aid of the oppressed Christians, would have soon turned the scale in favour of the Turks. Pius takes a business-like view of the proposed conversion:—

"If you desire to extend your empire among the Christians, and to make your name as glorious as possible, you need neither gold nor arms, neither fleets nor armies. A little thing can make you the greatest, the most powerful, and the most illustrious of all men now living. Do you ask what that thing is? It is not hard to be found, nor have you far to look for it: it is to be met with all the world over; a little water to baptize you, that you may submit yourself to the rites of Christians, and may believe the Gospel. If you will do this, there is not a prince in the world who will surpass you in glory, or be able to equal you in power. We will call you Emperor of the Greeks and of the East, and, what you now occupy by force, and hold with injustice, you shall possess by right. * * *

"If you were baptized, and would walk with us in the house of the Lord as friends, neither would they stand in so great dread of your empire, nor should we lend them help against you. But we should rather implore your aid against those who sometimes usurp the rights of the Roman Church, and lift up their horns against their mother." (P. 874-5.)

Whether Mahomet was displeased with a slight which Pius had cast upon the "Bull's Paradise," as he rudely styled it (the garden of the Houris), or whether he did not choose to bow down to the Pope for all the kingdoms of the East and the glory of them, history does not tell. The hint thrown out about helping the Pope against the heretics, may well excite a grateful feeling to that Providence which frustrated the impious counsel, and delivered Europe from the terrors of an Inquisition, backed by the combined powers of Pope and Turk.

The Apocalypse was next taken up by another Carthusian, James of Paradise. This monk was among the many who longed for a Reformation; but to the fulfilment of that wish there existed a great obstacle. "To me," says Paradisus, "it seems scarcely possible that the Church in general can be reformed, unless the court of Rome be reformed first. And how difficult that is, present events show: for no people or nation of believers make such resistance to the reformation of any church as the Italians."*

His plan of the seals, almost copied from Anselm, does no great violence either to history or to Scripture. According to Paradisus, the Church is seen, first, white, in its Apostolic purity, then red with martyrdom, black with Arianism, still pale with hypocrisy, and henceforth expectant till the end shall come. The sixth seal will bring in Antichrist; the seventh, the rest that remaineth to the people of God.

At this point the invention of printing puts to flight the last lingering visions of the middle ages, marking the beginning of a new chapter in the history of man. Here, then, the historian takes leave of the mediæval church, preparing himself for the bursting forth of that light which Rome, with all her arts, was no longer able to suppress.

* De Septem Ætatibus Ecclesiæ, App. ad Fasciculum Rerum, p. 106.

CHAPTER V.

REMAINS OF THE PRIMITIVE INTERPRETATION IN MODERN TIMES.

"A woman seated. And still she is sitting, that city of Rome, which rules over all the faithful, and yet is called a harlot. For thus says Isaiah, How is the faithful city become a harlot."
Sermones super Apoc., A. D. 1512.

THE Reformation, though it ultimately restored the lost portions of the primitive interpretation, produced that effect more slowly, and far less generally, than might have been expected. First, the reformed churches began to proclaim afresh the Babylonish character of Rome, and the Jesuits, stepping in with much prudence and learning, forced their church to admit partially the identity of the two cities. Next, the dreamy belief in a present millennium began to give place to the renewed hope of a literal Sabbatism, a hope which first appeared among the reformed, and which, after receiving strength from the enthusiasm of the Jesuit Lacunza, finally spread among the students of prophecy in all countries. Lastly, the prospects of the Jews attracted a degree of attention not granted them since the Apostles' time.

From this slight sketch of the modern revival the Jesuits appear to have been the most prominent actors in the scene. The object and motive of their interference admits of an easy explanation.

There existed in Pagan Rome a certain class of augurs to whom belonged the task of observing and interpreting the thunder. Of these fulguratores it was required, that they should watch the play of the lightning, visit the spot where the bolt had fallen, and, from the signs of times and places, expound, in order to avert, the threatenings of the offended gods. What those augurs were to ancient Rome, Papal Rome possessed in the Jesuits; upon whom, by their own choosing, devolved the task of interpreting the Apocalyptic thunders, so as to explain away those portentous omens that struck terror into the adherents of the Papal church. And, if the prophetic bolts had fallen thickly upon the harlot city, if her seven hills had been conspicuously smitten, if the smell of fire had passed upon her purple, if her "pearls and gold and precious stones" had been dimmed by the fiery stroke, — then, difficult was the task, and important the assistance, of her new allies. But, in the end, the prophecy proved too strong for them: vainly did they invent distinctions, labouring to avert the threatenings while they encouraged the sins, till the latest of their number, abandoning the unequal contest, exclaimed in despair, "O my people, they which call thee blessed cause thee to err, and destroy the way of thy paths." *

Two symbols, neither of which had been thoroughly explained in the primitive age, now received the attention of some distinguished expositors. By a combination of what all ages have contributed towards the explanation of the Scarlet Beast and of the Sun-clothed Woman, the primitive outline may be thus filled up: —

* Benezra's Coming of the Messiah, Irving's Translation, vol. i. p. 252. Benezra is the Jesuit Lacunza in disguise.

First, as to the Scarlet Beast. That monster so inactive and so silent, giving no signs of life beyond the names of blasphemy which break out upon its hide, whose very existence appears to be suspended, whose home is the bottomless pit, and its end everlasting ruin;—that empire, so mysterious and unearthly, whose is it, and where, over men or devils, is it established?

A beast in prophecy represents a kingdom: " The fourth beast is the fourth kingdom." Red, also, is the satanic colour, for the red Dragon is the Devil and Satan. For fifteen centuries, therefore, nearly the whole Church agreed to understand by this beast the kingdom of "the Devil and his angels:" or, according to the language of Apoc. xii., " the Dragon with his angels." Ribera, affecting more precision, styles it " the Devil Regnant."

It is, they say, that kingdom of Satan which the Pharisees of old thought to be divided against itself, attributing to our Lord a share in its administration. That kingdom, so often spoken of, but now for the first time seen in vision, comprising the principalities and powers which were spoiled openly, the invisible object of the Christian's warfare, while he wrestles not against flesh and blood, but against (as it runs in the Greek) " empires and powers, against the cosmocrats of the darkness of this world."

We speak of the prince of darkness, of the prince of this world. In the red Dragon he was seen to be crowned; but, if he be a king, where is his kingdom? To meet this question, as it seems, the Scarlet Beast is allowed to flit before us:—

The Beast that thou sawest, was, and is not. Said,

either prophetically; for, shall soon come to an end; as it was said of Troy shortly before its fall, "Troy was." Or contemptuously (Irenæus) : — It is beneath taking into the account, so precarious and fleeting is its existence. Or, in contrast to the name of Christ. As He was, and is, and is to come, so the kingdom of His enemy was, and is not, and yet is (as some read) to come.

And fourthly (by most) it is taken historically. It was, in great power, before Christ's first coming, when the strong man armed kept his palace, and his goods were in peace: when devils were suffered visibly to possess mankind, and every country, Judæa partially excepted, resounded with the praises of the demon herd. When the Gentiles universally worshipped devils, and Satan became, not indeed by right of creation, as the Manicheans pretend, but by adoption on the part of his worshippers, God of this world. (T. Aquinas.)

But this empire is not: its supremacy ceased when the prince of this world was cast out; when the strong man was surprised by the stronger man, who entered his palace and spoiled his goods. For not only upon earth did Christ ravage the possessions of Satan, but carried the war into the very fortress of the grave: through death destroying him that had the power of death, that is, the Devil. At that time the prince of this world was judged; and soon after he was suffered to exert no more *visible* power over our redeemed race.

And shall ascend out of the bottomless pit, in the time of Antichrist. Shall ascend, to earth, when their leader with his angels is cast down to earth,—

when it is said, Woe to the inhabiters of the earth. Out of the bottomless pit, the abode of demons, whither the legion of devils prayed that they might not be sent — εἰς τὴν ἄβυσσον. Shall ascend, perhaps, in the form of those fiery locusts that come up out of the bottomless pit.

They shall come out of the bottomless pit: but worse shall befall them, for they shall go into perdition, their own place, being prepared for the Devil and his angels.

And they that dwell on the earth shall wonder: all but the elect, whom it is not possible that he should deceive, their names being written in the book of life from the foundation of the world. But the rest shall wonder, ignorantly, saying, Who is like unto the Beast, and who is able to make war with him? and, secondly, profanely; admiring the triumph of anti-Christian principles, and rejoicing to see Revelation, as they will think, plainly refuted by common sense. For that power which Christianity boasts to have conquered, saying of it that it was and is not, yet is. Declared to be on the verge of final ruin, it is nevertheless, to all human calculation, acquiring stability, and flourishing more than ever.

And to the mind that hath wisdom; that desires to understand the meaning of these symbols; for the wise shall understand, — the seven heads have two meanings. First, when bearing a city, they are seven hills: Mount Palatine, Quirinal, &c.; secondly, when spoken of as wounded, or when seen with crowns, they are seven kings.

Now Daniel's "four kings" proved to be four great kingdoms entering into the history of the Church from his own time. So these "seven kings" may be the same series, reckoned from the beginning, thus: Altogether, past, present, and future, there are seven church-molesting kingdoms, each made the subject of prophecy: Egypt under the Pharaohs; Syria under Sennacherib, Hazael, and Rezin; next, Daniel's four; and lastly, the empire of Antichrist, or the little horn.

Five are fallen: Egypt, Syria, Assyria, Persia, and Greece (Bachmair and Croly), and one is, the Roman status, or order of things. And the seventh, Antichrist, is not yet come; for he who now letteth (the Roman) will let, till he be taken away; and when he cometh, he *must* continue. No prayers and groans on the part of the Church, no insolent defiance on the part of the usurper, shall induce the Creator to retract that permission by which the forty and two months' possession of the world is secured to Antichrist. But, a short space: made so for the elect's sake: for, unless those days were shortened, no flesh should be saved.

And the beast that thou sawest is himself an eighth: that is, according to the classical Greek idiom, there are seven besides him. Either, first, the seven horns, three of the ten being then rooted up. (Irenæus and Prosper.) Or, secondly, thus: there are seven that oppress the Church, yea, eight that make war against it. As the body is to the seven heads, so is the spiritual satanic kingdom to the seven persecuting empires founded upon it. It is reckoned, therefore, an eighth, and is of the seven, their common stock and parent: for, through them it acts, as it was said to Polycarp: "The Devil shall cast some of you into prison." And goeth into perdition, being entrusted to the Son of perdition, when the

Dragon gives him his power, and seat, and great authority: it goeth into perdition, when the Beast and the false prophet shall be cast into the lake of fire.

II. That the history of the sun-clothed woman does in some way express that of the Church immediately before the coming of Antichrist, nearly all are agreed; but whether this Church is to be considered Jewish or Christian, remains a question. Of the ancients, Hippolytus takes it to be the Church in general; Victorinus, that of Judea especially. Methodius and Augustine suppose the woman to be the Zion of the prophets, but typical of the Christian Church: Lacunza, thinking this a defrauding of the Jew, takes it to be the ancient Zion, literally restored in the last days.

There appeared, it says, a great wonder, in heaven: perhaps a method of showing that the fulfilment (until the scene changes to earth) will not be visible to mankind. In heaven, behind the scenes, in the spiritual and invisible world.

A woman clothed with the sun: what to her is a glory is to the rest of the world a light. Either, first, the Jewish Church, restored before the great and terrible day of the Lord. The woman once forsaken and grieved in spirit, but now shining, because her light is come, and the glory of the Lord is risen upon her. Clothed with the sun, of Righteousness; at once a light to lighten the Gentiles, and the glory of His people Israel. And the moon under her feet, as useless; neither for brightness shall it give light unto her. And upon her head a crown of twelve stars.

The stars of Joseph's dream: the twelve patriarchs. (Lacunza.)

Or, secondly, the Christian Church, clothed with, or having put on, the Sun of Righteousness:—that true light which lighteth every man that cometh into the world. (Eusebius.) Having the moon under her feet; not easily explained with precision, though at times supposed to be a symbol of the Synagogue, or of change, or of things sublunary. And on her head twelve stars. The Twelve. (Hippolytus.) By these she conquered the world, therefore with reason she now wears them in her crown. (Deacon Anselm.)

Or thirdly, the Church universal, made one fold under one Shepherd: displaying the twelve Apostles, seated on twelve thrones, judging the twelve tribes of Israel.

And she, being with child, cried; being engaged in achieving some great work, she struggled earnestly. Perhaps at this stage crying out, We have been with child, we have brought forth wind, we have not wrought any deliverance in the earth, &c.

And there appeared, in the same region of things spiritual and invisible, another symbol. A red Dragon, representing Satan: seen in heaven, either to represent the spiritual wickedness in heavenly places: or, seen as prince of the power of the air, conducting, as yet unperceived on earth, the mystery of iniquity. He is called the Devil and Satan: that is, Diabolus in the Septuagint, and Satan in the Hebrew: for St. John is in the habit of giving proper names in both languages.

And his tail drew the third part of the stars of heaven: either, he seduced by his antichristian agents the third part of the bishops of the church universal: for the seven stars were angels of seven churches, that is, seven bishops; according to the saying of Malachi in the LXX., "the priest is the angel of the Lord Almighty." These stars, drawn from their orbit, may be those wandering stars described by St. Jude, the apostate teachers of the last time, referred to in the prophecy of Enoch. Or, he was permitted to comprise in his army, ("the Dragon and his angels") one third of the invisible hosts frequenting our earth. And he, going about seeking whom he might devour, stood before the woman, to destroy the fruit of her labours, as soon as accomplished.

And she brought forth a man-child. Either, first, Christ. She who had been His executioner, now acknowledged Him as her son. She accomplished in the face of Satan a good confession of Him who came of her own flesh. Of whom it was said that He should rule all nations with a rod of iron; even Him who was caught up, formerly, from the Mount of Olives, to the throne of God, to be welcomed with these words, Sit thou on my right hand, till I make thy foes thy footstool.

Or secondly (and more usually,) a man child: a valiant offspring, a body of confessors and martyrs, to whom Christ promised that having overcome, they should rule the nations with a rod of iron, even as He had received of His Father. And they were caught up, by martyrdom, to heaven, and to God's throne, according to the promise: To him that overcometh, will I give to sit with me on my Throne. (Apoc. iii. 21.)

And there was war in heaven. Michael, the great prince that stands for the Jewish people, opposes the powers of Satan, still in the invisible world. The Devil is cast down from the office which he now holds as accuser of the brethren: but, while losing some invisible influence against the elect, he appears to receive in exchange an increase of visible power over the rest of men. Perhaps he is now suffered to exercise his special deceivableness of unrighteousness, God sending upon men the strong delusion, that they should believe the lie. Here begins Antichrist. (Victorinus Martyr.)*

Satan, knowing that his opportunity is short, even three years and a half, loses no time in raising his fiercest persecution against the Church. For, after Michael's standing up, there comes a time of trouble, such as never has been. The scene now changes to earth, the persecution and the flight of the Church being things visible to mankind.

There was war, it was said, in heaven: and now peace is taken from the earth. The Church flies to the wilderness: she receives the wings of "that great eagle:" probably God Himself, who bears her, as of old, on eagle's wings, that under the shadow of those wings may be her refuge, till this tyranny be overpast. They that are in Judæa now flee to the mountains: perhaps then entering into their

---

* A writer of the fifth or sixth century, known as the Pseudo-Ambrose, connects this casting down of Satan with the removal of the letting power: "The Devil, perceiving that his ruin draws near, at the time of the Roman empire's failing, he himself being cast down to earth, as it is said in the Apocalypse," &c. — In Ep. ii. ad Thess.

chambers, till the indignation be overpast. And lest they should there perish of want, they will be, as it seems, miraculously supported during the forty-two months, as were the Israelites of old during the forty years.

That they should feed her there. As it was promised to the Israelites, when restored to Jerusalem, that "bread shall be given them, their waters shall be sure:"— so, to these, who in obedience to the divine injunction flee from Judæa to the mountains, the fulfilment of the promise is, by a special provision, miraculously secured.

And I stood upon the sand of the sea. Having been admitted behind the scenes, to witness both the causes and the effects in connection, I now took my stand as an ordinary spectator, to behold the effects alone, as they will appear to those who will be living when God doeth this. And I saw a beast, the empire of Antichrist represented by its head, (as Nebuchadnezzar stood for the head of gold,) rising up out of the sea of the nations.

A. D. 1512.

What the first Leo beheld but dimly in the mirror of his own ambition, the tenth Leo witnessed in reality, and possessed to his heart's content. Rome now ruled as widely by spiritual despotism, as before by the arts of war. On the accession of this Leo, Rome presented a spectacle as closely corresponding to the Babylonish pageant of the prophecy as can easily be imagined.

St. John had seen in vision, a woman mounted, seated on seven hills, clothed in purple and scarlet, and adorned with gold and precious stones. In the year 1512 a triumphal procession wound along the seven hills;—the Pope and Cardinals, mounted, dressed in purple and scarlet, and adorned with gold and precious stones. Nor was there wanting a certain spectator, who, like St. John, wondered with great admiration, and afterwards wrote an account of what he saw.* The parallel fails in one particular; there was no angel to say to the Italian, Wherefore didst thou wonder? or to tell him the mystery of the woman, and of the beast that carried her.

This spectator was one Penni, a Florentine, by profession a physician, but at heart a milliner. A good and simple man he seems to have been, taking for granted all that they tell him, and believing that Christ is truly carried on that very white horse, under the little canopy of cloth of gold that protects the Eucharist.

The Pope is mounted on another white horse. By the scarlet cloak, the crown of gold, and the "many other jewels and precious stones," he preserves a due resemblance to the prophetic type. In other respects the procession displays little that is remarkable; the Pope is preceded by the Swiss guards, rapturously described by Penni, as having a green stripe all up one leg, and all down one arm; the bishops and cardinals are in their scarlet cloaks, their horses being covered with white housings, "excepting the eyes out of which they saw," says Penni: for the Pope did not care to hoodwink his brute subjects.

"Next followed a very white horse, having upon its back

---

* This very scarce tract is reprinted by Roscoe, in the appendix to his Life of Leo X.

a little tabernacle adorned with cloth of gold, within which was placed the holy Eucharist; and above it was a most beautiful canopy, surrounded by about twenty-five squires, carrying lighted tapers of the purest white wax. Behind them came a sacristan, carrying a wooden staff, as a guard to Christ."

The Pope passed beneath devices and inscriptions scarcely to be acquitted of an idolatrous meaning. As the crowd shouted " Long live Pope Leo," Penni's thoughts were wandering to Jerusalem; by a strange illusion he seemed to hear the hosannahs of the multitude, while in the fluttering draperies of the pageant he beheld the palm branches of the Mount of Olives. For Penni was intoxicated, but not with wine; he had been drinking of that golden cup, which long before had taught the Abbot Rupert to read Zion in place of Babylon.

The pope proceeded to the Lateran, of which he was to take formal possession. On reaching the gate there was enacted a dramatic ceremony,—one of those scenic effects in which the Church of Rome ever delights, and which in this instance comes in not amiss, to support a distinction between the vain assumptions of the popes, and the rabid blasphemies attributed to Antichrist. Leo dismounts from his horse and seats himself beside the way. From this humble resting-place the cardinals raise him up; and, while he ascends the Lateran steps, they chant over him the words of Hannah, " He lifteth up the poor from the dust, that He may set him among princes." Thus the pope, in his proudest hour, still ascribes his exaltation to God: whereas Antichrist, opening his mouth against heaven, will set himself above all that is called God or that is worshipped.

The same year produced an anonymous collection of " Sermons on the Apocalypse." These, though founded on the commentary of Bernardine, were interspersed with some new and important remarks. The following sentence contains the germ of the theory afterwards worked out by the Jesuits, supposing a future apostacy of the city of Rome : —

"And the woman which thou sawest is that great city; the union of the reprobate, or, the city of the Romans. Which reigneth over the kings of the earth, that is, over all who possess dominion and empire. John is speaking of the time when idolatry flourished in Rome, or of a future time, when perhaps all heresy and unfaithfulness will be reigning in her." [*]

A. D. 1531.

To this year belongs the " Onus Ecclesiæ," a work attributed to John, Bishop of Kemnitz. Chemensis, or Chemnicensis, as he is usually styled, was a member of the Romish communion, but scarcely to be reckoned a Papist, since he could give it as his opinion, that " Ambitious popes decree, and credulous fools believe, that Rome is the head of the universal church." [†]

Chemensis mostly follows the Franciscans, making Francis and other reformers to be types or precursors of the two witnesses. Like them he expects two Antichrists; one real and major, the other mystic and minor. The latter is to be the idol or false Pope. With great inconsistency he interprets the seat of the

---

[*] Sermones super Apoc. Paris. 1512. fol. 201.
[†] Onus Ecclesiæ, cap. xlix. sect. 15.

beast as Jerusalem typifying Rome. Fragments of various systems abound in the work: he notices, in passing, the new year-day scheme, counting the time declared to Daniel as 1335 years: but from what time the taking away of the daily sacrifice should be reckoned, he says, " I am utterly ignorant."

The sixth seal he applies to his own time, the " Status Reformativus" of the Church. This state was to include the coming of Antichrist, an event thought likely to follow soon: for the falling away, said the bishop, is already begun, not only from the empire, but also from the faith, and from the Roman Church. " As under the Roman Empire the Church began, so under the same will it come to ruin. And although the Roman Empire will last till the time of Antichrist, yet at some time or other it will certainly be taken from the Germans, together with the Church; for the kingdom and nation that will not serve God shall perish."*

" The third ruin of the Church is that by which the Catholic faith will fall. As Antichrist will execute the judgment and sentence pronounced by God against Babylon the great harlot, so will the Church also at that time be almost made desolate by Antichrist. Perhaps it would altogether be exterminated, but for the assistance to be rendered it by those preachers of the truth, Enoch and Elias, who will be the heralds or precursors of the second advent of Christ, then closely impending."† * * *

" Now this harlot, that is, the modern perverse Church, is rebuked by the Lord through Isaiah, saying, How is the faithful city become a harlot! Once it was full of justice. Such at this day appears the Church of the malignant. * * * And the merchants of the earth were made rich by the abundance of her delicacies. So at the present day some

---

* Cap. xlviii. sect. 6.   † Cap. lxi. sect. 5.

Florentine merchants are lifted up and made rich by the patrimony of St. Peter, and by the bounty of the Roman Church."*

A. D. circ. 1560.

The Reformation, so long hoped for, came at last. The continental Protestants fell into various excesses in the interpretation of prophecy, applying almost every prediction in turn to the Pope, the Turk, and the Roman emperor. The Reformers of England kept closest to the primitive teaching, recognising Rome as Babylon, and yet so respecting her worship of the Father and the Son as to abstain from treating her as Antichrist. On the subjects of the eastern Antichrist and the millennium, they remained, for the most part, silent.

Hooker endeavours to maintain the important distinction between the orthodoxy and the corruptions of the Roman Church:—

"Some there are, namely, the Arians, in Reformed churches of Poland, which imagine the canker to have eaten so far into the very bones and marrow of the Church of Rome, as if it had not so much as a sound belief; no, not concerning God Himself, but that the very belief of the Trinity were a part of Antichristian corruption. And that the wonderful Providence of God did bring to pass that the bishop of the see of Rome should be famous for his triple crown: a sensible mark whereby the world might know him to be that mystical Beast spoken of in the Revelation, to be that great and notorious Antichrist in no one respect so much as in this, that he maintaineth the doctrine of the Trinity." †

In this matter our Reformers showed themselves marvellously free from the spirit of party. Although,

* Cap. xliii. sect. 4, 5.
† Hooker's Eccles. Polity, book iv. ch. 8.

in the heat of controversy, being themselves but mortal, they might be led to employ vehement language, yet they recognised Rome's orders and apostolic succession*, as well as her claim to be reckoned among the Churches. "The Church of Rome," says their nineteenth article, "hath erred, and that in matters of faith."

For herself our Church claims no infallibility, assumes no menacing attitude. She is satisfied to declare herself Reformed: content, by that name of a penitent, to acknowledge her wanderings. She is not ashamed to confess that, for her own part, whatever may be the boast of others, she had wandered into a far country, and had wasted her living upon the Harlot; but now, having arisen and come to her Father, she feeds upon the fatted calf: she was dead, she owns, but rejoices that she is alive again; she was lost, but is found.

A. D. circ. 1590.

The year-day theory, now rising into general notice, was first attacked by Bellarmine. The cardinal seems to have gone out of his way for the purpose: perhaps tempted by the prospect of an easy victory, or hoping to strengthen his cause by having Scripture, for once, fairly on his side. By that prince of Romish controversialists the fallacy of the year-day

---

* Mr. S. R. Maitland has placed this matter in a forcible light: "It is difficult to imagine that the Church of England would admit a man to serve at her altar, because Antichrist had ordained him — because the son of perdition had laid hands on him — because the man of sin had given him holy orders." —Remarks on a Review in the Christian Guardian, p. 109. On the subject of Babylon, see the Homily against Peril of Idolatry, part third.

theory was placed in the clearest light: he called attention to the rule, that, whatever analogies between two periods of time may exist in Scripture, there is no instance in which a day is said, when a year is intended. The controversy was left by him exactly as it stands at present:—

"Nor can any objection be drawn from the words of Ezekiel iv., I have given thee a day for a year: for it does not mean that those days literally signified years, since, in that case, Ezekiel must have lain upon his left side 390 years, which is impossible. For God commanded him to lie upon his left side 390 days, and added, I have given thee a day for a year. Now, if these days are taken for years, he must have lain 390 years; but he did not live so long. We conclude therefore that these days are truly *taken* as days, but are said to be *given* instead of years: for the days of Ezekiel's lying symbolized the slumbering of God's wrath, when he bore with the sins of Israel for 390 years.

"But Chytræus objects from Luke xiii., I must walk to-day, and to-morrow, and the day following. To which I answer, that this does not mean, as our opponents pretend, that Christ would preach three years after He spoke those words, for they were uttered in the last year of His life. Since, as Jerome remarks (Script. Eccles., in Johannem), and as the thing speaks for itself, Matthew, Mark, and Luke, wrote Christ's sayings and doings, not of the first two years, but of the third only. Therefore by these three days the Lord either meant the three days which He would spend in walking to Jerusalem, as Albert and Cajetan expound it, or at least by that mode of speaking signified that He would live and preach a little while longer, as Jansen well remarks.

"Therefore Illyricus and Chytræus have still to look for their angelic days and months, since in Scripture they are nowhere to be found."*

To make out the Pope's title to the name of Anti-

* Bellarminus de Rom. Pont., lib. iii. cap. 8.

christ, it was thought necessary by some to deny the continued existence of the Roman Empire. Thus they hoped to prove that the removal of the letting power had been already accomplished. Bellarmine is now as much befriended by history as before by Scripture:—

"This sign was not fulfilled at the time in which the Transylvan Antitrinitarians place the coming of Antichrist, that is, about the year 200: for the Roman Empire was then at its height, and continued so for long after.

"Nor has it yet been fulfilled at any time: for the name and the succession of the Roman emperors still remain; and, by God's wonderful Providence, when the empire failed in the West, which was one of the legs of Daniel's statue, it remained safe in the East, which was the other leg. But because the Eastern Empire was to be destroyed by the Turks, as we have seen, God once more set up in the West the first leg, that is, the Western Empire, by Charlemagne; and this empire still exists." (Cap. v.)

To shorten the argument: Bellarmine contends that the possession of Rome is not necessary to the existence of a lawfully constituted Roman emperor; otherwise none of the sovereigns from Valens to Justinian could enjoy the title. Also that the Lutherans boasted the support of three electors of the Roman Empire. Therefore, concludes Bellarmine, they at least must not deny its existence.

The cardinal is here supported by our Homily against Peril of Idolatry, the second part of which declares that "all authority imperial and princely dominion of the empire of Rome remained continually in the right and possession of the emperors, who had their continuance and seat imperial at Constantinople." And that so it remained till Leo the Third, when "he by his papal authority doth translate the government of the empire, and the crown, and the name imperial, from the Greeks, and giveth it unto Charles the Great." The whole Romish communion still offer up, on Good Friday, a prayer for the welfare of the Roman Empire.

The new school of interpreters had gone on to say that Rome was the seat of the Beast; and here Bellarmine once more falls back upon the Apocalypse. Chytræus, he complains, takes no notice of the words, "Where also their Lord was crucified." Moreover Antichrist is to destroy Rome, not to reign in it. "The ten Kings who will share among them the Roman Empire, and in whose reign Antichrist will come, — these will hate the purple-bearing harlot, that is, Rome, and will make her desolate, and burn her with fire. How, therefore, can she be the seat of Antichrist, if at that very time she is to be overthrown and burnt?"*

Bellarmine allows that Rome is meant by Babylon: but Rome future, not Rome present. This future falling away of Rome seems to be incompatible with the infallibility of the Roman see: but Bellarmine judges otherwise; "It matters not," he argues, "that in the time of Antichrist Rome seems destined to be wasted and burnt, as appears from Apoc. xvii.: for this will not happen till the end of the world; and moreover at that time the Pope will be styled, and will in truth be, Pope of Rome, although not living in Rome: for so it happened in the time of Totila, king of the Goths."† The case of Bellarmine makes it probable that even in the hour of Babylon's de-

---

* Cap. 13. † Lib. iv. cap. 4.

struction by Antichrist, there will be Papists so infatuated as to be planning how to retain the title of Roman; that, deaf to the voice which cries "Come out of her," they will be fondly looking back to the accursed city. If such there be, will they, like Lot's wife, suffer a separate ruin? or will they be permitted to escape to those that cast dust upon their heads, and cry, "Alas, alas, that great city?"

A. D. 1592.

The suggestion of the anonymous homilist was next carried out by Ribera. The power and learning of the Jesuits enabled them to hold out the menace to Rome, that she would one day fall away from the faith, and, despite her boast of perpetual purity, become the mother of harlots and abominations of the earth.

On ground so dangerous Ribera treads lightly: he seems to fear even the sound of his own footsteps. "It may be," he suggests, "that some Christians not conspicuous for holiness may at some time be suffered to live in Rome."* The state of corruption prevailing in Rome early in the sixteenth century helps to bring this supposition within the range of possibility. But Ribera will allow nothing to the discredit of Rome in her present papal character:—

"Babylon whose fall is here predicted, Babylon the empurpled harlot, Babylon the mother of harlots and abominations of the earth, she that has made all nations to drink of the wine of the wrath of her fornication, this is indeed Rome; but not Rome Christian, not Rome obedient to the Pope, not Rome retaining and preserving within herself the see of the Apostle Peter; for this is not the mother either of abominations or of filthiness, but the mother of piety, the pillar of

* Ribera in Apocalypsin, cap. xiv. num. 47.

the Catholic faith, the mistress of sanctity. On the contrary, it is Rome the author and preserver of superstitions, the head of idolatry, the sink of all iniquity, the most bitter enemy of the Christian name, the murderer and slaughterer of the saints, such as she once was under heathen emperors, and such as she will be in the end of the world, after she has fallen away from the Pope." (Num. 39.)

Ribera lays it down that when Rome again becomes Babylon, " there will be in her the greatest idolatry." As the fathers of Trent have sanctioned the decrees of the second Nicene council, it is difficult to imagine more gross idolatry than that which the Church of Rome now supports. With better effect he replies to those who would make Rome in the end of the world, to suffer merely for the sins of Rome ancient and Pagan:—

" Great Babylon came into remembrance. Because Babylon's old sins are to be visited upon her together with the new, our Apostle speaks as of a thing done long ago, — Great Babylon came into remembrance before God, to give her the cup of the wine of the fierceness of His wrath. She came into remembrance, because her old sins had been already consigned to oblivion on account of the faith which she had embraced; but when fresh and similar offences are added, the former also come into the memory of God: — For her sins have reached unto heaven, and God hath remembered her iniquities.

" Now Jerusalem would not have been laid waste by the Romans on account of her old sins, unless she had afterwards heaped upon them new and very heavy offences, not knowing the time of her visitation, as the Lord said, but killing Him through whom she was to be saved. And so Rome, after the worship of so many idols, after incredible superstitions, and after shedding the blood of so many martyrs, might yet remain till the end of the world, having become the seat of Christ's vicar, were it not that she will equal her former impiety with new sins and horrible wickedness.

"Therefore not for her former sins alone will she burn with so great a burning, as was said before, but also on account of those which she will commit in the last times; and this we learn so distinctly from the words of the Apocalypse, that the greatest fool cannot deny it."*

There being in Scripture no notice of the change from Babylon to Zion, and then back again to Babylon, the Jesuits have been forced to turn prophets themselves, and to invent a little history of Rome future. That history is slightly sketched by Ribera: "It cannot be doubted," he begins, "that Babylon will become a workshop of all idolatry and crime: if then we believe that Rome is called Babylon, we cannot doubt that Rome will become all this near the end of the world; and as, while she continues Christian and obedient to her Pope, this cannot happen to her, we are forced to say that she will at that time fall away from the faith and from the obedience of Christ's vicar." †

In this matter the Jesuits acted with their usual sagacity. By allowing Rome to be Babylon, they made the Apocalypse comparatively easy of exposition; and, while they contrived to evade the dangerous consequences of their admission, they were entitled to insist upon the literal meaning of the city where the Lord was crucified. They could tie down their opponents to the Calvary of the spiritual Sodom, as rigorously as they themselves consented to abide by the Palatine of the mystic Babylon. By this concession the revival of the primitive system was advanced: Ribera had already come nearer to it

---

* Cap. xiv. num. 44. † Ibid.

than Augustine. The latter explained Babylon vaguely enough: Ribera insists that it is Rome past and future, present occupants always excepted.

A. D. 1602.

Ribera is supported by the next Jesuit commentator, Blasius Viegas:—

"From these words it appears that, by the Babylon of the Apocalypse, Jerome understood Rome. But the name of Babylon is to be applied, not to that Rome which, under the Popes, now professes the name of Christ, but to that Rome which, before she received Christianity, worshipped idols, and to that which will exist in the time of Antichrist, which John, in this and the next chapter, describes as about to fall away from the Pope, and therefore from the faith. I think, therefore, with Tertullian and Jerome, that throughout the Apocalypse, and especially in this chapter and the next, the name of Babylon and the Harlot do describe the city of Rome under that twofold state, and that this passage foretells the future calamity and destruction of the city about the time of Antichrist. * * *

"Now, as the angel here declares to John that the *ten* Kings will hate the Harlot, and will entirely desolate and burn her, it may be gathered plainly that, a little before Antichrist's coming, or at least in the beginning of his reign, the city of Rome will be overthrown and burnt by those ten Kings: for, when Antichrist rules, there will be, not ten Kings, but seven."*

In making these concessions to the requirements of prophecy, the Jesuits received no check from their superiors. Rome therefore may be considered as acknowledging, for the time, her past and future iden-

* In Apoc. cap. xvii. sectio 3. For the real sentiments of Jerome see in cent. v.

tity with Babylon. To pass over the cause that forced her to admit an interpretation so fraught with danger, would be to tell but half the story.

The tyranny of the Popes had latterly acquired a certain likeness to the fury of the predicted Antichrist. As that likeness continued to become more and more glaring, the outcry raised against the Papacy increased in strength. A simple denial of the resemblance was clearly insufficient: it was, therefore, thought prudent to stand by the plain sense of prophecy, and to admit, with certain restrictions, the identity between Rome and Babylon. For the crimes in which the Roman Church had latterly taken part were of startling magnitude. Quite recently the Pope had approved of the massacre of 29,000 Huguenots, striking a medal to record the event. "That this slaughter," says the papal numismatist, "was not perpetrated without God's help, and the divine counsel, Gregory shows by the medal struck, in which an angel armed with a cross and a sword attacks the rebels."*

When Rome's power began to diminish, she was reduced to the resource of boasting of her former cruelties. And as, in the history of certain arts and sciences, the appearance of systematic treatises notes the arrival of a period known as "the decline of art," so was the decline of persecution marked by the appearance of several works on the Inquisition, commemorating its exploits, and spreading abroad the fame of those whose names had as yet scarcely resounded beyond the tribunal and the torture-

---

* Bonanni, Numismata Pontificum.

chamber. Of these works, the treatise of Paramus, already mentioned, may serve as a specimen.

Luis à Paramo, a Spaniard, and an inquisitor of distinction, wrote on the history, dignity, and utility of the "Holy Office." In that office he includes Old and New Testament saints, and even two Persons of the blessed Trinity. He claims God the Father for the first inquisitor, and Christ for the chief inquisitor; not as mere honorary members, but as active labourers in the work. The records of his office go back as far as the garden of Eden, in which Adam and Eve were the first heretics. The process on that occasion is shown to have been duly and formally conducted: " Deus primus inquisitor se ad instructionem processûs contra primos parentes accingit." * Adam and Eve are condemned to wear the *san-benito*, made, for the occasion, of skins; as convicted heretics they are deprived of their earthly possessions, their home, and their garden; and finally they are sentenced to hard labour for the remainder of their lives. "Following which example," says Paramus, "the most holy tribunal of the Inquisition confiscates by just proscription the goods of heretics, and cuts them off from all their goods and fortunes." †

The inquisitors take for their motto these words,— "Arise, O God, and judge thine own cause." By this passage they profess to think themselves warranted in attempting to wrest the power out of God's hands, that they may judge it according to their own imaginations. A worse motto they could scarcely have chosen, unless it were the text of Chrysostom's

* Lib. i. p. 26. † Page, p. 45.

sermon against persecution,—"Let both grow together until the harvest."

This subject must not be supposed to have no connection with that of Babylon; for, says Paramus, "The inquisitors of heretical pravity, by whomsoever delegated or nominated, are always delegates of the Pope, and receive from him jurisdiction and power."* One point especially can scarcely be passed over in this place; that strange sort of weak and wicked logic which the Church of Rome so assiduously cultivates, and which she employs in justification of her rebellion and bloodshed.

The inquisitors, when they forgive a recanting penitent, scourge him before dismissal. This custom Paramus finds very much to his taste:—

"It is said,—The Lord shall send the rod of His power out of Zion. This is the power of Christ, the chief inquisitor, which He delivered to Peter, and Peter to the inquisitors. Moreover, the inquisitors use rods very suitably and appropriately. For as the rod at its beginning is naturally flexible, tender, and soft, but at its end, hard, thick, and stiff, so the inquisitors, when they reconcile to themselves penitents who had lapsed through frailty or ignorance, are tender and merciful; but if afterwards the heretics, overcome of evil, fall back again into their former sins, they strike them and smite them stiffly, even to the burning with fire. They try first, whether, by placing the rods before their eyes, the penitents may conceive, and bring forth a variegated offspring, even the fruit of good works."†

Paramus has a favourite theory about rods:— "The Inquisition expects fruit from the rods, but, finding none, it casts the dry tree into the fire." Sometimes they looked long for the fruit, as in the

* Page 525. † Page 383.

case of the Abbess Mary. It was part of her sentence that "Every Wednesday and Friday throughout a whole year she shall publicly enter the chapter-room of the nunnery, and shall there be whipt during the singing of the psalm, 'Have mercy upon me, O God.'" *

Well does Paramus remark that "it is the nature of heresies to brutalise the mind, and to make men altogether inhuman."

A. D. 1627.

The præterist scheme, which had now spread from Calvin to the Jesuits, failed to infect their great ornament, Cornelius A Lapide. Of this commentator, and the respect paid to his opinion by the learned of every communion, the Romish Church has some reason to boast. In the matter of Babylon, A Lapide follows the earlier Jesuits:—

"Ch. xvii. I say that Babylon, both in this chapter and the following, is Rome; not Christian, as she now is, but unbelieving and Pagan, as she was in St. John's time, and as she will be again in the time of Antichrist. This may be proved; first, because Pagan Rome is that great city which had dominion over the kings of the earth; and in the last verse St. John says that the woman Babylon is that city. She has, moreover, seven hills, as it is said in verse 9, which agrees with no other city than Rome. Secondly, St. John declares that the name of Babylon is not to be taken here literally, but mystically, for he says, — A mystery; Babylon the great." †

In his commentary upon the Epistle to the Thessalonians, A Lapide enters into controversy with the new Papal-Antichrist school:—

* Pages 303. 379.   † A Lapide in Apoc. cap. xvii. v. 1.

"Who opposeth and exalteth himself above all that is called God. The Apostle here explains the name of Antichrist; namely, that he is one who will oppose himself to Christ, and to God, and to all divinity. Ridiculously, therefore, does Wolfgang Musculus say;—Antichrist means Vicar of Christ, which the Pope pretends to be, therefore he is Antichrist. * * *

"Moreover, if Antichrist means Vicar of Christ, then Peter and Paul, and all the Apostles, were Antichrists, for they acted as vicars of Christ. 'We are ambassadors for Christ, as though God did beseech you by us; we pray you in Christ's stead.' Now an ambassador performs his embassy in the stead of a king, and is a king's vicar."*

The arguments against Wolfgang's translation may be thus summed up:—

First. The vast majority of the Church in all ages have agreed to translate Antichrist, by "opposed to Christ." No other explanation has ever been suggested except for controversial purposes.

Secondly. The Greeks, whose opinion must be decisive in the meaning of their own language, unanimously translate the word by,—opposed to Christ.

Thirdly. The use of the words antipope and anti-cardinal proves the mediæval acceptation of the compound. No one ever thought of an antipope acting in subordination to, or as vicar of, his rival.

Fourthly. St. Paul appears to fix the meaning of the word by using in its place ἀντικείμενος; "who opposeth himself." Also Daniel: "he shall speak great words *against* the Most High," he shall speak "*against* the God of Gods."

Fifthly. None of the reformed lexicographers have

* In D. Pauli Epistolas, in locum.

ventured to suggest *Vice-Christ* as the meaning of the word.

Lastly. The interpretation, "Vicar of the Son of God," contradicts St. John's paraphrase of the word, "denying the Father and the Son."

In proportion as the life of the Reformation declined, Rome relaxed those efforts that had enabled her to hold her ground in the great theological strife. The Jesuits, no longer thinking it needful to grant so much, shut up the Apocalypse, and devoted themselves to those political intrigues that have made their name infamous in modern history. And though the causes that prevented the further progress of the Reformation still remain a problem for the historian, among them he can scarcely fail to reckon that rationalism which ate out the vitals of continental Protestantism, delivering Rome from all fear of subversion from that quarter, — that is, from all fear of them in the character of Christians. But a new danger now menaced the city of the seven hills. The growth of infidelity made it evident by what connecting link the kings of Europe might be so joined together in an Antichristian league, as to consume the Harlot, and at the same time to give their power to the beast. Hitherto this state of things had been visible in prospect to faith alone; it now began to fall within the range of common sense and of daily observation.

For a long time the Romanists contented themselves with an occasional jest at the expense of their opponents; at length, Walmsley attempted, in more serious earnest, to retort upon the Reformed. The fifth-seal-martyrs he found in those traitors who suffered under Elizabeth; but these, being few and unsatisfactory, were helped out by the sufferers in Japan. This writer, who appeared under the name of Pastorini, is best known for his blunder in making the locusts to be the Protestants, whereas they must sting those who have not the seal of God, that is, the members of the Church of Rome. The deplorably low state of the controversy may be illustrated by this,—that Walmsley, while he took the other periods literally, made the five months to be the 150 years following the Reformation.

A. D. 1792.

So stood matters at the outbreak of the great French Revolution. That shock, so sudden and so violent, dispelled many an expositor's dream, and sent the Church back to Scripture for the true character of the predicted Antichrist. By the exploits of Napoleon, by his attack upon Babylon, by the kings that he subdued, and by his temporary suppression of the Roman empire, the microscopic interpretations of the day were fairly thrust out of sight; there flashed upon many a suspicion, that the things said about Antichrist might yet be fulfilled not less literally than the prophecies about Antiochus or Alexander the Great. The popular style of exposition now became less grovelling: it was no longer a question how many inches the Pope's footstool was raised above the surface of the high altar;—here was a nation proposing to write after the sacred name of Jesus, "late God." While men had been discussing whether claiming to act for the Son was, or was not, denying the existence of the

Son, here had risen a nation who literally denied both the Father and the Son, setting up Reason above every God. And whereas it had been taken for granted, for want of something better to say, that the Pope, while crying out for help against the Goths and Lombards, had been engaged in plucking up three kings, here was Napoleon, fighting real battles, dethroning living kings, and doing every year what would have made the reputation of any expositor who could have discovered such incidents in the history of the Popes. Therefore men began to look on in reasonable terror, waiting to see the end of the great words which this man spoke.

And well was it for those who had patience to wait; for some at once concluded that Napoleon was the wilful king, and the French atheism Antichristianity itself. Events, as it now appears most plainly, did not warrant the tone of certainty with which these assertions were put forth; for Napoleon worked no miracles, nor did he exalt himself above every god. Yet in the year 1815 Mr. Frere thus stated his expectations, — "Bonaparte, on hearing the intelligence from the north and the east, will return into the Holy Land, and will there plant his tabernacles in the valley of Megiddo, between the glorious holy mountains. There the treading of the winepress will take place, and there he and all his army will perish, under the manifest vengeance of God."*

This school of expositors came to a violent end. Those that survived the flight from Moscow, either fell at Waterloo, or dragged out a precarious ex-

---

* Frere's Combined View of the Prophecies, p. 468.

istence during the imprisonment at St. Helena.* Their last hopes centered in the son of Napoleon, who might yet turn out to be the son of perdition; and, though at present but a gentle boy, might ripen into that rampant and infernal king. The Duke of Reichstadt's early death cut short these expectations, and prepared the way for a new and composite system, destined to flourish a little longer than its predecessor.

This scheme was based upon a supposed connection between the Pope and the French Revolution; for, from Justinian to Robespierre was precisely 1260 years. But at this point the learned differed, some reckoning the Pope on the same side with the Revolution. Mr. Croly paraphrased thus, — " The spirit of Popery, in its shape of infidelity, shall publicly abolish the doctrines of Christianity." † The majority, however, seeing clearly that Popery and infidelity were deadly foes, set themselves to solve the question, whether the subversion of Popery was

---

* It would be well if all expositors would cling to the inspired interpretations as resolutely as these did to their own. When Napoleon was beaten at Waterloo, his defeat was given out to be that wound, from which he was destined certainly to recover: when he was shut up in St. Helena, the Atlantic was pronounced to be that sea from which the Beast was once more to arise. But he died in May, 1821: unfortunately for Mr. Hoblyn, who had, in the course of that year, published this prediction : — " Behold! the arrogant, contemptuous boaster has received a wound by a sword: yet he lives, and is gone into captivity. But now do we look for his return, and anticipate his entrance even into the land of Sabaeim, the land of glory. See! the beast who received a wound by a sword and did live, again advances, emerging from the ocean."— Hoblyn, on the Numbers of Daniel, p. 142.

† Croly on the Apocalypse, ch. xi. 7.

the fall or the rise of the beast from the bottomless pit. But here again they were divided, for this question involves another of equal magnitude, — whether the saints are still in the hands of the little horn or not? whether the kingdoms of this world have yet, as announced at the sounding of the seventh trumpet, become the kingdoms of Christ, or are still under the sceptre of the Devil, swayed by the hands of the Beast? In a word, whether the saints are still worn out, slaughtered, and forbidden to buy or sell, or whether the judgment has already sat, to take away the dominion of the tyrant to the end. So delicate is the question, that several who have ventured a journey to the seat of their Beast, and have enjoyed the best possible means of procuring information, have returned home still undecided about the slaughtering of the saints.

But difficulties of this sort were for the most part kept out of sight. It was safer to say generally that Paris, and not Vienna, was the city where the Lord was crucified. The foreground of the scheme was occupied by the figure of Napoleon; at one moment flaming in mid-heaven[*], at another emerging from the bottomless pit.[†] Anon, his artillery shakes not Europe only, but the very fabric of the exposition itself: next, he is seen expiring, smitten with a

---

[*] Mr. Fysh, in 1837. On the power to scorch men with fire: "Buonaparte was indeed the sun of France, and not only the sun of France, but the sun of Europe also."—Beast and his Image, page 179.

[†] Mr. Habershon, in 1844: "The Beast of the early French Revolution, described in Apoc. xi. 7., as ascending from the abyss, and which came to be a head under Napoleon, is to re-ascend, and to be the eighth, and of the seven."—On the Apoc. chapter xx.

" deadly wound " upon the Belgian plains. But we must not forget, in looking back upon the failure of these writers, that what they have suggested concerning the probable issue of Napoleon's antichristian principles, is daily receiving from passing events important confirmation.

A few, though without much life or enthusiasm, still held fast by the system of the ancients, that Rome was Babylon, and the city of the Crucifixion, Jerusalem. These seemed to have been, by the force of circumstances, compelled to take refuge in antiquity; the winds of doctrine which had driven them to that shore, left them there stranded, high and dry indeed, but yet in comparative tranquillity, at leisure to watch the tossings of their unstable neighbours.

Of this small class a specimen is to be found in the annotator of Reeve's Bible, from which the following sentences are taken:—

"Apoc. xiv. 9. Rome was to be destroyed by the beast Antichrist, as appears in ch. xvii.; who, after having thus put down the Romish Church, shall oppress Christians in a more grievous manner, and set himself up, not as Christ's vicar, but agreeably with his name, in direct opposition to Christ. . . . .

"V. 10. The harlotry of Babylon is here plainly distinguished from the worship of the Beast, and it is plain that the latter is to succeed the former. Again, of the former it is only said that she is fallen, but the followers of the latter are sentenced to dreadful punishments.

"Ch. xvii. 16. These shall hate the harlot. This, together with v. 13, 14, are a proof that the harlot, or Popish Rome, is not the Beast, or Antichrist properly so called: she must otherwise hate herself, eat her own flesh, and burn herself with fire. 18. That great city is a description which is applicable to none but Rome: so the great city mentioned at ch. xi. 8. can mean none but Jerusalem."

A. D. circ. 1800.

With far more vitality was that teaching enforced by the Jesuit Lacunza, notwithstanding some irregularities in his exposition of the beasts and metals. Perhaps, of all modern writers, Lacunza has the most deeply influenced the study of prophecy. Although a Jesuit, he takes Babylon to be the existing Church of Rome, while with the primitive Christians he believes in an infidel Antichrist, the restoration of the Jews, the resurrection of the saints, the literal millennium, and the final restoration of the earth to be the eternal dwelling of Christ and His Church.

Ben-Ezra's "Coming of the Messiah,"—for under that title the author has disguised his name,—is known in this country chiefly through the translation of Mr. Edward Irving. For the performance of this task we are much indebted to our countryman, especially as the Inquisition, by labouring to suppress the original, has rendered it scarce on the Continent.

From a treatise so well known, a few extracts must suffice. Hitherto the Jesuits had pretended that Rome must yet fall away from the faith in order to become Babylon: this theory is attacked by Lacunza:—

"Rome, not idolatrous, but Christian, not the head of the Roman empire, but the head of Christendom and centre of unity of the true Church of the living God, may very well, without ceasing from this dignity, at some time or other incur the guilt, and before God be held guilty of harlotry with the kings of the earth, and amenable to all its consequences. And in this there is not any inconsistency, however much her defenders may shake the head. And this same Rome, in that same state, may receive upon herself the horrible chastisement spoken of in the prophecy: nor is it necessary thereto that she should previously be taken by the infidels, — that she should return to become the court of the infidel Roman empire, arisen from the grave with new and greater grandeur; nor that the new emperors should root out of her the Christian faith, and reconstitute idolatry. All these extravagant ideas, all these imaginary suppositions, are indeed consolations of no worth, and cannot fail to be of the greatest injury to Rome, if she repose upon them. * * * O that it were possible to speak in her ear, in such a way as should profit her, those words which God spake to His ancient spouse (I mean only with a reference to this particular point), O my people, they which call thee blessed cause thee to err, and destroy the way of thy paths!" *

From the prevailing infidelity of the Spanish clergy, Lacunza expects them to take a prominent part in the affairs of Antichrist. Still further, he gives out with great confidence that the Romish clergy will become the second Beast of the Apocalypse: an opinion deserving notice when advanced by one of themselves.

Lacunza had chosen the name of Ben-Ezra, the better to plead the cause of the Jews. Like Methodius, he makes the sun-clothed woman and the Zion of Isaiah to be one: but unlike him, he interprets both in the most literal manner as the Jewish Church restored in the last days: even —

" Zion the mother, with all the wrecks of her family, who, be the number determinate or indeterminate, are to be '144,000 sealed of all the tribes of the children of Israel;' being enlightened or clothed with celestial light; having opened the inward eye and the inward ear to see and hear what till then, by the just judgment of God, she had not seen or heard. And she shall at once conceive in her womb, that is, figuratively, Jesus Christ and Him crucified; who, through the

* Irving's Benezra, t. i. p. 252.

fault of her doctors, has ever been to her a true scandal. And Christ Jesus shall begin to form himself in her very womb, still in a figure, and there also shall he proceed and grow into the perfect day." *

Thus far Lacunza has appeared as a restorer of the primitive belief; in other matters he must be ranked as an innovator. By a new arrangement of Daniel's symbols, he endeavoured to show that the iron kingdom was the Gothic, and the fourth beast still future, the kingdom of Antichrist. This arrangement is the basis of the Futurist scheme, the latest novelty in the interpretation of prophecy. Its supporters lay great stress upon the temporary residence of Darius in Babylon, as tending to prove the continuity of the Babylonian and Persian monarchies. But they seem to have forgotten the speedy removal of the empire to Shushan and Persepolis, after which Babylonia became but a conquered province, according to all the histories yet written, and, what is still more to the purpose, according to the accounts given in the Scriptures themselves.

A. D. circ. 1825.

The Futurist scheme, including a large portion of the primitive belief, now received the support of two clergymen of the English church, William Burgh and Samuel Maitland. To the latter belongs the honour of having effected a partial reformation in the manner of conducting prophetic investigations. For, before the appearance of this second Valla, it was the custom to quote authorities at second or third hand, or even to

* Vol. ii. p. 87.

rend half a sentence from its context, with little regard to the intention of its original author. All this he would have reformed altogether, routing up traditional references, and printing in italics long-suppressed clauses. These ghost-like apparitions startled many, so that desertions from the year-day camp followed in quick succession. Under this iron dictatorship it fared hard with many who had unsuspectingly repeated the statements of their predecessors, who had copied lists of the fallen kings, or had made free with the names of Bernard and Fluentius. Still harder were the times for those who with easy confidence had talked of the prophetic style, and given out that the prophets were in the habit of saying days when they meant as many years. Not long before, Mede had challenged the world to find an exception to this rule: the inexorable critic now demanded, but demanded in vain, to be shown a single instance in support of it.

The Futurists, when they borrowed from Lacunza the great elements of their system, rejected that which had cost him dearest, the admission that the Romish Church is Babylon. In preference to this they joined Bellarmine in the expectation that Rome will fall away from her present faith before the days of Antichrist.

In the production of this system there were seen the usual effects of a violent and sudden reformation: Scripture was made paramount, but tradition, even primitive and apostolic, was rejected. On the present occasion, as in the great convulsion of the sixteenth century, matters did not stop at that point: there was yet standing-room for another body of men, who could be content to receive Scripture as supreme, but with it to accept the aid of primitive tradition: who could allow with St. John that the Red Dragon is Satan, and yet agree with the Church at large that the fourth beast is the kingdom of the Romans. The ground thus prepared was soon occupied; but, strange to say, was almost as quickly deserted: for, of those that then expounded the prophecies according to the primitive system, scarcely one continued to pursue the subject after the year 1840.

A. D. 1832.

To finish the story, it remains only to compare with a passage from one of these writers, the sayings of those who represent to us the teaching of the Apostles. And lest our modern author should be supposed to have copied from the ancients, we must choose one who professes not to follow them; it being his belief, that " on prophecy they could know but little: the time was not come for unfolding the scroll, it was therefore to them as a sealed book." *

REV. C. D. MAITLAND.

"The Infidel power, the Beast under his last head, while running its desolating career, devours Popery; burns that great city Babylon down to the ground; yet it breaks not friendship with this false prophet, who continues his confederate and powerful auxiliary to the last. And being thus helped by this lying prophet,

VIRI APOSTOLICI.

" He will become the eighth among them, and they shall desolate Babylon, and burn her with fire, and give their kingdom to the Beast. * * * And of his armour-bearer, who is also called the false prophet, it is said, 'He spake like a Dragon; and he exerciseth all the power of the first beast before him.' This is said that all may

* Sermon on Christian Assurance, by Rev. C. D. Maitland, p. 5. (1831).

REV. C. D. MAITLAND.

and both being holpen by the Dragon, even the Devil, they will, I apprehend, slay God's witnesses, chase the mystic woman, the mother Church, into the wilderness, and do great feats.

"For I fear it will be found that all these bitter dregs are yet in the cup, and remain to be wrung out.

"And then, when they shall have afflicted the earth, and made it a scene such as we may shudder but to think of, Christ will burst forth upon them, and hurry them off the stage on which they had played the part of Antichrist so fearfully. He shall come and hurry them away, and they shall go together into the pit, and lie down side by side, with the fire and the undying worm for their companion. * * * Then shall the earth have rest a thousand years." *

VIRI APOSTOLICI.

know his miracles to be done, not by divine power, but by magic art. * * * And they will put to flight the Church." (Irenæus.)

"The consummate tribulation, as it is written, and as Daniel says, draws near. For the Lord has cut short the times and the days, that His beloved may hasten to His inheritance. For the prophet says, 'Ten kings shall reign on the earth, and after them shall arise a little one.'" (Barnabas.)

"And when this Antichrist shall have laid waste all things in the world, reigning three years and six months, and sitting in the temple of Jerusalem; then the Lord shall come from heaven with clouds, in the glory of the Father, and shall cast him and them that obey him into the lake of fire * * * And he will bring about to the just the times of the kingdom, that is, the rest, even the seventh day made holy." (Irenæus.)

"In six days, my brethren, even in six thousand years, shall all things be accomplished. And he rested the seventh day: that is, when His Son shall come and shall abolish the time of the Wicked one, and shall judge the ungodly.' (Barnabas.)

---

* Maitland's Noah's Day, pp. 186, 187.

The author of "Noah's Day," it appears, has not borrowed from the ancients; neither can the ancients be supposed to have borrowed from him. Yet from their close agreement, both he and they appear to have availed themselves of some common source of information. This common source, which neither of them will be ashamed to own, is the Bible: and that the Bible, taken as it stands, is able to make men wise, not only to salvation, but even to a knowledge of the future, appears from this: — that what the ancients gathered from it may be now repeated, word for word, confirmed rather than falsified by the lapse of ages. Nothing has yet occurred to contradict the expectation that Antichrist will come, to destroy Babylon, to put to flight the Church, to slay the witnesses, and, while denying the Father and the Son, to set up himself above every God.

So much for the history of the past: the present, in which we are at least equally interested, demands also a moment's notice.

Of late years, the field of prophetic investigation has been materially and rapidly enlarged. Through the recent revival of ecclesiastical learning, the expositor now finds himself in possession of almost all that has been written upon the subject since the lifetime of the prophets themselves. Thus the very character of the study promises to undergo a change; but, whether for the better or for the worse, remains to be seen. Yet the question cannot long continue undecided; succeeding expositors will either be encouraged, by the example of the ancient Church, more closely to follow Scripture, or will attempt to justify, by that extravagance of which history affords so many instances, their own departure from the track of the inspired interpretations.

The host of newly recovered commentaries offers a dangerous facility for the construction of eclectic systems. It has now become easy to select a scheme of trumpets from the thirteenth century, and of seals from the twelfth: a millennium from the fourth, and a city of the crucifixion from the fourteenth. In this manner many systems may be framed, all differing widely from each other, yet all professing a close agreement with the belief of the ancients. This practice will not assist in clearing up the vague opinions already entertained concerning the belief of the ancients, who in turn pass for præterists, year-day expositors, futurists, and even mystics.

Yet this mischief is more than counterbalanced by a happy result, already partially realised.

A few years back, it was not uncommon to meet with announcements of a "new and original exposition" of the book of Revelations. But, if all are to be original, where shall we find that body of believers who will agree to trace in any part of history, to the glory of the Lord of the prophets, the fulfilment of His word? Moreover, this "original" method was not found to repay, even to the expositor, the labour bestowed upon it. It was but a poor satisfaction that his scheme should be for a few months wondered at as a novelty, to be thenceforward forgotten, or even quoted as a proof of the folly of studying prophecy, and of attempting to penetrate the mysteries of Holy Writ. But now, by almost common consent, originality of interpretation has ceased to be the expositor's aim:

he is better satisfied that his system should seem true than new: and best of all is he pleased when he can point to some ancient and time-worn page, on which the reality of the fulfilment, and therefore the divine character of the prophecy, has been recorded of old.

Yet even here he is left to the guidance of his individual taste. He may be led to seek, from the suffrages of the past, that support which his opinions have failed to command from the incredulous present. He may labour to collect, what to his undiscriminating taste seems to be not less precious than the teaching of the highest antiquity, the random suggestions of degenerate monks and friars. For it is possible, in constructing a table of the seals, to find, somewhere or other, enough to take off the appearance of absolute novelty from the wildest speculations. Or, on the other hand, he may aspire to share the belief of the primitive Church, instructed by Apostles, fresh from the contemplation of miracles, and grounded in the elements of the faith by daily conflict with the Pagan and the Jew. It may be his delight to collect testimonies to that Divine foreknowledge which could inscribe upon the shield of a religion persecuted and trampled on, "Conquering and to conquer;" he may feel his own faith strengthened by the example of that martyr-church which waited not for temporal prosperity till it could venture to accept the omen: and he may joyfully follow through history the predicted conquests of that Truth, the success of which has long since passed into a proverb, "Magna est veritas, et prævalebit."

We seem to be living not far from a time in which an acquaintance with the subject of prophecy will be reckoned among the safeguards of a Christian's faith: when the question will be often and anxiously asked, What system of interpretation is safe and trustworthy? But which, of all the systems that modern ingenuity has constructed, may be expected then to obtain the sanction of the Church at large? Not one of them, in the opinion of all but its immediate supporters, is worthy to be named in connection with the "*sure* word of prophecy:" not one of them will bear historical examination, much less maintain its credit in controversial strife. They crumble before the daylight, how then shall they weather the storm?

CONCLUSION.

THE TIMES OF ANTICHRIST.

" That Antichrist's reign against the Church will be of the utmost severity, though continuing for a very short time, even till by God's final judgment the saints receive the eternal kingdom ; — he who reads these things, though half asleep, is not allowed to doubt."

AUGUSTINE.

THE Church of Rome, before finally taking leave of the prophecies, thought proper to foretel a yet future apostacy of the Papal city. In this prediction there may be a larger proportion of truth than we, whose thoughts naturally turn to her past bloodshed and idolatry, may be, at first sight, disposed to allow.

It will be granted by many, and those not eager to take undue advantage of an opponent now beginning to taste the bitter fruits of past iniquities, that, in the present aspect of that Church, there are important indications of a deep-seated change for the worse. It was with a new feeling of surprise that the world beheld her suspicious acquiescence in the recent insurrection in France, when she stood foremost in applauding the subversion of a peaceable monarchy, though effected by a half-infidel assemblage, ill deserving the name of government. From such a coalition, the casual observer might be led to suspect the existence of some secret principle, held in common by the infidel and Papal powers : a suspicion, as it will presently appear, not altogether unfounded or unjust.

There is at the present day no principle more widely diffused throughout the civilised world than that which is met with under the names of progression, development, and the cumulative perfection of human wisdom. On every side we behold Scripture, together with the primitive belief founded on it, treated as an antiquated system, profitable only for the world in its leading-strings, and ill adapted to the present enlightened condition of the human race. This principle, in one of its various forms, modern Romanists appear to have supplied to the rationalists of the day. Meeting on this common ground, both parties show themselves alike desirous of escaping from the bondage of the written rule. They cannot endure that the faith should continue, like its founder, "the same yesterday, to-day, and for ever." And though the one would for the most part add to, while the other would exclusively take from, the articles of faith contained in Scripture, yet, from a comparison between the curses denounced in the Apocalypse, these crimes appear to differ little either in nature or degree. Not more substantial is the further distinction, that the one vests the right of developing in the Church, the other in the world. For, let the principle of development be once granted, and the very ground of that distinction bids fair speedily to vanish.

The experience of past ages warns us against presuming to foretel confidently the issue of existing conflicts, or to announce a necessary connection between times present and times to come. But, without offending against the spirit of this caution, we may still follow out the intentions of the Giver of prophecy, by attempting to concentrate upon the present the light reflected back from the revealed future.

Prophecy, that has said so much about Rome's doings in the day of her pride, now leaves us to gather from herself the course that she will pursue in the day of her distress. And with evident reason: for while, in the full enjoyment of liberty, we are able freely to observe and to comment upon the aspect of affairs, we require far less the aid of prophecy than when called upon to struggle against the triple array of learning, genius, and the power of the secular arm. Therefore, free from preconceived expectations, and with a tacit permission to hope for the best, we now await her own decision, whether she will resist or will encourage the spirit of the age. Looking forward to a general rebellion of physical and intellectual power, we wait to see whether or not that Church, ever versatile and unscrupulous, will then think fit to abandon her ancient principles of blind obedience, in the hope of thereby securing a hold over the insurgent masses.

The Jesuits, two centuries ago, decided that Rome future cannot justly be punished solely for the offences of Rome past; but that she must, to the end, continue to heap up iniquities, and to merit vengeance. Till this reasoning has been satisfactorily disproved, let it be ours to guard against the contagion of her example, and jealously to preserve that distance which a happy Reformation has placed between ourselves and her.

Of the yet remaining length of Rome's career we know nothing certain from prophecy. It may be that the sorceress has still before her long ages of iniquity:

it may be that we are now resisting her latest arts, the last insidious smiles that shall cross her withered features. For though, to delay the fatal hour, she should form fresh compacts with the kings of the earth, she must soon reach a point in compliance, beyond which she cannot follow them. The truce, so hollow and interested, will then no longer avert their vengeance; the hatred wherewith they will hate her will be greater than the love wherewith they have loved her; " they shall make her desolate and naked, and shall eat her flesh, and shall burn her with fire."

The world, already beginning to confound the corruptions of Rome with the faith which she professes to support, will doubtless hail in her ruin the downfall of Christianity itself. But to clear up whatever difficulty that judgment may present to the Church, an angel has been commissioned to explain its cause: — " Babylon is fallen, is fallen, that great city, because she made all nations to drink of the wine of the wrath of her fornication." (Apoc. xiv. 8.)

Were Babylon, as some have fondly hoped, but a symbol of the wickedness of the world, the Church's troubles would be, at that time, happily ended. But such dreams will be rudely dispelled: Babylon is indeed fallen; the enemy has struck his camp; but it is that he may occupy a more commanding position. The worst trials of the Church, far from being ended, have still to come: — " The third angel followed, saying with a loud voice, If any man worship the beast and his image, the same shall drink of the wine of the wrath of God." (v. 9.)

For the principles that appear to be now hastening

the downfall of Babylon are of a nature to bring on, with almost equal rapidity, the coming of Antichrist. Man, in the opinion of these modern rationalists, having grown in wisdom and experience, now requires a revelation suited to his augmented powers. The Old Testament, they admit, might have been well adapted to the exclusive spirit of the Jew: the New to the unlearned simplicity of the early Christian. Popery suited well enough the darkness of the Middle Ages; the half sceptical, half superstitious creeds of the Continent, have hitherto met the requirements of modern times. But these, they object, were external forms of religion, requiring miracles to enforce them, tradition and the testimony of antiquity to support their credit. Something is now demanded that shall be felt to spring from the heart of man himself, something that reason will suggest and common sense accept; that shall reveal to man the divinity within, shall raise him from the dust of creeds and systems, and shall emancipate him from those fetters which the ignorance and timidity of former ages have cast around him.

This longing for a new revelation and a new intellectual religion, where may it be expected to end? What, if those who are dissatisfied with a God of mercy, be suffered to create for themselves a god of power; if despising a Saviour, they be permitted to set up a Destroyer: if, receiving not the love of the truth, that they might be saved, they become the subjects of strong delusion, that they should believe a lie? Such a result will not be without a parallel in the physical world.

There are certain states of the atmosphere, in

which a man, by turning his back to the light, and following the pointing of his own shadow, may behold a false and phantastic counterfeit of the sun. Such, in the last days, will be the origin of the counterfeit Messiah suffered to mock the despisers of the Sun of Righteousness. For the individual apostate it is doom enough that there remains no more sacrifice for his sins: but, for a world of rebel malcontents, a new and special confutation shall be prepared. Scorning the warmth and brightness of the noonday sun, they seek in empty space a luminary of their own: they are mocked with a phantasm, a cold and cheerless image of the star of day.

Though the coming of Antichrist will be a consequence of the unbelief of the world, the Church is no more permitted to reckon herself free from a share in the guilt, than to expect an exemption from the terrible punishment. For all her misrepresentations of Christianity to the world, for every act of neglect in publishing the Gospel, for all backwardness to warn others or to deny herself, for every cherished corruption and every selfish schism, she will then, in one form or another, suffer severely. Nor may she hope to neglect with impunity the great task committed to her care, the circulation of Holy Scripture, accompanied by the steadfast inculcation of its divine and infallible inspiration. Those who *actively* employ their powers in subverting its authority, where, but in the foremost ranks of Antichrist, may we shortly expect to find them? And those who, from a repugnance to support what is termed an obsolete and exploded doctrine, now suffer this form of infidelity to spread unchecked, from what, in the approaching trial, do they hope to regain their courage? He who would then face terrors, let him learn now to endure a smile.

For, in that day of unequalled trouble, besides death, and perhaps bodily torment, there will be the torture of sickening doubt, withering and racking despair. The grounds of faith will be so obscured as to render argument hopeless: the counter-evidence apparently so overwhelming as to place all opposition in the light of wilful blindness. For that counter-evidence, as the Pagan[*] long ago remarked with triumph, will appear to defy refutation: the only safety will lie in refusing to behold or to listen: " If they say, Here is Christ, believe it not; if they say, He is in the desert, go not forth." In former persecutions there has ever been an easy answer to the blasphemer; but now it will be a man's first difficulty to realise the faith for which he is called to suffer. Intellect, miracles, the course of Providence itself, all will appear to be ranged on the side of the delusion: to doubt it will seem unbelief: to receive it, an act of required submission to the Giver of reason. For when God, in fulfilment of His threatening, curses our blessings (Malachi ii. 2.), the greatest blessings will prove the heaviest curse: reason and common sense, intended to incline man to the Gospel, and to teach him his need of a Saviour, will then seem to rise up as an impassable barrier between him and his God.

As certain prophecies, besides their direct reference to the times of Antichrist, admit of a secondary application to all periods of trial, so do others, not especially descriptive of the coming persecution, nevertheless allow of a partial adaptation to that crowning

---

[*] Celsus; see sub anno 150.

event. On this principle it has been proposed to expound a passage in the Canticles, where the spouse, beaten and insulted, is described as wandering in search of her Bridegroom, though by so doing she seems to forfeit the honoured character of bride; for, to complete her disgrace, the keepers of the wall take from her her veil, as a token of purity, to which she no longer enjoys a title.*

But to begin in the middle of the story, and to apply to the case in hand the punishment without the previous offence, would be against all fair principles of expounding Scripture. If therefore, by the night-wandering celebrated in the Song of songs, we choose to understand the Church's distress in the times of Antichrist, let us also be prepared to allow that shortly before that time she is shown to have abandoned herself to untimely repose: whether by settling down upon the good things of this world, as though she had now reached the time for securely enjoying them: or, which seems more probable, by settling down upon the forms

---

* So Hortolanus in Cantica, c. iv. " In this passage, under the figure of the Bride, the Church relates the cruel hardships which she will then incur in seeking and calling upon her Bridegroom. Terrible, indeed, will be the sequel to the 'beginning of sorrows,' as Christ himself has thus foretold:—Then shall they deliver you up to be afflicted, and shall kill you. But he that shall endure to the end, the same shall be saved." In reference to the "keepers of the walls," the reader may consult the Jesuit Lacunza, who expects the Romish clergy to become the priests of Antichrist:—
" Our priesthood it is, and nothing else, which is announced for the last times, under the metaphor of a beast with two horns like a lamb. Our priesthood, which like the good shepherd should defend the flock of Christ, and for it lay down their own lives, shall prove in those times its greatest scandal and most perilous snare. . . . They that regard such iniquity as incredible in persons so sacred, will likewise regard the iniquity itself as goodness." Ben-Ezra, vol. i. p. 220.

and externals of her ancient faith, its evidences unrealised, its spirit supplanted by the letter, the very soul of her devotion chilled and dormant. Yet even this error might be remedied: she still has a friend to awaken her, to bid her descend from that bed of repose to the dust and the humiliation of her hours of toil. But this call she refuses, at the moment, to obey, and her refusal will cost her dear.

That last trial of her faith will be also the most searching. It is not without increased severity that she is asked for the last time, Lovest thou me? Yet she has one consolation left her, that she shall in the issue answer to the test as she has never answered before. Of all the false Christs and the false prophets of the day, she will suffer none to be compared with her beloved: He is of heaven, they are of hell: the new object of delight, glittering with miracles and rich in universal homage, this is a son of perdition: the Man of sorrows, the despised and rejected, though now so distant, seeming to have deserted her even in her darkest hour, "This is my beloved, and this is my friend, O ye daughters of Jerusalem."

But at that time she may no longer hope, as of old, to call forth the reply, "Where is thy beloved, that we may seek him with thee?" For, as none of the elect shall then be deceived, so, it seems, none but the faithful, already based upon Scripture and supported by the Divine purpose, shall be enabled to resist the delusion. A consideration, which, if in any degree probable, ought to have weight with all who are entrusted with the education of others. Now, if ever, let them labour to propagate a steadfast belief in the truth and the inspiration* of Scripture, not shunning the labour of forming a practical acquaintance with the fallacies of the age, well knowing that each generation of scorners plans new attacks upon the faith, requiring to be met by new and ever-varying exercise of the ancient weapons.

For in that day Christianity will seem to the world to have been a dream. They will wonder, unless all power of wondering should be absorbed by the object of universal wonder, how, for so long a time, a system could prevail, in their estimation so manifestly false, so deservedly exploded. In their new Messiah, they will, in their own estimation, both perceive what Christianity ought to have been, and learn by the contrast what it was not.

For, when compared with Antichrist's temporary success, our blessed Saviour's mission will appear to have been a failure. And, lest the comparison should

---

* The truth, as well as the inspiration. It is the latest insult that a presumptuous age has offered to its Maker, to suppose His Word, though inspired, not absolutely true. The reasonableness of absolute and miraculous inspiration, a question which some now labour to represent as one of intricacy, may still be reduced to the old form. For it is reasonable to suppose,

I. That the Being who spent such labour upon our creation, should have created us for some definite purpose, not to be thenceforth cast aside and abandoned to ourselves.

II. That, being our sovereign, He should constitute us His subjects, informing us of His existence, and giving us laws.

III. That the Creator, at the time of delivering those laws, might, as a means of establishing a visible connection between Himself and them, suspend in some manner the ordinary laws of creation.

IV. That to a revelation so sanctioned we should be expected to submit, neither charging it with incorrectness, nor with imposture in professing to be a message from God himself.

then miss its effect, Antichrist has even now his forerunners, who declare openly that the assent of the human race is the divine testimony to a divine mission. By this theory, so flattering to human pride, they are already preparing his way: doubtless they will not forget their argument when its force is at the highest. Your Messiah, they may say, was rejected by the very people to whom he was sent: he came to his own, and his own received him not: the ordained priesthood refused him; the multitude that saw his miracles, even they cried out "Crucify him." But this man has only to appear and to work miracles, when he obtains, not merely the homage of that one people, but the universal assent, the instant and profound reverence of a world. The followers of the Nazarene, even after the end of his career, could be gathered together in an upper chamber: but a continent is too narrow for the subjects and the worshippers of this new Hero. See how in the beginning of his reign all the world wonders after him: how from every kindred and tongue and nation arises the universal chorus, "Who is like unto our king, and who is able to make war with him?"

Blessed he whose faith, in that dark hour, will be based upon the sayings of Holy Writ. That man will understand, better than all who have gone before him, the parable of the house builded on a rock. His only danger will be in applying it too exclusively to himself, as if, before his time, the floods could never truly have been said to descend, the winds to blow, or the stream to threaten. Blessed he who, in the prospect of a violent death, will be enabled boldly to impugn the universal lie. Not that he may hope to convince others; enough, and yet only enough, if he can maintain his own conviction. He will have to fight over again the battle of Stephen, disallowing man's claim to be considered supreme judge of a Messiah's credentials. Least of all will he suffer the Jews to be appealed to. The people that rejected Moses, saying, Who made thee a ruler and a judge? it were strange if they did not reject the prophet who was to be raised up like him. They that took up the tabernacle of Moloch and the star of their god Remphan, no marvel that they now follow this new idol, that they delight to receive his mark, and to bear the number of his name. The assent now witnessed is indeed unparalleled, the union of heart and soul a new thing among mankind: but not new to him who knows it all beforehand, whose Bible at that time will open of itself at the place where it is written, "These have one mind, and give their power and strength to the beast."

To resist that torrent of enthusiasm, his foundations will need to be laid in actual contact with the substance of the rock itself. There may be, between him and Scripture, no shifting stratum of vague and second-hand traditions. The stream will indeed shake his faith who has been content to receive as an evidence of Christianity the bare testimony of temporal success: the argument will then be found to tell equally against it: he must seek in haste some finer touchstone of the heavenly and the true.

It will be well, if, in the dismay of that moment, men will be able to distinguish clearly the true ground of the Apostles' boasting:—not their conquests, but the manner of their conquests. " In these things we are more than conquerors:" that is, in being killed all the day long, and counted as sheep for the slaughter. And this is no new refinement upon the ancient sense, no sophistry dressed up to meet the demands of the hour. Long ago, before even the Saracen enforced his teaching by the sword, the words of the Apostle had called forth this exclamation:—" O marvel! The servants bound, the Master crucified, still the doctrine daily prospering: the very causes expected to extinguish it, these most of all contribute to spread the flame."*

The delusion, though of supernaturally rapid growth, will not be altogether the work of a moment. Many shall come, saying, I am Christ. There will be vague reports that a Christ is here, or a Christ there. Bede thinks that Antichrist himself will spread these rumours, in order to accustom men to the expectation of a new Messiah: but that at the beginning of the three years and a half he will say openly, I am Christ. For a time several prophecies may seem to be in his favour: it will be a question, (to him at least who has then to make his first acquaintance with their literal meaning,) who it is that most truly builds again the ruined tabernacle of David: the Nazarene, whose coming was followed by the destruction of David's city, and by the departure of the sceptre from his tribe, or he who makes the holy city the seat of universal empire. And who is it that is set up as king upon the holy hill of Zion? The Nazarene, set up as a malefactor on the hill

---

* Chrysostomi Homilia xvi. ad Populum.

of Calvary, or he who, like a king, plants the tabernacles of his palace in the glorious holy mountain? In this way will be felt that sign of the latest days, "perplexity."

Though the craftiness of Antichrist may at first lead him to employ these arguments, his pride will not long suffer him to appeal to the word of Another. He will hasten to set up himself above every god, and will open his mouth against the God of gods: even against His name, His tabernacle, and them that dwell in heaven. The style and character of his blasphemies we are not told: whether he will imitate the coarser forms of the French Atheists, or the more polished defiance of ancient Rome:—

> "Shut up, thou God, the solid gates of high Olympus,
> Fortify, O Jove, the sacred citadel of the sky:
> Already Rome's lance has vanquished land and sea,
> The path to heaven still remains untrodden." *

Yet, in the absence of fuller particulars, two general expressions present themselves to our notice. The first, — " He opened his mouth:" an idiom foreign to classical Greek, and used by the Evangelists in prefacing a set speech, such as the Sermon on the Mount. Of this character was the proclamation of Sennacherib, the closest parallel afforded by Holy Scripture: "Whom hast thou reproached and blasphemed? Even the Holy One of Israel." And, secondly, " There was given him a mouth." A phrase used elsewhere to express direct inspiration: " I will give you a mouth and wisdom;" but seeming here to imply a peculiar satanic gift of blasphemy, far exceeding in malignity the efforts of unassisted man.

* Alphœus of Mitylene.

"He shall speak marvellous things against the God of gods." All this God shows to be mainly directed against Himself: doubtless that, from the example of His own long-suffering, we also may learn patience.

But how, taking up a position contrary to the instincts of human nature, will the impostor support his pretensions?

"He doeth great miracles." Upon this passage the Church has evermore kept her finger; noticing, with undisguised dismay, that the very words used to describe the Saviour's miracles are likewise applied to those of Antichrist. Some writers have proposed a qualification, but in vain; for St. Paul speaks of " *all* power and signs and lying wonders." Even the word *lying*, on which they have built hopes, does not occur in the other passages: therefore we are forced to conclude, that even if unreal in essence, they will be proof against detection by human vision. The false prophet will call down fire from heaven, and will "deceive those that dwell on the earth by the miracles which he hath power to do in the sight of the beast."

At these miracles all the non-elect then living shall wonder, that is, they shall be deceived. The elect also would be deceived; but it is not possible, and for that reason alone they stand. The Church has long desired to know how near a doubt will be suffered to approach the mind, before it is repelled by the stern front of the eternal purpose. On this subject the first Gregory thought deeply: and, if it may be said without disparagement to his faith, his courage quailed at the prospect:—

"While the elect behold with horror such signs and miracles

wrought by the ministers of Antichrist, even they, though despising life, will feel a mist of uncertainty rising in their hearts. For as, through its miracles, the imposture flourishes, so in some degree does their steadfast vision grow dim. . . . Therefore, by the influence of his lying wonders, a shadow of doubt will obscure the sight of the righteous; and, in the hearts of the elect, at the sight of the terrible miracles, a dark thought will gather form and substance."*

Compared with the history of our Saviour's life, faith and unbelief will seem, in that day, to have changed sides. What it was blasphemy to say of the first, it will be soul-saving truth to think of the second: he truly "hath a devil, and is mad;" he lives and reigns "by the operation of Satan †," for it is the Dragon that gives him that power, and seat, and great authority. For the heaven-sent messenger must be backed, not by miracles alone, but by every word of God. The same Scriptures that foretold good things of Christ have declared bad things of Antichrist. Seen by this light, his very miracles will resolve themselves into a fulfilment of prophecy: the great signs and wonders by which he will think to style himself God, will stamp him "Man of Sin:" for, if he did no miracles, he would not be the Antichrist of prophecy: if that prophet called down no

---

* Gregorius Maximus, lib. 33. in Job.

† Regarding the "Operation of Satan," the remark of La Haye is at least ingenious: "Has Satan," he asks, "never done such things before? Did not he, when power was given him to tempt Job, cause fire to descend from heaven in the sight of men? The fire of God! exclaimed the messenger, not knowing what was done, or what Satan intended. And did not the same Devil once give sense to an image of himself, and cause that the image of himself should speak, when the serpent uttered deceitful and death-bearing words?" In Apoc. xiii. tom. ii. p. 622.

fire from heaven, he would not be the false prophet of the Apocalypse.

It has been usual to attribute to Antichrist the possession of transcendent universal genius; and, with the apostolic definition before us, "all power, and all deceivableness," it seems impossible to overshoot the mark. Therefore each age, according to its peculiar taste, has boldly speculated upon his acquirements. The ancients, thinking of Simon Magus and the Egyptians, expected a magician of matchless supernatural power. The schoolmen looked for the most subtle of disputants: the monks, a man famous for his austerities. Malvenda anticipates a profound knowledge of Scripture, with eloquence so fascinating as to make it unsafe for the best instructed Christian to listen to him.* A few years ago, when physical science was popular, many supposed that he would gain ascendency by means of science: but, now that the cry is for genius, we may tremble at the prospect

* Malvenda de Antichristo, p. 411. "Antichrist," he says, "will dispute in public with the most learned of the faithful, and with such subtleties and smoothness of speech will he, Proteus-like, shift his ground, that to all present he will seem to have proved as with the light of day, by all reasons human and divine, that our Lord Christ was nothing else than a mad deceiver. Meanwhile the Christian will be driven out with laughter, hisses, and the noise of hands and feet. Then that proud one, inflated with his new triumph, will thus arrogantly address the Christians:— 'Wretched men, cease now to believe in your Crucified Impostor: see you not how clearly I have proved him to be the sorriest of pretenders? Now open the eyes of your understanding, and at length acknowledge me to be the very God.'" But La Haye suggests the caution, that in inventing such things about Antichrist, we give him the opportunity of disproving them:— "For, being so profoundly learned, he will convince the Christians of that time that he is not the son of perdition, since the things which they themselves have predicted, are not fulfilled in him." Tom. ii. p. 587.

of his vivid imagination and persuasive eloquence. For such a one the way is fast preparing by the efforts now made to Pantheise our race, and to represent the intellect of man as the evidence of an indwelling divinity. Ye shall be as gods, said Satan at the first; Ye are as gods, Satan now begins to say, preparatory to teaching one man to say, I am above every god.

The strength of Antichrist's persecution will not lie in torture, for there is no death foretold but by decapitation (Greek, the stroke of the axe. Apoc. xx. 4.). This state of things reminds us of the French revolution, in which two millions of persons perished by instant death: the ancients, however, taking Nero and Diocletian for their guides, overlooked the omission of the torture. But, in place of bodily torment, there will be a new and peculiar source of distress: a universal conflict in the heart of each country, each city, and each home. Without doors, the certainty of instant death; within, no refuge from the maddening anxiety, but at the fireside savage hatred and deadly revenge. The daughter is at variance with her mother: some word or gesture betrays that their God is not the same God, and the executioner is called in to end the dispute. "Children shall rise up against their parents, and shall cause them to be put to death." In this desolation of hearth and home, one sanctuary, as it appears, shall be spared, for nothing is said of treachery between husband and wife. Nor need we attempt to supply the omission, since the worst is professedly revealed: "Behold, I have foretold you all things."

To the severity of that tribulation the prophets oppose its shortness. Its duration is reckoned in three ways: by God, by His Son, by the angels, and even by Satan, it is reckoned as short: but to the souls under the altar, and to the elect crying day and night, it will seem long. Therefore, as a common standard of reference, its actual length is given: and to suit the readers of all times, its duration is laid down in months, and in years, and in days. It will last 1290 days of Jewish reckoning; 1260, Gentile style, without the intercalary month; each number making, when reduced to modern time, 1279 days, or two and forty months.*

It must be for some higher end than to gratify an idle wonder, that the limits of this trial have been so strictly defined. To know, when things are at the worst, how much longer the worst will continue, is a consolation, which, till that day of rebuke and blasphemy, the believer cannot learn to estimate aright. For that knowledge, though it must preclude false hopes of an instant deliverance, will as certainly supply true hope, and banish utter despair. The tyranny, in proportion as by the lapse of time it appears to be gaining stability, will thus be known to be most surely hastening to its fatal hour. The towers rise proudly, but their base is crumbling; the torrent foams madly, but its source is failing; "the ungodly is in great power, and flourishing like a green bay-tree:" but with equal truth shall it soon be added, — " I went by, and lo, he was gone; I sought him, but his place could no more be found."

* This period is still further refined upon in the "Ascension of Isaiah," a work of the second or third century. "The power of his prodigies shall be displayed in every city and country. In every city also shall his image be erected. And he shall have power three years, seven months, and twenty-seven days."— Ch. iv.

Meanwhile Israel's Keeper is neither slumbering nor sleeping. The earth is His, and the fulness thereof; though, for His own purposes, He has seemingly abandoned it to this ruinous tenant. And, first, to provide for his own: the Church, which now in her worst troubles longs for the wings of a dove, will then, as Bede remarks, both need and receive the wings of a great eagle. Next, unveiling the secrets of His eternal purpose, God proceeds to show the world who are His, and who Satan's. This is done, perhaps invisibly, by the sealing angel; but beyond the possibility of mistake, by the plague of locusts. Before that plague is let loose, each monarch marks his own: all will have either the sign of the Beast or the seal of the living God; (at least throughout the land of Judea, for none but Jews are sealed). And, as the angel once passed by the bloodstained threshold, so will the locust, during those five months of woe, pass by the seal-bearing forehead.*

* The book of Jeremiah appears to contain the earliest notice of the locust plague. In the following passage, translated from the Septuagint, some points of resemblance to the Apocalypse will be perceived: —

JEREMIAH, viii. (LXX.)	APOCALYPSE.
"Out of Dan shall we hear the sound of the swiftness of his horses. At the sound of the neighing of his cavalry the whole earth is shaken. He shall come and shall devour the earth with its fulness, the city and them that dwell therein. Therefore, behold, I send you death-bearing serpents, which cannot be charmed, and they shall bite you incurably, with torment and	Omission of Dan among the sealed. "As the sound of chariots of many horses rushing to battle." Treading under foot the holy city. "Their tails were like unto serpents." "The men which were not killed by these plagues." "In those days men shall seek death, and shall not find it."

But the high office of witnessing for God in times so critical will not be left to the locusts only. "I will give power to my two witnesses." They shall prophesy, it says, twelve hundred and sixty days. It seems impossible to go far wrong in anticipating the substance of their discourse: that, like their Master, they will begin at Moses and all the prophets, showing that, as He must needs suffer those things and enter into glory, so Antichrist must needs achieve *these* things, and go into perdition: that while boasting himself supremely free, he is toiling slave-like to fulfil the Scriptures; that the duration of his power has been fixed to a day, and the letters of his name have been all numbered.

The cry of the elect still goes up to heaven. The gale, charged with their sighs and unspeakable groanings, is further laden with the curses of the Antichristian herd. At heaven's gate both speak the same language, "How long, O Lord?"

But there is yet a triumph reserved for the powers of hell. The witnesses, though proof against human violence, fall before the infernal part of Antichrist's

JEREMIAH viii. (LXX.)	APOCALYPSE.
perplexity of your heart. Behold the cry of the daughter of my people from a far country: Is not the Lord in Zion, or is there no King in her? Wherefore have they grieved me with their graven images, and with their foreign vanities? The summer is past, the harvest is over, and we are not saved."	"The woman fled to the wilderness." "They repented not, that they should not worship idols of gold and silver and brass and stone." Five months, supposed to mean the summer season, when the scorpions appear.

kingdom. Thus far it had seemed a drawn battle: miracles against miracles; fire breathed out, against fire called down from heaven. But now Satan is victorious at all points; the witnesses of truth have been slain: the foundations, it seems, are destroyed, and what shall the righteous do?

The season for divine interference has at length arrived. Till all else had failed, it was too early for the Son to quit the throne: but now earth, mastered by hell, has no helper save in Him who took of her substance, and who, from the right hand of the Father, beholds the unequal struggle. "For when," asked one of old, "when else should the true King come, but to dethrone a tyrant, to avenge his country, to restore a world? The alien Herod had usurped the Jewish sceptre, had subverted liberty and rule, had profaned the sanctuary, and had confounded the rites of worship; therefore, when things human were found failing, the Divine drew near to succour: the helper, denied in man, appeared in God Himself. In like manner will Christ again come, to destroy Antichrist, to throw open Paradise, to strike off the fetters of a world, and, in the place of bondage, to establish eternal freedom." *

Meanwhile the world prepares to take its fill of joy. There is now none to say to the fools, Deal not so madly; nor to the ungodly, Lift not up your horn. They send presents one to another: everywhere the word is, "Peace and safety." A bad omen, for then sudden destruction is to come upon them.

Immediately after the tribulation of those days

* Chrysologus, sermo 156.

shall the sun be darkened, and the moon shall not give her light, and the stars shall fall from heaven. Upon earth there is distress of nations with perplexity: a suspicion of the fatal truth strikes terror into the hearts of all. In that suspense and deathlike syncope, a portentous sound adds horror to the gloom: " The sea and the waves roaring." Inanimate nature conceives a hope of the manifestation of the sons of God: therefore the floods clap their hands, as if remembering the ancient saying, " Let the sea make a noise, and all that therein is, for the Lord cometh to judge the earth."

But why this darkened hemisphere and these extinguished lights? The bright sign of the Son of man is about to be displayed in heaven. By that sign all doubt is at once removed: the true Christ is none other than the Nazarene. He whom His enemies made sure to have seen for the last time, as He hung between two thieves, now reappears in glory amidst ten thousand saints.

They shall look on Him whom they pierced. By the wound of their own inflicting He condescends once more to be known. In that mark of the Roman spear they read all that they dread to know;—that their Judge is no new comer, essaying for the first time a reception among men, but a sojourner of old, who has already trodden their paths, and has carried away with Him a token of their hate. But others, in that pierced side, will see mercy as well as judgment,—the sin and the salvation, the rebellion and the pardon, the warfare and the triumph,—all written with that iron pen in the Rock for ever.

With supernatural firmness the impostor supports

the blow: upon his heart, blasted by the operation of Satan, no dew of repentance may descend. In that hour he justifies the election of his master, in his madness defying heaven, and hastening to decide, at the sword's point, who is God of gods and Lord of lords. For this moment Satan has long been preparing; and at once the Dragon, the Beast and the false prophet beat to arms. (Rev. xvi. 13, 14.)

All great battles receive a name: this is called "the battle of that great day of God Almighty." Of this encounter what prophet has not sung? At the thought of that conflict Habakkuk trembled; and Enoch, who dwelt beyond the flood, even he caught the din of that warfare, the thunder of those captains and their shouting. Then it was, that, regarding neither the trackless distance nor the sounding flood between, he uttered the exulting cry, "Behold the Lord cometh with ten thousand of his saints."

The kings of the earth stand up, each at the head of his army. The rulers take counsel together, how they may break His bonds in sunder, and cast away His cords from them. At their matchless folly He that sitteth in the heavens shall laugh: the most merciful, that willeth not the death of a sinner, even He shall have them in derision. Like the disdainful warriors of old, He invites the fowls of heaven to feed upon their flesh.

The white-robed army is now marshalled upon the heavenly plain: but to fight with equal forces is beneath the purpose of their Leader. He must win some glory now, having been so long known as the despised and rejected of men. Therefore this great host shall not go down with Him to the slaughter. Who then shall accompany Him? Any that shared the agony in Gethsemane: any that stood by Him before Pilate. Any who helped him to redeem, let them now claim a share in the glory of avenging. But He sees that there is no man; He wonders there is none to uphold: therefore His own arm shall bring salvation, His own fury shall sustain Him.

The fighting is soon ended. The Beast is taken alive, and translated to the lake of fire. And whither he goes, his disciples do not follow him now, but they shall follow him afterwards. For death and hell shall be cast into the lake of fire, and all who have worshipped the Beast and his image shall be tormented with him. Yet down that steep and flaming road the King of Pride goes not alone: the False Prophet, still his companion, shares with him the precedence in eternal fire. From that time it is said, as a synonym for the place of torment, " Where the Beast and the false prophet are."

And the remnant were slain with the sword of Him that sat upon the horse, and all fowls were filled with their flesh.

" And I saw the souls of them that were beheaded for the witness of Jesus, and for the word of God, and which had not worshipped the Beast, neither his image, neither had received his mark upon their foreheads, or in their hands, and they lived and reigned with Christ a thousand years."

APPENDIX.

SKETCH OF THE LEADING COUNTER-INTERPRETATIONS.

Table of Inventors.

Scheme.	Author.	Date.
Antiochus the little horn.	Porphyry	290.
Mahomet the little horn.	Joachim	1190.
The Pope the little horn.	Eberhard.	1240.
The Turks the little horn.	Luther.	1520.
Julius Cæsar the little horn.	Calvin.	1550.
The Turk the Beast.	Innocent III.	1213.
The Persians the Beast.	De Lyra.	1320.
Modern Roman Empire the Beast.	Walter Brute.	1390.
The Pope the Beast.	Luther.	1520.
The Pope Antichrist.	The Cathari.	1160.
Trinitarians Antichrist.	Polish Arians.	{ 1550 to 1600.
The 1260 years scheme.	Joachim.	1190.
Præterist scheme.	Calvin.	1550.
Futurist scheme.	Lacunza (Ben Ezra.)	1800.

The scheme of Porphyry, the most formidable as well as the most ancient of those classed above, was at first based upon the supposed spuriousness of Daniel's prophecies. In this he has been followed by the infidels Gibbon and Collins, also by the late Dr. Arnold.* But this assumption is not necessary to the interpretation which Porphyry thought proper to put upon the visions themselves.

* Arnold's Life, p. 505. Sixth edition.

SECT. I.—*Antiochus the Little Horn.*

In order to get rid of the Roman Empire, Porphyry confined the third kingdom to Alexander in person, reserving the fourth for the Lagidæ and Seleucids. From among these he chose eleven kings, the last of whom is Antiochus Epiphanes.

The Jews, perhaps from respect for their own prophet, remained proof against the seductions of their new ally. But among the Christians he succeeded better, drawing after him, here and there, a straggler of no ignoble name. Before his time there had appeared no commentary upon Daniel, except that of Hippolytus Martyr: no marvel, then, that the prophetic creed seemed shaken by the treatise of Porphyry, in which the pupil of Longinus poured forth his eloquence, exhausted his historical learning, and, with incredible success, laboured to clothe in the very language of the prophet his own perversion of the prophet's meaning. It was now time for the Church to take the field: accordingly, during the next two centuries there appeared a host of orthodox Greek commentaries on the book of Daniel.*

The mischief was entirely confined to the East. In Assyria, or at least on its borders, James of Nisibim supported the new arrangement of the empires, and was copied by his scholar, the Syrian Ephrem.† Next came the Syriac version of Daniel‡, possibly executed under the direction of Ephrem: and from these, or, as Eudoxius thinks, from Porphyry himself, Polychronius§ the Syrian caught the infection. An anonymous Greek ‖, likewise belonging to the fifth century, completes the list of the ancient *Porphyriogeniti.*

---

* For the Commentary of Polychronius, together with the remaining fragments of fourteen others, see the Greek Chain, published by Mai, Vet. Script. t. i.

† Nisibenus, an Armenian writer of 340. His sermons are published, with a Latin version. Ephrem's commentary on Daniel is published in Syriac, but not in Greek.

‡ Walton's Polyglott Bible.

§ Mai, Vet. Script. t. i. ; Polychronius in Danielem.

‖ Ibid., Catena Græca in Danielem.

The venom of reptiles, when for a few years it has lain dormant, is supposed to lose its force: but this infidel poison, after lying dormant for eleven centuries, came forth with undiminished power. About the year 1590 Broughton discovered the long lost work of Polychronius, and soon, upon his own extravagancies, he grafted the Porphyrian scheme of the kingdoms and the horns. But Broughton fell into the hands of Ben Jonson, not the first poet that has come forward to support the cause of prophetic orthodoxy. In the "Alchemist," the heroine is made to discharge a torrent of the expositor's undigested learning:—

> "*Doll.* For after Alexander's death ——
> *Mammon.* Good lady!
> *Doll.* That Perdiccas and Antigone were slain;
> The two that stood, Seleuc' and Ptolemee, ——
> *Mammon.* Madam!
> *Doll.* Made up the two legs and the fourth beast.
> *   *   *   *   *
> *Face.* How did you put her into it?
> *Mammon.* Alas, I talked
> Of a fifth monarchy I would erect
> With the philosopher's stone, (by chance,) and she
> Falls on the other four straight.
> *Face.* Out of Broughton!"*

When reproached with having seconded the attempts of a professed infidel, Broughton retorted upon his opponents that they themselves followed the Jews. But here he overlooks the difference between a sceptic labouring to disprove Revelation, and a nation, chosen to receive the prophecies, recognising in the divine dealings the fulfilment of those prophecies. Nor, when we find the Apostle Barnabas among the supporters of the orthodox system, can we assent to the censure of Broughton:—"They that make the legs of the statue, and the fourth beast, to be the Roman government, show themselves witty to their own punishment, and the ruin of Christianity."†

---

* Ben Jonson's Alchemist, act iv. scene 5.
† Broughton on Daniel.

The followers of Broughton were F. Junius, Grotius, Venema, and Caspar Abel. They had recourse to various shifts for extricating themselves from the difficulties which follow: as a specimen may be taken the exposition of the stone and of the Son of Man, given by Grotius:—

"I beheld till the beast was slain, and his body destroyed. He now shows how the change took place. . . . . One like unto the Son of Man—the Roman people having no king among them. Private individuals are called sons of men, as in Ps. lxxxii. Here understand *private* as opposed to *kings*. He came with the clouds of heaven: with the utmost swiftness, moving rapidly in every direction. . . . . His power is an eternal power. For, to this day, the name and the majesty of the Roman empire remain, destroyed in some places, but augmented in others."*

SECT. II.—*Mahomet or the Turks, the Beast or the Little Horn.*

This scheme owed its origin to the Crusades. Joachim, when on a visit to the Holy Land, imagined the fourth beast to be the Saracens, and the little horn Mahomet.† Within fifteen years Innocent the Third made the beast and the false prophet each to be Mahomet. In 1320 De Lyra and Aureolus made the first beast the son of Chosroë, the false prophet being Mahomet.

In 1480, these speculations were consolidated by Nannius. His strong point was the woman Babylon, which he took to mean the city Babylon, as rebuilt by the Turks under the name of Bagdad. The seven hills seem to have given him no uneasiness. He made Mahomet the man of sin and Antichrist: but Genebrard, in 1580, was the first to make the 666 out of Maometis.

Luther made the Turk the little horn, but allowed him the Pope as partner in the kingdom of Antichrist. In the "Table-Talk," the following sentences are preserved:—

* Grotius on Daniel, c. vii.
† Joachim in Apoc. (on the fourth seal).

"The head of Antichrist, said Luther, is together the Pope and the Turk. . . . . I cannot define the prophecy, a time, times, and a half. I would willingly draw it upon the Turks, who began to rule, after Constantinople was overcome, in the year 1453, which is 85 years ago. Now, when I reckon the *time*, according to the age of Christ, thirty years, so maketh this sentence 105 years. . . . If a time be called a year, then it maketh three years and a half, and hitteth just upon Antiochus, who exercised tyranny even so long among the people of Israel. . . .

"The Pope's kingdom shall stand 666 years, according to the number of the beast, in Rev. xiii. The Pope is the right Antichrist."*

In his commentary on Daniel he attempts to work out the problem of the ten horns:—

"Daniel vii. In the description of the Roman kingdom, the ten horns mean the ten kingdoms into which it was to be divided; namely, Syria, Egypt, Asia, Greece, Africa, Spain, France, Italy, Germany, England, &c. And by the little horn which plucked up three of the ten, is meant Mahomet or the Turk, who now possesses Egypt, Asia, and Greece."

Luther was supported by Melancthon, and afterwards by the monk Pinto. The ten horns still presented some difficulty; but, says Pinto, "Mahomet conquered three horns, that is, three parts of the world formerly subject to the Roman Empire: Asia, Africa, and Europe. Not indeed the whole of them, but a part."†

This scheme has been lately advocated in the British Magazine, No. 36. The plucked up horns are there said to be Syria, Egypt, and Northern Africa.

SECT. III.— *The Papal-Antichrist and Year-day scheme.*

A part of this system had its origin in the twelfth century among the Cathari, a sect holding the tenets summed up by

---

* Luther's Table Talk, Bell's translation.
† Hector Pinto, in Danielem.

the Apostle as "forbidding to marry and commanding to abstain from meats." They reckoned that, in eating flesh, a man ate damnation to himself: also that in wedlock there is no salvation. The forbidden fruit was Adam's marrying Eve. They denied Christ's having come in the flesh, allowing only that He seemed to have a body. Having upon them these palpable marks of Antichrist, they gave out, as if in self-defence, that Pope Sylvester was Antichrist; and the Cross, the symbol which refuted their impious scheme, the mark of the beast.

For a summary of their opinions we are indebted to Bonacursus, once their teacher, but afterwards converted to the Trinitarian faith:—

"They do not believe that the body of Christ rose again, nor that it was taken up into heaven, nor that there will be a resurrection of the flesh, nor that Christ descended into hell. They do not believe that the Son is equal to the Father, because He said, The Father is greater than I. They say that the Cross is the mark of the Beast spoken of in the Apocalypse, and the abomination standing in the holy place. They say that St. Sylvester was the Antichrist, of whom it is said in the Epistles, The son of perdition, who exalteth himself above all that is called God. From that time, they say, the Church was lost. They believe that no person can be saved in the married state."*

The idea of a Papal little horn was first struck out by Archbishop Everard, in 1240. The orator, perhaps, meant nothing more than a rhetorical flourish, for he was speaking against the temporal encroachments of the Pope. He attempted to show, for the first time on record, that the Roman empire had been divided into ten kingdoms, of which the Pope had conquered, or was conquering, three. These were Germany, Sicily, and Italy.†

Another improvement was that of Joachim, who reckoned 1260 years from Christ to Antichrist. Our countryman Brute, well pleased with this theory, carried it out in a con-

---

* Dacherii Spicilegium, ed. quarto, t. xiii. p. 63.
† Aventini Annales Boiorum, lib. vii.

nected system of exposition. His date is fixed by the record of his recantation, which took place in 1393.

According to Walter Brute, the Beast of the Apocalypse represents the Roman empire from Julius Cæsar to Frederick, a period of about 1260 years. This power, under Adrian, set up the abomination of desolation in the temple of Jerusalem, which abomination was to remain 1290 years, to be followed by the appearance of the Papal Antichrist.*

Brute was anxious to reduce the times and half time to 1290 years:—

"A time, times, and half a time. Behold, how unfitly they did assign this time by three years and a half, which, they say, Antichrist shall reign. For whereas it is said, a time, times, and half a time, there is a going down from the greater to the part, because it is from a time to half a time. If therefore there be a going downward from the whole to the part, by the *middest*, (which is greater than the whole itself,) the going downward is not meet nor agreeing. And this is done when as it is said that a time, times, and half a time, is a year, two years, and half a year."

On this plan the *time* is taken to mean a millennium; *times*, a century each; and half a time, 60, or 90 years.

Down to the year 1500 this school of prophecy made little progress. Joachim lived to abandon his wildest speculations: Brute, and even Wickliffe, recanted; but the genius and the wrath of Luther were not so to be diverted from their mark. The great Reformer, waging deadly warfare against the Papacy, availed himself of such weapons as his zeal and sincerity of purpose first supplied. Prophecy was all before him where to choose: and, considering the violence of the times, his moderation, rather than his vehemence, should excite our surprise. The little horn he reserved for the Turks: the locusts he let loose upon the schoolmen. The star fallen from heaven was Thomas Aquinas: the king of the bottomless pit, Aristotle. The schoolmen had power to torment men during their natural

* Foxe's Acts and Monuments, sub anno.

life, expressed by five months, that is, the duration of the five senses.*

It is Luther's great point that the Pope is Antichrist. With this he identifies the man of sin, the king of fierce countenance, and the wilful king. The Mahuzzim he translates by *Missam*, the Mass: the holy mountain he takes to be Rome, called holy from the number of its martyrs. Most of his explanations are equally at random. "The Pope," he says, "raised up a new Roman empire, transferring it, as he styles it, from the Greeks to the Germans, which, among the other signs of Antichrist, is the principal and greatest."† But transferring empire to *another* seems scarcely a mark of Antichrist, whose sole aim will be to "exalt and magnify himself."

Melancthon follows with little variation. Zwingle is satisfied with making the man of sin to be the Pope: "not Julius nor Alexander alone, but the whole kingdom."‡ In this track followed most of the continental reformers, and soon after the Polish Arians, who looked upon the Pope as the main support of the Trinitarian doctrine. Slichtingius shall speak for them all: "God shall send them strong delusion, that they should believe a lie. They refused to believe the pure truth, therefore they deserve to believe a lie. They refused to believe that the man Jesus is a God, made by the one God; therefore let them believe that he is the one very God himself." (In 2 Thess. ii.)

Meanwhile the year-day theory was assuming a definite form. Luther allowed the possibility of 1290 years, from A.D. 38 to 1328. Melancthon, by adding 1290 to 1335, obtained a sum total of 2625 years, reaching from Daniel to the second Advent. For the three times and a half, he proposed a theory with his usual want of success: "I understand," he says, "in a general way, a long time, and then a sudden and unexpected decline. For it says, Half a time: as much as to say, When the Turkish power has reached its height, hoping to enjoy universal empire, and beginning to

---

* Lutherus in librum Ambrosii Catharini.
† Ibidem.   ‡ Zwinglius in 2 Thess.

promise itself endless rule, suddenly it will begin to decline." (In locum.) Calvin, on the other hand, disdains to count the days: "In numeris non sum Pythagoricus." (In Dan. c. xii.) Upon this, the year-day writers, finding their cause still in need of support, constructed the famous theory of "angelic days."

The prophetic periods, it was noticed, are for the most part revealed by the medium of angels. But angels, looking down from their heavenly watch-tower, might have lost sight of the *rotatory* motion of our planet, and thus have been led to measure the terrestrial day by the only movement visible to them, our circuit round the sun. Thus when an angel spoke of a day, he might fairly be supposed to mean a year.

We can place no reasonable confidence in the prophecies, if the prophets, whether men or angels, are permitted to commit such gross mistakes in delivering their message. Could we suppose this ignorance on the part of those who sang together when the evening and the morning made the first day, we should still have to get over the declaration that "All Scripture is given by inspiration of God," and is therefore warranted to have been free from all mistakes at the time of its first reception by mankind.

Illyricus attempted to adapt the *times* to the Interim of three years and a half. Others, giving up as hopeless all regular and fair methods of exposition, had recourse to the suggestions of individual fancy. Foxe, the Martyrologist, hearing Daniel call seven years a week, felt himself authorised to call seven years a month. Thus the forty-two months made 294 years; and these, reckoned from 1300 (the end of the millennium), would expire in the year 1594.*

These failures, for such they were soon acknowledged to be, gave rise to a method of explaining the times, which raised the Papal-Antichrist school to its highest point of credit. According to some of the more sagacious, the period of 1260 days represents, by way of parable, a certain time accurately fixed in the Divine purpose, though not definitely revealed to man. Aretius, leader of this section, allows the

* Foxius in Apoc. c. xii.

possibility of a further year-day fulfilment. The forty-two months, he remarks, make three years and a half: —

"Therefore it signifies that this affliction will last but a short time, which is limited with God, though to us its bounds are not clearly apparent, except by the event. Yet, if we take the number to mean angelic days, that is, a day for each year, the treading down will have now lasted 1260 days, that is, so many years, down to our time. For, during exactly so many years, beginning from Constantine the Great, the Papacy ruled over that court which was cast out and condemned by God. If to these years we add the number before Constantine, that is, 312, we shall arrive at the year just expired, A.D. 1572. So that at length we may expect, confidently, the end of this tyranny." (Aretius in Apoc. xi.)

In the locusts he differs little from Brute and Luther. His fallen star is the eighth Boniface, who, walking upon earth, obtained from Phocas the primacy. The key of the pit is the counterfeit key of Peter: the smoke is vanity and theological pride, darkening the Sun of righteousness. Out of it come swarms of monks and clergy, having over them a king, Apollyon, either the Devil, or (which seems to amount to the same thing), the Pope.

The theory, now supported by numerous and discordant writers, began to be embarrassed by increasing difficulties. It was a question, whether the first ten centuries after Constantine should be considered as the reign of Christ, or of Antichrist. Since history gave them no assistance, they were left entirely to the guidance of imagination. Luther, in his Chronology, counted the millennium from Christ to A.D. 1000. Foxe reckoned it from Constantine to 1300. Now Foxe must be allowed to know something about martyrs, especially those that suffered under the Papacy: he may be worthless as an expositor; but, after a life spent, and well spent, in recording the sufferings of the faithful, his historical opinion must be of weight. And his opinion is this: that for a thousand years after Constantine, the true Church was visibly triumphant.

On the other hand it was maintained by Brightman, Napier, Aretius, Cocceius, and others, that the same thousand years were not the reign, but the humiliation of the saints, being four-fifths of that time during which the little horn prevailed against them and wore them out. Latterly, the theory of Foxe has become antiquated, and the beginning of the 1260 years is pushed on three or four centuries later than Constantine.

The inconvenience was avoided by Pareus, through some judicious concessions to Scripture, and an entire abandonment of the year-day calculation. By making the times indefinite, he escaped a world of mortification. The red Dragon was boldly expounded in agreement with St. John: at least he takes it for granted that "who the Devil and Satan is, nobody is ignorant." (In Apoc. xii.) One saying is too remarkable to be passed over: " This Dragon has nothing in common with the beast of Daniel, excepting the ten horns." A degree of attention to the prophecy, not usual among Papal-Antichrist expositors, many of whom imagine that the "Beast" and Daniel's fourth beast are the same. But it seems unlikely that the prophet, while describing the animal down to the colour of its nails, should omit so important a feature as the seven heads.

The talents and moderation of Pareus procured him, as it appears, a follower in our James the First. The royal pamphleteer, regardless of the importance divinely assigned to dates and numbers, abandons all that cannot be traced in history. Unable to find precisely ten kings in Europe, he takes the number as indefinite; and as for the whole arithmetic of days, months, and times, "Any one," he says, "though but slightly acquainted with St. John's style and mode of speaking in the Apocalypse, will readily observe that he is accustomed to put a certain number in the place of an uncertain."

His treatise is addressed to Rodolph II. Emperor of the Romans, and to his fellow-sovereigns of Europe. All these, his " Dilectissimi Fratres," together with himself, he reckons as horns of the scarlet beast. Not that he means them to go into perdition, having a plan for their conversion, of which it could only be desired that its ingenuity might be equalled by its success. In their unreformed state, he admits, they give their power to the beast, the Pope; but now they are invited to turn round upon the Romish harlot, to strip her naked, that is, to lay bare her pretensions, and to burn her with fire. Hitherto, by persecuting the Church, they have fought against the Lamb; but now He is to conquer them by converting grace. Thus does James, mistaking his pen for a sceptre, right royally rule the sense: but Alexander's cutting the Gordian knot is a dangerous precedent for royal theologians.

The system fares worse in the hands of the infuriated Brightman, whose treatise bears the arrogant title of a "Revelation of the Apocalypse." And a new revelation was indeed required, if we are meant to discover that Constantine is at once the seal-bearing angel, the man-child, the angel standing by the altar, a horn of the beast, and the Archangel Michael. " And so," he concludes, " there is a marvellous consent of the history with the prophecy."

To any one who undertakes the history of this school, it will be mortifying (unless he shall have far better success than the author of these pages) to find himself always unable to convey to his reader a distinct idea of their system. Never will he be able to say what they understand by the Beast: never to point out the Pope's actual place in their prophetic scheme. Every explanation hitherto proposed among them has been negatived by a decided majority: for, if anything may be expected to be fixed amongst them, it is that the Pope is the Beast: yet, out of thirty expositors collected indiscriminately from that school, ten think the Pope the Beast, twenty deny it: the Beast being in turn claimed for the old Roman Empire, the new Roman Empire, the Church of Rome, and the Pope. As for the Pope himself, ten vote him the Beast, fourteen the false prophet, and six the image of the Beast.

LEADING COUNTER-INTERPRETATIONS. 439

Expositor.	Beast.	False Prophet.	Image of the Beast.
Walter Brute.	Roman Emperors, from Julius Cæsar to Frederick.	The Pope.	
Aretius.	Old Roman Empire.	The Pope.	Electorate, or Image of the Empire.
Foxe.	Heathen Roman Empire.	The Pope.	Roman See.
Lord Napier.	Modern Roman Empire.	Papacy.	Papal confirmation of Emperors.
Broughton.	Old Roman Empire.	Pope.	New Roman Empire.
King James I.	The Pope.	Apostate Church.	Papal Power.
Brightman.	Pope.	Pope.	Pope.
Pareus.	Pope.	Pope.	Images.
Gerhard.	Old Roman Empire.	Papal Kingdom.	Modern Roman Emperors.
Mede.	Modern Roman Empire, as ten kingdoms.	Pope and Clergy.	Idolatrous power.
Cocceius.	False Church.	False Hierarchy.	Church Representative (probably as Pope).
Mulerius.	Papacy.	Roman Doctors.	Scholastic Theology.
Piscator.	Roman Emperors.	Pope.	Papal confirmation of Emperors.
Vitringa.	Rome Papal	Franciscans, Dominicans, &c.	Inquisition.
Daubuz.	Gothic Roman Empire.	Ecclesiastical Empire.	Pope.
Sir I. Newton.	Latin Empire.	Greek Church.	Men like the first Beast.
Bishop Newton	Modern Roman Empire.	Roman Church.	Pope.
Lowman.	Papal States.	Holy Roman Empire.	Deification of the Pope.
Gill.	Pope.	Pope.	Popery.
Bachmair.	Papal Empire.	Roman Clergy.	Saint-worship.
Fraser.	Papacy.	Roman Clergy.	Pontifical supremacy.
Galloway.	Pope.	French Republic.	Convention of Paris.
Cunninghame.	Roman Empire.	Pope and Clergy.	False Church.
Clarke.	Modern Roman Empire.	Spiritual Roman Empire.	Pope.
Faber.	Roman Empire.	Papacy.	Image-worship.
Croly.	Papacy.	Dominicans.	Inquisition.
Woodhouse.	Roman Empire.	Papal Power.	Tyrannical power.
Fysh.	Pope.	Jesuits.	Council of Trent.
Habershon.	Modern Roman Empire.	Papacy.	Papal Hierarchy.
Elliott.	Pope.	Papal Clergy.	Papal General Councils.

F F 4

The scheme, faring so badly in the matter of dates and doctrines, rests a defence upon a supposed resemblance between the Papacy and the Antichristian powers of Apoc. xiii. These powers the year-day expositors pronounce to resemble wonderfully the Papacy and the Roman Empire. Then, turning to the history of Europe, Here, they say, we find the Beast, the false prophet, and the image of the Beast: how perfect is the likeness! how accurately does each feature of the portrait correspond! But which is the Beast, and which is the false prophet? And now it turns out that though so fully agreed about the likeness, they are entirely at variance about the identity of the features: what ten had taken for the eyes, fourteen had guessed to be the mouth, and six had all along vainly imagined to be the nose: for in that proportion have we seen them divided as to the Pope's place in the apocalyptic portrait.

But the dates have proved, if possible, still more difficult to fix. The following list comprises a large proportion of those writers who have either applied the 1260 days to the Papacy, or have attempted any other mystical explanation of the period.

Expositor.	His date.	End of 1260 days.	Beginning of 1260 days.	
Joachim	1195	1260	1	
Walter Brute	1393	1394	134	
Luther	1530	{ 1558	1453	{ 3 times and a half.
		1328	38	1290 days
Melancthon	1530	2000	660	
Aretius	1573	1572	312	
Illyricus	1580	1551	1548	
Foxe	1586	1594	1300	
Napier	1593	1576	316	
Pareus	1600	indefinite	—	
King James I.	1600	indefinite	—	
Brightman	1600	1546	304	
Mede	1630	does not say	—	
J. Artopæus	1665	1520	260	
Cocceius	1669	1552	292	

LEADING COUNTER-INTERPRETATIONS. 441

Expositor.	His date.	End of 1260 days.	Beginning of 1260 days.
Fleming	1701	1848 / 2000 / 2742	606 / 758 / 1407
Vitringa	1705	not definite	
Daubuz	1720	1736	476
Bishop Newton	1750	uncertain	uncertain.
Bengel	1750	1836	1058
Lowman	1770	2016	756
Gill	1776	1866	606
Bachmair	1778	1500	1150
Fraser	1795	1998	756
Galloway	1802	1849	606
Cunninghame	1813	1792	533
Clarke	1814	"rather	difficult to say."
Faber	1814	1866	606
Frere	1815	1792	533
Croly	1828	1793	533
Woodhouse	1828	1882	622
Fysh	1837	1987	727
Habershon	1843	1844	584
Elliott	1844	1789 / 1793 / 1864 / 1868	529 / 533 / 604 / 608

Not less difficulty do they find in the seventh head of the scarlet beast.

Expositor.	Seventh Head.
Foxe.	Foreign Emperors.
Aretius.	Trajan and other foreign Emperors.
Pareus.	Constantine and Successors.
Brightman.	Popes.
Bishop Newton.	Exarchs of Ravenna.
Gill.	Popes.
Clarke.	Patricians.
Bachmair.	Lombards.
Cunninghame.	Napoleon.
Cocceius.	Popes.
Habershon.	Napoleon.
Elliott.	Diocletian and colleagues.
Croly.	Charlemagne and successors.

Expositor.	Seventh Head.
Faber.	Carlovingian Patriciate.
King James I.	Bishops before Popes.
Fysh.	Dukes.
Napier.	Popes.
Gerhard.	Goths and Vandals.

In the attempt to discover, by force, fit representatives of the two witnesses, it would be hard to decide whether these writers have simply done themselves injustice, or have betrayed, by their struggles, the desperate state of their cause. Among the sects which they have dignified with the name of "the witnesses," two of the most conspicuous are the Paulikians and Orleanists.

The Paulikians were a warlike race of Bulgarians, sometimes employed as mercenaries by the emperors of the East. Their history is told by Petrus Siculus, who visited them in the eighth century, and preserved some fragments of their writings in the original Greek.

Few of these sects rejected the whole Bible. The Paulikians retained the Gospels, and even the Epistles of St. Paul. All historians ascribe to them certain semi-Manichæan tenets. Sergius, their principal ornament, was a laborious and zealous teacher, though filled with that spirit of arrogance which, in the Western world, afterwards distinguished the more ambitious pontiffs. Of his Epistles, a few sentences remain: —

"Let no man deceive you by any means. Having these promises of God, be of good cheer: for, having confidence in your hearts, we write to you, that I am the Porter and the good Shepherd, the leader of the body of Christ, and the lamp of the house of God; and I am with you always, even to the end of the world; for though I am absent from you in body, yet I am present with you in spirit."

To Leo Montanus he writes: —

"Far be it from me to hate you, but rather to admonish you, that as you have received the apostles and prophets which are four" (probably meaning the evangelists), "you would also receive pastors and masters, lest you become a prey to beasts. * * * We are the body of Christ: and if any one fall away from the traditions of the body of Christ, that is, from mine, he sins, because he turns aside to those that teach otherwise, and is not obedient to sound words."*

At this sentence the historian expresses horror, and is on that account vehemently blamed by the year-day writers. They seem to forget that Petrus, being a Greek, and living before the time of Hildebrand, could not have grown accustomed to such arrogance. Nor can he be expected to acquiesce in the distinction preserved by our expositors, who reckon *that* but mild language in a sectarian which in a Pope they would call outrageous blasphemy. Petrus, recognising no such distinction, roughly styles Sergius a precursor of Antichrist.

Since the Paulikians never came into contact with the Church of Rome, it is difficult to see how they belong to the list of anti-papal witnesses. This objection does not apply to the Orleanists, who, if they could, in the faintest sense, be styled Christians, might fairly be admitted as witnesses against Rome. But, since they witnessed chiefly against the doctrines of the Atonement, the Incarnation, the Sacraments, and the saving character of the Bible, rather than against the corruptions of the Romish Church, we must suppose that the angel who is made to speak of them as "my witnesses," is speaking in the character of Antichrist, attributed to him by some year-day expositors.

The Orleanists were charged with teaching these and other errors: "that Christ was not born of the Virgin Mary; that He did not suffer for man, neither was He truly laid in the grave, nor did He truly rise from the dead." After admitting the truth of this accusation, they sustained a conversation which is thus reported:—

"The president then put it to them, That Christ chose to be born of a virgin, because He was able: also, that He suffered in human nature for our salvation, and, after overcoming death, rose again the third day in Deity, teaching us that we also should arise in the regeneration. To which with viper's mouth they answered, Neither were we present, nor can we believe these things to be true.

* Petri Siculi Historia. Gr. et Lat. Ingoldstadt, 1604.

" The president then asked them, Do you believe, or not, that you had parents after the flesh? Upon their allowing this, he answered, If you believe that you were begotten of parents, when you did not exist, why refuse to believe that God, begotten of God without a mother before the world, was in the end of time born of a virgin by the overshadowing of the Holy Spirit? But they said, What nature owns not has no part in creation.

" The President then answered, Do you not believe that, before anything existed by nature, God the Father made all things out of nothing by His Son? To which, as aliens from the faith, they answered: You may tell these things to such as savour the earthly, and believe the fictions of carnal men written upon parchment. But to us, who have the law written in the Spirit by the inner man, and who savour nothing but what we have learnt from God the Maker of all, you vainly speak of things superfluous and unbefitting the Deity. And now cease talking, and do with us what you will. Already we behold our King reigning in heaven, by His right hand conducting us to immortal triumphs, and granting us heavenly joys." *

But the greatest feat of the year-day expositors has been the construction of ten kingdoms out of the offshoots of the Roman empire. Three of these, they say, were conquered by the Pope.

Perhaps it may be safely asserted, that no two of them agree in a list of the ten kingdoms. Napier counts twenty-six, but of these he rejects sixteen as unsuitable. He rejects Ireland, but includes Scotland; he rejects Poland, but includes Hungary. The number of kingdoms since collected for this purpose is said (perhaps incorrectly) to exceed sixty.

In 1728 Bishop Chandler finds " Ten kingdoms, neither more nor less, whose names, Machiavel, little thinking what he was doing, gives us." The ten he quotes thus : " 1. Vandals; 2. Alans and Sueves; 3. Visigoths; 4. Burgundians; 5. Franks; 6. Angli and Saxons; 7. Ostrogoths; 8. Gepidæ; 9. Huns; 10. Heruli and Thuringi." †

* Dacherii Spicilegium, ed. quarto, t. ii. p. 675.
† Bishop Chandler's Vindication of his Defence, vol. i. p. 253.

Bishop Chandler, having made out this list, as if from Machiavel, is soon quoted by Bishop Newton: from Bishop Newton, Mr. Faber quotes, as he fondly imagines, the list of Machiavel. Had Bishop Newton, or Mr. Faber troubled themselves to consult the Florentine, they would have found his list to contain, not ten kingdoms, but five, exclusive of the Byzantine Roman empire. For thus writes Machiavel himself: " Zeno held the Eastern empire. The Ostrogoths governed Mysia and Pannonia; the Vestrogoths, Suevi, and Alani held Cascovy and Spain. The Vandals possessed Africa; the Franks and Burgundians, France. The Heruli and Thuringhi had Italy." — (Historiæ Florentinæ, lib. i.)

The Machiavellian list of ten kingdoms is therefore a fiction. It is no less a fiction that he made out "ten kingdoms, neither more nor less," than that the prophets wrote day for year, or that Justinian delivered up the saints.

SECT. IV. — *The Præterist Theories.*

When a man starts with the assertion that these prophecies were fulfilled in the first ages of Christianity, he is met by this difficulty: that the prophecies were not found sufficiently plain to enable the Church to recognise their fulfilment until some fifteen centuries afterwards. But where lies the fault? in the obscurity of the predictions, or in the dulness of the Church? It is the business of the Præterist to vindicate the Scripture, and to leave the entire blame with the Church. He is bound to point out in history some fulfilment, so obvious as to show that the believers of that age might fairly have suspected it to be a fulfilment. But, far from this, scarcely two Præterists have as yet agreed about even the outline of their supposed fulfilments.

Though Alcassar was the first to apply the Præterist principle to the Apocalypse, the rest of the prophecies had been so treated one hundred years before.

In the eleventh of Daniel, Calvin finds Crassus and the

Parthians, with a continuation of Roman history down to the birth of Christ: at this point he brings in the standing up of Michael and the great tribulation suffered by Christ's first followers. Having made the little horn to be Julius Cæsar, the three years and a half remain to be got rid of: —

"They shall be given into his hand for a time, and times, and the dividing of a time. Here the interpreters are in difficulty: I will not repeat all their opinions, since it would be needful at the same time to refute them. Though, if I chose to refute each of them, it would give me little trouble; but I will follow my usual method, that is, I will briefly explain the genuine sense of the prophet, and then no difficulty will remain. Those who think that a time here means a year, are, in my opinion, mistaken. They quote from the Apocalypse the forty-two months, which make three years and a half; but this is by no means decisive. For, even if I should grant that a time may be called a year, those years are not to be reckoned as containing 365 days in each, but the year itself is taken figuratively for some indefinite time. It is better to abide by the words of the prophet." — (In Danielem, vii.)

Calvin's idea of abiding by the words of the prophet amounts to making 1290 days to mean any time except 1290 days. But, if Calvin condemns everybody else, everybody else has judged him with the same judgment: he has not had, to this day, a single follower in the original parts of his system.

The Præterists may be said to require no refutation, since they condemn and expose each other. The only exception is in the case of Calmet, who thought proper to follow Bossuet.

Expositor.	Date.	Name of the Beast.	Fulfilment of the Three Years and a Half.
Alcassar.	1614	The Pride of Life.	Persecution by Jews.
Mariana.	1618	Maometis.	Nero's persecution.
Grotius.	1630	Ulpius (Trajan).	Domitian's persecution.
Hammond.	1680	(Doubtful).	Domitian's persecution.

LEADING COUNTER-INTERPRETATIONS. 447

Expositor.	Date.	Name of the Beast.	Fulfilment of the Three Years and a Half.
Bossuet.	1690	Diocles Augustus.	Julian's persecution.
Clericus.	1714	"I belong to Jove or Juno."	
Calmet.	1720	Diocles Augustus.	Julian's persecution.
Wetstein.	1752	Titus (Teitan).	Jewish war.
Lee.	1830	Probably the number is inserted by a copyist.	Pagan persecutions.
Moses Stuart.	1845	Nero Cæsar.	Nero's persecution.

In making out the Beast and false prophet, they are less at variance, the heathen religious power answering without much difficulty to the false prophet.

Expositor.	Beast.	False Prophet.	Image.
Alcassar.	Roman Empire.	Fleshly Wisdom.	Majesty of Roman Empire.
Mariana.	Roman Empire.	Mahometanism.	Imitation of Paganism.
Grotius.	Idolatry.	Magic.	Image of Apollonius.
Hammond.	Idolatry.	Apollonius.	Flavian Temples.
Bossuet.	Roman Idolatry.	Philosophy.	Image of Julian.
Calmet.	Roman Empire.	Porphyry, Hierocles, &c.	Julian's restored idolatry.
Wetstein.	Roman Empire.	Empire of Vespasian.	Standards.
Lee.	Roman Empire.	Heathen Priesthood.	
Moses Stuart.	Roman Civil Power.	Heathen Priesthood.	Statues of Nero.

SECT. V.— *The Futurists.*

This small but energetic school dates no farther back than the beginning of the present century. Its members agree to receive as final the inspired explanations: but, while thus adhering to Scripture, they reject all ancient tradition, however Catholic in its reception or Apostolic in its source. But, since in other respects they are no Puritans, nor disposed to reject the traditions of the Church, it may be hoped that they will soon abandon their opposition to the ancients, and give in their adhesion to Barnabas and Irenæus.

Their system involves the following variations from the ancient belief: —

That the third beast, or none at all, is the Roman empire, and the fourth the kingdom of Antichrist, still future.

That the first seal represents Christ's future triumph at the close of this dispensation : " The beginning of the end."

That Rome is not yet Babylon, but will be. (Bellarmine.) (Lacunza thinks that the Church of Rome is now Babylon.)

That the " Revelation " means, not a revelation *by* or *about* Jesus Christ, but the Revelation, or Second Advent, of Jesus Christ Himself.

Within the last year this system, adapted to the expectation of a Jewish Antichrist, has been advocated in an anonymous work, entitled the " Jewish Missionary." With a general disregard of the ancient belief, its author combines an endeavour to carry out, to the utmost, the literal sense of Scripture; with what measure of success, it may be, as yet, premature to decide : —

"If the view here taken of this epistle be correct, it will enable us to explain that very difficult passage, 'the sin unto death,' of which if a brother be guilty, we are not even to pray for him. This sin, the writer thinks, is the crowning sin of the latter times, the completion of the apostacy, the idolatrous worship of the idol Messiah. For any sin short of this, there may be hope; for this there is none. It is commonly supposed, indeed, that this expression refers to that sin against the Holy Ghost, which our Lord himself declared should never be forgiven; which consisted in ascribing the miracles of Jesus to the power of the devil. The writer thinks, that this sin and the worship of the idol Messiah are essentially the same, though in different stages of its growth. The rejection of Jesus, ' who came in his Father's name,' and the attributing his miracles to the agency of the devil, will end in the receiving and worshipping His rival, the idol Messiah, who 'will come in his own name:'—the former marked 'the green tree,' the latter will distinguish 'the dry.' . . .

"For, when the idol Messiah shall fulfil St. Paul's words, and 'sit as God in the temple, showing himself that he is God,' there will be no middle course between openly and boldly maintaining that Jesus is the true Messiah, the Son of God, and bending in prostrate adoration before the impious usurper of his throne. Well, therefore, might the inspired apostle conclude his prophetical warnings with this solemn admonition: 'This, Jesus, is the true God: little children, keep yourselves from idols.' . . .

"In the mind of every man who believes these things, these prophecies must awaken a feeling of the most solemn interest. But in the Jew, this feeling will be yet more solemn — an intense and overwhelming anxiety. In the approaching contest, the Gentile Christian may perhaps be able to stand aloof, in comparative security; but the Jew will be called to the fore-front of the battle; he must be enrolled either in the ranks of Jesus of Nazareth, or in those of the idol king; for him there will be no escape. Let every Jew, who reads these lines, fly from the approaching trial — while flight is in his own power."

There still remain the Mystics, Swedenborg's followers, and all others who can see in the Apocalypse nothing else than a highly coloured picture of the Christian's life. But setting aside their systems, the above are the most popular counter-interpretations of the Bible prophecies. After detailing their points of difference, there still remains the more pleasing task of noticing in what they agree. The Futurist and the Turk-Expositor, the Year-day and the scholar of Porphyry, when they have differed on all besides, and have fought over every inch of the debateable ground of Scripture, will yet with one accord hold up their hands for this principle: — That prophecy means something definite and tangible: that when the future is professedly revealed, it is for man to seek diligently a visible fulfilment: and that the simple and unlearned shall not prove to have been so deluded by the splendour of the visions as to mistake, for the history of thrones and nations, a mere parable of the every day experience of the human heart.

INDEX

TO

PASSAGES OF SCRIPTURE EXPLAINED.

		Page
Genesis iii. 5.	Ye shall be as gods	419
xli. 32.	The dream is doubled unto Pharaoh twice	27
xlix. 10.	The sceptre shall not depart from Judah	96. 135
„ 16, 17.	Dan shall be a serpent by the way	155–159
Exodus xiii. 10.	From year to year	85
Numbers xiv. 33.	Your children shall wander forty years — each day for a year	35
xxiv. 17.	There shall come a star out of Jacob	133
Deut. xxxii. 8.	(Septuagint.) He appointed the bounds of the nations according to the number of the angels	84
Job i. 16.	The fire of God is fallen from heaven	417
Psalm xlv. 4.	Ride prosperously, &c.	52
lxxii.	A psalm for Solomon, &c.	229. 232
xc. 4.	A thousand years, &c.	114
cxxxvii.	O daughter of Babylon, &c.	349
Song of Solomon ch. v.	My beloved had withdrawn himself, &c.	409, 410
viii. 8.	We have a little sister	84
Isaiah i. 10.	Ye rulers of Sodom	160. 283
viii.	Mahershahal-hash-baz	232
xi. 4.	With the breath of his lips he will slay the wicked	83
xxvi. 20.	Enter into thy chambers	164
xxvii. 1.	The dragon that is in the sea	209
xxxiii. 16.	Bread shall be given him, his waters shall be sure	366
xlix. 17.	(Sept.) Thou shalt soon be rebuilt by thy destroyers	228
Jeremiah viii. 16.	(Sept.) From Dan shall we hear the sound of his horses	157

INDEX TO PASSAGES

		Page
Jeremiah viii. 17.	I will send you death-bearing serpents (Sept.)	421
xxii. 8.	This great city (Jerusalem)	74. 283
xxv. 11.	They shall serve the King of Babylon seventy years	24
xxv. 18.	Jerusalem and the cities of Judah, . . . and Pharaoh	283
Ezekiel iv. 6.	Each day for a year	35. 373
xiv. 21.	My four sore judgments upon Jerusalem	182–183
xvi. 17.	Thou hast taken thy fair jewels of my gold	289
xxiii. 4.	Jerusalem is Aholibah	283–284
xxxviii. 12.	The midst of the land; (umbilicus terræ, Vulgate and Septuagint)	283
Daniel.	General notices of the prophecy, 26. 72. 192–195. 223–225	
ii.	Vision of the metallic statue, 78. 87. 95. 226. 257–262	
33.	Legs of iron and clay	375
34.	The stone cut out without hands,	82. 259–261
42.	Ten toes, part of iron and part of clay, 233. 244. 257–259	
iv.	Nebuchadnezzar's abasement	79
16.	Seven times	37
vii.	Vision of the four beasts	87–95. 227
7.	Fourth beast	120
8.	Little horn	111
,,	Eyes like the eyes of a man	45. 228
,,	There were counsels in the horns (Sept.)	147
17.	The four beasts are four kings	26. 74
25.	He shall think to change times and laws	13
viii.	Vision of the ram and goat	80
12.	An host was given him, &c.	152
14.	Two thousand three hundred days,	77. 80–83
20, 21.	The ram having two horns is the kings of Media and Persia, &c., 19. 26. 68. 76. 85.	
23.	A king of fierce countenance	171
ix.	Seventy weeks (Sept. " of years" p. 72.) 31. 165. 167. 170. 204. 253	
25.	The street shall be built again	284
27.	The one week and the half week, 136. 166. 172. 202–204	

			Page
Daniel	x. 2.	Three full weeks	85
	xi. 6.	The king's daughter of the south, &c.	73
	21.	A vile person - - - - 195.	229–233
	30.	Ships of Chittim shall come / (Sept.) The Romans shall come	73
	xi. 34.	A little help	228
		(Rest of the chapter)	229–233
	xii. 1.	Michael shall stand up	365
		(See Apoc. xii. 7.)	
	,, ,,	A time of trouble - - - 115–118.	196
Hosea	vi. 2.	After two days he will revive us	30
Habakkuk	iii. 17.	Although the fig-tree shall not blossom	83
Zechariah	ii. 18.	Four horns	83
	ix. 9.	Lowly, and riding on an ass	20
	xii. 10.	They shall look on me whom they have pierced	424
Malachi	ii. 7.	The priest is the messenger (Sept. angel) of the Lord	74
	iv. 5.	I will send you Elijah the prophet	139
Matthew	vii. 24.	Which built his house upon a rock -	412, 413
	xvii. 10.	Why say the Scribes that Elias must first come?	172
	11.	Elias truly shall first come, &c., 86. 129. 139–141. 224.	240
	xxiv.	The prophecy delivered on the Mount of Olives	213–215
	5.	Many shall say, I am Christ	414
	7.	Famines, pestilences, and earthquakes	180
	8.	The beginning of sorrows	98
	14.	The Gospel shall be preached in all the world	52
	15.	The abomination of desolation, 103, 104. 150.	189. 219
	16.	Let them that are in Judea flee to the mountains - - - - - 110. 187.	212
	19.	Woe unto them that are with child	244
	21.	For then shall be great tribulation 216–218.	274. 419
	24.	Lo, here is Christ - - - - 408.	414
	25.	They shall show great signs and wonders 137.	170
	27.	As the lightning, so shall be the coming, &c.	216

INDEX TO PASSAGES

			Page
Matthew xxiv.	29.	Immediately after that tribulation, &c.	183, 184. 224. 423
	30.	The sign of the Son of man	129. 424
	„	Coming in the clouds of heaven	86, 87
	34.	This generation shall not pass	224
xxvii.	29.	A crown of thorns	55–57
Mark xiii.	32.	That day and hour, &c. — Neither the Son, &c.	38. 144
Luke xi.	24.	When the unclean spirit goeth out of a man	192
xiii.	33.	I must walk to-day, and to-morrow, &c.	36. 394
xv.		Parable of the prodigal son	66
xviii.		The unjust judge	152, 153
xxi.	20.	When ye see Jerusalem compassed with armies	104. 160. 219
	24.	Jerusalem shall be trodden down of the Gentiles	104. 161
	36.	Pray that ye may escape those things	218
John i.	1.	In the beginning was the word	78
	43.	If another shall come in his own name	152–154
xi.	48.	The Romans shall come	8. 74
Acts i.	7.	It is not yours to know the times and seasons	254. 353
viii.	10.	This man is the great power of God	124
xiii.	46.	Lo, we turn to the Gentiles, &c.	55
Romans viii.	19.	The earnest expectation of the creature, &c.	191. 424
	37.	In all these things we are more than conquerors	53. 414
1 *Corinth.* iii.	4.	I am of Paul, and I of Apollos	123
2 *Thess.* ii.		(The subject of the whole chapter)	3. 7. 23, 105. 150. 162. 221–223. 242–244. 416–418
	3.	A falling away first	306. 318. 344. 366. 405–411
	6.	Ye know what withholdeth	7. 131
	7.	The mystery of iniquity	222
	„	He who now letteth	7. 23. 160. 162. 198. 374–375
	9.	The working of Satan	417
	11.	For this cause God shall send them strong delusion	407
	12.	That they all might be damned	223
	15.	Hold the traditions which ye have been taught, &c.	3

OF SCRIPTURE EXPLAINED. 455

			Page
2 *Timothy*	ii. 18.	Saying that the resurrection is past already	161
Hebrews	iv. 9.	There remaineth a rest - - - -	113
1 *Peter*	v. 13.	The church that is in Babylon - -	106
1 *John*	ii. 18.	Ye have heard that Antichrist shall come -	106
	„	Even now there are many Antichrists -	124
	22.	He is Antichrist that denieth the Father and the Son - - 47. 123.	384–386
	iv. 3.	This is that spirit of Antichrist - -	126
Jude	14.	Of these Enoch also prophesied, saying, &c.	425
Revelation		(General notices of the book) - 107. 177.	296
	i. 4.	Which was, and is, and is to come - -	179
	20.	The angels of the seven churches - -	74
	ii. 8.	To the church of Smyrna write -	141–143
	10.	Ten days - - - - - -	143
	18.	To the church of Thyatira - - -	108
	20.	That woman Jezebel - - - -	108
	iv. 7.	Four living creatures - - - -	181
	v. 1.	The sealed book - - - -	179. 268
	9.	A new song - - - - - -	179
	vi.	The seven seals 98. 180–184. 296.	315. 400
	1.	Come and see - - - - - -	180
	2.	The first seal - - - 50–58.	181. 400
	3.	The second seal - - - -	181
	5.	The third seal - - - - -	181
	8.	The fourth seal - - - - -	182
	9.	The fifth seal - - - -	162–164
	12.	The sixth seal - - - 174.	183, 184
	vii.	Sealing of the Jews - - - -	421
	„	Omission of Dan - - - -	155–159
	viii. 1.	The seventh seal - - - - -	181
	2.	Seven trumpets - - - - -	185
	ix. 1.	A star fallen from heaven - - -	44
	3.	The locusts - - - - - -	61
	11.	Abaddon - - - - - -	84
	xi.	The two witnesses 63. 140, 141. 168. 199. 218. 268. 280–285.	422
	6.	To shut heaven that it rain not - -	129
	7–12.	Their death and resurrection - -	280–282
	8.	Their dead bodies shall lie — spiritually called Sodom and Egypt 16. 160. 188. 234. 238. 283–285.	391
	11.	After three days and a half 186. 248. 271.	333

			Page
Revelation xi. 12.	They ascended in a cloud		268
xii.	Vision of the sun-clothed woman 169. 186–188, 189–191. 362–367. 393		
	3. A red dragon		130
	9. Called the Devil and Satan		15
xiii.	2. Like unto a leopard		269. 277
	3. All the world wondered after the beast		49
	,, Whose deadly wound was healed		133
	4. Who is like unto the beast?		412
	5. A mouth speaking great things		415
	,, Forty and two months		154. 420. 435
	6. He opened his mouth in blasphemy		415
	10. Here is the patience and the faith of the saints		145
	11. The second beast		151. 409
	13. He doeth great wonders		416
	,, He maketh fire to come down from heaven		417
	14. An image to the beast		189. 417
	18. His number is six hundred and sixty-six 146–150. 168. 422		
xiv.	8. Babylon is fallen, is fallen		405
	9. If any man worship the beast or his image 323. 391. 405		
	20. Blood to the horse-bridles		134
	,, Sixteen hundred furlongs		234
xv.	1. Seven vials		64. 152. 185
xvi.	12. The kings of the East		70
	13. Three unclean spirits like frogs		263
	19. And the great city was divided		269. 283
	,, Great Babylon came into remembrance		378
xvii.	The vision of Babylon 23. 126. 167. 239. 264–267. 311. 358. 376–380		
	1. The great harlot		340
	,, That sitteth		357
	,, Upon many waters		343
	2. With whom the kings of the earth, &c.		295
	,, Made drunk with the wine		338. 354
	3. Sitting upon a scarlet beast full of names, &c. 285, 286		
	,, Having seven heads and ten horns		341. 344
	4. Purple and scarlet		293
	,, Gold and precious stones		293. 368

OF SCRIPTURE EXPLAINED. 457

		Page
Revelation xvii. 4.	Having a golden cup	- 351
5.	And upon her forehead	- 242. 289
„	Mystery	- 188. 384
„	Babylon the great	160. 188. 234. 270. 342. 392
„	Mother of harlots	- 331. 377
6.	Drunk with the blood of the saints	- 48. 188
7.	Wherefore didst thou marvel?	- 367, 368
8–11.	The scarlet beast	45. 188. 269. 336. 358–362
8.	Was and is not	- 359
„	Shall ascend out of the bottomless pit	- 360
„	They that dwell on the earth shall wonder	361
„	Was, and is not, and yet is	- 361
9.	Seven mountains	18. 22. 102. 188. 361
10.	Seven kings	- 336. 362
„	Five are fallen	- 362
11.	The eighth, and of the seven	- 362
12.	Ten kings	198. 445. 413
14.	The Lamb shall overcome them	- 425. 437
16.	They shall hate her and make her desolate	41 162. 323. 339. 380. 391. 396. 405
17.	To give their kingdom to the beast	43. 147. 151
18.	The woman is that great city	- 277. 318. 384
xviii. 3.	The merchants of the earth	- 300. 371
4.	Come out of her, my people	- 376
7.	How much she hath glorified herself	- 347
„	I sit a queen	- 340
23.	By thy sorceries were all nations deceived	292
xix. 11–21.	The battle of that great day of God Almighty	- 425, 426
xx. 2.	The dragon bound	- 162
4.	The souls of them that were beheaded	175–176. 419
„	They reigned a thousand years	113. 122. 137. 163. 168. 173. 201. 250–252.
xxi. 1.	A new heaven and a new earth	- 119
10.	That great city, the holy Jerusalem	- 283

INDEX

TO

AUTHORS AND PROPER NAMES.

Abbo, 304.
Aben-Ezra, 84.
Ado, 276.
Adso, 300-302.
Africanus, 194.
Ageruchia (Gerontia), 244.
Albertus Magnus, 54. 196. 278.
333, 334.
Alcassar, 150. 445.
Algasia, 241.
Alphœus of Mitylene, 415.
Ambrose of Milan, 219.
Ambrose of Camaldula, 342.
Ambrose, Pseudo, 366.
Ammianus Marcellinus, 228.
Ammonius, 138. 262.
Anastasius, Bibliothecarius, 275. 286.
Andreas Cæsariensis, 23. 265-269.
Anselm of Havilsburgh, 315.
Anselm of Laon (Laudunensis), 306. 364.
Ansbert, Ambrose, 300.
Antiochus, Prince, his easy Catechism, 215.
Apollinarius, 81. 95. 220.
Aquinas, Thomas, 333-336. 360.
Aretas Cæsariensis, 276.
Aretius, 17. 436.
Armillus (Jewish name of Antichrist), 83.
Arnulphus, 265.
Articles of Church of England, 50.
Athanasius, 38. 211.

Athenæus, 73.
Augustine, 246-257. 402.
Aureolus, 349.

Baldwin (Jesuit), 265.
Barnabas, St., 33. 111-114.
Baronius, 276.
Bartoloccius, 33. 219.
Bede, 296. 414. 421.
Beguins, 341.
Bellarmine, 12. 150. 373-376.
Ben-Ezra (See Lacunza).
Ben Jonson, 429.
Ben-Sirach (Ecclesiasticus), 77.
Berengaud, 349.
Bernard of Clairvaux, 313.
Bernard of Jacma, 341.
Bernardine, 57. 353.
Bonacursus, 432.
Bonanni, 381.
Bridget, 345.
Brightman, 438.
Broughton, 429.
Bruno of Ast, 310. 319.
Brute, Walter, 433.
Bulengerus, 143.
Burgh, Rev. William, 394.
Buxtorf, 83. 184.

Calmet, 46. 283.
Calvin, 63. 435. 446.
Cassiodorus, 184. 270.
Catenæ, notice of, 335.
Cathari, the, 432.

INDEX TO AUTHORS AND PROPER NAMES.

Celsus, 136. 170. 172.
Chaldee paraphrase, 84.
Chandler, Bishop, 445.
Charlemagne, 294.
Chrysologus, 186. 246. 423.
Chrysostom, 81. 221-225. 414.
Cicero, 143.
Clarke, 15.
Clemangis, 347.
Clement of Alexandria, 166.
Clement XI., 264.
Constantine, 208-210.
Constantine's donation, 292.
Croly, Dr., 389.
Cyprian, 174-177. 183.
Cyril of Jerusalem, 212-215.

Damascenus, John, 297.
Daniel, the prophet, evidences of his authenticity, 26. 102-104.
Dante, 343.
Dionysius of Alexandria, 173. 202.
Dionysius Carthusianus, 57. 60. 353.
Donatists, the, 246, 247.

Eberhard of Salzburg, 330. 432.
Ecclesiasticus (See Ben-Sirach).
Elliott, Rev. E. B., 16. 37. 45. 53.
Ephrem Syrus, 81. 216-219. 427.
Epiphanius, 108. 110. 249.
Esdras, Pseudo, 70. 119.
Eudoxius, 89. 94. 95. 197. 260.
Eusebius, 12. 88. 110. 122. 207. 210. 284.
Everaclus, 305.

Fleming, Mr., 39. 45. 441.
Fluentius, 312.
Foxe, 435, 436.
Franciscans, 337-342.
Freculphus, 299.
Frederick, Emperor of the Romans, 46.
Frere, Mr., 388.
Futurists, the, 394-396.
Fysh, Rev. Mr., 55. 64. 390.

Galatinus, 134. 136.
Galloway, Mr., 16.

Gaudentius, 220.
Genebrard, 431.
Geroch, 317.
Gherbert, Pope, 303. 306.
Gibbon, 427.
Godell, 305.
Greathead, Bishop, 332.
Gregory of Nazianzen, 220.
Gregory the Great, 273, 274. 416.
Gregory VII., 308. 330.
Gregory of Heimburg, 353.
Grotius, 430.
Gualternus, 45.

Habershon, Dr., 390.
Hales, Alexander de, 338.
Harvey, 23. 344.
Haye, La, 417, 418.
Haymo, 300.
Hermes, 114-119.
Hesychius, 252-255.
Hilary, 178. 211.
Hildegarde, Abbess, 315.
Hippolytus, 92. 95. 166-170.
Hoblyn, Rev. Mr., 389.
Homilies, of Church of England, 375.
Hooker, 372.
Hortolanus, 409.
Hugo, Cardinal, 333-336.
Hugo Etherianus, 319.
Hyrcanus (first book of the Maccabees), 75.

Jaddus, 68.
James I. of England, 437.
Jerome, 72. 136. 206. 225-245.
Jesuits, 357. 386. 404.
"Jewish Missionary," the, 149. 448.
Ignatius, 97. 124.
Innocent III. 324-326.
Joachim, Abbot, 311. 320-323. 337. 431.
Jonathan Ben-Uzziel, 157.
John Chemnicensis, 370.
John of Paris, 341.
Josephus, 68, 69. 78. 82.
Irenæus, 144-155. 157. 181.
Isaiah, "Ascension of," 420.
Isidore the Pelusiot, 262.

Judas, 165.
Justin Martyr, 133. 137–139.
Justin, historian, 69, 70. 232.
Justinian, 272.

Lacunza (Ben-Ezra), 357, 358. 363. 392–394. 409. 448.
Lactantius, 10. 197.
Lanfranc, 306.
Lapide, Cornelius A, 383–385.
Layard, Mr., 26. 90.
Lee, Professor, 46.
Leo I., Pope, 264.
Leo X., Pope, 367.
Liege, church of, 312.
Luther, 61, 62. 431. 433.
Lyons, church of, 144.
Lyra, Nicolas de, 60. 63. 349. 431.

Maccabees, see Hyrcanus.
Machiavel, 445.
Maitland, Rev. C. D., 43. 396–398.
Maitland, Rev. S. R., 17. 372. 394.
Malvenda, 43. 231. 418.
Marcella, 236–241. 245.
Marsilius of Padua, 291.
Martin of Tours, 258.
Matthew Paris, 331.
Mede, 15.
Melancthon, 62. 431. 434.
Melito, 177.
Methodius, 189–191.
Milan, first council of, 352.
Missale Romanum, 12.
Morinus, 327.

Nannius, 431.
Nepos, 173.
Newton, Bishop, 15.
Nice, second council of, 290.
Nisibenus, James, 32. 90. 204. 427.
Norbert, 314.

Œcumenius, 306.
Onkelos, 156.
Onus Ecclesiæ, see John of Kemnitz.
Oremius, 347.
Origen, 170–173. 202.
Orleanists, 443.

Orosius, 262.
Otto Frisingensis, 295. 318.
Oveto, council of, 299.

Pagi, 294.
Pantænus, 24.
Papias, 121.
Paradisus, 356.
Paramo, Luis à, 326–329. 381–383.
Pareus, 437.
Paschal II., Pope, 312.
Pastorini, see Walmsley.
Paul, the deacon, 275.
Paula and her daughter, 236–240.
Paulikians, 442.
Penni, 368.
Peter Casinensis, 324.
Peter Comestor, 318.
Peter John of Olivi, 23. 337–340.
Peter Lombard, 318.
Peter Siculus, 442.
Petrarch, 342, 343.
Phocas, Emperor, 275.
Philo Judæus, 71. 77. 155, 156.
Pius II., Pope, 354.
Polycarp, 126, 142.
Polychronius, 81. 197. 284. 428, 429.
Pontius, deacon, 176.
Porphyry, 191–197. 228. 427.
Potter, Dr., 47.
Primasius, 270.
Prosper, 262.
Prudentius, 221.

Quinet, M., 331.

Rabbi Eleazar, 96.
Reeves' Bible, 391.
Ribera, 359, 377–399.
Richard St. Victor, 319.
Richard I., of England, 322.
Roger of Hovedon, 321, 322.
Ruffinus, 220.
Rupert, 311. 315. 319.

Sergius, 442.
Sermones super Apoc., 357. 369.
Seventy Translators, 70–75.

Severianus, 105.
Sibylline Oracles, 126–131.
Simon Magus, 124.
Slichtingius, 434.
Stella, 303.
Stephen, Pope, 287.
Suetonius, 51. 132.
Sulpitius Severus, 257.
Symmachus, 18.

Tacitus, 31. 51. 132.
Targum, of Onkelos, 156.
Targum, of Jonathan, 157.
Targum, of Jerusalem, 157.
Targum, of Pseudo-Jonathan, 83, 87.
Telesphorus, 341.
Tertullian, 135. 159–165.
Theodore, 222.
Theodoret, 89. 158. 258–260, 284.
Theophanes, 286.

Theophylact, 306.
Thiota, 298.
Titus Bostrensis, 9. 94.
Tychonius, 162. 247. 249. 281.
Tyrinus, 18.

Ubertinus, 341.

Valentine, 124.
Valla, 294.
Victor of Antioch, 95.
Victorinus, 177–189.
Vergas, 379.
Vincent of Ferrers, 351.
Volkuin, 351.
Voragine (Golden Legend), 346.

Walmsley (Pastorini), 61. 386.
Woodhouse, Dean, 16.

Zohar, 138.

THE END.

www.ingramcontent.com/pod-product-compliance
Lightning Source LLC
Chambersburg PA
CBHW071433300426
44114CB00013B/1414